Global Perspectives on Recruiting International Students

Global Perspectives on Recruiting International Students: Challenges and Opportunities

EDITED BY

BELAL SHNEIKAT
University of Kyrenia, Cyprus

CIHAN COBANOGLU
University of South Florida, USA

&

CEM TANOVA
Eastern Mediterranean University, Cyprus

United Kingdom – North America – Japan – India – Malaysia – China

Emerald Publishing Limited
Howard House, Wagon Lane, Bingley BD16 1WA, UK

First edition 2021

Editorial matter and selection © 2021 Belal Shneikat, Cihan Cobanoglu, Cem Tanova.
Published under exclusive license by Emerald Publishing Limited. Individual chapters
copyright © 2021 Emerald Publishing Limited.

Reprints and permissions service
Contact: permissions@emeraldinsight.com

No part of this book may be reproduced, stored in a retrieval system, transmitted in
any form or by any means electronic, mechanical, photocopying, recording or otherwise
without either the prior written permission of the publisher or a licence permitting
restricted copying issued in the UK by The Copyright Licensing Agency and in the USA
by The Copyright Clearance Center. Any opinions expressed in the chapters are those
of the authors. Whilst Emerald makes every effort to ensure the quality and accuracy of
its content, Emerald makes no representation implied or otherwise, as to the chapters'
suitability and application and disclaims any warranties, express or implied, to their use.

British Library Cataloguing in Publication Data
A catalogue record for this book is available from the British Library

ISBN: 978-1-83982-519-4 (Print)
ISBN: 978-1-83982-518-7 (Online)
ISBN: 978-1-83982-520-0 (Epub)

ISOQAR certified
Management System,
awarded to Emerald
for adherence to
Environmental
standard
ISO 14001:2004.

Certificate Number 1985
ISO 14001

INVESTOR IN PEOPLE

Contents

About the Editors   *vii*

About the Contributors   *ix*

Preface   *xiii*

Chapter 1   Key Factors in the Selection of an Educational Tourism Destination   *1*
Melissa Rikiatou Kana Kenfack and Ali Öztüren

Chapter 2   Study Hard but Do Tour to See the World: Tourism of Chinese Students who Studied in the United States   *37*
Carol Huang and Connie Chuyun Hu

Chapter 3   The Role of Social Media Marketing Activities on International Students' Brand Preference: A Study on English-Speaking Universities of Germany   *51*
Hasan Evrim Arici and Nagihan Cakmakoglu Arici

Chapter 4   Use of Web Analytics and Social Listening to Attract International Students   *65*
Rakhi Tripathi

Chapter 5   Promoting the Internationalisation of Students in University Strategic Goals: A Case Study   *81*
Carla Del Gesso

Chapter 6   Exploring Institutional Culture and Its Impact on International Student Recruitment Capabilities   *97*
Melissa James

Chapter 7   Recruiting Educational Tourists from Countries Under International Sanctions: The Case of Iranian Education Market   *111*
Cahit Ezel

vi Content

Chapter 8 Geopolitics and Global Events: International Student Recruitment in a Time of Disruption *125*
Joseph M. Stokes

Chapter 9 Challenges to Admission for Indonesian Sponsored Applicants to a US Graduate Program in Education *139*
Adrian Rodgers

Chapter 10 The Qualitative Study of Factors Influencing to International Students' Satisfaction: The Case of a Private University in Turkey *155*
Ayşe Collins, Zeynep Goknil Sanal and Aygil Takır

Chapter 11 Are Chinese Students Studying at European Universities Satisfied? Performance and Challenges *173*
Marta Melguizo-Garde and Ana Yetano

Chapter 12 How to Integrate International Students into the Local Society and How That Will Affect Their Satisfaction Level *187*
Janet M. Howes

Chapter 13 Living Closely Together but in Parallel - Multi-dimensional Challenges to the Integration of International Students in a Danish 'Muscle' Town *197*
Annette Aagaard Thuesen and Eva Mærsk

Chapter 14 The Impact of Cultural Adjustment on International Student Recruitment and First-Year Success *215*
Clayton Smith

Chapter 15 International Chinese Students' Cultural Experience and Cultural Support in the UK *231*
Yimeng Zhang

Chapter 16 The Future of International Student Recruitment *245*
Belal Shneikat

Index *257*

About the Editors

Belal Shneikat is an Assistant Professor in Business Administration at The University of Kyrenia. He holds BSc in Regional Planning and MBA from Al- Balqa' Applied University in Jordan and PhD in Business Administration from Eastern Mediterranean University in North Cyprus. He served as International Admissions Recruiter for several years and recruited thousands of international students from Asia, Africa and Europe. His areas of interest are educational tourism, entrepreneurship and human–computer interaction. His research appeared in journals like *The Service Industries Journal*, *Online Information Review*, *Tourism Management Perspectives* and *Journal of the Knowledge Economy*.

Cihan Cobanoglu is the McKibbon Endowed Chair Professor School of Hospitality and Tourism Management, Muma College of Business at the University of South Florida, who also serves as the Director of the M3 Center for Hospitality Technology and Innovation and coordinator of International Programs for the School of Hospitality and Tourism Management. He is a renowned hospitality and tourism technology expert. Dr Cobanoglu is a Fulbright Specialist commissioned by the Fulbright Commission which is part of the US Department of State's Bureau of Educational and Cultural Affairs (ECA) and World Learning (2018–2021). He is a Certified Hospitality Technology Professional (CHTP) commissioned by Hospitality Financial & Technology Professionals (HFTP) and Educational Institute of American Hotel & Lodging Association (AHLA). He is the Editor of the *Journal of Hospitality and Tourism Technology* (JHTT) (Indexed in SSCI and Scopus), Editor of the *Journal of Global Business Insights* (JGBI), Associate Editor of *Tourism Review* (world's oldest tourism journal, indexed in SCCI and Scopus) and a co-author of 6 books and 10 conference proceedings. He is also currently serving as the President of the Association of North America Higher Education International (ANAHEI).

Cem Tanova is currently a Professor of Management in Eastern Mediterranean University. After completing his Bachelor's in Management and Master's in Public Administration degrees in Northern Michigan University in Michigan, USA, he received his Doctorate in Management and Organizations from Cukurova University in Adana Turkey. Dr Tanova held many academic leadership positions in his career. He has served as the Vice Rector for International Affairs, Dean of the Faculty of Business and Economics, the Department Head of Business Administration and the Chair of the Continuing Education Center in Eastern *viii*   *About the Editors*

Mediterranean University. His research interests include human resource management, recruitment methods, voluntary turnover, organisational justice and cognitive styles. His research appeared in journals including *International Journal of Human Resource Management*, *International Journal of Hospitality Management* and *Service Industries Journal*.

About the Contributors

Hasan Evrim Arici is a Lecturer at EU Business School. His current research interests include leadership, HRM and organisational behaviours. His work has been published in international journals, such as *Journal of Hospitality Marketing & Management* and *International Journal of Contemporary Hospitality Management*.

Nagihan Cakmakoglu Arici studied PhD in Tourism Management. She is currently working for the T.R. General Consulate Stuttgart, Germany. Her research interests are in consumer behaviours, tourist experiences, e-marketing and business administration. She also carried out a number of international projects funded by EU.

Ayse Collins is an Associate Professor at Bilkent University, Ankara, Turkey. She has her PhD from the Middle East Technical University, Ankara, Turkey, where her thesis won the 'Thesis of the Year' award. Her research interests cover human resources management, labour law, curriculum development, performance evaluation, inclusion, social inclusion, disability, and arts. She is the member of editorial boards of several international and national journals.

Cahit Ezel, PhD in Tourism Management, is an Assistant Professor at Eastern Mediterranean University, Faculty of Tourism. Dr. Ezel had worked at various administrative positions at EMU Rector's Office and travelled extensively in Middle-East, Asia and Europe. Dr. Ezel has special interest in internationalization of higher education, developing international academic partnerships and strategic planning at higher education institutions. His current research interest focus on educational tourism, internationalization of higher education, and student satisfaction.

Carla Del Gesso, PhD in Business Administration, is an Adjunct Professor of Public Management and Accounting at the Department of Economics, University of Molise, Italy. She has significant experience in teaching and research in the field of management and accounting of public organisations and social enterprises. Her primary research interests include public sector governance and performance information disclosures.

Janet M. Howes, PhD, is an Assistant Professor of Business Administration and the Director of the Sport Management and Promotion Program at the University of Saint Joseph in West Hartford, CT. Dr Howes' PhD is in Sport Administration and teaches in the business and sport management programs.

x   About the Contributors

Connie Chuyun Hu is a PhD Candidate (ABD) in the Department of Educational Leadership and Policy Studies and a Graduate Teaching Assistant in the School of Education and the Department of East Asian Literatures and Cultures at the University of Kansas. Her research is on IT and IT instruction.

Carol Huang is currently teaching at the City College of New York and CUNY Graduate Center. She used to serve as the research director for Asian American and Asian Research Institute of CUNY. Her research interests include educational policy, Asian American education, multiculturalism and dual language schools.

Melissa James is an Associate Professor at the University of Prince Edward Island's Faculty of Business and specialises in research, strategy and marketing. Her current research focuses on public sector marketing in higher education with a focus on the impact of internationalisation on higher education institutions.

Melissa Rikiatou Kana Kenfack is an enthusiast of sustainability in tourism. Aside from receiving her Bachelor's degree in tourism and hospitality management and master's degree in Tourism Management at Eastern Mediterranean University, North Cyprus, she participated in some laudable projects on tourism sustainability. She is currently pursuing her second master's degree in marketing.

Eva Mærsk is a PhD student at the Danish Centre for Rural Research at the University of Southern Denmark and department of Cultural Geography at Groningen University. Her PhD project research is about student mobility and youth culture in the context of peripheral urban study cities.

Marta Melguizo-Garde, PhD, is a Senior Lecturer in Applied Economics at the University of Zaragoza, is the Vicedean for Quality and belongs to the Public Economics research group (http://www.economiapublica.net/). Her research interests include the tax planning, public policy and taxes, education and social policies. She has published in leading academic journals.

Ali Öztüren is a Professor of Tourism Management and currently working as vice dean in the Faculty of Tourism at Eastern Mediterranean University. He is on executive boards of various national and international academic projects and events, on referee boards of many international and national journals, and advisory boards of academic and social organisations.

Adrian Rodgers is an Associate Professor in Teaching and Learning at The Ohio State University. His areas of interest are pre-service and in-service teacher education with a focus on literacy, international education and qualitative research. He has published books with Teachers College Press and Pearson and in journals such as *Teaching and Teacher Education*.

Zeynep Goknil Sanal is a freelance researcher and activist based in Ankara, Turkey. She completed her PhD at the Middle East Technical University on curriculum development; however, her research and activism is focussed on human rights issues including women's rights, children's rights and disabled rights.

Clayton Smith has held senior enrolment management positions at four postsecondary institutions in the United States and Canada. He is currently Associate Professor in the Faculty of Education at the University of Windsor. Over the course of his career, Dr Smith has amassed significant knowledge and expertise in strategic enrolment management.

Joseph M. Stokes is the University Registrar at Ontario Tech University, and an Adjunct Professor in the Faculty of Education. His portfolio includes the leadership of strategic enrolment management, and the university's international office Dr. Stokes has led work across the post-secondary sector on governance, strategic enrolment management, and student retention and success.

Aygil Takır is an Education Scholar with professional experience in some of the public, nongovernmental and academic institutions. She earned her PhD in Curriculum and Instruction in Middle East Technical University. As a researcher, Dr Takır's research mainly focuses on curriculum studies, migration, contemporary issues in education and higher education.

Annette Aagaard Thuesen, PhD, is an Associate Professor at the Danish Centre for Rural Research at the University of Southern Denmark. Her current research lies in governance and democratic aspects of student migration, partnership organising for change, community-led local development, co-creation of village plans and rural health.

Rakhi Tripathi is an Associate Professor in Information Technology and the Head of the Centre for Digital Innovation at FORE School of Management, Delhi, India. Her areas of research are Digital Technologies, Social Media Analytics, Social Listening and E-government. The primary objective of her research is to use Digital technologies to serve the society. Several research papers have been published in national as well as international reputed journals, conferences and books. She has been awarded 'Outstanding Women in Science' in the field of Information Technology in 2018 by Venus International Foundation, Chennai, India.'

Ana Yetano, PhD, is Professor in Accounting at the University of Zaragoza, is the Vicedean for Internationalisation and belongs to the Gespublica Research Group (http://gespublica.unizar.es). Her research interests are in public sector performance measurement, accounting and auditing. She has published in leading international journals.

Yimeng Zhang is a current PhD Candidate in Education (Teaching English to Speakers of Other Languages, TESOL) at the University of Exeter. Her research interest includes internationalisation in education, second language acquisition, as well as gender equality in education.

Preface

As we observe the tremendous growth in the internationalisation of higher education, we not only see larger number of students who wish to study abroad but also institutions that wish to attract international students. This book provides an in depth look at the competition among countries and universities in the process of recruiting international students. Thus, it can provide invaluable information for policy makers, researchers as well as students who wish to understand internationalisation of higher education.

Recruitment of international students provide numerous benefits and opportunities for both the host communities and the students. While the international students contribute to the cultural, economic and social welfare of the host community, they gain from being exposed to a new environment, develop their skills in adaptability and their proficiency in a new language which will improve their prospects for employment. Overall, the opportunities from meeting of ideas and cultures will spark innovation and open many opportunities.

The book brings together the most up-to-date and comprehensive scholarly contributions on recruiting international students written by authors representing a variety of geographical and academic backgrounds. The book covers a wide range of topics such as educational tourism, role of social media in recruiting international students, internationalisation and institutionalisation, challenges to admission, satisfaction of international students, and integration and cultural adjustment.

Chapter 1

Key Factors in the Selection of an Educational Tourism Destination*

Melissa Rikiatou Kana Kenfack and Ali Öztüren

Abstract

It is salient to be acquainted with the key elements that determine educational tourists' decision in selecting an overseas destination while considering the rise of international competition amidst nations concerning international students. There has been a growth in the number of nations committed to attracting educational tourists. This issue is evident in countries involved in higher education (HE), such as Northern Cyprus, identified as an edu-tourism destination. Northern Cyprus can attract a whopping number of tourists, and the higher population is most likely to be made up of international students regardless of its interdiction on direct flights and political pressure. This chapter centres on analysing educational tourists' motivators in selecting a tourism education destination abroad and on revealing effective recruitment and promotion plans towards attracting them.

The chapter includes the descriptions and discussions of educational tourism, the HE industry over the years, globalisation and internationalisation of educational tourism, factors influencing educational tourists' decision-making process and key elements influencing educational tourists' decisions in HE institutions.

At the end of the chapter, a case study is presented that reports the findings of interviews with educational tourists, overseas recruitment agents and Eastern Mediterranean University staff responsible for promoting the institution. The results identified eight factors affecting educational tourists' decisions on study destination. Those factors comprise cost, ease of access,

---

*This chapter is based on the first author's Master of Science thesis in Tourism Management.

Global Perspectives on Recruiting International Students: Challenges and Opportunities, 1–36
Copyright © 2021 by Emerald Publishing Limited
All rights of reproduction in any form reserved
doi:10.1108/978-1-83982-518-720211001

location, social factors, quality of education, instruction language, cultural environment and communication quality. The sub-factors of the main eight factors are scholarships, destination's scenery, safety, friends' and relatives' influence and cultural differences.

This chapter brings a significant knowledge about the motives that affect educational tourists in selecting at a particular HE destination. Based on the study's findings, educational institutions may consider various recommendations to redesign their strategies towards attracting educational tourists more effectively. Generally, this study promotes an apprehension about the diverse elements that affect educational tourists' selection of a destination study. An in-depth understanding of these factors will help education institutions' decision-makers better develop plans of action to provide desired services to educational tourists, attract and keep them in return.

Keywords: Educational tourism; higher education institutions (HEI); educational tourists; motivation; destination choice; North Cyprus

1. Introduction

The trade in international educational services in advanced countries constitutes a vital aspect of their economy. It has become a multibillion industry to those countries, thus, constituting their primary means of revenue (Cheung, Yuen, Yuen, & Cheng, 2011). International students have, therefore, become a feasible target for many countries.

Travelling with the aim of learning is not a new concept. Nevertheless, few studies have been conducted in this regard (Paul, 2010). The number of studies carried out to acquire an understanding of educational tourists' travel decisions and motives behind destination preferences is very few. Abubakar, Shneikat, and Oday (2014) affirmed that studies were done by tourism researchers' in-depth apprehension of educational tourism components in terms of choice motives, and recruitment strategies are few. Educational marketers' in the higher education (HE) industry need to obtain an in-depth understanding of educational tourists' preferences and motives behind their preferences to achieve their primary aim, which is to attract international students and acquire benefits.

Deciding to further education in a foreign land is a sensitive and compound decision, deriving from a set of motives from 'why deciding to leave a country', and 'where to go'. It is a whole process in which some desires are birthed, arising from a need, and followed by the eagerness to satisfy the need. Many factors are involved in this process: the reasons behind the decision to travel abroad for educational purposes, the desired attractiveness in the future country and HE abroad, and the process of selection of the final country and higher education institution (HEI) (Eder, Smith, & Pitts, 2010). Therefore, educational marketers need to get acquainted with the specific needs of educational tourists to know how to provide them with services that will enhance their satisfaction.

Marketers may use various ways to gain knowledge of the educational tourists' needs and wants (Joyce, 2012). According to studies, one significant tendency in the HEI is online marketing, targeting students' needs and wants with regards to HEI. In reaction to this, hosting countries like the United Kingdom, United States, and Australia inculcate effective marketing techniques to attract international students (Taplin, 2012). Hence, education marketers need to be fully acquainted with the needs of students (Eder et al., 2010). The merge of tourism and education rightfully birth the Educational Tourism, adding to the tourism industry (Lam, Tong, & Ariffin, 2016).

HEI communicates the messages they want to convey through various media mediums, hence, the need to reckon these ways is due to the increase in the importance of marketing communications. HEI mostly use e-mails, websites and other digital channels to disseminate information amongst students, lecturers and the university. The first medium of information for prospective students and parents generally is often a website (Pugsley & Coffey, 2002). Websites are critical when it comes to choosing a study destination. By this, HEI has to review many areas in setting up messages that will be efficacious in passing the right knowledge needed digitally to those in need. This includes students from different cultural backgrounds and languages. This brings the necessity to consider culture while setting recruitments plans (Bagautdinova, Gorelova, & Polyakova, 2015). Studies have revealed the importance of protecting the information directed to various groups of students. The different communication methods and mediums used for student interaction need to be identified concerning cultural, linguistic and communication quality. In respect to this, modern-day studies can be termed to be a critical interrogation to highlight conditions that influence the decision of prospective students.

In light of the increasing competition between countries and institutions for international students, new ways to market post-secondary education progressively become more critical (McCarthy, Sen, & Garrity, 2012).

Recent studies have pinpointed that the three major English-speaking study destinations are Australia, The United Kingdom and The United States of America (Abubakar et al., 2014), predominantly in HEIs. Thus, various academicians from the aforementioned English-speaking nations have examined educational tourists and HEI recruitments plans (McCarthy et al., 2012; Taplin, 2012). Northern Cyprus, as a developing destination, currently is dealing with a lack of research dealing with understanding the needs of international students and deciphering efficacious mediums to reach out to these students. Therefore, there is an urgent need to interrogate the factors influencing the students' decision and mobility, specifically for the student, agent and staff. Knowledge of these factors will facilitate HEI institutions to establish effective plans for inducing educational tourists. Therefore, this study attempts to fill the lacuna in the research about international students marketing strategies and international students' decisions for an educational tourism destination like a Northern Cyprus.

Tourism actors are increasingly focussing on enhancing consumer information due to the rapid increase in world tourism (Brown & Hall, 2008; Tefera, 2015). In the same manner, the educational tourism sector has also expanded in size, and the growth has been attached to globalisation, increased global correctness, political freedom, civilisation and relative peace (Webster & Ivanov, 2014). There is a visible growth in the travel for the education sector, undisputed, but it remains largely ignored by both industry and academia (Abubakar et al., 2014). There is a need for academic institutions to align their services to meet the needs of the various international students' segments and to take hold of the educational tourism market. To make the student's experience enjoyable, students' attractions to specific areas in the country have to be reviewed to meet their expectations. This helps the institutions to know how to configure their curriculum to meet the needs of overseas students. More importantly, institutions need to know the need to equip students with boundary spanning skillsets across industries, cultures and countries (Abubakar et al., 2014). A growing niche market cannot be ignored due to the population of students from various countries in the HE sector in Northern Cyprus (Abubakar et al., 2014). This research would be of great interest to academic institutions in the country and local governments of North Cyprus. Lai et al. (2014) noted the international students' market to be highly heterogeneous and requires effort to the segment. This study will help the country and universities develop appropriate strategies that incorporate international students' needs as a market segment. Educational tourism is an important economic activity for developing countries and all countries generally. As more and more governments are privatising or commercialising HEI (Antra & Seema, 2018; Kwong, 2000), HEI's financial tenacity can be improved by the benefits of educational tourism (Antra & Seema, 2018). The attraction of several students coming into a particular destination can help institutions redeem poverty and foster economic growth (Hipsher & Bulmer, 2016). By this, the multi-dimensional facet of educational tourism can help to acquire a lot and draw interest from a diverse audience (McGladdery & Lubbe, 2017). The combination of education, tourism and movement of students for study purposes and the interrelationship with other economic variables make the research area appealing to interdisciplinary scholars (Lesjak et al., 2015). Moreover, Pitman et al. (2010) call researchers from various disciplines to explore this research scope.

2. Literature Review

The following section focusses on reviewing the relevant literature on educational tourism, putting an accent on educational tourists' motives and preferences in choosing a destination for studies.

2.1. Educational Tourism

We may have been regarded as 'tourists' at some point in our lives. Conceptualising tourism varies depending on the source and person. There is no consensus with regards to the definition of tourism, and nearly every institution defines tourism differently (Lai, Gibson, & Muthaly, 2014); based on expatiating tourism with the basic terms, it can be seen as follows.

Tourism can be seen as the movement of people in or out of a country, with the intent of leisure and trade (Holden, 2000). A visitor can be taken to be someone who travels to a new destination outside his/her usual environment for a specific purpose and for a stipulated time. This includes holidays, leisure and recreation, business, health, education or other purposes. This scope is much broader than tourists' traditional perception, which included only those travelling for leisure.

McIntosh et al. (1995) endorsed this view by stating that tourism is:

> The sum of the phenomena and relationships arising from the interaction of tourists, business suppliers, host governments, and host communities in attracting and hosting these tourists and other visitors.

To prevent the disaccords from defining tourism, UNWTO equally posits that

> Tourism comprises of the activities of people staying in new places outside their natural environment for not more than one consecutive year for leisure, business, and other purposes. (UNWTO, 2010)

There is a major distinguishing between mere travel and tourism. For tourism to happen, a displacement has to occur, an individual has to travel, using any means of transportation.

Tourism comes in two aspects, which are domestic or international. International tourism consists of incoming and outgoing movement of people considered as tourists. One active constituent of tourism is its diverseness of sectors, which aid in providing products and services to both visitors and locals. Tourism is a constantly changing industry that demands the capacity to adhere to customers' needs and desires, since customer's pleasure, safety and satisfaction are the tourism industry's primary concerns.

Over the last few decades, travelling has become part of our daily lives. Individuals from different origins shuffle between countries for acquiring new experiences, knowledge or skills. These activities are regarded as educational tourism (Larson & Ankomah, 2004).

Due to the growing recognition of teaching and learning and enhancing technical excellence, educational tourism is developed. Visiting another country to learn about new cultures, study tours or work and practice locally acquired skills in a different environment such as international training programs (World Tourism Organization, 2012) is one of the main focus of the educational tourism activities.

Ritchie, Carr, and Cooper (2003) gave a more encompassing definition of educational tourism as

> Tourist activity is undertaken by those who are engaging in an overnight vacation and engaging in an excursion for whom education and learning are a primary or secondary part of their trip. This can include general educational tourism and adult study tours, international and domestic university and school students' travel, including language school, school excursion, and exchange programs. Educational Tourism can be independently or formally organized and can be undertaken in various natural or human-made settings.

2.2. HE Industry over the Years

Transformation is often described as a complex, open-ended concept (Venter & Tolmie, 2012). One of the significant global boomings in the industry has been the growth of HEIs (McGladdery & Lubbe, 2017). International education was recognised as one of the more significant service industries between the 1980s and 1990s (Mazzarol, 1998). According to Venter (2015), the implication is that 'knowledge transmission and production should be pursued in dialogue with global contexts'. Thus, Mazzarol, Soutar, and Sim (2003) determined three flows of globalisation in the HEI area. The first flow had to do with students travelling to a foreign country at a specific academic institution. At the start of the twentieth century, it became standard and equally gained ground currently. The second flow was when academic institutions established cooperation through 'exchange' programs with other institutions to be known in the international market. This became popular in some continents such as Asia, as many scholars moved to another country to gain their degree. They have to know about these institutions through information provided in their school because of the exchange program agreement. Regarding the third flow, it was ushered in when courses started to be delivered online, known as 'distance learning', and it gained ground in the higher institution market (Mazzarol et al., 2003).

Several reasons could be attached to international education demand. Traditionally, it was compelled by intentions to raise the graduate's economic and social status, especially within the HE sector (Mazzarol & Soutar, 2002). Besides, low access to HE in many countries in Africa and Asia, for example, as well as educational tourists colonial tie amid his home country and the study destination country has played a massive role in birthing educational tourist's displacement and choice of study destination (Chou, 2008; Mazzarol & Soutar, 2002).

Thus, considering the fast escalation of HEIs, gaining the knowledge of various ways of attracting international students has become considerably necessary (McGladdery & Lubbe, 2017). Researchers have grouped the factors influencing students to travel abroad for study purposes into 'push' and 'pull' factors between their home and host country (OECD, 2017). Mazzarol and Soutar (2002) define the 'push' factors as domestic factors and pull factors as external influencers; in other words, push factors are domestic factors encouraging outward mobility and pull factors are vital external factors in the educational tourist's destination preference. In brief, studies point out that painful economic and social conditions dominant in the home country mainly play a role in pushes students in a foreign land; meanwhile, educational tourists' choice in preferred HEI abroad is dependent on several 'pull' factors. Going by this, deciding where to study is crucial for both educational tourists and parents (Mazzarol, 1998). The HEI in countries like the United States, Australia, Canada and the United Kingdom, which receives a massive number of students from across the world, have come to be market-oriented by adopting professional marketing strategies to admit international students (Mazzarol et al., 2003). The number of students studying abroad has been recorded at 150,000 approximately in 1955 (Naidoo, 2009) to 2.8 million in 2007 (UNESCO, 2009), 5 million in 2014 (ICEF, 2015), and is expected to reach 8 million by 2025 (OECD, 2017).

The influx of international students in North Cyprus still maintains the status as a valuable topic. The United States, Canada, United Kingdom, Australia, Germany and France are the significant educational tourism destinations (Lee & Sehoole, 2015). North Cyprus has striven to be acknowledged as an edu-tourism destination regardless of the impediment on a direct flight and unbearable political conditions North Cyprus is capable of attracting more than 103,000 edu-tourists (TRNC Ministry of Education and Culture, 2021a).

Registered at 21 universities in Northern Cyprus (TRNC Ministry of Education and Culture, 2021b). Three decades ago, The Turkish Republic of Northern Cyprus was proclaimed unrecognised by many countries except Turkey; yet thousands of young people coming from more than 100 countries study at its universities, despite its economic and political segregation from the world by international trade sanctions and travel interjections; education has, therefore, become the significant pitch of its economy.

Therefore, comprehending the significant conditions that influence the choice of study destination has become salient for HE administrators. Abubakar et al. (2014) posit:

> Specific factors related to the choice of North Cyprus as a location for higher education have not been the focus of prior research. However, the location has been noted as an important factor in international students' choice related to higher education.

2.3. Globalisation and Internationalisation of Educational Tourism

Deciding to leave a country of origin to another one is a whole process, and there are many motivators attached to it (in both making the decision to leave the country and deciding where to go to) (OECD, 2017). Due to digital globalisation and the rise in competition in the educational tourism sector, there has been an increment in the inquisition of the mechanism faced by educational tourists in selecting an HEI destination (Alsharari & Nizar, 2018). Because of this, recruitment and promotional activities in HEI have escalated beyond the ordinary. Thus, HEI has been transformed from a dormant marketing domain to a highly marketed sector (Petruzzellis & Romanazzi, 2010). Alsharari et al. (2018) asserted that globalisation and internationalisation are not similar. Internationalisation emphasises strategically established relationships; internationalisation in HEI comprises partnerships with other HEI, exchange programs and educational tourist's recruitment. Meanwhile, globalisation is a picture of the competitiveness and the intensified collaborations in the world (Heather & Haydn, 2010).

2.4. Apprehending Educational Tourists' Decisions

International educational tourists' preference is an exciting aspect to study; this is because of the demand for HEI abroad and competition. Hence, education marketers need to know and understand prospective students' influencing factors in their decision-making. Ivy (2010) highlighted the three dimensions of the choice model. The total amount of money spent on a student's studies and the choice of education instead of work is what is being regarded as the economic model of student choice. At the same time, the social part has to do with the student's family relationship, personal motivation, ability and other areas of life. When the monetary aspect of the model of a student's choice blends with the student's family relationship and other aspects of life, it is then regarded as the information processing model for the student's choice. This is what determines the decision of a prospective student (Ivy, 2010). Researchers assume that it is quite uneasy about distinguishing educational tourists' choices. Maringe (2006) posits that a student's choice is not based on fact or reason; instead, it is based on feeling so. Therefore, the process is not rational. Petruzzellis and Romanazzi (2010) opine that choice is a concept of complexity, which is a fusion of three elements. All three are connected. These concepts are the following: the context, the key influencers and the choosers.

The primary focus of research into education choice behaviour is to focus on the key elements that influence decision-making (Doria, Mohd, & Abdul, 2017). Foskett and Hemsley-Brown (2001) point out differences in the mannerism of students' choice. This is majorly due to the foregrounding and emphasis on the belief of spending so much money on good services in HEI as a medium of preparing for the future career. Maringe and Carter (2007) have categorised general decision making into a five-stage process. This has identified problems that need their solution to recognition, discovering the information, examining the option, deliberating on the purchase choice and finally weighing the purchase decision. Some other researchers equally identify a consecutive sequence in the way educational tourists decide to further their studies overseas. The first resolution comes when an individual prefers institutions outside his country instead of their home country; after this, the individual begins to consider a study destination and then resorts to a particular institution (Chen, Chen, & Lee, 2010). Some students do not go through searching and choosing an institution but instead directly select an institution (Chen et al., 2010).

Nevertheless, many students go through various stages when choosing an HEI abroad (Abubakar et al., 2014). In the first level, the student chooses to go abroad to study with the influence of the 'push' factors within the motherland. In the second stage, the student decides on the study destination and examines the conditions that make the host country more attractive with 'pull' factors. Lastly, the student gets to select the institution in the final and third stage, with an additional 'pull' factors, deriving from what makes an institution preferable and attractive over its opponents, such as the institution image, accreditations, range of courses offered and staff professionalism (Abubakar et al. 2014; Wong, Daisy & Peggy, 2018).

2.5. Factors influencing Educational Tourists' Decision-Making Process

Recent studies have identified numerous factors affecting educational tourists' choice of learning destination (Doria et al., 2017). Amongst them are the 'push' and 'pull' factors that are regarded as what influences the international educational tourists' decision of study (Dann, 1977; Doria et al., 2017; Foskett & Hemsley-Brown, 2001; Mazzarol & Soutar, 2002). The principal theory that leads the discussion is based on the 'push and pull' theory of Dann (1977).

2.5.1. 'Push' and 'Pull' Factors. Travelling is an activity that has been placed with high esteem by tourism researchers; as such, the researchers have accorded studying the motivations, aims and understand the attitudes and behaviours of travellers towards their intended destination. Theses, amongst others, have necessitated the conceptualisation and application of travel theories in academics.

In 1959, Tolman developed a theory that was initially called the sign-gestalt paradigm. After several researchers used the concept, Dann (1977) described it as the push–pull theory to answer the question, 'What makes tourists travel?' This theory has been accorded great attention from scholars in the field of tourism research. The literature on what motivates travellers to stipulate that the use of push and push factors theory in the bid of understanding travellers' motivations has been overall adopted or validated.

Generally, the pull factor may be classified as the 'motivation for choosing a particular place'. In contrast, the push factor is classified as the undefined or invincible factors that bring about the tourist's need to seek something in another destination (Dann, 1977). For example, the push factors for an international tourist may be the lack of adequate facilities in his/her country or low standard of education. In contrast, the pull factor may be the quality of instructors, facilities and the international recognition or accreditation of the various programs in an HEI.

While classifying the most significant reason/s behind the acts and actions were taken by tourists, the most significant thing that comes to mind is the motivation (Jang & Cai, 2002). Motivation may be classified as the 'push' factor behind every step and action taken by tourists (Uysal & Jurowski, 1994). Regarding the push and pull factor, it is essential to state that the need for the gratification of needs and desires is the primary motivation behind tourists migrating from one place to another. When a person is motivated, he/she takes actions based on his/her innermost feeling to achieve satisfaction. For instance, when an educational tourist is emotionally attracted to a university to study, he/she will most likely be fulfilling certain factors and needs that are non-physical but will drive him/her to achieve a target goal or aspiration.

Understanding the motivation behind tourists' actions and choices cannot be overemphasised because motivation is an essential part of the reason the choice for the destination was made (Masserini et al., 2018). The tourism sector will also develop mainly due to proper organisation, which will also facilitate higher motivation amongst potential tourists. Understanding motivation in tourism is essential, and scholars such as Petruzzellis and Romanazzi (2010) argued that when tourists' motivations are well understood, there will be higher competition and more significant provision of tourists' needs in the market, tourist's contentment and primary stimulus are inter-related. Educational tourism marketers most distinguish travellers' motives before providing them with a destination choice.

Scholars have also called for the segmentation of the various markets and potential tourist destinations; this is to facilitate easy and direct accessibility for tourists (Dann, 1977; Tolman 1959). For instance, if the education sector is well segmented, educational tourists will access the potential markets and destinations (Uysal & Hagan, 1993). However, it will also improve the visibility of new and upcoming markets, invariably bringing about healthy competition. To achieve appropriate marketing that directly meets the target audience, it is essential to begin by understanding the audience's motivation. By that, appropriate measures will be taken, and customer satisfaction will be achieved. This reemphasises the importance, and unique role motivation plays in the field of tourism.

According to Dann (1977), when the wants, needs and, most importantly, the motivations of tourists are understood, it will improve the tourism sector and boost satisfaction and help tourists achieve satisfaction and have value for their choice.

A compilation of all the factors that have been discovered by scholars are illustrated in Table 1.

2.5.2. 'Push' and 'Pull' Factors.   Amid the 1960s–1970s, Cohen (1972) and McMahon (1992) expatiated on the excess flow of students from many developing countries and still expanding worldwide in general and to Canada, United Kingdom and United States specifically. The motives behind this expansion are categorised as 'push' and 'pull' factors. Several motivators were determined in literature. 'Push' factors encompass the failure in the home country's entrance exam, the desire to acquire a better life, better education abroad and a better future career. While the 'pull' factors comprise the location attractiveness, the HEI abroad reputation, the desire to acquire a better English knowledge, the desire to discover new cultures (Finch, McDonald, & Staple, 2013; Petruzzellis & Romanazzi, 2010). These factors are inter-related; there cannot be a pull without a push. There is first the birth of a desire to travel abroad due to psychological and societal factors. In selecting a destination, individual perceptions of how the desired destination should be have been put forward.

2.5.3. Influences from Social Network.   Another vital role for international tourists while deciding for HEI is the influence and recommendations from family members, relatives and friends (Doria et al., 2017; Eder et al., 2010). Pugsley and Coffey (2002) suggested that the main influences are commendations from currents and graduate students from educational tourist networks. Students eventually decide where they study, but their relatives, friends and family severely influence their decision by giving them pre-information and suggestions (Doria et al., 2017). Pimpa (2003) has made it known that the influence Taiwanese students gained from their families was different and dependent on the standard they had aspired. The more substantial part of the study interrogated the influence on family-based on finance and recommendation.

Furthermore, Mazzarol and Soutar's (2002) highlighted that parents have a more substantial influence on students in their first degree when selecting a learning destination abroad, particularly in Asian students. Lee and Morrish (2012) suggest that HEI marketers' primary target should be students and parents. The way to go about this is by emphasising the institution's capability to provide only the best and see the child through to getting the best in the institution (Doria et al., 2017).

2.5.4. Educational Destination Image. Key elements affecting the choice of an HEI destination have been identified by Mazzarol and Soutar (2002). He mentioned the information received by educational tourists about the country from commendations from the network, monetary concerns, scenery, location and relatives and friends.

According to Wilkins, Butt, and Heffernan (2018), an international student's institution's choice is influenced by a city or an institution's image. Its safety, scenery, cultural values, better living, international environment and ease of access are related to living in a host country (Counsell, 2011; Lee & Morrish, 2012). Rather than developing infrastructures and other facilities, a university should focus instead on meeting up with service towards international students and having a bonding relationship with them (Petruzzellis & Romanazzi, 2010). Masserini et al. (2018) highlighted student comfort and satisfaction as a driving force in choosing a study destination and an institute in particular. According to Wilkins et al. (2018), an institution's attractiveness and student needs have a connection. Students' cultural needs were taken into account, which helped to increase the reputation of the HEI because when the students leave, their satisfaction is displayed in a confident manner (Wong et al., 2018).

The reputational image of an institute will be one of the most considered options in the choice of study destination by students (Petruzzellis & Romanazzi, 2010; Wong et al., 2018). It is most definitely going to remain a salient medium to guide the choice of a study destination. Wong et al. (2018) present the influential factors that affect international students in deciding over an institution for studying: the quality of an institution and its repute, an HEI affiliation with other recognised institute as well, the professionalism of the staff, the number of students enrolled at the institution and students' qualifications being recognised. Ayantunji (2018) has indicated that the recognition of the UK HEI by many other countries contributes to why students choose to study in the United Kingdom. In brief, the reputation and destination image constitute a plus in choosing a study destination (Wong et al., 2018).

2.5.5. Cost of Program. The total sum of money required for studying a course is the most considered factor in preference of institutions with a similar course (Hemsley-Brown & Oplatka, 2015; Price, Matzdorf, Smith, & Agahi, 2003). When a person is selecting an institution abroad, the first thing they consider is their income. Educational tourists always consider the different costs (tuition fees, living expenses, scholarship availability) in choosing an HEI (Petruzzellis & Romanazzi, 2010). To Gupta and Kaushik (2018), students' motivation is also conditioned by securing their future career and personal success. Binsardi and Ekwulugo (2003) pointed out those students who are 'buying' the benefits that a degree can be beneficial in providing employment, status and lifestyle. The cost of a program, career prospect is an essential factor (Eder et al., 2010; Hemsley-Brown & Oplatka, 2015; Maringe & Carter, 2007).

2.5.6. Cultural Environment. As identified by some scholars, a destination's cultural environment plays a role in students' selection of a study destination (Kan, Cliquet, & Gallo, 2014). The thought of meeting other students from different nationalities entice many students in choosing a specific destination

(Abubakar et al., 2014). Underwood (2016) underlined that culture has to do with people's beliefs and views. Culture comprises language, behaviour and beliefs (Ayantunji, 2018). The Chinese educational tourists' motivation to study abroad and pick the UK aside other study destinations in the quest for a higher standard of education and a longing to advance and develop not only their language skills but the discovery of new cultures as well (Ayantunji et al., 2018). Chen and Zimitat (2006) discovered that the Taiwanese educational tourists believe that the HEI's attitude and sagacity in the study destinations is a factor that influences their decision to prefer some countries over others. Chung et al. (2009) also suggested that Asian students easily blend into any society and live in unity with one another, which is another strong factor that helps students make decisions to study abroad.

2.5.7. Online Communicating Culture. If there were sensitivity to cultural values, HEI would attract many more international student groups (Lee & Morrish, 2012). For this to be made possible, communication must be taken seriously. In this present day, online platforms have been used as a medium of interaction with educational tourists, resulting from globalisation and digitalisation (Chirkova, 2011).

In HEI marketing, communication and culture are inter-related. Barnes and Lescault (2013) assert that culture is an instrument, which affects the behaviour of a person also, the ideology, values, norms and social practices. They also establish the relationship between culture and communication, which defines intercultural understanding and competence (Nyangau & Bado 2012).

Some aspects of culture are always infused when communication occurs across the Internet. Furthermore, on the Internet, there is the space to allow that marketing mould information, which has been set aside for different cultures, including non-verbal and verbal communication (Nyangau & Bado, 2012; Usunier & Lee, 2009). The researchers mentioned above opine the presence of many languages on a website creates a tie and serves as respect for the different cultures. More so, they discuss how crucial online communication is, that during the exchanging of messages, the sender should consider the recipient's belief. Due to globalisation, awareness of culture has expanded (Barnes & Lescault, 2013). As those who can turn out to be customers in the future and other general users, come from all parts of the world, the emphasis is ben put on culture. In this regard, information shared on websites to target various cultures must be critically reviewed, and it is essential for effective interaction with educational tourists (Bodycott, 2009; Gupta & Kaushik, 2018; Lee & Morrish, 2012).

2.6. Edu-tourism and Online Marketing

With globalisation, competition and education, marketers have evolved into a new way of meeting the desires of educational tourists, which is online marketing (Adam & Alison, 2018). Binsardi and Ekwulugo (2003) argue that the medium for meeting consumer satisfaction is by making all marketing activities consumer-centred. HEI researchers in marketing have gradually recognised the marketing theories and concepts that are effective in the world of business (Hemsley-Brown & Oplatka, 2015). Adam and Alison (2018) determined the importance of marketing HEI online. Bornschlegl and Cashman (2018) posit that HEI should use online platforms for marketing their products to educational tourists.

The essence of describing the surge of globalisation previously is in the bid of expressing evolvement in the marketing of educational tourism destination. The invention and application of technology have established a significant effect on HEI destinations (Nyangau & Bado, 2012). Using information and communication technology in HEI (Kolowich, 2013; Skinner & Blackey, 2010) paves the way for HEI marketers to consider online for promotion purposes. The Internet plays a vital role as these industries require severe information, including the HEI sector. Thus, HEI vendors can set up valuable information online to incorporate a set of information attractive to educational tourists (Nyangau & Bado, 2012). Nowadays, international students now get attracted in due course with the appropriation of Australian institutions' technological advancements like the Internet in their marketing patterns and strategies. Since online marketing is regarded as a lower-cost strategy, it is now a significant alternative for education (Nyangau & Bado, 2012).

One of the technologies used by students when it comes to decision making is the website and e-mail. It gives a wide range of communication with prospective students, and the institution must not meet with the person. This aids in the decision process of the student, mostly (Aldridge, 2010). For this to be realised, education marketers need to get a comprehensive understanding of what the prospective students need. For this reason, relationship marketing is vital in the competitive HE sector (Pingping, 2014).

Social media has done a great deal by enhancing the channel of communication for educational marketers. With the invention of Facebook, Instagram and Twitter, marketers of education can now reach out to prospective students. Wong et al. (2018) and Adam and Alison (2018) explained how social media could aid educational learning in HEI. In recent times, individuals are conversant with the Internet and computer-based collaborations. Students are now taken to be digital natives because they had already been involved with the online world since they were young (Wankel, 2009). One of the advantages of social media is that it makes room for HEI to communicate with prospective students, regardless of the place or time, without costing so much money. Social media, in general, and Facebook in particular, should be used as a tool towards marketing HEIs (Adam & Alison, 2018).

2.7. Resume of the Key Elements influencing Educational Tourists' Decision in HEI

Table 1 underpins the main determinants of educational tourists' preferences or HE choices as pinpointed by early researchers. These determinants are presented in alphabetical order; meanwhile, that of analysts are presented in chronological order.

14   Melissa Rikiatou Kana Kenfack and Ali Öztüren

Table 1.   Main Determinants for Educational Tourism.

Factors			
Push	**Researchers**	**Pull**	**Researchers**
Career prospects	Counsell (2011) and Gupta and Kaushik (2018)	Cost	Abubakar et al. (2014) and Petruzzellis and Romanazzi (2010)
Instability in the home country		Environment (attractiveness)	Chen (2010)
Immigration prospects	Counsell (2011) and Lee and Morrish (2012)	Culture	Bodycott (2009) and Lee and Morrish (2012)
Lack of access to HE at home (failure to entrance exam)	Abubakar et al. (2014) and Bodycott (2009)	Marketing and promotion	Pingping (2014) and Phoebe et al. (2018)
Quality of life	Bodycott (2009) and Lam et al. (2016)	Quality of overseas HE system	Counsell (2011)
Instability in the home country		Social Network (Family, friends)	Lee (2014) and McCarthy et al. (2012)
		Safety	Wilkins, Butt and Heffernan (2018)
		Visa application process (ease of access)	Eder et al. (2010)

3. A Case Study in Northern Cyprus

3.1. Description of the Case and the Methodology

This research was carried out at Eastern Mediterranean University (EMU), the largest university in North Cyprus, with 1,200 academic staff from over 20 different countries worldwide, and around 20,000 both local and international students. There are 100 undergraduate and school programs in EMU, and 81 postgraduate and doctoral degree programs provided by 11 faculties, 5 schools and Foreign Languages and English Preparatory School (EMU, 2018). Amongst all universities in North Cyprus, EMU is the only HEI featuring in the United Kingdom on a list (Times Higher Education (THE)); THE features 2,150 HEIs from 93 countries (THE, 2020). EMU has been ranked 46th in the Global Ranking of Academic Subjects 2020 of China-based Shanghai Ranking. This independent organisation has been the official publisher of the Academic Ranking of the World Universities since 2009 (http://www.shanghairanking.com/

Shanghairanking-Subject-Rankings/hospitality-tourism-management.html).
As the only university from Cyprus appearing on the said list, EMU is also the
top-ranking university amongst the universities of Turkey (https://www.emu.edu.
tr/en/news/news/emu-appears-in-shanghai-rankings-once-again/1206/pid/3443).

A qualitative approach was chosen for the research due to the nature of the
study. This method allows researchers to have a deeper understanding of the
research area; besides, it is time-saving; it lessens social pressure (Qu & Dumay,
2011). Besides, a qualitative research approach is the most favourable while
attempting to answer the questions 'why' and 'how', and online qualitative
research has been becoming frequent in researches (Qu & Dumay, 2011; Strzoda,
2006). Therefore, a qualitative study design was adopted for this exploratory study
utilising semi-structured interviews. Educational tourists were asked to state their
motivators ranking from the most important according to their preferences.

A qualitative approach was chosen for the research due to the nature of
the study. This method allows researchers to have a deeper understanding of
the research area; besides, it is time-saving and lessens social pressure (Qu &
Dumay, 2011). Besides, a qualitative research approach is the most favourable
while attempting to answer the questions 'why' and 'how', and online qualitative
research has been becoming frequent in researches (Qu & Dumay, 2011; Strzoda,
2006). Therefore, a qualitative study design was adopted for this exploratory study
utilising semi-structured interviews. Educational tourists were asked to state their
motivators ranking from the most important according to their preferences.

The authors sourced for literature in the field of HE and international educational
tourists' motivations through libraries and online search before the data collection
was carried out. A more significant part of the new literature search was done through
the EMU database (Özay Oral Library) with academic online journals.

The data collection was carried out in three stages, with three groups of
respondents:

1. Interviews with international students in North Cyprus
2. Interviews with the university staff
3. Interview with oversees recruitment agents.

According to the three sets, as mentioned above of respondents, the interviews
focussed on gathering information on the causes that make students decide on
their study destinations. In this order, three specific sets of interviews were framed
to carry out the present study. Semi-structured interviews were used as a tool to
acquire information from people on particular issues and topics on individual and
personal experiences (Salmons, 2014). This study used semi-structured interview
design with the same questions to compare the respondents' answers for exploring the similarities and differences. This research approach requires a clear topical
focus and a well-developed understanding of the topic (Cohen & Crabtree, 2006).

The sample size is influenced by many factors, of which time and cost are two
considerable factors (Bryman, 2008). This research sample size was restrained due
to participants' unavailability, with time also been a constraint. Participants in
this research were retrieved through the researcher's university network, resulting in a convenience sampling. The authors first contacted the staff dealing with

16   Melissa Rikiatou Kana Kenfack and Ali Öztüren

promotion for the university. Furthermore, potential interviewees implicated in promotions at EMU were distinguished. Invitations to participate in the research study were done via e-mail, phone call, and face to face to the EMU staff, international students and representatives.

Twenty invitations were sent to each group to take part in the interview. However, 15 international students, 15 staff and 15 representatives agreed to participate in the research. The target respondents were the leaders, who are representatives of students from their nationality before the university (EMU), staff who are involved in promotions and EMU 'VIP' representatives or agents, who are those who have been dealing with EMU for more than 5 years and are continually sending a considerable amount of students to EMU each semester.

The analysis of this research was done through thematic analysis (Braun & Clarke, 2006). Thematic analysis is done into various phases. First, data are collected, then coded and grouped into themes and sub-themes. Responses to interviews were compiled and arranged or transcribed concurrently. Once all interviews had been compiled and transcribed, the researcher started developing codes. Hennink et al. (2011) defined a code as a subject discussed or underlined by participants in the interviews and can be pinpointed while analysing data.

Upon coding, information received, repeated subjects were grouped into themes, which were, in turn, analysed and distributed into sub-themes. The same patterns were used to scrutinise responses from EMU agents and staff. The researcher used Student 1 as 'S1', Student 2 'S2'…Student 15 as 'S15' to cite responses from students. Similarly, Agent 1 (A1), Agent 15 (A15) for agents, and Staff 1 were (E1), Staff 15 (E15) for staff.

3.2. Findings and Discussion of Results

This section unveils findings from the data analysis of the interviews. It pays attention to underlining the key elements influencing international educational tourists' decisions in selecting North Cyprus as their study destination 'pull'.

In our findings, the pull factors are emphasised more. This is because push factors are relatively similar for educational tourists and amongst countries. Nevertheless, they will be highlighted in Table 2. Table 2 underlines the summary of Factors, and Table 3 compiles comparative results of the research factors motivating international students to travel abroad for study purposes.

Upon analysis of responses from the 45 participants in this research of which 15 were students from Algeria (1), Azerbaijan (1) Cameroon (2), Congo (1), Iran (2), Lebanon (1), Libya (1), Morocco (1), Nigeria (1), Palestine (1), Yemen (2), Zimbabwe (1), 15 were staff dealing with promotion at EMU and 15 were Educational agents from Azerbaijan (1), Egypt (1), Iran (3), Libya (1), Nigeria (2), North Cyprus (1), Palestine (2), Saudi Arabia (2), Syria (2), many factors have been identified to power international educational tourists' decision in choosing North Cyprus as their study destination. Those determinants are grouped into eight categories that are cost, ease of access, social factors, location, quality of education, the language of instruction, cultural environment and quality of communication.

Participants in this survey were asked to rank the factors according to what they considered the most important. More details will be given in Table 2.

Table 2. Summary of Motivators.

Push	Pull
Lack of desired programs	Cost
Poor quality of education	Ease of Access
Desire to obtain a better future career	Social Factors
Instability in home country (political and economic)	Location
	Quality of Education
	Language of Instruction
	Cultural Environment
	Quality of Communication

The cost factor relates to the relatively low tuition fees compared to other countries, and the availability of scholarships. The ease of access here entails the easy accessibility of North Cyprus in terms of visa and application fees. The location factor entails the North Cyprus environment, safety and attractiveness. Social factors refer to respondents' relationships and social networks. Quality of education has to do with the accreditations, and programs, diploma recognition worldwide. Language of instruction refers to the desired medium of instruction convenient to international students despite a country's national language. Cultural environment refers to the diversity of the population.

3.2.1. Cost.   The interview responses showed that the cost factor plays a vital role in attracting educational tourists to North Cyprus. The cost here entails the relatively low tuition fee compared to the quality of education and accreditations and the scholarship opportunities. Many students, while considering a study destination, might be sometimes refrained by the cost of education.

According to S1:

> The educational system is Similar to UK & USA but much cheaper.

This is clear that cost has a direct impact on student choice of study destination or institution. Besides the tuition fees, the availability of scholarship equally constitutes an aspect of cost considered by the respondents.

S3 specified that:

> I decided to come to EMU because I found the tuition affordable … In addition to that, the 50% weaver scholarship the school offers.

In other words, the cost factor has a significant impact on students' study destination decisions. The availability of scholarships and low tuition fees provides more direction to students while deciding on their future HE locations.

3.2.2. Ease of Access.   Many students travel to North Cyprus without having to apply for a visa. North Cyprus is a visa-free destination for some countries, and

18   Melissa Rikiatou Kana Kenfack and Ali Öztüren

Table 3.   Motivators in Selecting an Educational Tourism Destination.

	Ranking	Educational Tourists	Staff	Agents
Motivators (ranking from most essential motivators according to each category of respondents)	1	Cost (93%)	Location (86%)	Quality of communication (83%)
	2	Ease of access (93%)	Quality of education (80%)	Quality of education (80%)
	3	Social factors (86%)	Cultural environment (80%)	Ease of access (66%)
	4	Location (80%)	Cost (66%)	Language of instruction (60%)
	5	Quality of education (66%)	Language of instruction (60%)	Location (53%)
	6	Language of instruction (53%)	Social factors (53%)	Cost (46%)
	7	Cultural environment (40%)	Ease of access (40%)	Social factors (40%)
	8	Quality of communication (33%)	Quality of communication (33%)	Cultural environment (40%)

some nationalities can obtain an e-visa at the airport. This is a significant factor for many respondents, as the visa is not easy to be obtained in many countries. Students are sometimes restrained from going to a specific destination to further their studies due to visa denial.

S6 expressed that choosing North Cyprus for her HEI destination was also influenced by the fact that:

> ......*No visa is required.*

Similarly, S9 buttress this assertion by stating that:

> *The fact that North Cyprus is easily accessible was a plus for me ...*

S7 also share his view with us by positing that:

> *I decided to come to North Cyprus because the process the get here was not as hard as other countries.*

Ease of access here also relates to the non-applicability of application fee and easy application procedure. The fact that the application is free, unlike in many other countries, and easy as well, entice prospective students to proceed and with the application process.

S14 rightly stated that:

> *I was enticed by the ease of student visa, low time in processing documents, the fast admission processing ...*

Many Respondents fall into this category. The fact that Northern Cyprus is easily reachable and the EMU application process is effortless, and no application fee applies.

3.2.3. Social Network. The social network was the main factor for the respondents. It entailed educational tourists coming to North Cyprus. It decided to enrol at EMU through family members and friends who form the majority, are already enrolled, or have studied in EMU. One of the respondents stated S4:

> *I knew about EMU through a friend... I was searching for a good university in a friendly environment to start my graduate studies; he suggested I came here....*

Their family members powered the decisions of S5 and S9:

> S5 stated: '*My elder sister was studying there, so I decided to come*'.

> S9: 'My *uncle graduated in EMU*'.

86% out of 15 respondents came to know about EMU and North Cyprus through family and friends, and 20% through agents and 7% through the exhibition. Therefore, we noticed from the responses that many students' decisions to travel to North Cyprus were influenced by the fact that they had friends or family members who were already enrolled at EMU or family members who graduated from EMU. Moreover, they should constitute a target market of HEI marketers.

3.2.4. Location. The location factor entails the environment, scenery, international population and safety dimensions.

3.2.4.1. Scenery. North Cyprus is well-known for its beaches, touristic and historical sites, mountains and scenery. Many respondents were attracted by the fact that North Cyprus is firstly an island, therefore, located beside the sea. Its natural beauty cannot be ignored. Results from our data show that the natural attractiveness of a place is essential in deciding on a study destination. One of the respondents (S1) described his first impression as follows:

> *Northern Cyprus is well-known for its monuments, historical places, and touristic places. I was born and grown in a seaside city, so the sea is essential for my well-being.*

> *To another respondent S2:*

> *EMU ... has a beautiful campus, and it is located in a coastal city.....*

20   *Melissa Rikiatou Kana Kenfack and Ali Öztüren*

3.2.4.2. Safety.   Many respondents see North Cyprus as an attractive country due to its renowned reputation regarding safety and relatively low crime rate.
S13 expressed this factor in these words:

> *The main reason I decided to study in Cyprus is due to the serene and peaceful environment which is convenient for study.*

A country's safety is a critical factor in selecting a study destination, as many come from a background where they have not been used to peace and safety. The safety environment is most definitely conducive to a successful education.
S11 well expressed his point of view on safety as follows:

> *I had many places in mind, but the most things that made up my mind were the location of Cyprus and, that it is a safe country to live in…*

Thus, it is evident from the results that aside from the natural beauty of a country, a safe environment is a propulsion in selecting a HE abroad.

3.2.5. Quality of Education.   The quality of education students receives of great importance, according to responses from our findings. Knowing that the courses educational tourists study are accredited, and diploma recognises worldwide bring of satisfaction and contribute to the decision-making process of selecting an institution.
S8 stated that:

> *In my case, I had to choose between France, Turkey, and North Cyprus. France has a quota for international students plus the major I was interested in was very hard. I made research and found out that EMU is one of the best universities in Cyprus and Turkey for what I intended to study, so my choice was easy.*

S11 and S15 similarly stated that:

> *… and I chose EMU because of the ranking and the accreditations that it has. The diploma is recognizable in all countries.*

> *S15: 'The advantage to me is I could get the education I could not get from home'.*

We, therefore, notice that the quality of education matters to many respondents; Knowing that the program they study is accredited, and they attend a university with international standards that constitute a significant element in their decision-making process of a HEI.

3.2.6. Medium of Instruction.   The language of instruction was a vital aspect to participants in our survey. Knowing that they could enrol in a program with English as the language of instruction was a prominent step in choosing North Cyprus and EMU as their study destination.

Key Factors in the Selection of an Educational Tourism Destination **21**

To S14, one of his motivations was the fact that:

'Programs are held in English'.

To interviewees, moving to a country where they are aware they will be taught in English is a plus in their decision-making process in choosing HEI. S1 underlined that:

EMU is well ranked worldwide … To be honest, it is one of the best places where you can study, with most of the programs been taught in English.

English is not the first language for many. The awareness that they will learn English entices them in selecting a HEI to acquire more knowledge of English and further pursue their education in the medium, as mentioned above of instruction.

3.2.7. International Environment. Another factor of location is the international environment. According to some respondents, the diversity of a place is essential for choosing a study destination. EMU presents itself as an institution with students from 106 countries. The majority of respondents see diversity in an institution as a significant advantage. It enables them to learn from different cultures and meet people from different nationalities and learn new languages. Besides, the internationalisation of an institution can be perceived via the availability of languages on its website.

S9 and S10 described the importance of internationalisation in an educational institution as follows:

S9 *'……for me it is a big advantage having friends from different cultures and countries'.*

S10 *'Meeting many international students and receiving huge experience of interacting with multicultural education was a plus in choosing EMU'.*

Therefore, we notice that the presence of international students in EMU from various countries entices other students in their decision-making process.

3.2.8. Quality of Communication. The communication determinant entails the medium through which students received information before arriving North Cyprus (website, social media, promotion) and the perceived quality received from communication exchange between the institution and the interviewees.

Responses from the interviews reveal that social media and online interaction platforms are crucial in connecting educational tourists and the university, before and after their arrival at the university. The communication factor can be dissected into two subcategories that are the online and offline communication channels.

3.2.8.1. Online Communication. After knowing about the university, many tried to get in touch with the university through phone, e-mail, social media and by gathering information through the website. The online communication factor

22 Melissa Rikiatou Kana Kenfack and Ali Öztüren

entails the accessibility of information from the website and social media and the quality of interaction between respondents and institutions.

S4 shared his experience with us on communicating with EMU:

> *I knew about EMU through a friend...... I started visiting their website frequently and contacting the international office. I would say the best that motivated me to apply EMU is the efficiency of the international office, the strategy of being very welcoming and answering whatever dumb question you throw at them.*

Information provided by the university on their website, e-mail and social media is critical. Some respondents highlighted that clear, simple and straightforward navigation of the website is essential.

S12 shared that:

> *It was a commercial video. It was so well made that I just wanted to reach that place and see it by myself.*

From these responses, we see that no aspect is to be left unconsidered. The e-mail responses, the easily accessible and straightforward information from the website, can play significant roles in influencing educational tourists' decisions while still in their home country.

3.2.8.2. Offline Communication.   The offline communication channel relates to face-to-face interaction that a student has with the educational institution's representatives through fairs and exhibitions before travelling to North Cyprus. This may play a huge factor in influencing students' study destination. However, from our research outcomes, few respondents have been influenced by an offline communication channel before travelling to North Cyprus. Those who could get in touch with the university representatives in their home country through exhibitions and fairs share their experiences as pleasant and informative.

S3 express that:

> *I first heard on EMU through some friends and family, but I got all the information needed to get convinced from a desk in the mall of Mersin.*

Many who came to EMU through agents first knew from their friends and relatives and then went to agents for direction on how to apply. Some were referred to agents through their friends, but the first-hand information was from their friends.

S10 stated that he has heard about North Cyprus and EMU:

> *'Through referral and promotional programs'.*

The fact that North Cyprus is an island, EMU, has a high international population with approximately 20,000 students, of which around 9,000 are international students. According to the respondents, one of the leading influencers for choosing North Cyprus as their study destination was its location.

3.3. Discussion of the Critical Factors

This section discusses the research results in line with the results of the past researches. Practical implications for HEI in general and HEI in North Cyprus, in particular, are equally proposed and outlined in this section.

There is a notable competition between HEIs all over the world. Therefore, there is a necessity for an in-depth understanding of what influences educational tourists' choice of study destination. As discovered from our findings, there might be a plurality of factors motivating students to select their study destination. However, eight main factors were dominants: cost, ease of access, social factors, location, quality of education, the language of instruction, cultural environment and quality of communication. The factors mentioned above will be discussed further, taking into account past researches.

3.3.1. Cost. About what influences international educational tourists' decisions, the evidence is shown via the data analysis and is backed up by earlier research. The cost is an important issue and has an impact on where educational tourists will go to. This factor could be a restriction to educational tourists in their decision-making process of a specific destination. The cost of the study could restrain many. Abubakar et al. (2014) reinstated that the provision of low tuition and more scholarship can be a medium for attracting more students. Respondents placed a severe concern to the program and cost. Considering the average individual's sensitivity to cost, it is highly understandable that students pay more attention to low tuition (Petruzzellis & Romanazzi, 2010). Based on this research finding, it becomes imperative for HEI to find ways to provide lower tuition costs if there is the intention to attract a higher number of students. However, suppose lower tuition costs do not seem feasible to the institution. Other measures of financial aids could be employed, such as providing various percentages of performance-based scholarships, student employment within the institution ecosystem, research and teaching assistantships, student loans and opportunities for payment of fees in instalments. HEI management also has to focus on making space for scholarships and financial aids because the cost is a vital factor (Abubakar et al., 2014). These measures could help alleviate the direct effects of the tuition fees on potential students and serve as incentives for attraction.

3.3.2. Ease of Access. Our findings noted that the ability to travel to a country easily is of great importance to educational tourists. In selecting an educational destination, some educational tourists may encounter the barrier of accessing the country, such as visa denial, a long process in admission (Abubakar et al., 2014). This is also argued by Eder et al. (2010). They assert that even if educational tourists are willing to further their education in a country, if they are denied accessibility in the country, they will not travel or enrol in the institution, despite their tenacious willingness to further their study abroad. For instance, after finding attraction in a country like Canada, for example, and after being given admission in an institution in Canada, may not enrol due to the visa barrier, despite the strong willingness to enrol. Besides, some educational tourists may be faced with the application fee charged by HEI. As highlighted in our research, students may be attracted to an institution. However, the institution's application fee may slow the student's motivation to apply in the institution (Lee, 2007). Therefore, this is an essential factor for educational tourists. Our interviewees found easy access to North Cyprus, both in terms of visa and application process. This was a pull in their decision-making process.

3.3.3. Social Network. The respondents placed a high priority on social factors. This goes in line with what was suggested by early research with regards to influence from family and friends (Doria et al., 2017; Gomes & Murphy, 2003). Getting hold of parents' attention, in education affairs and renditions in countries like Taiwan and China, leads to setting both parents and educational tourists as primary targets. This could turn out to be a plan for increasing educational tourist's presence in a country or institution.

In selecting their study destination, the majority of the educational tourists interviewed leaned on their friend's recommendations and experiences. To them, knowing the experiences of their friends who are already enrolled in an institution helps them in their decision-making process. Furthermore, their decision could also be based on having an acquaintance or relative enrolled in an institution. The opinions, recommendations from social network enable them to know in advance where they are heading to; and also, going to an institution where their relatives or friends are enrolled make them feel more comfortable. HEI institutions have to pay more attention to their student's needs and wants to attend to them, which will result in a continuous increase in positive word of mouth.

3.3.4. Location. The location has a force on which is essential in the decision of educational tourists' study destination (Kan et al., 2014). One of the attractions of our educational tourist's respondents to North Cyprus is the country's location, safety and attractiveness. Northern Cyprus is well-known for its monuments, historical and touristic places. The idea of studying in an environment surrounded by beaches is an enticement to educational tourists. This is supported by Chen et al. (2010), who argue that a country's physical appearance, climate, historical buildings, beaches and overall geographical characteristics are attractive tools to educational tourists. In our research, interviewees did not dither or waver in mentioning the geographical location and physical appearance of North Cyprus as a motivator in their decision process. This was indicated by 80% of the respondents.

Nevertheless, it was not amongst the first two factors. Some were born and grew in a seaside city, so the sea is essential for their well-being. Besides the geographical location and country's attractiveness, safety was imperative to more than half of the participants. Educational tourists expressed their necessity of living in a safe environment, as many came from countries where there is political instability, war and social dangers. Knowing North Cyprus as a safe environment, with a relatively low crime rate was crucial to many respondents.

3.3.5. Quality of Education. The information a person has about a study destination quality of programs or courses plays a role in their decision-making process. From our responses, EMU accreditations, institution ranking and diploma recognition are essential to educational tourists. Previous studies show that the importance of HEI quality and image in terms of institution ranking, recognition, employment opportunities after graduation, and adequate facilities, is a great tool in attracting international students (Aldridge, 2010).

Several respondents regarded EMU's accreditations as a critical factor while deciding on their study destination. It is essential to choose an institution that diplomas are recognised worldwide, as this will aid in their future career prospects. What is the essence of studying in an institution where the programs are not accredited, neither diploma recognised? It may have a future long term negative impact in the career world. Wong et al. (2018) also posit that students do not choose where to study based on the love of the course or discipline; however, there is a particular factor that influences the choice of prospective students which further draws their attention to the quality of program and course of study.

Therefore, an institution's reputation in terms of ranking and accreditation is an imperial factor to educational tourists. HEI management has to keep creating awareness of its features in terms of ranking and accreditations and work towards the continual improvement of their quality of education to attract more prospective educational tourists.

3.3.6. Medium of Instruction. Despite not being an English-speaking country, HEI's in North Cyprus, such as EMU, offers a plurality of courses with English as the language of instruction. The medium of instruction was a significant issue for respondents of this survey. First, gaining knowledge of the English language for some and, second, learning a chosen English course constituted a motivator for educational tourists. This supports Finch et al. (2013), who argue that educational tourists travel abroad with the quest to gain knowledge of English. This stands as both a pull and a push factor. It is well-known that English is the most spoken language worldwide, both in the social and career world. It is an international language and a link of communication with tourists all over the world. English is no more used as just a primary language, and it is equally used in creating connections, relationships and connecting to the world. Respondents of this survey support that English is not a 'should know' language, but a 'must know' language. Therefore, choosing an institution with English as the language of instruction is elementary. Besides, some job offers require knowledge of English. Educational tourists desiring to acquire their professional careers in countries like the United States, United Kingdom, or Canada, for example, most have a good knowledge of English. Therefore, choosing an institution with English courses is elementary to educational tourists, and providing courses with English as the language of instruction is a plus towards attracting educational tourists.

3.3.7. Cultural Environment. Culture has been identified in the HEI sector as an issue (Counsell, 2011; Lee & Morrish, 2012). Amongst the critical factors that affect respondents' decisions, culture has usually been unimportant factors to consider. Therefore, this study has indicated that culture is an implicit issue when it comes to choosing study destinations (Lee & Morrish, 2012).

One of the numerous factors considered in HEI abroad is culture. Educational tourists who were interviewed tended to indicate knowing a culture different from theirs as a motive for their decision, even though not the primary motive. The chance to learn new cultures, discover new ways of living, influenced their choice of destination. Culture should be buttressed upon during marketing HE because of international students' desire to meet other students from all over the world. HEI marketers might consider findings from early studies by acknowledging

26 *Melissa Rikiatou Kana Kenfack and Ali Öztüren*

cultures in designing their marketing strategies (Würtz, 2006). As found in our research, the multiculturalism of North Cyprus is an enhancement in educational tourist's choice of North Cyprus as their study destination.

3.3.8. Communication. The Internet has been regarded as the enormous umbrella of communication. In this age of digitalisation, the Internet today has emerged as an essential tool for communication. This study has revealed that one significant influencing factor of educational tourists' decision is the communication factor. Respondents searched for information regarding the institution that they were interested in. This ideology supports past research underlines that institutions are located through search engines by the students (Gomes & Murphy, 2003; Gottschall & Saltmarsh, 2017). To recruit more international educational tourists, HEI has to make avail of their websites on the search with the most traffic (Asle & Gheorghita, 2013).

Communication between educational tourists and institutions plays a significant role in educational tourists' decisions (Asle & Gheorghita, 2013). This could be done by phone, chat, or e-mail correspondence. After finding an institution, students go online to search for information about the institution. The quality of responses they receive from e-mail, phone calls, or social media platforms is valuable to them. This implies that the HEI needs to place providing personalised, polite and prompt messages, preferably e-mail messages. The educational quality of the university would not be doubted. If the respondents received no response from the university they inquired on, slightly, the university's administrative competence would be doubted. This only has one interpretation: the image of the university is represented by the correspondence, which plays a useful role in the educational tourists' choice of institution.

Furthermore, the respondents indicated that a university should have a clear website, attractive videos and be more interactive on social media platforms such as Facebook, Instagram and other instant messaging channels. Surprisingly both educational marketers and staff of EMU buy the idea. Researches have shown that most of these educational tourists are frequent users of social media (Adam & Alison, 2018; Asle & Gheorghita, 2013). This will enable the university and the prospective edu-tourists to have real conversations when needed (Adam & Alison, 2018). The majority of the prospective students who were privileged to have communicated with EMU appreciated the quality of interaction, facilitating their decisions towards study destination.

In the data analysis, it has been indicated that various components affect educational tourists' study destination choice, and these factors have also been argued out. Understanding the driving forces and the reasons international students choose a specific study destination is essential. This would help the university to appropriate them in the HEI sector. This study further shows that academic collaboration with other institutions is keen to bring more educational tourists. While taking care of their cost, nevertheless, North Cyprus is an enticing study destination for international educational tourists. Despite the fact of challenges, which include decentralisation, embargo, political pressure. All these factors act as a motivator to international educational tourists in choosing North Cyprus as their study destination. Knowing that they will obtain a quality education at an

Key Factors in the Selection of an Educational Tourism Destination   27

affordable price, while enjoying the scenery of North Cyprus, living in it a safe environment.

Nevertheless, to maintain a continuous increase in the recruitment of international students and for the betterment and smooth recruitment, some recommendations were made by students, EMU representatives and staff. Institutions can use some tools in redesigning their promotional approaches towards the recruitment of international students, and they will be discussed in our next section.

3.4. Conclusion and Recommendations

This section concludes our research in light of our findings. Furthermore, the recommendations for future research are equally proposed and outlined in this section. In conclusion, this research brings about a response to what motivates educational tourists to choose North Cyprus as their study destinations.

There is an evolution in education in the world today, which is studying outside of one's home country. Study abroad involvement is on the increase, and it is at an all-time high and will continue to increase. However, before a student studies abroad, they must first make a firm decision that they want to study abroad, and then they must choose their final study destination. This study centres on identifying the major causes and influences of students in the process of their decisions of selecting an Edu-tourism destination.

Our results showed that there are pull concealed behind every educational tourists' choice of destination. Many of those pulls were mentioned during our interview; nevertheless, the redundant ones were cost, ease of access, location, social factors, quality of education, the language of instruction, cultural environment and quality of communication. This study contributes further to the validation of the push and pull factors theory. The low standard of education in the home country, the desire to obtain better education push educational tourists to seek education abroad. EMU has provided a high-quality standard of education, in an appealing and international environment, making it attractive to educational tourists.

Furthermore, pull them to travel to North Cyprus and further their studies in EMU. Besides, educational tourists mentioned the ease of access to North Cyprus as an essential factor in their decision-making process. They asserted that many countries such as '...' do not readily accept students in their countries. They set rules and regulations, making it hard for educational tourists to easily enrol in institutions in their countries, as mentioned by a respondent, thus creating a barrier to many other educational tourists. Countries that wish to be educational tourism destinations should consider this aspect, as it is one of the main factors that affected the educational tourist's final decision to further their studies in North Cyprus. The ease of access factor has been limitedly discussed in past researches as a motive to educational tourists.

Therefore, it is vital for HE marketers and countries. They wish to be educational tourism destinations to take those critical factors into account in the establishment of their marketing strategies. Also, as identified in this research, many interviewees came to know about EMU and North Cyprus through their

28 Melissa Rikiatou Kana Kenfack and Ali Öztüren

relatives or friends who were already enrolled in EMU; they, therefore, proceeded in searching for more information online and through educational representatives. Word of mouth plays a great role in attracting educational tourists. Therefore, EMU could alleviate their work and have their students assist them in the marketing process by improving the key elements already mentioned in general, and paying critical attention to students' recommendations and complaints in particular since they constitute a crucial element or tool prospective students' decision making. The contrast between responses from the different participants in this study adds to the knowledge about educational tourists' motives from the point of view of the three main stakeholders in the educational tourism industry.

In general, this study support results from past literature with regards to educational tourism destination motivation. It emphasises the ease of access, social network factor and contrast between responses from various participants in this study as critical elements in motivation, which should be taken into great consideration. This knowledge is a great tool for HE marketers and institutions in developing specific marketing strategies for attracting Educational Tourists.

Recommendations from educational tourists, EMU staff, educational agents, and recommendations for North Cyprus HEI are provided in this part. The possible future development for North Cyprus HEI is that education marketers need to grasp and consider factors influencing educational tourists' decisions and know how to make utilise them.

Tuition fees: In setting up tuition fees, HEI should consider the intricacy of students towards tuition fees if they intend to attract and retain a considerable number of students. Consideration of the low or non-availability of job opportunities should not be neglected. Nevertheless, in case keeping a low tuition fee seems to be unachievable to HEI, other actions could be implemented such creating more job openings for students in HEI, having an agreement with the government in encouraging a percentage of employment of educational tourists every year with a minimum wage, a well-planned followed up and organised social funding for students with the intent of assisting those who are unable to provide for their tuition cost. These measures put into action, will lessen the immediate sequel repercussion of the tuition costs on potential students and serve as incentives for attraction.

Collaboration with other HEI abroad: North Cyprus HEI should establish more collaboration with other countries and have affiliations with their HEI, to attract international educational tourists; for instance, collaborations with high schools and universities in other countries (Lee & Morrish, 2012). This may also result in sending their staff (lecturers) for training in those HEI abroad they agree with. In turn, those lecturers may play a role in attracting educational tourists by these last been aware of the institution the lecturers came. Besides, North Cyprus HEI needs to establish more exchange programs agreements with other HEI abroad. This put into place may serve as incentives for attraction.

Student's needs and wants: HEI should pay more attention to student's needs and wants, as to increase their satisfaction, which will result in 'indirectly' attracting educational tourists. This is obvious from our findings that educational tourists first knew about EMU and North Cyprus through their friends and relatives, and further proceeded in acquiring more information about EMU through its website and other communication mediums. It is notable that the first-hand information and knowledge came from the social network, and mainly students who are already enrolled in EMU. These students acted as 'indirect marketers' to the university. Therefore, working towards the satisfaction of these could result in attracting more educational tourists. This could be done by deriving information from students and parents about the advantages and uses of these for effective marketing while improving the disadvantages students may face.

Quality of communication: HEI should pay to consider the quality of communication with educational tourists'. It is evident from our findings that educational tourists resort to websites, social media, or e-mail to access more information after hearing about the university. In North Cyprus, HEI should develop a relationship-building bond and quality service provision while attending to educational tourists online and offline. This increases educational tourists' satisfaction and will be of significant influence in their decision-making process. Quality of communication also serves as attributing an image to an institution (Adam & Alison, 2018).

Thus, training employees to provide adequate and immediate answers to educational tourist requests from various social media platforms becomes paramount. There should be skills acquisition for employees based on communication (Wong et al., 2018). Due to globalisation, the Internet has taken over the communication sector; in this light, HEI's communication mediums to interact with educational tourists on platforms such as Facebook, Instagram, e-mail chat, could be focussed on (Adam & Alison, 2018). Also, offline communication on no account should not be neglected to attract international educational tourists. Just as for online communication, promotional staff needs to be continuously trained in attending to students' inquiries during exhibitions, fairs, promotional tours. (Mazzarol & Soutar, 2002).

The majority of HEI Websites in North Cyprus already have various languages besides English to target international educational tourists. North Cyprus HEI could simply regularly update its website and keep it as simple as possible and straightforward to enable educational tourists to navigate (Asle & Gheorghita, 2013) swiftly.

Online Marketing: Mediums of communication such as Facebook, e-mail, have been identified as an essential medium of communication for educational tourists to get in touch to HEI. Respondents discussed the importance of Facebook as a means for interaction with the university; in this case, a constant presence of qualified and well-informed staff will affect educational tourists' final decisions.

Although most of the interactions with educational tourists are done 'online', interviewees underline that offline interaction such as HEI promotional tours, taking place in various nations, plays a significant function in attracting international educational tourists.

Exchange programs: Exchange programs are already held at EMU. Nevertheless, more collaboration with other universities in other countries was recommended by students. Respondents suggest more cooperation with other HEI enhances educational tourist's choice. Besides, awareness of these collaborations should be advertised by the university. Also, an exchange program for master's students should be put in place. Master's students may further their study in North Cyprus, prepare their thesis in another country, have a limited period been assigned to them, and return to EMU to defend their work. This will create an open the door to international students in opening their scope to other places and may lead to job opportunities after graduation. This will also lead to attracting more educational tourists, as they will hope to visit other countries in the bid of broadening their scope of learning.

Government: The government should come up with a set of policies friendly towards international students. We noticed throughout our research that the main point of knowledge of North Cyprus in general and EMU, in particular, was through 'word of mouth' from educational tourists' relatives and friends who, however, complained of low job availability, and low-income off-campus. To some students, it is essential to have something doing while studying. To keep increasing word of mouth, the government should set up rules and regulations that are favourable to international students in terms of rent and job availability.

Besides, encouraging jobs to be offered to international students, with a maximum working hour per week, to set the minimum wage for international students, encourage proper treatment of foreigners at the workplace by the government, as it was a concern from some respondents.

The government can also set up rental agreements that are to be followed both by students and house owners, such as monthly payment options, yearly checking of houses conditions by owners.

Lastly, North Cyprus is a country populated by central youths. The government should put in place attraction places, artificial sites and amusement parks for the enjoyment of both local and foreigner youths.

Scholarships: Grants and tuition cost have been identified as necessary to educational tourists. A well-organised system for grants, social aids and funds for educational tourists should be established. Better services which would help the welfare of international educational tourists like scholarships and accommodation supports and other costs could be provided.

Reaching out to high-school institutions in the third world: EMU could focus their marketing strategies on targeting educational tourists in high schools in third world countries. This is because they are at the point of graduating, and besides, they are prompt in desiring to leave their country for better education and due to instability in their home country. Therefore, organising more educational fairs in such countries will aid in attracting more educational tourists. This could also be done by establishing partnerships with high schools in those countries, in which advertisement of EMU could be done by the management of high school institutions in those countries.

EMU accreditations awareness: Feedback is a vital part of marketing. In the advertisement, new products or services have to be emphasised. In educational tourism, new programs, new accreditations, have to be widely advertised. A constant, simple and straightforward update on a new agreement with EMU and other universities must be broadcasted. The feedback the university renders to the student can condition the decision-making process of the educational tourists.

Key Factors in the Selection of an Educational Tourism Destination 31

Attending to student's plea: To attract more educational tourists, EMU management should listen and pay attention and work towards reducing their student's complaints. This is because these students turn to be potential marketers for EMU; therefore, their satisfaction and fulfilment should be premium to EMU. Besides providing quality education, institutions should equally look into their student's happiness and contentment. Implementation of these suggestions will create more positive word of mouth, and bring about an increase in educational tourists in EMU.

Affiliation with schools abroad: Affiliation with other institutions abroad will help keep the current students and attract others. More collaborations and partnerships with universities in other countries are created not only for bachelor students but also for master students. The suggestion for affiliation here has to do with more collaboration for exchange programs, and more aware of those collaborations need to be created. Both students have emphasised this factor, and EMU staff, thus, appears to be critical.

A showcase of EMU facilities and standard of education: EMU has great features that could be assimilated to high-standard institutions in countries attracting the most international educational tourists. A showcase of these features in terms of quality of education, ranking, classroom standard, lecturers' presence from famous universities abroad, and accreditations should be done. A comparison of this standard with the cost of tuition should be emphasised. Many educational tourists, while selecting a study abroad destination, consider these factors. Thus, great emphasis should be accorded to these elements, in the bid of attracting educational tourists. Agents do not seem to be concerned with the cost of education, unlike students and staff.

References

Abubakar, A. M., Shneikat, B. H. T. & Oday, A. (2014). Motivational factors for educational tourism: A case study in Northern Cyprus. *Tourism Management Perspectives*, *11*, 58–62.

Adam, P., & Alison, B. S. (2018). Marketing your university on social media: A content analysis of Facebook post types and formats. *Journal of Marketing for Higher Education*, *33*, 1–17.

Aldridge S. (2010). Strategy matters more than budget in student recruiting. *The Chronicle of Higher Education*, *57*, B50.

Alsharari, N. M., & Nizar, M. A. (2018). Internationalization of the higher education system: An interpretive analysis. *International Journal of Educational Management*, *32*(3), 359–381.

Antra, S., & Seema, S. (2018). Expansion of private engineering institutions. *Higher Education for the Future*, *5*(1), 20–39.

Armstrong, G., & Kotler, P. (2007). *Marketing, an introduction* (8th ed.). Upper Saddle River, NJ: Pearson Education, Inc.

Asle, F., & Gheorghita, G. (2013). Co-creation of value in higher education: Using social network marketing in the recruitment of students. *Journal of Higher Education Policy and Management*, *35*(1), 45–53.

32 Melissa Rikiatou Kana Kenfack and Ali Öztüren

Ayantunji, G. (2018). The anatomy of international students' acculturation in UK universities. *Industry and Higher Education, 32*(2), 129–138.

Bagautdinova, N. G., Gorelova, Y. N., & Polyakova, O. V. (2015). University management: From successful corporate culture to effective university branding. *Procedia Economics and Finance, 26*, 764–768.

Barnes, N. D., & Lescault, A. M. (2013). *Higher Ed documents social media ROI: New communications tools are a game changer*. Dartmouth, MA: The Center for Market Research University of Massachusetts. Retrieved from http://www.umassd.edu/cmr/socialmedia/socialmediagamechanger/. Accessed on February 13, 2013.

Binsardi, A., & Ekwulugo, F. (2003). International marketing of British education: Research on the students' perception and the UK market penetration. *Marketing Intelligence & Planning, 21*(5), 318–327.

Bodycott, P. (2009). Choosing a higher education study abroad destination: What mainland Chinese parents and students rate as important. *Journal of Research in International Education, 8*(3), 349–373.

Bornschlegl, M., & Cashman, D. (2018). Improving distance student retention through satisfaction and authentic experiences. *International Journal of Online Pedagogy and Course Design, 8*(3), 60–77.

Braun, V., & Clarke, V. (2006). Using thematic analysis in psychology. *Qualitative Research in Psychology, 3*(2), 77–101.

Brown, F., & Hall, D. (2008). Tourism and development in the Global South: The issues. *Third World Quarterly, 29*(5), 839–849.

Bryman, A. (2008). *Social research methods*. (3rd Ed.). New York: Oxford University Press.

Chen, C. H., & Zimitat, C. (2006). Understanding Taiwanese students' decision-making factors regarding Australian international higher education. *International Journal of Educational Management, 20*(2), 91–100.

Chen, C. M., Chen, S. H., & Lee, T. H. (2010). Assessing destination image through combining tourist cognitive perceptions with destination resources. *International Journal of Hospitality and Tourism Administration, 11*(1), 59–75.

Cheung, A. C. K, Yuen, T. W. W., Yuen, C. Y. M., & Cheng, Y. C. (2011). Strategies and policies for Hong Kong's higher education in Asian markets: Lessons from the United Kingdom, Australia, and Singapore. *International Journal of Educational Management, 25*(2), 144–163.

Chirkova, A. (2011). Pepsi *Across Culture: Analysis and Cross-cultural Comparison of Pepsi Websites*. (Master Dissertation). Sweden: University of Gothenburg.

Chou, C. P. (2008). The impact of neo-liberalism on Taiwanese higher education. *The Worldwide Transformation of Higher Education (International Perspectives on Education and Society), 9*, 297–312.

Cohen, D., & Crabtree, B. (2006). *Qualitative research guidelines project*. New Jersey: Robert Wood Johnson Foundation. Retrieved from http://www.qualres.org/index.html. Accessed on November 1, 2011.

Cohen, E. (1972). Toward sociology of international tourism. *Social Research, 39*(1), 164–182.

Counsell, D. (2011). Chinese students abroad: Why they choose the UK and how they see their future. *China: An International Journal, 9*(1), 48–71.

Dann, G. M. S. (1977). Anomie, Ego Enhancement in tourism. *Annals of Tourism Research, 4*(4), 184–194.

Doria, A., Mohd, I. A. A., & Abdul, L. M. I. (2017). The stories they tell: Understanding international student mobility through higher education policy. *Journal of Studies in International Education, 21*(5), 450–466.

Eastern Mediterranean University (EMU). (2018). *About us*. Retrieved from emu.edu.tr: https://www.emu.edu.tr/north-cyprus-universities. Accessed on August 28, 2018.

Eder, J., Smith, W. W., & Pitts, R. E. (2010). Exploring factors influencing student study abroad destination choice. *Journal of Teaching in Travel & Tourism, 10*(3), 232–250

Finch, D., McDonald, S., & Staple, J. (2013). Reputational interdependence: An examination of category reputation in higher education. *Journal of Marketing for Higher Education, 23*(1), 34–61.

Foskett, N. H., & Hemsley-Brown, J. V. (2001). *Choosing Futures: Young people's decision-making in education, training and careers markets.* London: Routledge/Falmer.

Gomes, L., & Murphy, J. (2003). An exploratory study of marketing international education online. *International Journal of Educational Management, 17*(3), 116–125.

Gottschall, K., & Saltmarsh, S. (2017). You're not just learning it, you're living it! Constructing the 'good life' in Australian university online promotional videos. *Discourse: Studies in the Cultural Politics of Education, 38*(5), 768–781.

Gupta P., & Kaushik, N. (2018). Dimensions of service quality in higher education – Critical review (students' perspective). *International Journal of Educational Management, 32*(4), 580–605.

Hemsley-Brown, J., & Oplatka, I. (2015). University choice: What do we know, what don't we know and what do we still need to find out? *International Journal of Educational Management, 29*(3), 254–274.

Hennink, M. M., Kaiser, B. N., & Marconi, V. C. (2017). Code saturation versus meaning saturation: how many interviews are enough?. *Qualitative Health Research, 27*(4), 591–608.

Hipsher, S., & Bulmer, J. (2016). Developing economy universities competing in a global market: Evidence from Thailand. In *International marketing of higher education* (pp. 139–169). New York, NY: Springer.

Holden, A. (2000). *Environment and tourism. Students' Satisfaction and Loyalty in Higher Education? Social Indicators Research* (Vol. 29). London: Routledge.

ICEF. (2015). ICEF the state of international student mobility in 2015.

Ivy, J. (2010). Choosing futures: Influence of ethnic origin in university choice. *International Journal of Educational Management, 24*(5), 391–403.

Jang, S., & Cai, L. (2002). Travel motivations and destination choice: A study of British outbound market. *Journal of Travel & Tourism Marketing, 13*(3), 111–132.

Joyce, P. (2012). Educational tourism empowerment: Implications for flexible learning and digital equity. *Pittman. Journal of Tourism Hospitality, 1*(4), 119–141.

Kan, G., Cliquet, G., & Gallo, M. P. (2014). The effect of country image on hypermarket patronage intention. *International Journal of Retail & Distribution Management, 42*(2), 106–130.

Kolowich, S. (2013). Universities try MOOCs in bid to lure successful students to online programs. *Chronicle of Higher Education.* Retrieved from https://chronicle.com/blogs/wiredcampus/universities-try-mooc2degree-courses-to-lure-successful-students-to-online-programs/41829

Kwong, J. (2000). Introduction: Marketisation and privatisation in education. *International Journal of Educational Development,* 20, 87–92.

Lai, A. P., Gibson, P., & Muthaly, S. (2014). Becoming an education provider of choice in Hong Kong: An inquiry into student decision making. *International Journal of Educational Management, 28*(5), 590–609.

Lam, J. M. S., Tong, D. Y. K., & Ariffin, A. A. M. (2016). Exploring perceived risk and risk reduction strategies in the pursuit of higher education abroad: A case of international students in Malaysia. *Journal of Studies in International Education, 21*(2), 83–104.

Larson, T., & Ankomah, P. (2004). Evaluating tourism web site complexity: The case of international tourism in the U.S. *Services Marketing Quarterly, 26*(2), 23–37.

34 Melissa Rikiatou Kana Kenfack and Ali Öztüren

Lee, C. (2014). An investigation of factors determining the study abroad destination choice: A case study of Taiwan. *Journal of Studies in International Education, 18*(4), 362–381.

Lee, C., & Morrish, S. (2012). Cultural values and higher education choices: Chinese Families. *Australasian Marketing Journal, 20*(1), 59–64.

Lee, J. J. (2007). Beyond borders: International student pathways to the United States. *Journal of Studies in International Education, 20*(10), 1–20.

Lee, J. J., & Sehoole, C. (2015). Regional, continental, and global mobility to an emerging economy: The case of South Africa. *Higher Education, 70*(5), 827–843.

Lesjak, M., Juvan, E., Ineson, E. M., Yap, M. H., & Axelsson, E. P. (2015). Erasmus student motivation: Why and where to go?. *Higher Education, 70*(5), 845–865.

Maringe, F. (2006). University and course choice: Implications for positioning, recruitment and marketing. *International Journal of Educational Management, 20*(6), 466–479.

Maringe, F., & Carter, S. (2007). International students' motivations for studying in UK HE: Insights into the choice and decision making of African students. *International Journal of Educational Management, 21*(6), 459–475.

Masserini, L., Bini, M., & Pratesi, M. (2019). Do quality of services and institutional image impact students' satisfaction and loyalty in higher education?. *Social Indicators Research, 146*(1), 91–115.

Mazzarol, T. (1998). Critical success factors for international education marketing. *International Journal of Educational Management, 12*(4), 163–175.

Mazzarol, T., & Soutar, G. N. (2002). Push-pull factors influencing international student destination choice. *International Journal of Educational Management, 16*(2), 82–90.

Mazzarol, T., Soutar, G. N., & Sim, M. Y. S. (2003). The third wave: Future trends in international education. *International Journal of Educational Management, 17*(3), 90–99.

McCarthy, E., Sen, A., & Fox Garrity, B. (2012). Factors that influence Canadian students' choice of higher education institutions in the United States. *Business Education and Accreditation, 4*(2), 85–95.

McGladdery, C. A., & Lubbe, B. A. (2017). Rethinking educational tourism: Proposing a new model and future directions. *Tourism Review, 72*(3), 319–329.

McIntosh, R. W., Goeldner, C. R., & Ritchie, J. R. (1995). *Tourism, principles, practices, philosophies* (7th ed.). New York, NY: John Wiley & Sons.

Naidoo, V. (2009). Transnational higher education: A stock take of current activity. *Journal of Studies in International Education, 13*(3), 310–330.

McMahon, M. E. (1992). Higher education in a world market. *Higher Education, 24*(4), 465–482.

Nyangau, J. Z., & Bado, N. (2012). Social media and marketing of higher education: A review of the literature. [RCET]. *Journal of the Research Center for Educational Technology, 8*, 38–51.

OECD. (2017). Charts a slowing of international mobility growth. Retrieved from http://monitor.icef.com/2017/09/oecd-charts-slowing-international-mobility-growth/. Accessed on September 2017.

Paul, W. (2010). Educational tourism: Understanding the concept, recognizing the value. *Tourism Insights, 3*(1), unpaginated.

Petruzzellis, L., & Romanazzi, S. (2010). Educational value: How students choose university: Evidence from an Italian university. *International Journal of Educational Management, 24*(2), 139–158.

Pimpa, N. (2003). The influence of family on Thai students' choices of international education. *International Journal of Educational Management, 7*(2), 178–92.

Pingping, H. (2014). A literature review on college choice and marketing strategies for recruitment. *Family and Consumer Sciences Research Journal, 43*(2), 120–130.

Pitman, T., Broomhall, S., McEwan, J., & Majocha, E. (2010). Adult learning in educational tourism. *Australian Journal of Adult Learning, 50*(2), 219–238.

Price, I., Matzdorf, F., Smith, L., & Agahi, H. (2003). The impact of facilities on student choice of university. *Facilities, 21*(10), 212–220.

Pugsley, L., & Coffey, A. (2002). Keeping the customer satisfied: Parents in the higher education market place. *Welsh Journal of Education, 11*(2), 41–58.

Qu, S. Q., & Dumay, J. (2011). The qualitative research interview. *Qualitative Research in Accounting & Management, 8*(3), 238–264.

Ritchie, B., Carr, N., & Cooper, C. (2003). *Managing educational tourism*. Clevedon: Channel View Publications.

Salmons, J. (2014). *Qualitative Online Interviews: Strategies, design, and skills*. London: Sage Publications.

Skinner, H., & Blackey, H. (2010). Globalisation of business education – A British course or a British educational experience? Comparisons from a UK university. *Journal of Applied Research in Higher Education, 2*(2), 22–32.

Strzoda, C. (2006). Online evaluation survey. General Online Research Conference. Retrieved from http://www.websm.org/index.php?fl=2&lact=8&list=no&vir=691. Accessed on January 31, 2008.

Taplin, R. H. (2012). Competitive importance-performance analysis of an Australian wildlife park. *Tourism Management, 33*(1), 29–37.

Taylor, J. (2003). Institutional diversity in UK higher education: Policy and outcomes since the end of the binary divide. *Higher Education Quarterly, 57*(3), 266–93.

Tefera, O., & Govender, K. (2015). Hotel grading, service quality, satisfaction and loyalty– Proposing a theoretical model and relationship. *African Journal of Hospitality, Tourism and Leisure, 4*, 1–17.

Times Higher Education (THE). (2020).Setting the Agenda in Higher Education for Five Decades. Retrieved from https://www.timeshighereducation.com/about-us. Accessed on 29 January 2021.

Tolman, E. C. (1959). Principles of purposive behavior. In S. Koch (Ed.), *Psychology: A study of a science* (Vol. 2, pp. 92–157). New York, NY: McGraw-Hill.

TRNC Ministry of Education and Culture. (2021a). *Distribution Tables of the Total Number of Students for the 2018 - 2019 and 2019 - 2020 Academic Years by Nationality*. Retrieved from https://yobis.mebnet.net/Downloads/Istatistikler/KKTC_%C3%9C niversiteleri_%C4%B0statistikleri/20192020/2018-2019_ToT_Nat.pdf. Accessed on January 19, 2021.

TRNC Ministry of Education and Culture. (2021b). *Universities in North Cyprus*. Retrieved from https://yobis.mebnet.net/frmUniversities.aspx. Accessed on January 19, 2021.

Underwood, M. J. (2016). Travel, emotion and identity: An exploration into the experiences of students in post 16 education for whom studying in English means working in a foreign language and culture. *New Trends and Issues Proceedings on Humanities and Social Sciences, 5*, 1016.

United Nations Educational, Scientific and Cultural Organization (UNESCO). (2009). *Trends in global higher education*. Paris: UNESCO.

UNWTO. (1995). *UNWTO technical manual: Collection of Tourism Expenditure Statistics*. Retrieved from https://pub.unwto.org/WebRoot/Store/Shops/Infoshop/ Products/1034/1034-1.pdf. Accessed on June, 2010.

Usunier, J. C., & Lee, J. A. (2009). *Marketing across cultures* (5th ed.). Harlow: Pearson Education Limited.

Uysal, M., & Hagan, L. A. (1993). Motivations of pleasure travel and tourism. In *VNR's encyclopedia of hospitality and tourism* (pp. 798–810). New York, NY: Van Nostrand Reinhold.

Uysal, M., & Jurowski, C. (1994). Testing the push and pull factors. *Annals of Tourism Research, 21*(4), 844–846.

36 *Melissa Rikiatou Kana Kenfack and Ali Öztüren*

Venter, R. (2015). Transformation, theology and the public university in South Africa. *Acta Theologica, 35*(2), 173–203.

Venter, R., & Tolmie, F. (2012). *Transforming theological knowledge: Essay on theology and the university after apartheid.* Bloemfontein: Sun Press.

Wankel, C. (2009). Management education using social media. *Educational Organization Management Journal, 6,* 251–262.

Webster, C., & Ivanov, S. (2014). Transforming competitiveness into economic benefits: Does tourism stimulate economic growth in more competitive destinations?. *Tourism Management, 40,* 137–140.

Wilkins, S., Butt, M. M., & Heffernan, T. (2018). International brand alliances and cobranding: Antecedents of cognitive dissonance and student satisfaction with co-branded higher education programs. *Journal of Marketing for Higher Education, 28*(1), 32–50.

Wong, P., Daisy, L., & Peggy M. L. Ng. (2018). Online search for information about universities: A Hong Kong study. *International Journal of Educational Management, 32*(3), 511–524.

World Tourism Organization. (2012). Retrieved from http://themis.unwto.org/. Accessed on April, 2012.

Würtz, E. (2006). Intercultural communication on Web sites: A cross-cultural analysis of Web sites from high-context cultures and low-context cultures. *Journal of Computer-Mediated Communication, 11,* 274–299.

Young, S. (2002). The use of market mechanisms in higher education finance and state control: Ontario considered. *Canadian Journal of Higher Education, 2,* 79–102.

Chapter 2

Study Hard but Do Tour to See the World: Tourism of Chinese Students who Studied in the United States

Carol Huang and Connie Chuyun Hu

Abstract

The study examines how the tourism concept developed amongst Chinese students in the United States from 1905 to current juncture. Through the contrasting views presented in two landmark mega-reviews of Chinese students in the United States and France, the authors concluded that tourism enhances understanding of the host countries resulting in more comprehensive and overall success of Study Abroad Program. After the reopening, China encouraged touring the host country but with extreme financial constraints in the beginning. Tourism of Chinese students became popular and fashionable only in late 1990s with China's economic prosperity and policy changes to open tourism to foreign countries. As tension with China grew during the COVID pandemic, Chinese students in the United States were used by the Trump Administration as a lever in trade and diplomatic negotiation, and touring became wishful.

Keywords: Tourism; Chinese students in the US; Chinese Study Abroad Program; the first 52 Chinese students in 1978; Chinese students as spies; Chinese students in the US under COVID

Introduction

Research on the tourism of foreign students emerges only very recently, particularly in the case of Chinese students. Much of the recent literature on Chinese foreign students and tourism stems from an attempt to understand the consumer power of international students outside their academic work. The tourism

---

Global Perspectives on Recruiting International Students: Challenges and Opportunities, 37–49
Copyright © 2021 by Emerald Publishing Limited
All rights of reproduction in any form reserved
doi:10.1108/978-1-83982-518-720211002

38   Carol Huang and Connie Chuyun Hu

of international students is a new area rarely researched before 2000, which is understandable in light of the recent dramatic decreases in funding for higher educational institutions in developed countries and corresponding increases in international student enrolment to solve their financial crises. For instance, the University of Illinois at Urbana-Champaign made history to buy a \$425,000 insurance against the drop in Chinese students (Bothwell, 2018). The economic impact of international students is analysed as a new cash flow limited not only to the institution where they study but also to the leisure attractions they visit during their breaks and their stay in the host nations. The article examines mainly Chinese students, from 1905 through the current juncture.

Tourism and Educational Tourism: Any Distinctive Differences?

Traditionally, Chinese call study abroad 'youxue', that is, study tour or touring/ travel learning. So broadly defined, students' sojourn in the host country is a tour or a journey or travel by itself. Educational tourism includes both international students using their privileges of longer stay to tour the host country in order to enhance professional knowledge (such as internships), and touring for enjoyment and adventure. The research examines both fully funded and self-supported students from China in degree granting institutions.

Theoretical Framework

Education as a means to shape Chinese students while they study in the western world can be framed as the soft power to attract and co-opt their preferences, as opposed to the hard power of coercing the Chinese intellectual and gentry class to admire western culture and technology (Nye, 2004).

Liao (2006) summarised travel writing in stages of development: (1) identifying with the host country; (2) differentiating between their own country and the host county; (3) reviewing and reflecting on their experience and what they learned; (4) critically evaluating the host country; and (5) readjusting or integration of their view and vision of the world and self. He concludes comparison is the most dominant characteristic in all stages of development.

Methodology

The study looks at archival documents in US higher educational institutions — namely, University of Illinois at Urbana-Champaign, University of Michigan, Michigan State University, Cornell University, Columbia University, and Wesley College — to locate the sources the students may have left in the United States: published books, travelogues, autobiographies, correspondence, diaries, journals, biographical data, online obituaries and newspapers. Published interviews of Chinese who studied in the United States on their travel experience, in Chinese and English, were consulted to help generate a sense of their collective experience.

Historical Background

Tourism in Chinese Study Abroad Program is not new, but historically only a few people could afford it. Chinese study abroad programs have a unique historical background and had a rather distinguished development in terms of tourism. The idea that international students should tour their host countries developed and evolved slowly over the century from the late Chin Dynasty in the beginning of the 1900s to most recently with the increasing population of China's middle class and their devotion to their only child's education.

The majority of Chinese students who studied in the United States were eager to finish their studies without delay, so touring was not one of their priorities. During the Chinese Exclusion Era from 1882 to its repeal in 1943 when only 105 Chinese were allowed to enter, the de facto exclusion was forced to open a narrow gate in 1905 through the Open Door Policy to ease the tension between the United States and China (Daniels & Graham, 2001; Huang 2001, 2015). The narrow gate was higher educational institutions' doors. The new type desired by the United States was Chinese students in contrast to the labourers. The program lasted more than a century and brought in the majority of Chinese students who studied in the United States before the end of the Korean War in 1954, followed by a total close-down of educational exchange until Deng reopened it after Nixon's visit in 1978.

Brief Literature Review

The main reason Chinese students rarely toured when studying abroad was China's financial difficulties. The lack of actual knowledge about the host country beyond their campuses was severely criticised by Wang (1966), who wrote an extensive evaluation of the Chinese who studied in the United States from its inception to 1949. Wang blames US-educated Chinese for their inability to reform China and the eventual loss of China to communism. Wang further accuses the higher educational system in the United States and its locations. Remote campus towns where Chinese were educated sheltered them to study hard to graduate soon and go home. The Ivory Tower of American academies during their studies—the campus towns—allowed very limited exposure to the social realities of US society, and narrowed their vision, hindered their ability to cope with Chinese tradition, and thwarted their capacity of building sustainable new infrastructure to create a new China. Wang called them the lost generation, though John King Fairbank (1966) criticises Wang as too harsh in his review of the book.

In 1993, another important thesis emerged. Levine (1993) praises those who went through the work study program in France, including communist leaders such as Zhou Enlai and Deng Xiaoping, as the Found Generation, in contrast to Wang's Lost Generation. To Levine, the work study in France where students needed to work in factories to earn their keep developed a much deeper understanding for French society, and their training as worker-organisers in France would eventually lead them to use those strategies to organise in France. When the Chin government's financial support became impossible, they were disillusioned

40   *Carol Huang and Connie Chuyun Hu*

and returned to China to organise in all fractions of the society. And they became the rulers of a new China. Travel and working in the host country were essential to their understanding of the West and a deciding factor whether they could carry out their mission to reform China.

Li (2008) examines the US–China educational exchange and concludes national policy was the most dominant power in shaping the experience of Chinese studying in the United States and also their ability to move around or tour the host country until 1950.

We might consider their evaluations of Chinese study abroad programs in the United States to be mostly ideologically oriented, but they opened the discussion of touring and experiencing the host country more. Due to resources available, the student touring pattern did not change much during the period of these major reviews and evaluations. But they did advocate educational tourism in the study abroad programs.

Stages of Tourism Development Amongst Chinese Students in the United States

There are distinct periods in the Chinese study abroad program: (1) pre-Boxer Indemnity; (2) the Boxer Indemnity period from 1915 to the Korean War in 1954; (3) a break from 1955 to 1977 when hardly any came; (4) Deng's reopening of educational exchange in 1978 until the current juncture of COVID 19 pandemic and crisis in US–China relations.

Before the Boxer Indemnity (1905–1912): Breaking Ground

The very first group Chinese students came in 1905 were under the stewardship and guardianship of the Chinese Legation under Ting-fang Wu. Wu served under the Chin Dynasty as Minister to the United States, Spain and Peru from 1896 to 1902 and again from 1907 to 1909. During a brief period of Wu's guardianship from 1905 to 1910, many brilliant students who later on became influential in China, came to study at UIUC. Wu's initiative eventually brought many Chinese students to UIUC, which up to the 1960s produced the highest numbers of Chinese PhDs (Huang, 2001).

The first group of Chinese students in the United States valued practical working experience in the field more than academic studies in the universities. One of the best examples was the first Chinese Railway Engineer and Management PhD in the class of 1910, Ching-Chuang Wang (Huang, 2001). Before Wang transferred to UIUC from Harvard after Wu's visit to Urbana, after he was granted admission to the graduate program, he wanted to postpone his admission for one semester because he was offered an internship at a railway engine company in Colorado. The Graduate School dean, David Kinley, later the president from 1920 to 1930, dissuaded him and suggested that he study first and then do the internship. He eventually went to Colorado internship after graduation. Upon his graduation, Wu offered Wang a travel grant so Wang was able to travel through Europe to investigate European railway systems for a year before he returned to

China in 1911. Wang eventually applied a new accounting system to unify China's railway divided by Western Sphere of Influence and completed the Beijing-Hankou Railway started by his mentor Ting-feng Wu decades before.

Another one who travelled extensively for the major he chose in the United States was Chien Sung Sung-shu Chien Shu, 钱崇澍 (1883–1965) AB Science of UIUC, class of 1914. Born to a famous literati family in Zhejiang Province, Chien earned the rank of xiu-cai in 1904 before the old civil examination was abolished in 1905. He decided to study botany when he came to Illinois in 1910. He received an AB in 1914 and went to the University of Chicago and Harvard to study and returned to China to teach. In 1949, he became the dean of the Botany Graduate School of the Chinese Science Academy. He was amongst the first to use Western methods to categorise Chinese plants. His prolific publication of research, including his co-authoring of the *Encyclopedia of Chinese Botany,* helped establish modern Chinese botany. He was a great organiser of research teams to gather samples from a wide range of geographical areas in China. With the breadth of his work, Chien is considered the founder of contemporary Chinese botany.

Their insistence on internship as part of their study plan would change the US policy of not allowing foreign students to work and paved the way for them to see the United States. They interned in their professional fields for up to one year before they returned home. With the right to conduct internship, foreign students extended their opportunities to see more of the country and tour at the same time because they were required to return to campus for evaluation and to extend their student status. The internship policy expanded foreign students' professional knowledge with practical experience and expanded their horizon for understanding US society and culture beyond the boundary of the Ivory Tower.

Boxer Indemnity Grantees: Touring to Find China's Future 1920–1945

Boxer Indemnity grantees received handsome financial support even though the grant was war payment levied from Chinese people after the eight Western powers took over its capital in 1900. The grantees excelled through national examinations and a strict screening mechanism in China, and most of them chose to attend Ivy League schools. All in this group are deceased by now, and their biographies are available either in book form or on-line. Their letters, papers, travelogues, autobiographies and biographies comprise the major part of modern travel literature on places outside China that mapped their developmental view of the world and how they positioned themselves to carry out the mission: 'to modernise China'.

This group chose their professions and developed their expertise in their studies in the United States. Many chose majors requiring extensive fieldwork to gather data and conduct experiments. For instance, Co-chin Chu (or Kezhen Zhu), the father of Chinese meteorology, was the youngest of the first group of Boxer grantees. He was 18 when he arrived at UIUC in 1910, the youngest one in the group. He got his BS in Agriculture in 1913 from University of Illinois at Urbana-Champaign before he got a PhD from Harvard in Meteorology in 1918.

42   Carol Huang and Connie Chuyun Hu

He loved the travel required by his profession and kept a diary as early as 1913. His diary of more than 60 years recorded his trips and became the most comprehensive record of weather and agricultural development in China. During his life time, he built more than 600 weather stations across China to enhance agricultural production.

One older self-supported student from Shanghai demonstrated study with a purpose and travelled to gather information that he desired to implement when he went home. Hsiang-yueh Moh 穆藕初was born into a cotton farmer's family. In 1909, his friend lent him $1,000 USD for him to study in the United States. His wife sold all her jewellery so he could come to Madison, Wisconsin, as a self-supported student before he came to UIUC. He earned his MS degree in Agriculture in 1915. Even though under great financial difficulties in the United States, he managed to travel one year in the United States before he returned to China. He toured throughout the Southern cotton plantations and zigzagged through fabric factories. He visited Fredrick Taylor before he died in 1915, translated his book *Scientific Management* into Chinese, and applied it in his cotton factories (Moh, 1930). Moh reformed the cotton industry by importing American cotton seeds and weaving machines made in the United States and became known as the Cotton King of China. He later sponsored many famous scholars to study in the United States and encouraged them to travel as much as they could when they were studying. During the Second World War, Moh invented a manual weaving machine that produced most of the fabric for the war effort. Mao praised him and made him the model of businessmen under communism (Huang, 2001).

In general, how did this group interpret their world through their touring experience? Evidence of their life stories asserts that by comparison they interpreted and decoded their experience (Liao, 2016). The process was to locate one's old world in the new world they found such that they might reach a fusion in blending both worlds, or perhaps become more in favour of their old culture but with a newfound lens. The majority of the first two groups of Chinese students to study in the United States went through Chinese traditional training, and some even achieved higher ranks through imperial national examination. The cultural products revealed in their social research, diaries, correspondence, and publications symbolised the epistemological development of China in the late nineteenth and twentieth century. In the 1930s, after they had returned home for a decade or two, they were changed. When UIUC's Dr. David Kinley visited China in 1930, he observed that

> The country which gives its wealth and its citizens to the development of another country, while met at first with applause and gratitude, in time finds itself looked on as imperialistic and as seeking to exact tributes from the people it has tried to benefit...[This antagonism] has not been lessened by the attitudes and remarks of some foreign, particularly American visitors to the country who have gone out as 'advisors'...There has been too often an assumption of superiority, of teaching the Chinese how to do things [in their ways]. (Kinley, 1930)

The returned Chinese students restructuring their thoughts and looking reflectively on their US experience became critical of the imperial educational project of the United States and became more nationalist and resistant to western domination. At the same time, their professors reflected on their vision in educating them and understood that their students had their own mind and situations to cope with. The tourism that developed amongst this cohort by the 1930s helped them rethink their world in finding ways to modernise China (Liao, 2013).

Post-War Cohort: Stranded and Exiled in the Host Country

Very few Chinese students came during the Second World War. After Japan surrendered, a huge flow of Chinese students was sent in 1945. Almost all studied engineering to speed up China's recovery, and when they graduated, the Bamboo Curtain came down. However, with the United States and China on opposing sides in Korean War, the students were told to pack and go home. Later the American Nuclear Society pleaded not to send them back to China to arm China and keep them in the United States (Huang, 2001). After the Immigration and Nationality Act of 1952, many returned to China but more stayed. They were the stranded generation of Asian (Chinese) Americans (Lee, 1958). Cut off suddenly from their families, friends and nation, stranded in the United States, they found support from their classmates. Members of UIUC class of 1949, for example, later recalled in a self-published memoir from 1998 their road trips visiting their old college classmates studying in the United States. The only way they could afford to travel was in an old car they bought and repaired themselves. Sometimes during their visits, they helped each other fix the visiting cars. The excitement of driving through the vast land of the United States to visit friends was amongst the most mentioned activities (UIUC Class of 1949, 1992). The collection commemorated their deceased classmate who decided to leave the United States to work at the Danish Nuclear Commission in order to keep his relationship with his family behind the Bamboo Curtain. He eventually married a Danish woman. When he died, the classmates sent their memories of him to his daughter and dedicated the collection to this member of their group who was able to visit his home before Nixon's visit. They were in exile in the United States, forbidden to get in touch with their families and friends in China. For them, touring was an unfilled dream of visiting their homeland, a remembrance of the good old days. They seldom told their own stories, but their American children started to write about them (Zia, 2019).

After Mao's Death: Reopening of China and Tourism in China

Immediately after Chairman Mao's death, Deng Xiaoping, China's most famous economic reformer, who had himself studied in France, saw the monetary potential in tourism and began to promote it in the wake of Nixon's visit. Deng also reopened the study abroad program in 1978. That year, about 1.8 million tourists entered China. Initially, the majority of tourists came from neighbouring

44 Carol Huang and Connie Chuyun Hu

Hong Kong, Macau and Taiwan. By 2000, over 10 million new overseas visitors came to China, mostly from Japan, South Korea, Russia and the United States (Zhou, 2019).

Reopening and the First 52 of 1978 (Sing Dong Feng, 2018)

During the Cultural Revolution from 1966 to 1976, no higher educational institutions in China were open. In 1978, Deng Xiaoping reopened the channel to send Chinese students to the United States. The first group were selected through an initial 800 recommended by their own institutions which had reopened only 2 years before. From these, two hundred were picked to go to Chinghua University in Beijing for an English proficiency exam, and from these, 50 were chosen for study in the United States (Chen, 2018, Universal People Magazine, 2018). Their schedule to leave was pushed forward after the confirmation of Deng's visit to the United States in 1979. They left China on 26 December 1978, and since there was no direct flight, they flew first to Pakistan and then Paris before flying to the JFK airport in New York. According to the group leader Bai-cheng Liu, who was interviewed in 2018 at age 85, he was given $50 USD for the whole group for the trip, which meant about $1 per person without taking into account the two added. During the layover in Paris, the Chinese embassy managed to send them meals so they did not have to spend money on food. Many walked all the way from the airport just so they could see the Eiffel Tower. Most of them spent their only dollar as a tip to the bellhop who took care of their luggage at JFK. Soon they went to Washington DC to live at the embassy, and on 29 January 1979, they joined Deng at the White House dinner with President Carter. What a grand entrance to the United States as the first group of Chinese visiting scholars after China reopened!

Most of them stayed in the embassy and studied English in Washington DC for several months before they landed in their designated university. The tourism they experienced initially was going to and from the embassy and campus. The funding was quite restricted in the beginning, so they did not even visit much in Washington DC. Several of them had relatives in the United States and planned to visit them on their way to their universities. Xiao-ping Cao visited his brother in Detroit on his way to UC Berkeley. It was the first time they met. His brother had been studying in the United States in 1949 when he was only 2 years old, and they were separated for 40 years (Hu, 2020). All were very careful living in the United States until imposed surveillance of each other was relaxed and they could go to places alone, after which they travelled more and participated in more activities (People's Daily Overseas Version, 2009).

In 1984, the Chinese government approved 'self-supported' study abroad as more Chinese students stayed in the United States after their graduation. The policy changes significantly reduced the government funded students and encouraged private individuals to invest in their study abroad program. More than 7,000 out of 38,000 Chinese students were self-supported, most of them in the United States. The chances for them to travel were slim due to the financial condition (Wallstreetclub, 2019). Both government sponsored and self-supported students lived very frugally with limited financial resources like their predecessors before 1954. Their touring experience was very slim.

One of the most famous travel stories of the time was Yin-her Li, sociologist on sexuality, gender and transgender studies and her husband, famous writer Xiao-po Wang in the 1980s. The couple coined the term 'qiong you' (travel in poverty or travel regardless of constraints or pushing travel to extreme) when they were studying at the University of Pittsburgh. They took trips in an old car, camping and cooking their own food across the United States visiting their relatives and friends or travel for travel's sake to explore the United States, and later after Li got her PhD, they went to Europe for a year-long trip before returning to China. Their travel experience was first published by a friend of Wong in 2007 (Li, 2007) and Li's autobiography *Lived, Loved, and Written* in 2020 (Li, 2020) detailed her days in the United States and abroad. According to their friend and Li's own description, their living arrangement was similar to pre-war and like the earliest group who came before 1954: living in a cheap China house near campus, cooking food to save money, trying to get extra work on campus and save money during their stay to buy goods to take home. But this couple was different: they saved to travel. They travelled to expand their horizons and vision of the world while they were studying abroad. They decided to return after rethinking their research and their artistic work, having concluded they had to be in China to fulfil their vision. In Liao (2013), hypothetical processes of travel that Li lived a fusion life to adopt what she believed in to break numerous cultural barriers in her research and lifestyle as one of few open lesbian/transgender couple with her partner Dasha after her husband died. Without her study in the United States and travel experience, she could not possibly have created such a life. Their experience set an example for many of their generation who came to the United States to study and wished for a road trip across the United States before their return. But touring was slow to develop against the economic pressure. In 1990s, brain drain became a serious issue for the study abroad program as the influence of US soft power expanded in China (Nye, 2004). But Deng insisted on keeping the direction of sending students to study abroad (Xinhuanet, 2018).

The group's legal status to stay in the United States was made possible by the 1965 Family Reunion Act, which allowed family members to migrate to the United States, and by an increase in professional visas such as H1-B visas (1992). The Chinese Student Protection Act of 1992 after the Tienanman Incident of 1989 granted permanent residence status to 70,000 Chinese students and their family members that triggered chain migration later. 'Study abroad to stay abroad' became obtainable. 'Beijinese in New York' in 1994 became the most popular soap opera of the year. Depicting a group of artists living in NY even with a lot of hardship was deemed worthwhile because their dream would come true. From 1990 to 2003, only one out of seven in the study abroad program returned to China, in contrast to the first group in 1978 — everyone returned. For the latter group, study abroad was a springboard to living in the United States. The concept of touring transformed to living abroad after study.

Overall, the Chinese students' concept of tourism developed along with the policy of tourism in China. First, domestic travel was encouraged to stimulate consumption. In 1999, over 700 million trips were made by domestic tourists. Many work-related domestic tours of other similar agencies were strongly encouraged. Also, international tourism to China increased. In 2000, more than 10 million overseas visitors came to China (Zhou, 2019).

Outbound tourism from China did not become popular until recent years with the rise of the Chinese middle class who had more disposable income and the Chinese government easing the restriction on international travel. At the end of 1999, only 14 countries, mostly in the southeast and east Asia, were open for Chinese to travel. By 2010, more than 100 countries were listed as approved destinations. This policy enabled parents to visit their children studying in the United States. Chinese students and their families travelled even more frequently in the countries their children were studying. When China joined the WTO in 2001, travel restrictions in the country were relaxed further (Zhou, 2019). Chinese students in the US travelled more and their trips became more touristic than ever before. They became the vanguard for discovering tourist attractions, tailored the tour for Chinese visitors with the Water Taxi tour of New York Harbor in 15 min, which used to be more than four hours in the Circle Line, and created a formula for touring the United States by inventing must-see tourist spots that included not just historical spots but also a string of other attractions from ice cream shops, street vendors to fancy steak houses. Without Chinese students' lived experience in the United States and policy changes enabling them to stay, China's tourist industry in the United States could not prosper in such fast speed.

The 2008 Beijing Olympic Games fostered an extraordinary increase in tourism in China through worldwide exposure. The Beijing Games put 'The Bird's Nest' and 'Water Cube' buildings on the centre stage, with opening and closing ceremonies that showcased to the world China's rich culture and history. It was designed by four renowned artists, all of whom except one had studied and lived in the United States for many years. For instance, composer Tan Dun, who wrote the official award music, artist Cai Gao Qiang, who designed the fireworks, film director Ang Lee, who codirected the opening ceremony, all had studied and lived many years in NYC. This is the climactic moment of tourism, of East mixed with West to create what Liao (2013) theorised as 'fusion', was showcased in the Beijing Olympics. The event marked the pivotal cultural moment in US–China educational exchange.

In 2018, over 3 million Chinese tourists came to the United States and each spent on average about $6,700 per trip, the highest amongst all tourist groups (Statistical Research Department, 2020). The Chinese students who study in the United States also travel widely and explore almost every place possible. But as tensions grew between the United States and China, higher educational institutions again came to the limelight as an area of contestation. The US administration began to express worry that Chinese students studying in the United States might be spying for China. Tighter monitoring of Chinese students by the US administration revealed a fraud scheme of Chinese students after graduation working for US-based companies that did not exist and raised the question of how well the government monitors and regulates the popular student work program in 2019 (Lighty, 2019). In 2019, there were more cases of Chinese students facing espionage charges and universities were alerted to pay attention to the potential Chinese students who might be spying for China or stealing business or science secrets (Lighty, 2019). Lately, there has been a string of US criminal cases accusing Chinese professors of spying for China in the academic world (Dilanian, 2020).

In addition to the criminalisation of Chinese students and professionals, the wide spread of COVID-19 in the United States led to closing of higher educational campuses in March 2020. Chinese students were instructed to leave campus housing and find their own shelter in places off campus. Many also felt the hostility towards Chinese across the United States. They were eager to leave the United States, but they were not welcomed by the Chinese government. According to China's Ministry of Education records for April 2020, an estimated 410,000 Chinese students were studying in the United States. Due to flight cancellations and flight bans to China, many Chinese students were stranded and many wished to leave after graduation. On 3 June 2020, a group of 21 Chinese, 17 of whom were students, plotted their circuitous way back from New York and boarded a flight to China via Zurich and Singapore. They learned in Zurich that Singapore denied their transfer visa (Xu, 2020). The Swiss Government wanted to deport them back to the United States but many of their visas expired when they left the United States. They feared they could not enter again. They camped out in the airport for days. Travel is dangerous at the time of pandemic. This nightmarish incident demonstrates how a tour went out of control during the pandemic amid increasing tensions between two countries. Worst of all, at the time of writing in July 2020, no new international students are being admitted to Harvard for the fall because it will be online-only instruction, despite Trump rescinding his order to expel foreign students. But with newly issued F1 visas, international students cannot enter if the schools they are going to attend are on-line in the fall. The estimated decrease of international students in the United States for fall 2020 compared to 2018–2019 is a decline of from 63% to 98% of new international enrolments (Anderson, 2020).

Conclusion

Chinese students came through a small door of higher education to ease the tension between China and the United States during the Chinese Exclusion Act. Their touring experience was encouraged and sponsored by the Chinese legation with limited financial resources. Their numbers increased with the Boxer Indemnity grant. The group toured more with more funding from their grant. Their overwhelming ideological switch from identifying with their host nation to Chinese nationalism in 1930s became evident in their life stories. Their changing worldview reflects their integration of western technology they learned and their identity realignments after returning home.

The reopening of 1978 brought several waves of Chinese students. Their touring experience in the host county developed along the path of China's tourism deregulation and expansion. And policy changes in the United States enabled them to stay. They reached higher achievement than the previous generation to create an artistic fusion that presented a new China during the Beijing Olympics.

48   Carol Huang and Connie Chuyun Hu

Overall, national policy in both countries has been and will be the most dominant influence steering their experience and journeys. As COVID-19 ravages the world, Chinese students are used again as at the time of Chinese Exclusion: a political chip to leverage the US–China relationship. The future of studying and touring in the United States is dim. The fate of 115 years of the US–China educational exchange and the future explorations of the United States by Chinese students depends on the development of the pandemic, on the results of US presidential election, and Chinese re-evaluation of the soft power and the value of US education.

References

Anderson, S. (2020, July 22). No new international students at Harvard due to immigration rules. *Forbes*. Retrieved from https://www.forbes.com/sites/stuartanderson/2020/07/22/no-new-international-students-at-harvard-due-to-immigration-rules/#97b78185cbb2

Bothwell, B. (2018, November 19). Insuring against drop in Chinese students: University of Illinois at Urbana-Champaign is paying $424,000 to protect itself in case of fall off. *Inside Higher Ed*. Retrieved from https://www.insidehighered.com/news/2018/11/29/university-illinois-insures-itself-against-possible-drop-chinese-enrollments

Chen, L. B. (2018, October 8). Fifty dollars and a new suit – On our way to study in the US. Interview with Lew Bai Chen, the leader of the first 52 people sent to the US to study in 1978 [Interview]. *Universal People Magazine*. Retrieved from https://xw.qq.com/cmsid/20181008A1J2N000

Cohen, Z., & Marquardt, A. (2019, February 2). US intelligence warns China using student spies to steal secrets. *CNN*. Retrieved from https://www.cnn.com/2019/02/01/politics/us-intelligence-chinese-student-espionage/index.html

Daniels, R., & Graham, O. L. (2001). *Debating American immigration, 1882-present*. Boston, MA: Rowman & Littlefield Publishing Inc.

Dilanian, K. (2020, February 2). American universities are a soft target for China's spies, say U.S. intelligence officials. *NBC*. Retrieved from https://www.nbcnews.com/news/china/american-universities-are-soft-target-china-s-spies-say-u-n1104291

Fairbank, J. K. (1966). Review of Chinese intellectuals and the West. *The American Historical Review, 72*(1), 261.

Hu, L. W. (2020, April 5). After Reopening, the first group sent to study in the U.S.—Their experience Interview of Chao. Retrieved from http://edu.sina.com.cn/a/2009-05-11/1450170703.shtml?from=wap

Huang, C. (2001). *The soft power of education and the formation of a Chinese American intellectual community at Urbana-Champaign, 1905–1954*. Doctoral dissertation, University of Illinois at Urbana-Champaign, IL.

Huang, C. (2015). *East meets Illinois: The dawn of China and midwest educational exchange, 1905 to 1920*. [Exhibit]. University of Illinois at Urbana-Champaign, Spurlock Museum.

Lee, R. H. (1958). The stranded Chinese in the United States. *The Phylon Quarterly, 19*(2), 180–194.

Levine, M. A. (1993). *The found generation: Chinese communists in Europe during the twenties*. London: University of Washington Press.

Li, S. (2007, April 12). Wang Xiaopoa's college and study abroad days. *Sina News*. Retrieved from http://news.sina.com.cn/c/cul/2007-04-12/145312762840.shtml?from=wap

Li, H. S. (2008). *US-China educational exchange: State, society, and intercultural relations, 1905–1950*. New Brunswick, NJ: Rutgers University Press.

Li, Y. H. (2020). *Lived, loved, written*. Beijing: Beijing October Literary Publishing Company.

Liao, P. H. (2002). Travel, memory and identity. *United Literature Magazine*, 2006, pp. 185–187.

Lighty, T. (2019, September 26). How a Chicago college student ended up in the middle of an FBI investigation into Chinese spying. *Chicago Tribune*. Retrieved from https://www.chicagotribune.com/investigations/ct-chinese-espionage-chicago-20190926-xh74yrhorzakjpsnojyx4aapfm-story.html

Moh, Y. C. 穆藕初 (1930). Autobiography at age 50. Retrieved from http://blog.sina.com.cn/s/blog_87a2ad830100wc7x.html

Nye, J. S. Jr. (2004). *Soft power: The means to success in world politics*. New York, NY: Public Affairs.

People's Daily Overseas Version. (2009, May 15). First group to study in the US – Unforgettable journey of a generation [interview of 王靖华]. Retrieved from http://edu.sina.com.cn/a/2009-05-15/1105171038.shtml

Statista Research Department. (2020). Number of visitors to the US from China from 2003 to 2024. Retrieved from https://www.statista.com/statistics/214813/number-of-visitors-to-the-us-from-china/

UIUC Class of 1949. (1992). The passing of waves. A collection of writings by UIUC engineering graduates of 1949. Self-published.

Wallstreetclub. (2019, January 15). Forty years after reopening: Reflection on Chinese study in the US. 改开40周年·回顾中国人赴美留学史. Retrieved from https://posts.careerengine.us/p/5c2f8eb4346fd3559a0b1eee

Wang, Y. C. (1966). *Chinese intellectuals and the West, 1872–1949*. Chapel Hill, NC: University of North Carolina Press.

Xindongfang. (2018, December 11). What happened to the first group to study in the U.S. in 1978? Retrieved from http://sz.xdf.cn./201812/118485567.html

Xinhuanet. (2018, December 25). *Forty Years of Policy Changes in Study Abroad Program*, Deng's insistence on "supporting studying abroad, encouraging their return to China and they are free to come or to leave", "支持留学、鼓励回国、来去自由". Retrieved from http://www.xinhuanet.com//globe/2018-12/25/c_137697887.htm

Xu, K. (2020, June 3). Chinese consulate helps stranded students at Zurich airport. *Global Times*. Retrieved from https://www.globaltimes.cn/content/1190470.shtml

Zhou, P. (2019, March 9). Tourism development in China. Retrieved from https://www.thoughtco.com/tourism-development-in-china-1434412

Zia, H. (2019). *The last boat out of Shanghai: The epic story of the Chinese who fled Mao's revolution*. New York, NY: Ballantine Books.

Chapter 3

The Role of Social Media Marketing Activities on International Students' Brand Preference: A Study on English-Speaking Universities of Germany

Hasan Evrim Arici and Nagihan Cakmakoglu Arici

Abstract

This study investigates the influences of social media marketing activities (SMMAs) on brand preference by focussing on the mediation influence of brand recognisability and the moderator influence of brand signature in higher education institutions in Germany. A total of 257 students were surveyed and the data gathered were tested through partial least squares structural equation modelling. The findings demonstrated that higher-education institutions' SMMAs had a significant effect on both brand recognisability and students' brand preference. The findings also empirically proved the significant mediator influence of brand recognisability and the moderator influence of brand signature upon the association of higher education institutions' SMMAs and students' brand preference. It is anticipated that the findings of this research could be utilised as a significant solution in the improvement of higher education institutions' SMMAs, specifically focussing on the significance of each component of SMMAs.

Keywords: SMMAs; brand recognisability; brand signature; brand preference; education tourism; higher education; Germany

Introduction

Tourism is a significant phenomenon regarding specially its huge revenue generation in the world. The social media has a crucial impact on promoting tourism

---

Global Perspectives on Recruiting International Students: Challenges and Opportunities, 51–64
Copyright © 2021 by Emerald Publishing Limited
All rights of reproduction in any form reserved
doi:10.1108/978-1-83982-518-720211003

52   Hasan Evrim Arici and Nagihan Cakmakoglu Arici

products and services through affecting decision-making processes of customers from pre-purchase to post-purchase stages (Irfan, Rasli, Sami, & Liaquat, 2017). Educational tourism is considered as a fast growing area of the tourism industry and has to date received little attention by practitioners and scholars (Savaşan, Yalvaç, Uzunboylu, & Tuncel, 2018). Traditional education marketing used to count on conventional promotion activities and avenues, such as press, TV and radio channels, education events and festivals, and official webpages to promote their institutions (Irfan et al., 2017). With the development in social media, these promotional activities have dramatically altered in educational tourism (Chamberlain, 2014). The phenomenon of social media, which refers to novel web tools, is under strong debate especially because of its commercial value. The background of this debate focusses on its influence on individuals' attitudes and behaviours (Barker, 2009; Kolbitsch & Maurer, 2006;), educational subjects (Augustsson, 2010; Greenhow & Lewin, 2016) and its role on marketing (Alalwan, Rana, Dwivedi, & Algharabat, 2017; Bruhn, Schoenmueller, & Schäfer, 2012; Grabs & Sudhoff, 2014). Zenith, a media agency, has predicted global social media advertising expenditure to rise 20% in 2019, with $84 billion and constituting 13% of total global expenditure ranking the third-largest advertising channel, following TV and paid search (Zenith, 2019). Facebook reported in 2019 that more than 140 million businesses used its family of apps (Facebook, Instagram, Messenger and WhatsApp) each month in order to find new customers, hire employees or engage with their communities (Zenith, 2019). In that vein, several scholars have pointed the positive impact of SMMAs on consumer behaviours. For example, Seo and Park (2018) found that SMMAs significantly influence brand awareness and brand image in the airline industry. In addition, a research investigating the event fans' attitudes and intentions found a significant effect of social networking sites on event fans' behavioural intention, leading to their actual behaviour (Harb, Fowler, Chang, Blum, & Alakaleek, 2019). A recent bibliometric study revealed that social media investigation in tourism and travel journals has mainly focussed on six areas, namely, electronic word of mouth, service recovery, visitor loyalty, company/destination image and perceived service quality (Nusair, Butt, & Nikhashemi, 2019).

Nonetheless, how SMMAs promote international students' brand preference has not yet been subjected to elaborate academic exploration with lacking parts. As an instance, SMMAs' direct effect on international students' responses is incomplete without any mediator effect; as suggested by Whetten (1989), it is necessary for researchers to explain causal relationships in a phenomenon by determining mediators between dependent and independent variables. Thus, studies have been recently exploring the SMMAs-brand preference model and considering in what way and whenever these marketing activities may conclude with higher or lower brand preference in higher education sector. First, we aimed to enlighten the situation by examining SMMAs concentrating upon the mechanism, resulting in brand preference. Focussing on the brand equity approach, we introduced the concept of brand recognisability. It is categorised under the concept of brand awareness together with brand familiarity in the literature, such that it is defined as 'a tool which emphases on defining and generating the familiarity and recognisability of a target audience towards a particular brand' (Foroudi, 2019, p. 275). That is, brand recognisability can be defined as customer's awareness about the presence and value of a brand, product or service. Brand recognisability is acknowledged as a key connecting SMMAs and international students' brand preference. Subsequently, following the attribution theory, focussing on how people try to understand the world, and suggesting that attitude of attribution defines the possibility of satisfaction of the customers and image favourability affects consumer behaviour, we attempt to expand the understanding of the determinants strengthening the influences of SMMAs on brand preference by focussing on the potential moderating role of brand signature, which is an unique, different format based on the brand personality and identity (Foroudi, 2019). This necessitates the study question to be empirically investigated.

To fill the above-mentioned gap, this study investigates the effects of SMMAs on international students' brand preference by focussing on the mediator effect of brand recognisability and moderating effect of brand signature in the higher education sector in Germany. Therefore, this research makes at least three contributions to the tourism, education and marketing literature. First, it makes contribution to the literature through investigating the relationship between SMMAs and brand preference in higher education sector. This empirical examination is crucial since social media is often considered as an important tool to promote and increase the attractiveness of a brand. Nevertheless, no studies to our knowledge has explored the potential outcomes of SMMAs from the perspective of international students in higher education institutions. Second, the current research contributes the study of brand equity and attribution theory through proposing and testing the impact of SMMAs (attribution method influences consumer satisfaction) affect international students' brand preference. By applying this theory, this chapter may highlight the black box between SMMAs and brand preference. Third, this research investigated international students' perceptions about the brand signature in the aspect of attribution theory, which has been rarely studied. It has been understood that brand signature is a complicated topic including different subjects to be investigated in detail. Thus, this study is among the first to gather empirical evidence so as to analyse if favourable appreciations of brand signature moderate the effects of SMMAs to enhance international students' brand preference in higher education institutions in Germany.

Literature Review and Research Hypotheses

Social media can be referred as 'a group of internet-based applications that build on the ideological and technological foundations of Web 2.0 and that allow the creation and exchange of user generated content' (Kaplan & Haenlein, 2010, p. 61). Compared with the conventional communication channels, such as TV, print media and radio, social media is appreciated as a quite more effective platform in branding thanks to its interactive attributes providing information sharing and online collective activities (Knoll, 2016; Kusumasondjaja, 2018). That is a very stunning point to be understood how communities rely on such a virtual world during their brand evaluations. The attribution theory (Heider, 1958; Weiner,

1972), which has been utilised commonly in consumer decision-making process studies (Mizerski, Golden, & Kernan, 1979), can explain this inquiry in some way. This theory tries to enlighten how people understand their world referring 'to the perception or inference of cause' (Kelley & Michela, 1980, p. 458). The way people manage in their communications and what makes them to behave in such a way in these interactions are the topics of this theory (Kelley & Michela, 1980). Social media and the marketing activities done through social media are closely related to the scope of the attribution theory in such a virtual world. This theory defines the possibility of consumer satisfaction behaviour and also brand favourability affecting customer attitudes, which is closely related to brand signature (Sen & Bhattacharya, 2001; Weiner, 2000).

As the second theoretical background of this study, brand equity approach (Aaker, 1992; Keller, 2009) has long been a noteworthy notion in marketing studies focussing on the consumer. This approach includes brand awareness, brand association, perceived quality, brand loyalty and other possession subjects, such as patents (Aaker, 1992; Huang & Cai, 2015). As one of the key elements of this theory, brand awareness is the one which is associated with the brand recognisability handled in this study. Brand awareness refers two main aspects, one of which is the ability of the customer in remembering, recognising and relating with the brand through name, logo, and symbol of the brand. The second aspect is the extent to which the consumers buy something remembering its brand, namely aware of the brand (Keller, 2009; Pappu, Quester, & Cooksey, 2005). Thus, higher brand awareness triggers consumer response in a positive way (Nah, Eschenbrenner, & DeWester, 2011). A study conducted by Caldwell (2000) has posed that when the more positively the brand of a museum is appreciated, the more loyal customers it attracts.

The Internet has both created the opportunity for the founding of new ways for communication and it changed the style and methods of commercialising products and facilities. Online purchasing has turned into very popular amongst consumers in the twentieth century. The importance of social networking sites as a tool of social media is anticipated to rise in the near future. In 2019, approximately 2.9 billion people were using social media worldwide, a number projected to increase to almost 3.43 billion in 2023 (Statista, 2020). Specifically, such an increase has been also witnessed in Germany. This country became the second in online shopping with 92% of all Internet users, after China (75%) and also the sales of e-trade in Germany increased by 27.000 million Euros in 2013, and this has been estimated to increase up to 77.000 million Euros in 2020 (Statista, 2018).

The Internet has caused the means of communication, which has in turn provided people to pass over geographical and temporal boundaries through linking globally at any time by the consumers (Harris & Rae, 2009). Online platforms enable consumers or users to meet virtually with different intentions, such as information search band share, discussions about collective topics and reviewing (Wang & Fesenmaier, 2004). Fast changing innovations in information technology, these virtual facilities are conducted through a novel kind of Internet or network technology, which is Web-2.0 and online media platform (Gretzel, Kang, & Lee, 2008). In that respect, all of these developments triggered various marketing strategies, which includes SMMAs. These are such marketing methods that they include sharing brand knowledge and communication with the customers in a social media platform (Schultz & Peltier, 2013; Tiago & Veríssimo, 2014). Social media marketing has a great role in moulding the perceptions of the customers about a brand and their information search process (Keller, 2009; Langaro, Rita, & de Fatima Salgueiro, 2018; Mangold & Faulds, 2009). During the purchasing process, the consumers use the information about a product or service online, through checking SMMAs of a brand with the aim of minimising their information gap about that product or service that may impact on their preference negatively. Hence, these online actions and SMMAs have great value for the higher education institutions and marketers working in the social media (Grabs & Sudhoff, 2014). The investigations on SMMAs and consumer behaviours in higher education institutions have been so current, however, rather scarce (e.g. Binsardi & Ekwulugo, 2003; Constantinides & Zinck Stagno, 2011; Tess, 2013; Yadav & Rahman, 2018; Zeng & Gerritsen, 2014). These limited studies suggest that within the concept of social media, there can be acknowledged consumer reviews, content community sites, forums and social platforms like Facebook, Instagram and Twitter. The reason behind the importance of the social media lies under the fact that several businesses, one of which is beyond dispute tourism and hospitality industry, make use of SMMAs to make their brand stronger and more easily recognisable through user-generated and personalised content (Alves, Fernandes, &Raposo, 2016; Phan, Thomas, & Heine, 2011) as well as developing committed consumers (Barreda, Nusair, Wang, Okumus, & Bilgihan, 2020).

When brand recognisability is of concern, many studies evaluated it under the topic of brand awareness together with brand familiarity (e.g. Aaker, 1991; Bae, Jung, Moorhouse, Suh, & Kwon, 2020; Foroudi, 2019; Keller, 2009). According to Keller (2009, 2013) brand awareness refers to a 'personal meaning about a brand stored in consumer memory, that is, all descriptive and evaluative brand-related information' regarding a brand's cognitional image. It is about the possibility that one can remember a brand and how easily this happens. Making the consumers aware about a brand is of vital importance in the process of decision and purchasing resulting in higher likelihood of impressing the idea, perception, relationship and cognition about a brand (Foroudi, Melewar, & Gupta, 2014). Drawing on this background, we claim that applying the SMMAs in an effective way may result in higher possibility of a more recognisable brand, which is an inquiry to be empirically tested. Thus, we posited the following hypothesis:

H1: SMMAs of a higher education institution increase its brand recognisability in the eyes of students.

Brand preference attributes to the tendency of the consumers for a specific product or service during the cognitive process of information search (Howard & Sheth, 1969). Namely, consumers' perceptions about a brand influence their preference and correspondingly impacts on their choice of a brand (Berger, Draganska, & Simonson, 2007; Streicher & Estes, 2015). It is the connection between information process and the intention to buy. Social media provides in this search process online reviews reflecting the experiences and evaluations of consumers about a brand.

A research claim that social media triggers the potential students to prefer a higher education institution (Constantinides & Zinck Stagno, 2011). Social media penetration rate is quite high among potential students, who are tech-savvy. Therefore, the use of social media actively by higher education institutions can contribute to the attracting and recruiting of potential students. Because extent literature shows that potential students extremely search information utilising social media, the relation between the level of SMMAs use by higher education institutions and the preference level of students is a crucial question to be addressed. This question needs to be empirically tested, thus, the following hypothesis was formulated:

H2: As SMMAs of a higher education institution enhance, the brand preference probability of students has a tendency to increase.

Brand recognisability is an important factor of brand knowledge, including the capability of future customers to recognise a brand, and so linking products to brands (Aaker, 1991). Despite its importance on branding, brand recognisability has been occasionally studied. For example, Keller (2009) has stated that brand recognition attributes to customers previous experiences about a brand. Furthermore, Naidoo (2017) specified recognisability in his study about consumer perceptions under the brand reputation factors together with differentiation, credibility, performance, responsibility, willingness to support, relevance and trustworthiness. More recently, Foroudi (2019) classified brand recognisability as one of the factors together with brand familiarity in his study in which a multidimensional measurement of brand signature was developed. Several scholars also suggested that brand recognisability is affected by a couple of elements, such as brand name, advertisements and communicative experiences (Datta, Ailawadi, & Van Heerde, 2017; Keller, 2013).

Although brand awareness plays a significant mediator role in the recent literature (e.g. Shabbir, Kaufmann, Ahmad, & Qureshi, 2010; Sharifi, 2014), scholars have disregarded the potential mediator effect of brand recognisability in the relationship of marketing strategies and customers' behaviours and attitudes. Therefore, to expand our knowledge of the potential mediation effects of brand recognisability in the relationship between SMMAs and brand preference of a higher education institution that has received little attention, this chapter proposed the following hypothesis:

H3: Brand recognisability will mediate the association between SMMAs and brand preference.

Brand signature has a notable role in getting competitive advantage for organisations through creating a valuable image for their reputation with their stakeholders (Olins, 1989). Furthermore, it is important for the decision makers willing to improve positive perceptions of a brand with the help of interactive elements, such as brand name (Dacin & Brown, 2002; Kapferer, 1997; Van Riel & Van den Ban, 2001). Brand signature can give an idea about the brand through its fame and related information to the consumers, enabling long-term positive awareness, attitude, idea and fame for a high performance (Van Riel & Van den Ban, 2001). Brand signature with a positive perception is pervasive and can be encountered many times a day by the consumers (Foroudi et al., 2014; Hagtvedt, 2011).

Consumers could buy a brand looking its logo and name if they have limited information about it. It can be seen in the literature that brand signature and brand awareness are of great importance. According to Kohli et al. (2002), it is an advantage for a brand to be associated with a product. The more familiar the customers with a brand are, the more trustworthy become the other products and services of the brand. When the consumers have high perception of brand signature, their awareness about that brand rises (Chadwick & Walters, 2009). Constructing common imagery identity (brand signature) has a positive effect on consumer awareness with more familiar and recognisable products and services (Melewar & Saunders, 1998). A well-constructed brand signature could arouse higher familiarity rising sales. Researchers of marketing state that brand signature has an important role in formation of a positive and recognised brand signature in the process of communication, and so the brand reaches a known and positive fame (Pittard et al., 2007; Van der Lans et al., 2009). Therefore, it is logical that a firm with positive and strong brand signature implementing in its SMMAs can impact its future customers regarding their feelings and buying intentions. Namely, it is likely that if the firms are able to use their brand signature in the SMMAs in an effective way, they give a positive impression towards to their potential customers and strengthen the demand for their brand. Given that examining the potential moderator role of brand signature on the effects of SMMAs on brand preference could make a considerable contribution to the education marketing studies, we posited the following hypothesis:

H4: Brand signature moderates the effects of SMMAs of higher education institutions on brand preference of students such that the relationship is stronger when the effect of brand signature is higher on the students rather than lower.

Method and Results

The data were analysed by using Smart-PLS software in this chapter. A convenience sampling technique was utilised, and survey instruments were delivered individually to the international students in the higher education institutions in Germany. By delivering questionnaires individually, we could prevent possible misunderstandings about survey items. Using questionnaires, we gathered data on study variables, like SMMAs, brand recognisability, brand signature and brand preference. A total of 400 questionnaires were delivered to international students who receive a business education in different English-speaking higher education institutions in Germany and, after omitting uncompleted surveys, 257 questionnaires were taken into consideration for further examination. Furthermore, the sample size efficiency was checked utilising the guideline of Hair et al. (2011), claiming that a sufficient sample has to be 'ten times the largest number of structural paths directed at a particular latent construct in the structural model' (p. 144). Applied to our research, 10 times of the 4 paths is 40.

The usage of partial least squares structural equation modelling (PLS-SEM) has importantly increased in tourism and marketing investigations (Ali et al., 2018). The PLS-SEM seems adequate for our chapter, because it is often used for theory building or expanding due to its strong statistical attributes (Hair et al., 2011). The conceptual framework proposed in the chapter is unique and makes a contribution to theory construction. Further, scholars have suggested several methodological developments including moderator impacts, non-linear influences, hierarchical linear modellings and heterotrait–monotrait ratio of correlations (HTMT) to evaluate discriminant validity (Ali et al., 2018). Hence, PLS-SEM seems as an adequate technique for testing the hierarchical and moderating effects proposed in the study model.

Common method bias (CMB) could influence the reliability of data as the data were gathered from a single source through self-administrated questionnaires. To mitigate CMB, we ensured participating international students that the knowledge obtained will be secret, and their personal information will be kept completely anonymous. One-factor analysis of Harman was performed as a statistical avenue, with the findings demonstrating that the initial construct (SMMAs) explained 41.92% of total variance, which did not exceed the threshold of 50% (MacKenzie & Podsakoff, 2012).

Furthermore, the reliability and convergent and discriminant validities were examined. The Cronbach's alpha values were higher than the commonly accepted cut-off level of 0.70. The results of composite construct reliability and rho_a also showed that the factors had internal consistency, ranging from 0.863 to 0.958. Moreover, average variance extracted (AVE) results of all factors were higher than 0.5 (between 0.654 and 0.782), showing sufficient convergent validity (Hair et al., 2016). The results of Fornell–Larcker criterion also demonstrated that the square roots of AVE results were more than the correlation exponents among the factors. Further, the results of discriminant validity did not exceed the threshold of Heterotrait–Monotrait criterion (HTMT), 0.85 (Henseler et al., 2015), which shows that multi-collinearity did not influence the study variables (Kline, 2011).

Primarily, multicollinearity issue was controlled by testing variance influence factor of each variable, and the findings showed that collinearity did not affect the study findings. Regarding coefficient of determination, R^2 coefficient values of the endogenous variables show the predictive accuracy of the structural model that the values of brand recognisability and brand preference were 0.164, and 0.402; the adjusted R^2 values were 0.160, and 0.392, respectively. To examine the predictive precision of the proposed framework, the Stone–Geisser's Q^2 was performed through utilising the blindfolding approach to calculate the cross-validated redundancy measure Q^2 for the endogenous variables of brand recognisability and brand preference. As per the findings, Q^2 values were higher than zero in all cases, demonstrating acceptability (Hair et al., 2019), with the scores gained being: brand recognisability (0.124) and brand preference (0.271). Furthermore, following the guidelines produced by Henseler, Hubona, and Ray (2016), the general model fit has been tested through utilising the result of standardised root mean square residual (SRMR). The SRMR score below 0.08 shows an acceptable model fit. Hence, the proposed framework yielded a good model fit (SRMR = 0.045).

The proposed hypotheses have been analysed based on the commonly accepted significance value of 0.05. As can be seen in Table 1, outcomes of the structural path coefficients demonstrated that all the hypothesised relationships were significant. First, the direct association between SMMAs and brand recognisability was statistically significant and positive ($\beta = 0.405$, $t = 6.377$, $p = 0.000$). SMMAs also had a significant and positive effect on international students' brand preference ($\beta = 0.444$, $t = 5.472$, $p = 0.000$). In addition, the mediation effect of brand recognisability and the moderation influence of brand signature were tested by using a bootstrapping procedure, using 1,000 resamples. The mediation role of brand recognisability on the relationship of SMMAs and brand preference yielded significant results, demonstrating the significant mediation effect of brand recognisability between these constructs ($\beta = 0.146$, $t = 4.236$, $p = 0.000$). The moderator role of brand signature between SMMAs and brand preference was also analysed. The results indicate that brand signature moderates the effect of SMMAs on international students' brand preference ($\beta = 0.106$, $t = 2.208$, $p = 0.027$). Hence, we can conclude that brand signature increases the strength of the positive impact of higher education institutions' SMMAs on international students' brand preference. In sum, the association is vigorously positive and significant if brand signature is effectively carried out in higher education institutions.

Table 1. Hypothesis Testing and Effect Sizes.

Hypothesised paths	Coefficients	t-values	p	Q^2	R^2 Adj.
Moderation effect—> brand preference	0.106	2.208	0.027		
SMMAs—> brand recognisability	0.405	6.377	0.000		
SMMAs—> brand preference	0.444	5.472	0.000		
SMMAs—> recognisability—> preference	0.146	4.236	0.000		
Brand recognisability				0.124	0.160
Brand preference				0.271	0.392

Note: This table is our original work.

Conclusion

This chapter examines the effect of SMMAs on international students' preference for a higher education institution by focussing on the mediator role of brand recognisability and the moderator effect of brand signature. The present study has a potential in guiding higher education institutions' online marketing activities to increase their brand recognisability and brand preference from the perspective of international students. The results demonstrated that SMMAs have a significant effect on brand recognisability, in line with our expectation. To our knowledge, this relationship has been first tested, and so this important finding adds to the literature. This chapter also calls for more research to expand the knowledge of the relationships between these constructs. Furthermore, congruent with the existing literature (D'silva, Bhuptani, Menon & D'Silva, 2011; Yang, Pan, Mahmud, Yang, & Srinivasan, 2015), this study showed that SMMAs can increase the brand preference of international students. Additionally, the findings endorse the mediator role of brand recognisability on the association between SMMAs and brand preference. The result concerning the mediation effect of brand recognisability is in line with the empirical findings of previous examinations conducted in the literature (Seo & Park, 2018). This study also proved that brand signature as a moderator has triggered the effects of SMMAs on brand preference.

The present research also provides higher education institutions helpful insights on how to better use brand signature and SMMAs as opportunities to improve their brand recognisability and brand preference. Since SMMAs are a good means of developing positive impact on brand recognisability and brand preference, which make a contribution to higher education brand image, higher education institutions need to encourage their students to utilise social media more by presenting more exciting and attractive SMMAs. Additionally, higher education institutions are to be aware of the important effect of the brand signature elements, including logo, name and colour, during their process of SMMAs towards the potential international students as these elements have a great potential to trigger the marketing activities in the eyes of the students.

The limitations of the chapter associate with the sample that has been limited to English-speaking high school students in Germany. Thus, with the involvement of more extensive spam of students could facilitate to generalise the results more significantly. Further research can also examine the potential impacts of SMMAs and brand signature on other outcomes, such as brand image and students' purchase intention. Future investigations focussing on the limitations would offer helpful knowledge for both higher education institutions and education tourism marketers, aiming to develop effective strategies in the SMMAs for improving their brand.

References

Aaker, D. A. (1991). *Managing brand equity*. New York, NY: Free Press.
Aaker, D. A. (1992). The value of brand equity. *Journal of Business Strategy*, *13*(1), 27–32.

Alalwan, A. A., Rana, N. P., Dwivedi, Y. K., & Algharabat, R. (2017). Social media in marketing: A review and analysis of the existing literature. *Telematics and Informatics, 34*(7), 1177–1190.

Ali,F., Rasoolimanesh,S. M., Sarstedt, M., Ringle, C. M., & Ryu, K. (2018). An assessment of the use of partial least squares structural equation modeling (PLS-SEM) in hospitality research. *International Journal of Contemporary Hospitality Management, 30*(1), 514–538.

Alves, H., Fernandes, C., & Raposo, M. (2016). Social media marketing: A literature review and implications. *Psychology & Marketing, 33*(12), 1029–1038.

Augustsson, G. (2010). Web 2.0, pedagogical support for reflexive and emotional social interaction among Swedish students. *The Internet and Higher Education, 13*(4), 197–205.

Bae, S., Jung, T. H., Moorhouse, N., Suh, M., & Kwon, O. (2020). The influence of mixed reality on satisfaction and brand loyalty in cultural heritage attractions: A brand equity perspective. *Sustainability, 12*(7), 2956.

Barker, V. (2009). Older adolescents' motivations for social network site use: The influence of gender, group identity, and collective self-esteem. *Cyber Psychology & Behavior, 12*(2), 209–213.

Barreda, A. A., Nusair,K., Wang,Y., Okumus,F., & Bilgihan,A. (2020). The impact of social media activities on brand image and emotional attachment: A case in the travel context. *Journal of Hospitality and Tourism Technology, 11*(1), 109–135.

Berger, J., Draganska, M., & Simonson, I. (2007). The influence of product variety on brand perception and choice. *Marketing Science, 26*(4), 460–472.

Binsardi, A., & Ekwulugo, F. (2003). International marketing of British education: Research on the students' perception and the UK market penetration. *Marketing Intelligence & Planning, 21*(5), 318–327.

Bruhn, M., Schoenmueller, V., & Schäfer, D. B. (2012). Are social media replacing traditional media in terms of brand equity creation? *Management Research Review, 35*(9), 770–790.

Caldwell, N. G. (2000). The emergence of museum brands. *International Journal of Arts Management, 2*(3), 28–34.

Chadwick, S., & Walters, G. (2009). Sportswear identification, distinctive design and manufacturer logos–issues from the front line. *The Marketing Review, 9*(1), 63–78.

Chamberlain, S. (2014). Economic development and social media: A strategic approach for success. *Papers in Canadian Economic Development, 14*(1), 55–73.

Constantinides, E., & Zinck Stagno, M. C. (2011). Potential of the social media as instruments of higher education marketing: A segmentation study. *Journal of Marketing for Higher Education, 21*(1), 7–24.

D'silva, B., Bhuptani, R., Menon, S., & D'Silva, S. (2011). Influence of social media marketing on brand choice behaviour among youth in India: an empirical study. Paper presented at the International Conference on Technology and Business Management, March, 28–30, in Dubai, U.A.E. (Conference Proceedings, pp: 756–763).

Dacin, P. A., & Brown, T. J. (2002). Corporate identity and corporate associations: A framework for future research. *Corporate Reputation Review, 5*(2–1), 254–263.

Datta, H., Ailawadi, K. L., & Van Heerde, H. J. (2017). How well does consumer-based brand equity align with sales-based brand equity and marketing-mix response? *Journal of Marketing, 81*(3), 1–20.

Foroudi, P. (2019). Influence of brand signature, brand awareness, brand attitude, brand reputation on hotel industry's brand performance. *International Journal of Hospitality Management, 76*(1), 271–285.

Foroudi, P., Melewar, T. C., & Gupta, S. (2014). Linking corporate logo, corporate image, and reputation: An examination of consumer perceptions in the financial setting. *Journal of Business Research, 67*(11), 2269–2281.

Grabs, A., & Sudhoff, J. (2014). *Empfehlungsmarketing im Social Web: Kunden gewinnen und Kunden binden (Relationship marketing in social web. Customers win and bind)*. Bonn: Galileo Press.

Greenhow, C., & Lewin, C. (2016). Social media and education: Reconceptualizing the boundaries of formal and informal learning. *Learning, Media and Technology*, *41*(1), 6–30.

Gretzel, U., Kang, M., & Lee, W. J. (2008). Differences in consumer-generated media adoption and use: A cross-national perspective. *Journal of Hospitality and Leisure Marketing*, *17*(1–2), 99–120.

Hagtvedt, H. (2011). The impact of incomplete typeface logos on perceptions of the firm. *Journal of Marketing*, *75*(July), 86–93.

Hair, J. F., Ringle,C. M., & Sarstedt,M. (2011). PLS-SEM: Indeed a silver bullet. *Journal of Marketing Theory and Practice*, 19(2), 139-152.

Harb, A. A., Fowler, D., Chang, H. J. J., Blum, S. C., & Alakaleek, W. (2019). Social media as a marketing tool for events. *Journal of Hospitality and Tourism Technology*, *10*(1), 28–44.

Harris, L., & Rae, A. (2009). Social networks: The future of marketing for small businesses. *Journal of Business Strategy*, *30*(5), 24–31.

Heider, F. (1958). *The psychology of interpersonal relations*. New York, NY: Wiley.

Henseler, J., Hubona,G., &Ray,P. A. (2016). Using PLS path modeling in new technology research: updated guidelines. *Industrial Management & Data Systems,* 116(1), 2–20.

Henseler,J., Ringle, C. M., & Sarstedt,M. (2015). A New Criterion for Assessing Discriminant Validity in Variance-based Structural Equation Modeling. *Journal of the Academy of Marketing Science*, 43(1), 115–135.

Howard, J. A., & Sheth, J. N. (1969). *The theory of buyer behaviour*. New York, NY: John Wiley & Sons.

Huang, Z. J., & Cai, L. A. (2015). Modeling consumer-based brand equity for multinational hotel brands – When hosts become guests. *Tourism Management*, *46*, 431–443.

Irfan, A., Rasli, A., Sami, A., & Liaquat, H. (2017). Role of social media in promoting education tourism. *Advanced Science Letters*, *23*(9), 8728–8731.

Kapferer, J. N. (1997). Managing luxury brands. *Journal of Brand Management*, *4*(4), 251–259.

Kaplan, A. M., & Haenlein, M. (2010). Users of the world, unite! The challenges and opportunities of social media. *Business Horizons*, *53*(1), 59–68.

Keller, K. L. (2009). Building strong brands in a modern marketing communications environment. *Journal of Marketing Communications*, *15*(2–3), 139–155.

Keller, K. L. (2013). *Strategic brand management: Building, measuring, and managing brand equity* (4th ed.). London: Prentice-Hall.

Kelley, H. H., & Michela, J. L. (1980) Attribution theory and research. *Annual Review of Psychology*, *31*(1), 457–501.

Knoll, J. (2016). Advertising in social media: A review of empirical evidence. *International Journal of Advertising*, *35*(2), 266–300.

Kohli, C., Suri,R., & Thakor,M. (2002), Creating effective logos: Insights from theory and practice, *Business Horizons*, *45*(3), 58–64.

Kolbitsch, J., & Maurer, H. (2006). The transformation of the web: How emerging communities shape the information we consume. *Journal of Universal Computer Science*, *12*(2), 187–213.

Kusumasondjaja, S. (2018). The roles of message appeals and orientation on social media brand communication effectiveness: An evidence from Indonesia. *Asia Pacific Journal of Marketing and Logistics*, *30*(4), 1135–1158.

Langaro, D., Rita, P., & de Fatima Salgueiro, M. (2018). Do social networking sites contribute for building brands? Evaluating the impact of users' participation on

The Role of Social Media Marketing Activities   63

brand awareness and brand attitude. *Journal of Marketing Communications*, *24*(2), 146–168.

MacKenzie, S. B., & Podsakoff, P. M. (2012). Common method bias in marketing: Causes, mechanisms, and procedural remedies. *Journal of Retailing*, *88*(4), 542–555.

Mangold, W. G., & Faulds, D. J. (2009). Social media: The new hybrid element of the promotion mix. *Business Horizons*, *52*(4), 357–365.

Melewar, T. C., & Saunders, J. (1998). Global corporate visual identity systems. *International Marketing Review*, *15*(4), 291–308.

Mizerski, R. W., Golden, L. L., & Kernan, J. B. (1979). The attributional process in consumer decision making. *Journal of Consumer Research*, *2*(1), 123–140.

Nah, F. F. H., Eschenbrenner, B., & DeWester, D. (2011). Enhancing brand equity through flow and telepresence: A comparison of 2D and 3D virtual worlds. *Mis Quarterly*, *35*(3), 731–747.

Naidoo, S. (2017). *Understanding the role that brand communication plays in influencing brand reputation from a consumer perspective against the Urde and Greyser Corporate Brand Identity and Reputation Matrix: Samsung South Africa.* Doctoral dissertation, The IIE.

Nusair, K., Butt, I., & Nikhashemi, S. (2019). A bibliometric analysis of social media in hospitality and tourism research. *International Journal of Contemporary Hospitality Management*, *31*(7), 2691–2719. doi:10.1108/IJCHM-06-2018-0489

Olins, W. (1989). *Corporate entity: Making business strategy visible through design.* London: Thames and Hudson.

Pappu, R., Quester, P. G., & Cooksey, R. W. (2005). Consumer-based brand equity: Improving the measurement – Empirical evidence. *Journal of Product and Brand Management*, *14*, 143–154.

Phan, M., Thomas, R., & Heine, K. (2011). Social media and luxury brand management: The case of Burberry. *Journal of Global Fashion Marketing*, *2*(4), 213–222.

Pittard, N., Ewing, M., & Jevons, C. (2007). Aesthetic theory and logo design: examining consumer response to proportion across cultures. *International Marketing Review*, *24*(4), 457–473.

Savaşan, A., Yalvaç, M., Uzunboylu, H., & Tuncel, E. (2018). The attitudes of education, tourism and health sector managers in Northern Cyprus towards Education on Health Tourism. *Quality & Quantity*, *52*(1), 285–303.

Schultz, D., & Peltier, J. (2013). Social media's slippery slope: Challenges, opportunities and future research directions. *Journal of Research in Interactive Marketing*, *7*(2), 86–99.

Sen, S., & Bhattacharya, C. B. (2001). Does doing good always lead to doing better? Consumer reactions to corporate social responsibility. *Journal of Marketing Research*, *38*(2), 225–243.

Seo, E.-J., & Park, J.-W. (2018). A study on the effects of social media marketing activities on brand equity and customer response in the airline industry. *Journal of Air Transport Management*, *66*, 36–41.

Shabbir, S., Kaufmann, H. R., Ahmad, I., & Qureshi, I. M. (2010). Cause related marketing campaigns and consumer purchase intentions: The mediating role of brand awareness and corporate image. *African Journal of Business Management*, *4*(6), 1229–1235.

Sharifi, S. S. (2014). Impacts of the trilogy of emotion on future purchase intentions in products of high involvement under the mediating role of brand awareness. *European Business Review*, *26*(1), 43–63.

Statista. (2018). Global Web Index. Ranking der Länder mit dem höchsten Anteil an Online-Käufern an allen Internetnutzern in ausgewählten Ländern weltweit im 1. Quartal 2015. [Online]. Retrieved from http://de.statista.com/statistik/daten/

studie/482490/umfrage/anteil-der-online-kaeufer-nach-ausgewaehlten-laendern-weltweit/. Accessed on February 2, 2020.

Statista. (2020). Number of social network users worldwide from 2010 to 2023. Retrieved from https://www.statista.com/statistics/278414/number-of-worldwide-social-network-users/. Accessed on April 8, 2020.

Streicher, M. C., & Estes, Z. (2015). Touch and go: Merely grasping a product facilitates brand perception and choice. *Applied Cognitive Psychology*, *29*(3), 350–359.

Tess, P. A. (2013). The role of social media in higher education classes (real and virtual) – A literature review. *Computers in Human Behaviour*, *29*(5), 60–68.

Tiago, M. T. P. M. B., & Veríssimo, J. M. C. (2014). Digital marketing and social media: Why bother? *Business Horizons*, *57*(6), 703–708.

Van der Lans,R., Cote,J. A., Cole,C. A., Leong,S. M., Smidts, A., Henderson, P. W., ... and Schmitt,B. H. (2009). Cross-national logo evaluation analysis: An individual-level approach. *Marketing Science, 28*(5), 968–985.

Van Riel, C. B., & Van den Ban, A. (2001). The added value of corporate logos – An empirical study. *European Journal of Marketing*, *35*(3/4), 428–440.

Wang, Y. C., & Fesenmaier, D. R. (2004). Modeling participation in an online travel community. *Journal of Travel Research*, *42*(3), 261–270.

Weiner, B. (1972). Attribution theory, achievement motivation, and the educational process. *Review of Educational Research*, *42*(2), 203–215.

Weiner, B. (2000). Intrapersonal and interpersonal theories of motivation from an attributional perspective. *Educational Psychology Review*, *12*(1), 1–14.

Whetten, D. A. (1989). What constitutes a theoretical contribution? *Academy of Management Review*, *14*(4), 490–495.

Yadav, M., & Rahman, Z. (2018). The influence of social media marketing activities on customer loyalty. *Benchmarking: An International Journal*, *25*(9), 3882–3905.

Yang, C., Pan, S., Mahmud, J., Yang, H., & Srinivasan, P. (2015). Using personal traits for brand preference prediction, Paper presented at the Conference on Empirical Methods in Natural Language Processing, September, 17–21, in Lisbon, Portugal (Conference Proceedings, pp. 86–96).

Zeng, B., & Gerritsen, R. (2014). What do we know about social media in tourism? A review. *Tourism Management Perspectives*, *10*(1), 27–36.

Zenith. (2019). Social media overtakes. [Online]. Retrieved from https://www.zenithmedia.com/social-media-overtakes-print-to-become-the-third-largest-advertising-channel/. Accessed on February 2, 2020.

Chapter 4

Use of Web Analytics and Social Listening to Attract International Students

Rakhi Tripathi

Abstract

International students make valuable educational and economic contributions in higher education institutions (HEIs) all across the world. They contribute to the diversity and add different perspective in classrooms. Attracting international students is one of the objectives of HEIs. International students being present all over the world access information about the university online. Hence, all the relevant information must be available on the HEI website. Institutions are also present on social media platforms for interaction purposes. The owned media, including website, social media, discussion forums, etc. of institutions must be regularly monitored and analysed. Equally important is to analyse what students are discussing online about institutions, that is, what are their sentiments. This chapter is an attempt to develop a guide for HEI to draw the interest of international students for an institution through web analytics and social listening. Web analytics will help in understanding the behaviour of the visitor to the HEI website. Key performance indicators that will help in achieve the objective of attracting international students will be identified. On the other hand, analysing social listening on different platforms will help in understanding international students' perspectives towards a specific institution.

Keywords: Higher education; international students; web analytics; key performance indicators; social media monitoring; Social media listening

---

Global Perspectives on Recruiting International Students: Challenges and Opportunities, 65–79
Copyright © 2021 by Emerald Publishing Limited
All rights of reproduction in any form reserved
doi:10.1108/978-1-83982-518-720211004

66 *Rakhi Tripathi*

Introduction

Studying abroad is described as an enriching experience for students leaving their home country (Yang, Webster, & Prosser, 2011). Nowadays, an increasing number of students from Asia participate in the global educational market. Figures show that Asian students occupy 52% of the international student population worldwide (Organization for Economic Co-operation and Development (OECD), 2011). China and India grab the highest positions of international students across the globe (Altbach, 2009). Most international students pursue their further studies in Western countries such as the United States, the United Kingdom, Germany, Australia and France (Institute of International Education, Open Door, 2014; OECD, 2011). Studying in a different country is a common practice, whether for short-term, typically a few months in another country to gain intercultural understanding and/or relocating to a separate nation to complete a degree. According to the Open Doors Report of 2011, there was a 5% increase in the world's total of international students getting admission to the United States. Table 1 demonstrates the top 10 places of origin of international students from 2016/2017 to 2017/2018. As shown in Table 1, the majority of international students are from Asian backgrounds. Chinese and Indian students together add 50% of the total international students' population. Except for a few countries, there has been an increase in the number of students who go for international studies.

From a higher education institution (HEI) point of view, international students are incredibly crucial to higher education for both academic prestige and financial benefits (Altbach & Knight, 2007; Li, 2016). It is essential to define the term international students. According to Andrade (2006), international students

Table 1. Top 10 Places of Origin of International Students.

		2016/17	2017/18	% of Total
	World TOTAL	**1,078,822**	**1,094,792**	**100.0**
1	China	350,755	363,341	33.2
2	India	186,267	196,271	17.9
3	South Korea	58,663	54,555	5.0
4	Saudi Arabia	52,611	44,432	4.1
5	Canada	27,065	25,909	2.4
6	Vietnam	22,438	24,325	2.2
7	Taiwan	21,516	22,454	2.1
8	Japan	18,780	18,753	1.7
9	Mexico	16,835	15,468	1.4
10	Brazil	13,089	14,620	1.3

Source: Open doors report (Institute of International Education, 2018).

are individuals enrolled in institutions of higher education who are on temporary student visas and are non-native English speakers (NNES). International students not only help in economic growth but also they promote cultural awareness at university. They also offer an opportunity to promote university and country through word of mouth. Competence for attracting international students has expanded to regional and national Governments.

While applying for HEI abroad and selecting the most suitable one, international students find difficulty in getting authentic and relevant information about the institution online. Higher education institutions, through their websites and social media pages, try to provide information pertinent to international students. Not only a compatible user interface is required, but also, these interactions on digital platforms need to be analysed. Web analytics for international students is essential. Moreover, the sentiments of international aspirants need to be analysed to understand the queries they have.

Intending to analyse the performance of academic institutions website and social media platforms concerning international students, this study focusses on the following research questions:

- What do international students search online before applying for HEI abroad?
- What are the key performance indicators for academic websites to understand the online behaviour of international students?
- What are the social listening strategies for institutions to attract international students?

Research Method

Exploratory qualitative research from the peer-review literature approach has been used. Through extensive literature, various features on the website to attract International students have been identified for higher education institutions. The literature review aimed at the following research question: *What do international students search online before applying for Higher Education Institution abroad?* Combining the objectives with the metrics of web analytic tools by Chaffey and Patron (2012) and Waisberg and Kaushik (2009), the second research question has been addressed: *What are the key performance indicators for academic websites to understand the online behaviour of the international students?* Finally, this study will attempt to find out how social listening strategies can be used.

Therefore, for the above research questions, the following research objectives have been identified:

- Through literature, identify the features of the website that international students are looking for in any reputed higher education institution.
- Identify key performance indicators for academic websites for international students.
- Identify social listening strategies for academic institutions to attract international students.

3. International Students and Academic Institutional Websites

Before applying to any university, students try to find information about the university in terms of the course curriculum, fees, faculties, etc. As far as international students are concerned, they are not only interested in the information as mentioned above but also would like to understand about institution's norms and acceptance for international student. With the Internet, students go online and collect information about the universities and desired courses before applying. University websites (owned media) become an authentic source of information. Not only the students get the information, but they can also interact with the university through the website by asking queries and feedbacks. The following (Table 2) website features have been identified and classified by the author(s) from the literature that is relevant for international students. These features play a vital role in international student decision making to shortlist an institution for admission.

Web Analytics for Understanding Online Behaviour of International Students

Web analytics refers to a combination of (a) measuring, (b) acquisition, (c) analysing and (d) reporting of data collected from the Internet with the aim of understanding and optimising web experience (Web Analytics Association, 2008). Understanding visitor activities through website backend and analytics organisations can better understand their target audience and, in return, approach them accordingly (Waisberg & Kaushik, 2009). According to Bekavac and Praničević (2015), web analytics is the analysis of qualitative and quantitative data on the website to continuously improve the online experience of visitors, which leads to the more efficient and effective realisation of the company's planned goals. Quantitative data provide insight into visitor behaviour, such as the previous web page,

Table 2.   Information Searched Online by International Students

Feature	Authors (year)	University website (author(s) remarks)
World Rank International students depend on global rankings. Sometimes between different countries and sometimes within a country. Rank correlates with placement. Students also look for rankings of the course they are willing to apply	Altbach (2015), Hazelkorn (2007), McDonagh, Lising, Walpole, and Perez (1998), Cebolla-Boado, Hu, and Soysal (2018) and Jabjaimoh, Samart, Jansakul, and Jibenja (2019)	On the university website, highlighting the rank and/or accreditation of the institution, usually on the homepage will help. Many institutions dedicate a separate page to rankings where details are mentioned

Feature	Authors (year)	University website (author(s) remarks)
Image and reputation Actual perceptions of an institution held by external stakeholders. Image profoundly influences the choice of students in selecting an institution. Faculty members and facilities play a crucial role – the image of cross-culture students on the website help in attracting students. Reputation is not limited to brand image, corporate image, destination image but can be extended to functional and emotional images	Brown, Dacin, Pratt, and Whetten (2006), Bakewell and Gibson-Sweet (1998), Ivy (2001), Binsardi and Ekwulugo (2003), Nguyen and LeBlanc (2001), Brown and Oplatka (2006), Mun, Aziz, and Bojei (2018)	Uploading articles, blogs written by stakeholders such as faculty, students, and alumni about the university to the website can highlight the reputation
Campus culture Socio-cultural adjustment is an issue with International students. Asian international students encounter obstacles when trying to acquire additional skills, which at times bring them a sense of 'study shock'. There are two factors at campus-level adjustment in communication and adjustment in campus life	Hung and Hyun (2010); Schweitzer, Morson, and Mather (2011), Wang and Mallinckrodt (2006), Westmont (2014), Morson and Mather (2011), Li (2016) and Wen, Hu, and Hao (2018)	Sharing information on the academic website and social media regarding campus culture such as cultural activities, hostel life, etc. helps the students in understanding the expectations of the institution
Language Language is a challenge for international students. Many international students from Asia, studying in Australia, face serious learning difficulties, and lack confidence in speaking and taking a proactive role in classrooms. Not only the interaction becomes difficult, but completing courses in different styles becomes a nightmare	Zheng (2010), Liu (2011), Terui (2011), Wu, Garza, and Guzman (2015) and Iwara, Kativhu, and Obadire (2017)	Information about language in institutions such as special language programs for international students is supposed to be posted on the website. Also, a translated version of the website will be useful. By using the this page, international students will feel comfortable and get the desired information

(Continued)

70   *Rakhi Tripathi*

Table 2.   (*Continued*)

Feature	Authors (year)	University website (author(s) remarks)
Fee structure and other expenses Education Fees of a particular country plays a vital role in aspirants' decision. Not only tuition fees but also the cost of living in the main elements taken into account. A majority of students are those who come out with their sponsorship and without receiving any scholarships.	Mazzarol and Soutar, (2002), Landes (2008), Parafianowicz (2009), Petruzzellis and Romanazzi (2010), Maringe and Carter (2007) and Kauko and Medvedeva (2016)	All details about the fee structure and other expenses such as hostel fee, transportation, canteen, etc. must be uploaded on the website. Navigation bars must have a separate tab for fee structure and costs
Immigration information Students after shortlisting the Higher Education Institution for admission find difficulty in getting information regarding the immigration process such as visa requirements and fee structure and mode of payment	Cummings and Bain (2015), Tran and Nyland (2011) and Ling and Tran (2015)	A separate web page on immigration or a direct link where all the information related to immigration is given must be available on the website. Offering aspirants an option of asking queries online can be helpful
Career and Institutional support International students have diverse careers, needs, and concerns. They want to know the scope of the course offered by any Higher Education Institution. They prefer countries and institutions where career certainty is provided. They compete with domestic students for on-campus jobs	Singaravelu, White, and Bringaze (2005), Kovacs Burns, Richter, Mao, Mogale, and Danko (2014), Calder et al. (2016) and Bulgan and Çiftçi (2018)	Details about placement such as companies visiting campus, historical data, etc. must be available on an academic website. Information on placement related to international students must be updated on the website regularly
Faculty Excellent faculty not only improves the rank of the institution but also attract aspirants. They not only add diversity in higher education culture but also bring a new area of research, perspectives, skills, and pedagogies that enhances the reputation of any university. International students consider the faculty profile before applying	Lee and Kuzhabekova (2017), Altbach and Yudkevich (2017) and Lawrence, Celis, Kim, Lipson, and Tong (2014)	Details of faculty on the website in terms of experience, expertise and resume will be beneficial. Adding email id will help the aspirant contact the academic directly which will help these students in taking a decision

time spent on the website, pages visited, etc. Continuous improvement of online visitors based on information obtained in web analytics is a vital aspect of the web analytics concept. The metrics that help in achieve the goals are considered as key performance indicators (Chaffey & Patron, 2012; Waisberg & Kaushik, 2009). Key performance indicators help in analysing the present performance of the website. For example, if students from other countries are not visiting the university's website, then the site requires attention. There might be different reasons for this: technical error, poor content on the website, etc.

In the last section, the information that international students search on the university website has been identified (Table 1). The following metrics have been identified as key performance indicators for the university website. Through web analytics, universities can analyse the online behaviour of international students and try to target them:

- *Location*: Web analytic tools can provide the place of the users in terms of country and city. Hence, with this KPI, the university can analyse from which country are the majority of international aspirants visiting the website.
- *Demographics*: This metric gives information about the age and gender of the user. Age is crucial here as it will help in understanding if the visitor is an aspirant or any other stakeholder. For example, a faculty might also visit the university website for applying. Even parents visit websites for necessary information.
- *Returning visitors*: Per Google analytics, if someone has visited the website within the past 2 years and returns from the same device, they are marked as a Returning Visitor. With this metric, the seriousness of the visitor can be estimated.
- *Landing page*: A landing page is the page of the website that the visitor lands on, that is, it is the first point of interaction with the visitor (Khopkar et al., 2014). The visitor may be coming from different sources, but the landing page will let the visitors decide to stay at the website or leave. This metric, when clubbed with conversion rate, depth of page metric can give helpful insights.
- *Bounce rate*: The bounce rate is the percentage of website visitors who visit only one page on the website. Kaushik (2009) states that the percentage of website visitors who stay on the site for a small amount of time (usually 5 s or less) is also considered as bounce rate. This metric is very crucial for any higher education institution website as it will estimate the percent of the visitors that bounced back from the site without further engagement. It shows that the visitors did not find adequate information. Also, clubbing this metric with traffic source metric it can give a useful insight if some sources of traffic are sending you particularly terrible traffic compared to others. If a substantial number of international visitors (clubbing location KPI) bounce back, then it will be a severe concern. Reason can be incorrect information, incorrect webpage, etc.
- *Page visits*: This metric gives the data on what pages did the visitor visit on the educational website. This KPI helps in understanding the information visitor is looking for. For example, the visitor visits the immigration page or international student admission page; then, it can be said that the visitor is interested in this information.

72   *Rakhi Tripathi*

- *Depth of visit*: Measured as the ratio of page viewed to visits, depth of visits is a measurement of interest in the content provided by the website. More significant numbers indicate more interest in the content provided (Clifton, 2012). The majority of visitors view a couple of web pages of a website. For example, if international students visit more than three web pages and stay on the website for some time, then it can be concluded that the student might be interested. Such visitors can be approached.
- *Time spent*: The amount of time a visitor spent on the website. If the aspirant is on the site and is visiting different pages, then he/she is looking for some crucial information. For example, an article on campus culture is uploaded on a website, whose reading time is 3 min. If a visitor visits this page and stays for more than 3 min on it, then it can be concluded that the visitor has read the article.
- *Measure downloads*: It is crucial to track how many times aspirants, students or any other visitor downloaded particular files as this act as micro-conversions (Rodden et al., 2010). It is crucial to track the number of times users downloads data from the University website. This metric can be clubbed with the location metric. For example, how many admission brochures or forms have foreign aspirants downloaded.
- *Tracking registered users*: Understanding the behaviour of the visitors that have registered themselves on the institutional website. Metrics such as behaviour flow, time of visit, number of visits, the time between each pair successive logins by the same user can allow detailed analyses and understanding of what different types of visitors are on the university website (Khoo et al., 2008). Moreover, once the visitor registers himself/herself on the academic institution website, the pattern of users becomes essential. Visitors can be contacted, and related information can be sent to them.
- Tracking incomplete transactions is a must. If the international student starts the process of the payment and abandons it before completing it, then it is essential to find the root cause and solve the issue. Funnels help in tracing the path to a goal (Clifton, 2012). The reasons behind incomplete transactions can be payment gateways, security concerns, technology issues, compatibility of two systems, etc.
- *Conversion rate*: Conversion rate is the percentage of visits that result in the visitor taking an action that has been defined as necessary to an organisation. Every website is created with a predefined goal (Kaushik, 2009). For university, the conversion rate is when the student pays the fee online, aspirants download a form, etc. Conversion rate is a useful KPI that helps to monitor the goals of the website. For the objective of fees and expenses, this metric will be beneficial. If an international student is trying to pay the payment online, and it is taking time, then the tool can identify the root cause. Some students download forms but never apply; some get admission and do not pay their fees. All this information can be checked.
- *Technology and device*: The technology being used and device information of the visitor is critical for any stage (Loftus, 2012). This information includes the device type, connectivity and operating system and is useful for decision-makers (Brown & Green, 2012). It will be helpful for universities to know what Internet speed is foreign visitors using. According to the content of the website

can be edited. If the user's Internet speed is high, then content with video and images can be added else, only text will be used.

- *Traffic source*: For any academic institution websites, it is crucial to know whether the visitors are coming directly to the site, from a search engine, through referral or social media. Based on this data, the Institutes can estimate the frequency of traffic sources. For example, if the majority of the international traffic is coming from blogs and social media, then the institutes need to work on its content on social media (Kaushik, 2009). Also, if the traffic is coming of search engines, then keywords can be analysed. Keywords help in search engine optimisation as well.

Social Listening of International Students

Social media are communication systems that allow stakeholders to exchange information along with dyadic ties (Peters, Chen, Kaplan, Ognibeni, and Pauwels, 2013). Social media platforms are extensively being used by higher education all across the globe. It is a platform where a university connects both formally and informally with its stakeholders. Students and aspirants have discussions on social media. Many influencer bloggers discuss and review the ratings and courses of academic institutions. For higher education, social media is owned, paid and earned media (Davis, Deil-Amen, Rios-Aguilar, & González Canché, 2015). Owned media refers to media that is owned by universities, that is, institutions have their own social media pages and control the content (Lovett & Staelin, 2016). Paid media refers to media that is used for a specific purpose, and monetarily transactions are involved. For example, institutions invest in Google ads. Finally, earned media is the interaction on owned media (Mattke, Müller, & Maier, 2019). The feedback, queries and suggestions about a university created by visitors on social media forms earned media of that university.

Social media can play a crucial role in attracting international students. Being a two-way communication; international aspirants can interact with institutions through social media platforms. For owned media, that is, the social media pages owned by institutions, information regarding the admission process, fees, campus culture, immigration, etc. can be provided.

There are broadly two ways of analysing social media: social media monitoring and social listening (Reid & Duffy, 2018). It is essential to investigate this interaction, which is called social media monitoring. Social Media Monitoring is defined as 'the continuous, systematic observation and analysis of social media networks and social communities' (Fensel, Leiter, & Stavrakantonakis, 2012). Usually, it is used by private sectors, but now governments and public sectors have started utilising it (Fensel et al., 2012; Loukis, Charalabidis, & Androutsopoulou, 2017). Social media monitoring can be beneficial for higher education in connecting with international students by analysis and their engagement with institutions, posts, and updates. Kaushik (2009) divided social media metrics into four categories:

- *Conversation rate*: When the audience comments on the posts. Through comments, one can analyse what the sentiments of the visitor are. Are they asking questions, providing feedback, appreciating or complaining, etc.?

74   Rakhi Tripathi

- The amplification rate is the rate at which your followers take your content and share it through their networks. By sharing, the content is reached in different networks, and the visibility improves. This is a useful metric for higher education targeting international students. With few shares, the content can reach various systems and hence different locations.
- *The applause rate*: The number of approval actions (e.g. likes, favourites) a post receives relative to the total number of followers. When a follower likes any of the posts, it is an acknowledgment that it is valuable for him/her. Knowing what percentage of the audience finds value in the things an organisation post provides insights which post is being appreciated well by the audience. For institutions, applause rate helps in understanding which posts are being recognised by international students. Hence, similar relevant content can be posted.
- The number of impressions, that is, how many people have viewed the content. All the above three metrics help in increasing the visibility of any post. Therefore, higher education needs to focus on all these metrics.

These metrics need to be combined with other parameters such as user ID, user location, age, number of followers, etc. These parameters will be key performance indicators for higher education to understand the behaviour and response of international students on the institution's social media platforms. For example, a post on the new admission policy has been updated on the institution's social media pages. Students all across the globe start asking queries and share the post. Through these metrics, it will be easy to analyse whether these visitors are authentic users, fake or bots.

Apart from social media analytics, sentiments of the students need to be captured. Stewart and Arnold (2016) define social listening as an active process of attending to, observing, interpreting and responding to a variety of stimuli through mediated, electronic and social channels. Social listening emerges in how we communicate and listen to others using a domain of social media and communication technologies that influence our interpersonal engagement (Stewart, Atilano, & Arnold, 2017). Social listening allows universities to track, analyse and respond to the conversations of its stakeholders on social media. Therefore, higher education institutions must analyse the tone of the students' comments regularly. Below steps are identified for understanding the sentiments of international students for a university:

- It is essential to extract data from various social media sources such as blogs, social networking sites, reviews, etc. regularly. These data may not necessarily be only from owned media. Students, apart from university websites and social media, also visit other relevant sources such as web blogs, other social media accounts, educational and career influencers, etc. Hence, extracting data from all sources are beneficial. Proper keywords must be used for extraction so that targeted data is received.
- *Volume*: Before running any tool for sentiment analysis, a considerable amount of data must be available. With insufficient data, the review will be incorrect. For example, if only a few students have commented on the university's

Facebook page, then there is no need for a tool to analyse. On the contrary, if there are considerable tweets on Twitter from an international location and are discussing higher education fee structure, then this data needs to be analysed.

- *Sentiment analysis*: Sentiment analysis is the interpretation and classifications of tones within text data. According to Medhat, Hassan, and Korashy (2014), sentiment analysis is the computational study of people's opinions, attitudes and emotions towards an entity. Sentiment analysis is broadly divided into three emotions: negative, positive and neutral. Positive words/sentences have a positive sentiment attached to them. Keywords indicating happiness, appreciation, satisfaction, etc., are classified as having a positive sentiment. Similarly, negative words, sentences have a negative sentiment attached to them. Keywords or texts indicating sadness, dissatisfaction, discrimination, etc. are classified as having a negative sentiment (Ferrara & Yang, 2015). The strength of the identified sentiment depends on keyword frequencies, co-occurrences, or a predefined assignment on specific words (Gaspar, Pedro, Panagiotopoulos, & Seibt, 2016). When no emotions are implied, they are classified as neutral. Neutral comments usually either provide information or are in the form of queries and discussions. This emotion, too, cannot be ignored. For example, aspirants are looking for information regarding the immigration process; then the university needs to address this query. If neutral sentiments are ignored, then they can form an emotion later.
- *Segmentation of sentiments*: Once the sentiment analysis has been conducted and the university has data on how many students are speaking in favour (positive sentiment) and how many comments are negative, a more in-depth study is required. Each sentiment can be further categorised, and priority for each sentiment can be assigned. This way, it will be easier to get close to the root cause. For example, there are negative comments about higher education institutions on social media. It is crucial to sub-segment these negative comments. Negative feedback can be about fees, image, faculty, etc. As stated above, the volume of each emotion is essential. If the quantity of any sentiment is low, then it not worth analysing further. Hence, combining with volume, issues can be prioritised and addressed. This step involves machine learning techniques.

Conclusion and Research Implications

This study analysed how web analytic tools and social listening strategies can be used to attract international students for any university. By focussing on international students, not only the culture and diversity of any university will improve but also it adds to the economic value of the institution. The contribution of this study is three-fold. First, through literature, relevant information that international aspirants search online is identified. Also, how, through the website, all relevant information can be provided to students is suggested. Second, through web analytic tools, how online behaviour of international students can be studied. Finally, social listening strategies have been identified. This study will be useful for higher education institutions. Through data from web analytic tools and social

76   *Rakhi Tripathi*

listening, they can target international students in a better way. Social listening will help in understanding the sentiment of aspirants, and, hence, universities can make changes in their digital presence accordingly. For future work, a focussed study can be conducted where real-time data of university can be collected and analysed.

References

Altbach, P. (2015). Perspectives on internationalizing higher education. *International Higher Education*, (27). doi:10.6017/ihe.2002.27.6975

Altbach, P. G. (2009). One-third of the globe: The future of higher education in China and India. *Prospects, 39*(1), 11–31. http://dx.doi.org/10.1007/s11125-009-9106-1

Altbach, P. G., & Knight, J. (2007). The internationalization of higher education: Motivations and realities. *Journal of Studies in International Education, 11*(3), 290–305.

Altbach, P. G., & Yudkevich, M. (2017). Twenty-first century mobility: The role of international faculty. *International Higher Education, 90*, 8–10.

Andrade, M. S. (2006). International students in English-speaking universities: Adjustment factors. *Journal of Research in International Education, 5*(2), 131–154.

Bakewell, C. J., & Gibson-Sweet, M. F. (1998). Strategic marketing in a changing environment: Are the new U.K. universities in danger of being stuck in the middle? *The International Journal of Educational Management, 12*(3), 103–107.

Bekavac, I., & Praničević, D. G. (2015). Web analytics tools and web metrics tools: An overview and comparative analysis. *Croatian Operational Research Review, 6*(2), 373–386.

Binsardi, A., & Ekwulugo, F. (2003). International marketing of British education: Research on the students' perception and the U.K. market penetration. *Marketing Intelligence & Planning, 21*(5), 318–327.

Brown, T. J., Dacin, P. A., Pratt, M. G., & Whetten, D. A. (2006). Identity, intended image, construed image, and reputation: An interdisciplinary framework and suggested terminology. *Journal of the Academy of Marketing Science, 34*(2), 99–106.

Bulgan, G., & Çiftçi, A. (2018). Career counseling for international students: using the framework of social cognitive career theory. *International Student Mobility and Opportunities for Growth in the Global Marketplace*. IGI Global, 203–213.

Calder, M. J., Richter, S., Mao, Y., Burns, K. K., Mogale, R. S., & Danko, M. (2016). International students attending Canadian Universities: Their experiences with housing, finances, and other issues. *The Canadian Journal of Higher Education, 46*(2), 92.

Cebolla-Boado, H., Hu, Y., & Soysal, Y. N. (2018). Why study abroad? Sorting of Chinese students across British universities. *British Journal of Sociology of Education, 39*(3), 365–380.

Chaffey, D., & Patron, M. (2012). From Web Analytics to Digital Marketing Optimization: Increasing the Commercial Value of Digital Analytics, *Journal of Direct, Data and Digital Marketing Practice, 14*(1), 30–45.

Clifton, B. (2012). *Advanced web metrics with Google Analytics*. John Wiley & Sons.

Cummings, W., & Bain, O. (2015). Where are international students going? *International Higher Education, 43*, 5–17.

Davis, C. H. III, Deil-Amen, R., Rios-Aguilar, C., & González Canché, M. S. (2015). Social media, higher education, and community colleges: A research synthesis and implications for the study of two-year institutions. *Community College Journal of Research and Practice, 39*(5), 409–422.

Fensel, D., Leiter, B., & Stavrakantonakis, I. (2012). *Social media monitoring*. Innsbruck: Semantic Technology Institute. Retrieved from http://oc.sti2.at/sites/default/files/SMM%20Handouts.pdf

Ferrara, E., & Yang, Z. (2015). Quantifying the effect of sentiment on information diffusion in social media. *PeerJ Computer Science, 1*, e26.

Gaspar, R., Pedro, C., Panagiotopoulos, P., & Seibt, B. (2016). Beyond positive or negative: Qualitative sentiment analysis of social media reactions to unexpected stressful events. *Computers in Human Behavior, 56*, 179–191.

Glass, C. R., & Westmont, C. M. Comparative effects of belongingness on the academic success and cross-cultural interactions of domestic and international students. International journal of intercultural relations, *38*(2014), 106–119.

Hazelkorn, E. (2007). The impact of league tables and ranking systems on higher education decision making. *Higher Education Management and Policy, 19*(2), 1–24.

Hung, H. L., & Hyun, E. (2010). East Asian international graduate students' epistemological experiences in an American University. *International Journal of Intercultural Relations, 34*(4), 340–353. doi:10.1016/j.ijintrel.2009.12.001

Institute of International Education, Open Doors (IIE). (2014). International student enrollment in the U.S. Retrieved from http://www.iie.org

Institute of International Education. (2018). Top 25 places of origin of international students. Open Doors Report on International Educational Exchange 2009/10-2010/11.

Ivy, J. (2001). Higher education institution image: A correspondence analysis approach. *The International Journal of Educational Management, 15*(6), 276–282.

Iwara, I. O., Kativhu, S., & Obadire, O. S. (2017). Factors hindering socio-cultural integration of international students: A case of University of Zululand and University of Venda. *Gender and Behaviour, 15*(4), 10628–10643.

Jabjaimoh, P., Samart, K., Jansakul, N., & Jibenja, N. (2019). Optimization for better world university rank. *Journal of Scientific Research, 8*(1), 18–20.

Kauko, J., & Medvedeva, A. (2016). Internationalisation as marketisation? Tuition fees for international students in Finland. *Research in Comparative and International Education, 11*(1), 98–114.

Kaushik, A. (2009). Web analytics 2.0: The art of online accountability and science of customer centricity. John Wiley & Sons.

Khopkar, C., et al. (2014, March 25). Monitoring landing page experiments. U.S. Patent No. 8,682,712.

Kovacs Burns, K., Richter, M. S., Mao, Y., Mogale, S., & Danko, M. (2014). Case study of a post-secondary institution and its response to student homelessness. *International Journal of Case Studies, 3*(9). 49–70. Retrieved from http://www.casestudiesjournal

Landes, D. (2008). Paper Study College Fee for Non-Europeans. *The Local-Sweden's News in English*. Retrieved from http://www.thelocal.se/12702/20080627/

Lawrence, J. H., Celis, S., Kim, H. S., Lipson, S. K., & Tong, X. (2014). To stay or not to stay: Retention of Asian international faculty in STEM fields. *Higher Education, 67*(5), 511–531.

Lee, J. T., & Kuzhabekova, A. (2017). Reverse flow in academic mobility from core to periphery: Motivations of international faculty working in Kazakhstan. *Higher Education, 76*, 369–386.

Li, J. (2016). A cultural hybridization perspective: Emerging academic subculture among international students from East Asia in U.S. *Universal Journal of Educational Research, 4*(9), 2218–2228.

Ling, C., & Tran, L. T. (2015). "hinese international students in Australia: An insight into their help and information seeking manners. *International Education Journal: Comparative Perspectives, 14*(1), 42–56.

Liu, L. (2011). An international graduate student's ESL learning experience beyond the classroom. *TESL Canada Journal, 29*, 77–92.

78   Rakhi Tripathi

Loftus, W. (2012). Demonstrating success: Web analytics and continuous improvement. *Journal of Web Librarianship, 6*(1), 45–55.

Loukis, E., Charalabidis, Y., & Androutsopoulou, A. (2017). Promoting open innovation in the public sector through social media monitoring. *Government Information Quarterly, 34*(1), 99–109.

Lovett, M. J., & Staelin, R. (2016). The role of paid, earned, and owned media in building entertainment brands: Reminding, informing, and enhancing enjoyment. *Marketing Science, 35*(1), 142–157.

Maringe, F., & Carter, S. (2007). International Students' Motivations for Studying in UK HE: Insights Into The Choice and Decision Making Of African Students. *International Journal of Educational Management, 21*(6), 459–475.

Mattke, J., Müller, L., & Maier, C. (2019, September). Paid, Owned and Earned Media: A Qualitative Comparative Analysis Revealing Attributes Influencing Consumer's Brand Attitude in Social Media. In *Proceedings of the 52nd Hawaii International Conference on System Sciences DOI* (Vol. 10).

Mazzarol, T., & Soutar, G. N. (2002). "Push-pull" factors influencing international student destination choice. *International Journal of Educational Management, 16*(2), 82–90.

McDonagh, P. M., Lising, A., Walpole, A. M., & Perez, L. X. (1998). College rankings: Democratized college knowledge for whom? *Research in Higher Education, 39*(5), 513.

Medhat, W., Hassan, A., & Korashy, H. (2014). Sentiment analysis algorithms and applications: A survey. *Ain Shams Engineering Journal, 5*(4), 1093–1113.

Mun, Y. W., Aziz, Y. A., & Bojei, J. (2018). Preliminary study of international students in Malaysia on perceived university and destination image towards intention to recommend. *Journal of Research in Business, Economics and Management, 10*(5), 2078–2091.

Nguyen, N., & LeBlanc, G. (2001). Image and reputation of higher education institutions in students' retention decisions. *The International Journal of Educational Management, 15*(6), 303–311.

Organisation for Economic Co-operation and Development. (2011). Access to education, participation and progression. Indicator C3 – Who studies abroad and where? In education at a glance 2011: OECD Indicators. Retrieved from http://www.oecd.org/education/preschoolandschool/educationataglance2011oecdindicators.htm

Parafianowicz, L. (2009). Foreign Student Fees Delayed Until 2011. *The Local-Sweden's News In English.* Retrieved from http://www.thelocal.se/19410/20090512/

Peters, K., Chen, Y., Kaplan, A. M., Ognibeni, B., & Pauwels, K. (2013). Social media metrics: A framework and guidelines for managing social media. *Journal of Interactive Marketing, 27*(4), 281–298.

Petruzzellis, L., & Romanazzi, S. (2010). Educational Value: How Students Choose University: Evidence From An Italian University. *International Journal of Educational Management, 24*(2), 139–158.

Rodden, K., Hutchinson, H., & Fu, X. (2010). Measuring the user experience on a large scale: user-centered metrics for web applications. *Proceedings of the SIGCHI Conference on Human Factors in Computing Systems.*

Reid, E., & Duffy, K. (2018). A netnographic sensibility: Developing the netnographic/social listening boundaries. *Journal of Marketing Management, 34*(3–4), 263–286.

Schweitzer, B., Morson, G., & Mather, P. (2011). *Understanding the international student experience. American College Personnel Association.* Baltimore, MD: American College Personnel Association.

Singaravelu, H. D., White, L. J., & Bringaze, T. B. (2005). Factors influencing international students' career choice: A comparative study. *Journal of Career Development, 32*(1), 46–59.

Stewart, M. C., & Arnold, C. L. (2016). Defining social listening: Recognizing an emerging dimension of listening.

Stewart, M. C., Atilano, M., & Arnold, C. L. (2017). Improving customer relations with social listening: A case study of an American academic library. *International Journal of Customer Relationship Marketing and Management (IJCRMM)*, 8(1), 49–63.

Terui, S. (2011). Second language learners' coping strategy in conversations with native speakers. *Journal of International Students*, 2(2), 168–183.

Tran, L. T., & Nyland, C. (2011). International vocational education and training-The migration and learning mix. *Australian Journal of Adult Learning, 51*(1), 8.

Waisberg, D., & Kaushik, A. (2009). Web Analytics 2.0: Empowering Customer Centricity. *The original Search Engine Marketing Journal, 2*(1), 5–11.

Web Analytics Association. (2008). Web Analytics Definitions. September 2008. Retrieved from http://www.digitalanalyticsassociation.org/Files/PDF_standards/WebAnalyticsDefinitions.pdf. Accessed on July 18, 2020.

Wen, W., Hu, D., & Hao, J. (2018). International students' experiences in China: Does the planned reverse mobility work? *International Journal of Educational Development, 61*, 204–212.

Wu, H. P., Garza, E., & Guzman, N. (2015). International student's challenge and adjustment to college. *Education Research International, 2015*, 1–9.

Yang, M., Webster, B., & Prosser, M. (2011). Travelling a thousand miles: Hong Kong Chinese students' study abroad experience. *International Journal of Intercultural Relations, 35*(1), 69–78. doi:10.1016/j.ijintrel.2010.09.010

Zheng, X. (2010). Re-interpreting silence: Chinese International Students' verbal participation in U.S. Universities. *International Journal of Learning, 17*(5), 451–464.

Chapter 5

Promoting the Internationalisation of Students in University Strategic Goals: A Case Study

Carla Del Gesso

Abstract

This chapter considers internationalisation strategies to promote international student recruitment and mobility as the central tools of contemporary universities operating in a global and competitive context. It presents an overview of these strategies in the public university context in Italy, which serves as a case study to highlight how universities increasingly give relevance to the internationalisation of education in their strategic plans to attract overseas students and encourage incoming and outgoing student mobility. The document-based analysis of the Italian case reveals a prominent commitment from public universities to promoting internationalisation through different strategic performance objectives that contribute to the internationalisation of students and fuel their mobility and recruitment on a global scale. This research provides empirical evidence of the saliency of the internationalisation of education within the strategic missions of universities. It also addresses the connection between the internationalisation of university education and performance-based funding.

Keywords: Internationalisation strategies; university international education; strategic performance objectives; strategic plans; international students; performance-based funding; public universities

1. Introduction

The presence of international students in the landscape of higher education institutions constitutes an expanding phenomenon of the last few decades

---

Global Perspectives on Recruiting International Students: Challenges and Opportunities, 81–96
Copyright © 2021 by Emerald Publishing Limited
All rights of reproduction in any form reserved
doi:10.1108/978-1-83982-518-720211005

82   Carla Del Gesso

(Guo & Guo, 2017; Guruz, 2011; Ryan, 2013). Worldwide, the student populations of such institutions appear to be ever more inclusive (Hegarty, 2014). Several influential factors are contributing to shape this growing global trend, which
is certainly an outcome of the emerging challenges created by the globalisation of
knowledge, skills, culture, values, people, economics, capital, services, and technology (Altbach & Knight, 2007; Guruz, 2011; Stromquist, 2007). Accordingly,
ongoing globalisation and internationalisation processes are leading the higher
education sector to produce and deliver their knowledge services in a globally oriented environment. This is playing a prominent role in shaping the cross-border
migration of undergraduate and graduate students worldwide (Altbach, 2016;
Brooks & Waters, 2011).

In particular, the intensification of global competitiveness amongst universities within and beyond national boundaries is one of the most crucial drivers
that leads universities to proactively attract international students (Choudaha,
Chang, & Kono, 2013; Rumbley, Altbach, & Reisberg, 2012). Pressures linked
both to the quality of university performance and the restrictions of budgetary
resources, especially in the case of public universities, have prompted university
administrations to implement and develop strategies for the internationalisation
of their activities, including education (Jogunola & Varis, 2018; Taylor, 2004;
Warwick, 2014). Consequently, the internationalisation of teaching and learning, which involves both domestic and international students and university staff,
appears to have emerged as a prominent goal in the strategic missions of universities around the world (Paige, 2005; Ryan, 2013; Soliman, Anchor, & Taylor, 2019).

Within this framework, this chapter considers internationalisation strategies
to promote international student recruitment and mobility as the central tools of
contemporary universities operating in a global and competitive context. It presents an overview of these strategies in the public university context in Italy, which
serves as a case study to highlight how universities increasingly give relevance to
the internationalisation of education in their strategic plans to attract overseas
students and encourage incoming and outgoing student mobility. This research,
therefore, aims to provide an empirical insight into how the internationalisation
of education has become a strategic priority for universities. The main planned
strategic performance goals with which universities boost the internationalisation of their students are discussed. The chapter also addresses the connection
between the internationalisation of university education and performance-based
funding.

2. A Rational Focus on Internationalisation Strategies for Education in Universities Through a Literature Review

Increasing competition amongst universities has led them to implement strategies for the internationalisation of their core activities relating to education,
research, and their third mission (Bartell, 2003; Soliman et al., 2019). Internationalisation is a process whereby universities incorporate an 'international, intercultural, and global dimension' (Knight, 2004, p. 11) into their strategic mission
and functions, encouraging an organisational transition towards the creation of

internationalised universities (Altbach, 2016; Robson, 2011). Indeed, in an effort to compete internationally in response to globalisation, universities worldwide are seeking to expand their institutional activities within and beyond domestic borders, by implementing a wide variety of international initiatives (Beelen & Jones, 2015; Hudzik, 2011). These range from encouraging international student and staff mobility, and greater cross-border recruitment of students and scholars, to international inter-university agreements, internationalised curricula, bilingualism, joint and double degree programs, and research collaborations (Rumbley et al., 2012; Stromquist, 2007). Although university internationalisation tends to reflect the political and socio-economic development dynamics of a country, it can be explained by some key universal performance dimensions, such as academic mobility and international student enrolment (Guo & Guo, 2017; Okalany, Chindime, Uwituze, Osiru, & Adipala, 2016; Paige, 2005). As Rumbley et al. (2012, p. 6) argue, the movement of students (as well as university staff) to and from different locations is the most important current manifestation of university internationalisation.

Three pillars distinguish strategic policies for internationalisation of education in universities at the national level: study abroad, internationalisation at home and partnerships (de Wit, Hunter, Howard, & Egron-Polak, 2015). While study abroad (or internationalisation abroad) encompasses all forms of international activity that occur across borders (such as mobility programs and transnational education), internationalisation at home includes activities that happen within the domestic learning sphere of a university (Beelen & Jones, 2015; Knight, 2004). In particular, internationalisation at home is an emerging alternative to study abroad; it consists in the internationalisation of the curriculum with the aim of developing the global and intercultural skills of all students (local and international) (Beelen & Jones, 2015; Soria & Troisi, 2014). Indeed, the enrolment in international courses provides opportunities for global citizenship to domestic students – even more so for those who do not experience study abroad – who, in addition to obtaining international learning outcomes, can benefit from the presence of international students by interacting with them and helping their integration (de Wit et al., 2015; Soria & Troisi, 2014). Furthermore, partnerships amongst universities – in order to develop student exchange, joint or double degrees and other cooperative projects – have become a 'key pillar' for both internationalisation abroad and at home, and for university collaboration and competitiveness (de Wit et al., 2015, p. 53). Arguably, because of the need of universities to develop a comprehensive, broad approach to internationalisation (Brennan & Dellow, 2013; Hudzik, 2011), the three strategic pillars of university internationalisation (study abroad, internationalisation at home and partnerships) are interdependent.

In short, there is an increasing socio-economic interest in the internationalisation of universities around the world in order to enhance their international profiles, their reputations and competitiveness and to improve their rankings both inside and outside the national context (Cattaneo, Meoli, & Paleari, 2016). Although with different timing, motivation and scope, university internationalisation has occurred across the globe, such as in Latin America, in the United

84   Carla Del Gesso

States and Canada, in Japan and Asia, in Africa, and in Europe (Berry & Taylor, 2014; Curaj, Matei, Pricopie, Salmi, & Scott, 2015; Guo & Guo, 2017; Hegarty, 2014; Kuroda, Sugimura, Kitamura, & Asada, 2018; Okalany et al., 2016). This is because internationalisation provides opportunities not only for personal development, the growth of expertise of academic students and staff, and for increasing the attractiveness and competitiveness of universities on a global scale, but also for national and regional development (Guo & Guo, 2017; Knight, 2013; Kuroda et al., 2018).

Furthermore, the internationalisation of students represents 'a source of potential revenue' for universities (Hegarty, 2014; Rumbley et al., 2012, p. 3). As highlighted by Hegarty (2014), international student enrolment has an important impact on the long-term financial sustainability of public universities, which are having to face a lack of governmental funding and the challenges of international competition. Therefore, university leadership, which plays a critical role in strategising and planning the active recruitment of international students, is called upon to sustain the distinctiveness and attractiveness of campuses from the point of view of overseas students (de Wit et al., 2015; Paige, 2005; Taylor, 2004). In other words, the central management of a university is forced to strive to recruit international students who wish to study abroad, for example, by offering graduate programs taught entirely in the English language, by improving international student services, assistance and accommodation, and by facilitating the integration of overseas students into the life of the host university (Hegarty, 2014).

In addition, performance outcomes related to the internationalisation of educational activities (as well as to the internationalisation of research and third mission activities) have an impact on the allocation of public funding to universities. Performance-based indicators related to international competition are taken into account in many universities in the European area operating in a performance-based financing regime, when funding is to be allocated (Pruvot, Claeys-Kulik, & Estermann, 2015; de Wit et al., 2015). These universities are, therefore, being encouraged to improve their internationalisation profile, for instance, by appealing to overseas students, by forging partnerships and cooperative networks, and by assessing the quality of international activities using performance indicators (Curaj et al., 2015). This is particularly topical in the case of the Italian public university system, which, in recent years, has experienced a managerial transformation due to the constraint of public funds. Changes have concerned university governance, the accounting and reporting systems and the ways in which state funding is allocated, by ensuring that ever greater attention is paid to the quality and efficiency of the activities and the related competitive performance achieved (Hunter, 2015; Mateos-González & Boliver, 2019; Salvatore & Del Gesso, 2018). In this framework, given the growing relevance of performance measurement and management, the internationalisation of research and education represents an important indicator of the effective functioning of universities, especially since the current criteria for assigning funds to Italian public universities include performance indicators related to internationalisation (Hunter, 2015).

Therefore, as highlighted by de Wit (2010), strategic approaches to internationalisation are 'filtered and contextualized by the specific internal context of the university, by the type of university, and how they are embedded nationally' (p. 5). Indeed, internationalisation strategies in universities can be determined both by internal (such as stakeholder pressures) and external forces (such as national policies) (de Wit et al., 2015). Nonetheless, de Wit et al. (2015) reported how two surveys on university internationalisation demonstrated that the increasing mobility of international students (especially outgoing students) 'is a key policy focus in institutional internationalization policies' (p. 28). These surveys also demonstrated that, besides international student mobility, European universities prioritise international strategic partnerships amongst their internationalisation activities for education.

It is important to emphasise that what matters is that the internationalisation of teaching and learning are conceived as an integral part of university strategic goals, since if internationalisation is integrated into the strategies of an organisation it means it will have priority, otherwise it will be marginalised (Hudzik, 2011). As Hudzik (2011) states, 'clear and measurable goals identify what is important, define intentions, provide the basis for accountability, and drive behavior' (p. 25). Strategic planning, therefore, assumes a key role within university governance for the internationalisation of education, considering that the internationalisation agenda has become strategic for the governance of university competitiveness and long-term sustainability (Soliman et al., 2019; Taylor, 2004). Accordingly, the strategic plan constitutes a managerial tool through which university leadership gives form and content to the internationalisation that will be operationalised (based on the established objectives, input, activities and timelines) and then monitored and assessed with appropriate performance indicators (Paige, 2005).

In light of the above, the present study focusses on the strategic plans as they help to recognise the extent to which internationalisation policies of education are embedded into a university's vision. Other studies have examined the strategic plans of universities to analyse their internationalisation strategies for education. Stromquist (2007) studied the case of a private US university to probe internationalisation as a lever with which to improve a university's reputation and appeal to students both domestically and abroad in response to globalisation. Jogunola and Varis (2018) evaluated two cases of Finnish universities to examine their internationalisation strategies regarding international student recruitment and retention. Grantham (2018) analysed Canadian universities to assess their strategic commitment to international student mobility programs, underlining the importance of strategic plans for any discussion of this commitment.

University internationalisation processes have seen a shift from the operational to the strategic only recently (Soliman et al., 2019). Consequently, despite the extensive literature on internationalisation in higher education (e.g. Knight, 2013; Wihlborg & Robson, 2018; Yemini & Sagie, 2016), relatively few studies have analysed this phenomenon from the perspective of university strategy, particularly in terms of teaching and learning policies and performance goals through which to promote internationalisation within university strategic plans.

86   Carla Del Gesso

3. An Empirical Focus on Internationalisation Strategies for Education in Universities Through a Case Study

Through an analysis of the Italian public university context, this section seeks to provide an understanding of the strategical significance of internationalisation activities for education in universities to develop their attractiveness internationally. The Italian case, therefore, can provide evidence of how the internationalisation of education (which empowers international students) is now an integral part of the current strategic missions of universities. This case also highlights how external forces such as national performance-based funding policies can determine it.

3.1. The Italian Case: Context and Methodology

The Italian higher education system is currently composed of 97 universities that are legally recognised by the Ministry for Education, Universities and Research (MIUR). These are: 67 'state universities' (or public universities); 19 'non-state universities' (or private universities); and 11 'non-state telematic universities' (or private distance learning universities). Public universities are, therefore, prevalent in Italy and are principally financed by state resources, whereas the non-state universities are mainly self-funding. State funding represents an important source of income for Italian public universities, although the latter are progressively forced to autonomously seek alternative resources given the decrease of public fund availability. In addition, the distribution of these public funds amongst universities is driven by performance-based mechanisms which put emphasis on the evaluation of the performance results of university activities, and hence, on the related performance indicators. In particular, the Italian state funding model for public universities focusses on the MIUR block grant (the so-called 'Fondo di Finanziamento Ordinario – FFO'). Since 2009, this grant has been distributed on the basis of meritocratic criteria which consider individual university performance. Indeed, the basic quota of the FFO, which is determined on a historical basis, is decreasing. However, a growing part of the grant (a 'performance-based rewarding share') is distributed on the basis of competition performance results that make additional resources available to the most 'virtuous' universities. The internationalisation of students is one of the determining factors for this additional state funding, which is intended to be used to promote the quality of university activities, such as the quality of research and education. Consequently, the Italian case may be a suitable environment in which to perceive how internationalisation activities in education are becoming a contemporary strategic issue.

Empirical data for the entire population of 67 public universities were obtained using documentary analysis that consists in a document review procedure for finding and organising information relevant to a particular investigation (e.g. Bowen, 2009). Mandatory university strategic plans for the 3-year period 2019–2021 were, therefore, reviewed in order to identify – with no preconceived set of ideas and taking an inductive research approach – the strategic objectives and related performance outcome indicators of international education. Indeed, these planning documents define the university strategies and goals relating to education, research and the third mission, through which the overall institutional mission is to be achieved. A specific section is devoted to internationalisation. Defining strategic objectives is the first stage of the performance cycle implementation which enables university performance to be evaluated.

3.2. Evidence of Strategic Planning for Internationalisation of Students from Italian Public Universities

All 67 Italian public universities include international education strategies in their current strategic plans. These strategies are pursued with the final goal of strengthening the quality of education through the improvement of an international dimension with which to increase the attractiveness of the university to international students. Table 1 gives a glimpse of the 10 different categories of strategic objectives concerning the internationalisation of teaching and learning activities (with the main related performance indicators) herein identified.

As can be seen from this table, the main strategic performance objectives Italian public universities plan to achieve within 3 years are: to increase the number of exchange students within mobility programs (with a greater attention to outgoing over incoming mobility); to intensify international university partnerships; to improve the internationalisation of home study paths at undergraduate and postgraduate level by increasing, for example, joint and double degree and PhD

Table 1. Mapping of Strategic Performance Objectives Concerning the Internationalisation of Education in Italian Public Universities' Strategic Plans 2019–2021.

Strategic Objectives	Main Performance Indicators	Total Count (Number of Universities that Plan Each Objective)	% (Percentage of Universities that Plan Each Objective)
Increase in number of outgoing exchange students within mobility programs	• Number of outgoing exchange students; • Proportion of educational credits earned abroad within mobility programs; • Proportion of graduates with at least 12 educational credits earned abroad	55	82
Intensification of partnerships with foreign universities	• Number of collaboration agreements with foreign universities	50	75

(*Continued*)

88   *Carla Del Gesso*

Table 1. (*Continued*)

Strategic Objectives	Main Performance Indicators	Total Count (Number of Universities that Plan Each Objective)	% (Percentage of Universities that Plan Each Objective)
Activation/ expansion of international graduate programs	• Number of international graduate programs; • Number of joint and double degree programs; • Number of graduate programs/courses taught in English; • Number of overseas professors involved in teaching activities	45	67
Increase in the internationalisation of teaching staff	• Number of incoming visiting professors from foreign universities; • Number of outgoing visiting professors to foreign universities; • Number of professors previously recruited by a foreign university; • Number of courses taught by overseas professors	45	67
Increase in the number of incoming exchange students within mobility programs	• Number of incoming exchange students	44	66
Increase in enrolment of overseas students	• Proportions of students enrolled in graduate programs with a previous degree obtained abroad	38	57

Strategic Objectives	Main Performance Indicators	Total Count (Number of Universities that Plan Each Objective)	% (Percentage of Universities that Plan Each Objective)
Activation/ expansion of graduate programs/ courses taught in English	• Number of graduate programs entirely taught in English; • Number of courses/ modules taught in English.	33	49
Improvement of the internationalisation of PhD programs	• Number of PhD students with mobility periods spent abroad; • Proportion of PhD students enrolled with an academic qualification from overseas; • Number of joint PhD programs; • Number of overseas professors involved in PhD programs	32	48
Enhancement of services for overseas students	• Number of services activated for overseas students	13	19
Promotion of recruitment of international students through specific projects	• Number of official projects	7	10

Source: Data analysed from the results of the review of the strategic plans of the 67 Italian public universities.

programs and courses in English; to improve the internationalisation of teaching staff by increasing incoming and outgoing visiting programs and the recruitment of overseas professors; and to increase the enrolment of overseas students by enhancing the attractiveness of the university (sometimes through specific and targeted projects) and reception services. Increasing outgoing student numbers within various mobility programs and intensifying international collaboration

90 *Carla Del Gesso*

agreements with foreign universities (planned by 82% and 75% of universities, respectively) are given priority by Italian public universities in their strategic plans. In contrast, specific internationalisation projects and services for overseas students, which aim to increase the recruitment of international students, are not yet widespread (planned by only 10% and 19% of universities, respectively).

However, all 67 universities include at least 1 of the 10 identified strategic objectives in their strategic plans; moreover, although only one university includes all 10 objectives, most universities have integrated at least 5. Therefore, although interpreted differently, the internationalisation of education in the strategic plans of Italian public universities can be summarised as student and teacher mobility, international university partnerships, integrated academic programs, international student recruitment, teaching in English, international doctorates and international student services.

Italian public universities are currently paying great attention to education internationalisation in their strategic plans. Each related performance objective promotes an increase in the internationalisation of both domestic and overseas students and/or an increase in the recruitment and mobility of international students, resulting in university student populations that are increasingly inclusive.

Some strategic objectives are also interrelated. Indeed, many universities plan to intensify partnerships with universities in one or more foreign countries (both European and extra-European) in order to develop different opportunities for internationalisation. In particular, bilateral and multiple collaboration agreements aim to encourage the following: student and staff exchanges, whereby mobility periods of study, work or apprenticeships are offered abroad; and/or integrated international programs for joint and double degrees; and/or other forms of cooperation and networking. However, most partnerships are mainly intended to advance inter-university mobility programs.

Furthermore, several universities plan to activate or expand one or more international graduate programs to internationalise their curricula at home. In addition to joint and double degree programs, this is also scheduled to be achieved by integrating an international perspective into teaching programs, by providing entire graduate programs or specific courses taught in English and by involving overseas professors. Internationalised curricula, which offer better opportunities for domestic students to improve their skills, also help to make universities more attractive abroad and promote student mobility internationally. The recruitment of overseas students, who are attracted by the international, intercultural environment of the campus, as well as by reduced linguistic difficulties, is, therefore, boosted. Indeed, as reported by some universities in their strategic plans, the internationalisation of curricula both through the recognition of joint degree programs and the activation of courses taught in English has led to an increase in both the enrolment of international students and the number of students on exchange. Thus, providing curricula, courses or even single modules taught in English can be an important strategic objective with which to increase international recruitment. Furthermore, increasing the internationalisation of teaching staff, by supporting incoming and outgoing teacher mobility or by recruiting overseas professors to whom the teaching of entire courses is entrusted, contributes to making universities more attractive to students and academics abroad.

An increase in overseas student enrolment is a planned goal for more than half of Italian public universities (57%); whereas an increase in the number of incoming exchange students is a goal planned by 66% of universities. In addition, in order to appeal to international students (both in terms of enrolment and incoming exchanges), some universities also plan to implement specific projects, such as calls for study and scholarships for candidates coming from abroad, educational paths to be activated in foreign universities, promotional campaigns and other student recruitment projects. However, only a small number of Italian universities are active in such initiatives. In addition, few universities are planning to enhance services to attract international students, such as the development of administrative and logistical support related to their reception, orientation, accommodation and stay in Italy.

3.3. How Internationalisation Strategies Matter to Performance-Based Funding Mechanisms in Italian Universities

The internationalisation of education is a must for Italian public universities who plan strategic performance objectives with a broad approach in order to implement and improve internationalisation both within their home institutions and abroad. These objectives are essential for the assessment of the quality of performance results of university activities, which in turn is essential for the performance-based funding of universities. Indeed, as the allocation of the FFO amongst Italian public universities is increasingly based on the evaluation of the quality of their activities, improving internationalisation performance outcomes allows universities to be awarded additional funding. In particular, a recent decree issued by the MIUR stated that from 2017, 20% of the 'performance-based rewarding share' of the FFO would be distributed to universities according to their results related to performance indicators concerning: the quality of research (first group of indicators); the quality of education (second group of indicators); and internationalisation strategies (third group of indicators) (MIUR decree n. 635/2016, paragraph 5). Each university must autonomously select two different performance indicators consistent with its strategic planning, within two of the above three groups. As some universities have reported in their strategic plans, specific performance indicators related to the internationalisation of education have been chosen as measurements of university best performance, which is used to award additional funding from the MIUR. Therefore, performance indicators associated with internationalisation strategies, such as the proportion of educational credits earned abroad within mobility programs, the proportion of overseas students enrolled and so on, appear to have acquired a growing relevance within the parameters used to selectively distribute performance-based funding amongst universities (Mateos-González & Boliver, 2019).

The development of internationalisation initiatives has a clear impact on public funding allocation, as better performance means more opportunities to receive funding to invest in enhancing university activities. The correlation between university internationalisation performance and public funding is, therefore, evident. Hence, seeking to obtain additional resources is important in order to enhance university activities, which include increasing the internationalisation of students.

92   Carla Del Gesso

As highlighted by Hunter (2015), however, 'Italian universities are now being required to internationalize in order to receive funding, rather than being funded in order to internationalize' (p. 99). Indeed, in Italy, the national approach to university internationalisation is recent (Curaj et al., 2015) and there is a development process in place. As reported by several universities in their strategic plans, internationalisation represents a weak point of their strategies. Therefore, these universities plan strong internationalisation objectives, such as the activation of one or more international graduate programs, in order to overcome this weakness. However, for other universities, internationalisation is a strength which allows them to rank best at a national and international level; these universities will continue, therefore, to expand and improve the internationalisation activities they have already implemented.

Italian public universities are pressed by institutional external forces to improve their international dimension in order to be proactively competitive and increase their autonomous financial sustainability. In particular, in Italy, increasing attention is being given to university internationalisation at a national level, which reflects trends at the European and global levels. Indeed, the 'Act of Address' of the MIUR (issued in December 2018), concerning the identification of national policy priorities, lists the internationalisation of university education and research amongst the strategic priorities for 2019 in order to improve academic attractiveness and inter-university co-operation. Therefore, the considerable planning for education internationalisation in Italian universities appears to be driven, above all, by a national systemic approach to internationalisation rather than constituting a spontaneous initiative at the university level.

4. Looking Forward: Concluding Remarks on Student Internationalisation

This study provides empirical evidence of the saliency of the internationalisation of teaching and learning activities within the strategic missions of universities. The analysis of the Italian case reveals a prominent commitment from public universities to promoting internationalisation through different strategic objectives that contribute to the internationalisation of students and fuel their mobility and recruitment on a global scale. The internationalisation of students is a recent phenomenon in the Italian public university system, although planning through the formulation of related strategic goals appears to be an emergent priority. In line with the trend emphasised in the literature (Soliman et al., 2019; Warwick, 2014), Italian public universities are now paying great attention to the internationalisation of education in order to ensure their long-term competitiveness and sustainability.

In Italy, as in other European countries, a strategic development of the internationalisation of educational activities began with the Erasmus mobility program during the 1990s and was subsequently reinforced by the Bologna process (de Wit et al., 2015). Currently, through a comprehensive approach (Brennan & Dellow, 2013; Hudzik, 2011), this strategic development is continuing within the Italian public university context. A growing number of universities plan to implement or improve their academic programs with an international dimension in their curricula, as well as to increase the number of courses taught in English and overseas professor involvement. Nevertheless, this does not yet apply to all Italian universities. As shown by the present study, increasing international outbound student mobility and international strategic partnerships constitutes the two main strategic objectives that Italian universities pursue. This is in line with international and European trends whereby institutions mainly give priorities to these two strategies (de Wit et al., 2015, p. 28).

However, internationalising university student populations does not mean merely mobility exchange programs which give home students the chance to study abroad. Similarly, international inter-university co-operation cannot be limited to increasing student exchanges. Therefore, the Italian case reinforces the concept of universities needing to paying more attention to the implementation of different international strategies (Warwick, 2014) in order to improve their own international profile and reputation, and rank better internationally (Cattaneo et al., 2016). Hence, universities need to focus more on internationalisation at home, on their graduate and PhD programs, on international student services and on the development of specific projects (potentially through international partnerships) with which to attract talented home and international students and scholars. This is because, in a university context strongly characterised by increasingly competitive dynamics and by a growing and persistent shortage of resources, it is essential to continue to recruit high-skilled international students from all over the world.

Given the growing pressures facing universities related to global competitiveness, international rankings and the difficulties of achieving lasting sustainability, the development of their international profiles through an expansion of their cross-border delivery appears to be yet another challenge for university education. Openness to the international dimension, by focussing on the quality and international accessibility of their educational delivery, can help universities manage these pressures in order to achieve or maintain their campus excellence, even beyond national borders.

In this framework, the elements that characterise the ever-changing dynamics of the university environment can be measured according to some key features, which include the role and results of universities relating to the internationalisation of their teaching and learning, their teaching staff and, finally, their students. Indeed, students are now moving readily to and from diverse geographical areas; a most evident consequence of university internationalisation (Rumbley et al., 2012). The global evolution of the dynamics of collaboration and competition amongst organisations, countries and cultures will lead more and more universities to actively compete as global players, to attract the best national and international talents (students and scholars). Being more attractive means being an appealing place of study for home and international students. Therefore, it is essential to increase the efforts of universities, by improving internationalisation activities (both on their home campuses and abroad) since the internationalisation of students can represent an important cornerstone of the competitiveness and financial sustainability of universities (Hegarty, 2014; Soliman et al., 2019). Universities are increasingly global environments because they are called upon

94 *Carla Del Gesso*

to form global citizens; therefore, improving internationalisation is not just an economic issue but a necessity for the creation of a global modern society. Hence, internationalisation is important for the social and financial survival of universities that owe their future sustainability to their students, who are now global citizens and players.

References

Altbach, P. G. (2016). *Global perspectives on higher education*. Baltimore, MD: Johns Hopkins University Press.

Altbach, P. G., & Knight, J. (2007). The internationalization of higher education: Motivations and realities. *Journal of Studies in International Education, 11*(3–4), 290–305. doi:10.1177/1028315307303542

Bartell, M. (2003). Internationalization of universities: A university culture-based framework. *Higher Education, 45*(1), 43–70. doi:10.1023/A:1021225514599

Beelen, J., & Jones, E. (2015). Redefining internationalization at home. In A. Curaj, L. Matei, R. Pricopie, J. Salmi, & P. Scott (Eds.), *The European higher education area: Between critical reflections and future policies* (pp. 59–72). Cham: Springer.

Berry, C., & Taylor, J. (2014). Internationalisation in higher education in Latin America: Policies and practice in Colombia and Mexico. *Higher Education, 67*(5), 585–601. doi:10.1007/s10734-013-9667-z

Bowen, G. A. (2009). Document analysis as a qualitative research method. *Qualitative Research Journal, 9*(2), 27–40. doi:10.3316/QRJ0902027

Brennan, M., & Dellow, D. A. (2013). International students as a resource for achieving comprehensive internationalization. *New Directions for Community Colleges, 161*, 27–37. doi:10.1002/cc.20046

Brooks, R., & Waters, J. (2011). *Student mobilities, migration and the internationalization of higher education*. Basingstoke: Palgrave Macmillan.

Cattaneo, M., Meoli, M., & Paleari, S. (2016). Why do universities internationalize? Organizational reputation and legitimacy. In D. Audretsch, E. Lehmann, M. Meoli, & S. Vismara (Eds.), *University evolution, entrepreneurial activity and regional competitiveness* (pp. 327–346). Cham: Springer.

Choudaha, R., Chang, L., & Kono, Y. (2013). International student mobility trends 2013: Towards responsive recruitment strategies. *World Education News & Reviews, 26*(2), 1–8. Retrieved from https://ssrn.com/abstract=2275946

Curaj, A., Matei, L., Pricopie, R., Salmi, J., & Scott, P. (Eds.). (2015). *The European higher education area: Between critical reflections and future policies*. Cham: Springer.

de Wit, H. (2010). *Internationalisation of higher education in Europe and its assessment, trends and issues*. Den Haag: NVAO.

de Wit, H., Hunter, F., Howard, L., & Egron-Polak, E. (Eds.). (2015). *Internationalization of higher education*. Brussels: European Parliament, Directorate-General for Internal Policies. Retrieved from http://www.europarl.europa.eu/studies

Grantham, K. (2018). Assessing international student mobility in Canadian university strategic plans: Instrumentalist versus transformational approaches in higher education. *Journal of Global Citizenship & Equity Education, 6*(1), 1–21. Retrieved from http://journals.sfu.ca/jgcee

Guo, Y., & Guo, S. (2017). Internationalization of Canadian higher education: Discrepancies between policies and international student experiences. *Studies in Higher Education, 42*(5), 851–868. doi:10.1080/03075079.2017.1293874

Promoting the Internationalisation of Students in University   95

Guruz, K. (2011). *Higher education and international student mobility in the global knowledge economy: Revised and updated second edition.* Albany, NY: State University of New York Press.

Hegarty, N. (2014). Where we are now – The presence and importance of international students to universities in the United States. *Journal of International Students, 4*(3), 223–235. Retrieved from https://www.ojed.org/index.php/jis/article/view/462

Hudzik, J. K. (2011). *Comprehensive internationalization: From concept to action.* Washington, DC: NAFSA, The Association of International Educators.

Hunter, F. (2015). Internationalisation as a lever for change: The case of Italy. In A. Curaj, L. Matei, R. Pricopie, J. Salmi, & P. Scott (Eds.), *The European higher education area: Between critical reflections and future policies* (pp. 93–107). Cham: Springer.

Jogunola, O., & Varis, K. (2018). The evaluation of internationalization strategies of Finnish universities: A case study of two universities in Finland. *Journal of Higher Education Theory and Practice, 18*(6), 95–109. doi:10.33423/jhetp.v18i6.152

Knight, J. (2004). Internationalization remodeled: Definition, approaches, and rationales. *Journal of Studies in International Education, 8*(1), 5–31. doi:10.1177/1028315303260832

Knight, J. (2013). The changing landscape of higher education internationalisation–for better or worse? *Perspectives: Policy and Practice in Higher Education, 17*(3), 84–90. doi: 10.1080/13603108.2012.753957

Kuroda, K., Sugimura, M., Kitamura, Y., & Asada, S. (2018). *Internationalization of higher education and student mobility in Japan and Asia.* Paris: United Nations Educational, Scientific, and Cultural Organization. Retrieved from https://www.jica.go.jp/jica-ri/ja/publication/other/l75nbg0000108nmr-att/Background_Kuroda.pdf

Mateos-González, J. L., & Boliver, V. (2019). Performance-based university funding and the drive towards 'institutional meritocracy' in Italy. *British Journal of Sociology of Education, 40*(2), 145–158.

Okalany, E., Chindime, S., Uwituze, S., Osiru, M., & Adipala, E. (2016). Enhancing internationalization and quality of African universities through academic mobility: Experiences from RUFORUM. *RUFORUM Working Document Series, 14*(1), 197–204. Retrieved from http://repository.ruforum.org

Paige, R. M. (2005). Internationalization of higher education: Performance assessment and indicators. *Nagoya Journal of Higher Education, 5*(8), 99–122. doi:10.18999/njhe.5.99

Pruvot, E. B., Claeys-Kulik, A., & Estermann, T. (2015). Strategies for efficient funding of universities in Europe. In A. Curaj, L. Matei, R. Pricopie, J. Salmi, & P. Scott (Eds.), *The European higher education area: Between critical reflections and future policies* (pp. 153–168). Cham: Springer.

Robson, S. (2011). Internationalization: A transformative agenda for higher education? *Teachers and Teaching, 17*(6), 619–630. doi:10.1080/13540602.2011.625116

Rumbley, L. E., Altbach, P. G., & Reisberg, L. (2012). Internationalization within the higher education context. In D. K. Deardorff, H. de Wit, J. D. Heyl, & T. Adams (Eds.), *The SAGE handbook of international higher education* (pp. 3–26). Thousand Oaks: SAGE.

Ryan, J. (Ed.). (2013). *Cross-cultural teaching and learning for home and international students, internationalisation of pedagogy and curriculum in higher education.* Abingdon: Routledge.

Salvatore, C., & Del Gesso, C. (2018). From financial accounting to management accounting in Italian public universities: Results of an empirical study. In *Proceedings of 7th Global Business and Finance Research Conference, Kuala Lumpur, Malaysia* (pp. 1–11).

Soliman, S., Anchor, J., & Taylor, D. (2019). The international strategies of universities: Deliberate or emergent? *Studies in Higher Education, 44*(8), 1413–1424. doi:10.1080/03075079.2018.1445985

96 *Carla Del Gesso*

Soria, K. M., & Troisi, J. (2014). Internationalization at home alternatives to study abroad: Implications for students' development of global, international, and intercultural competencies. *Journal of Studies in International Education, 18*(3), 261–280. doi:10.1177/1028315313496572

Stromquist, N. P. (2007). Internationalization as a response to globalization: Radical shifts in university environments. *Higher Education, 53*(1), 81–105. doi:10.1007/s10734-005-1975-5

Taylor, J. (2004). Toward a strategy for internationalisation: Lessons and practice from four universities. *Journal of Studies in International Education, 8*(2), 149–171. doi:10.1177/1028315303260827

Warwick, P. (2014). The international business of higher education – A managerial perspective on the internationalisation of UK universities. *The International Journal of Management Education, 12*(2), 91–103.

Wihlborg, M., & Robson, S. (2018). Internationalisation of higher education: Drivers, rationales, priorities, values and impacts. *European Journal of Higher Education, 8*(1), 8–18. doi:10.1080/21568235.2017.1376696

Yemini, M., & Sagie, N. (2016). Research on internationalisation in higher education – Exploratory analysis. *Perspectives: Policy and Practice in Higher Education, 20*(2–3), 90–98.

Chapter 6

Exploring Institutional Culture and Its Impact on International Student Recruitment Capabilities

Melissa James

Abstract

This chapter compares how three institutions from three countries, Canada, Hong Kong and the United Kingdom, use international student recruitment as an institutional capability. Institutional capability to recruit students from international markets is determined by a mix of national policy, internal cultures and institutional resources and capabilities. This chapter explores the complex nature of institutional operations in higher education institutions (HEIs) by considering the perspectives of senior leaders, administrators and international student recruiters and how they implement their international student recruitment plans while facing increasing competition and unstable government policies. The results show what is needed is for institutions to improve their institutional capabilities to respond to national policies and to adapt to the changing global landscape

It also discusses the importance of understanding highly localised, institutional culture and practice and how national policy is one dimension that shapes international student recruitment. International case study allows you to draw these conclusions and to examine how strategy and policy contexts shape individual institutional capability. Institutional context shows capabilities in international student recruitment practice are unique and institutional responses to policies and competition are based on their internal cultures. Institutional actors view government policy as the 'playing field' to achieve their institutional strategies; however, there is more to international student recruitment than merely national policies such as the ability to communicate and coordinate activities within institutions.

Global Perspectives on Recruiting International Students: Challenges and Opportunities, 97–110
Copyright © 2021 by Emerald Publishing Limited
All rights of reproduction in any form reserved
doi:10.1108/978-1-83982-518-720211006

98 *Melissa James*

This chapter highlights the importance of understanding the capabilities of the institutions themselves as they attempt to recruit students from international markets. This chapter reinforces the notion that it is not only what the policies say or do, but also how these policies are interpreted at the practice level that shapes international student recruitment.

Keywords: Institutional culture; government policies; institutional capabilities; marketing; international comparisons; international student recruitment

Introduction

Countries and higher education institutions (HEIs) have various motives to recruit international students such as attracting fee-paying students for revenue, creating a diversity in their student cohorts or developing the local labour market (Knight, 2015; Walker, 2013). Many of these policies are described as neo-liberal and are commonly used by countries and HEIs around the world to attract income and economic benefits from students (Onk & Joseph, 2017). In response to global and local forces, HEIs are evolving their strategies to market themselves to prospective students and student recruitment has become an important consideration that requires adjustments and changes to practice as the landscape is constantly changing for HEIs (Findlay, McCollum, & Packwood, 2017). Choudaha, Chang, and Kono (2013) suggest that unpredictability in the global environment poses challenges for all institutions and that effective student recruitment requires institutions to engage with this volatility and to develop capabilities. Institutional capability is particularly important during times of global crises such as COVID-19 and political unrest around the globe. This study contributes to understanding institutional reaction and responses to internal and external forces by examining practitioners and their perceptions on their practice.

This chapter compares HEIs from different parts of the world to understand what influences their international student recruitment practices. It argues that international student recruitment for HEIs is complex and nuanced due to their unique institutional cultures and these cultures shape how recruiters respond and react to international students. Most importantly, it shows that institutional culture shapes coordination of the practice of international student recruitment. There is much unknown about how actors involved in international student recruitment activities conceptualise and respond to their external environment. Other studies argue for greater understanding of international student recruitment activities in HEIs from the supply-side and the challenges faced by those involved in the practice as institutions aim to manage government policy changes, internal strategies, and other forces on their practice (Findlay et al., 2017; O'Connor, 2018; Zinn & Johansson, 2015). There is a need for more critical perspectives on international student recruitment practice to offer accounts and descriptions from those involved and how institutional culture shapes daily practice. This chapter will provide these perspectives and will further our understanding of how institutional culture shapes international student recruitment from the supply-side perspective.

Literature Review

Institutional policy, such as programming and marketing, influences student mobility and affects the recruitment of international students to HEIs (Ross, Grace, & Shao, 2013). One common focus of institutional policy or strategy is internationalisation. Internationalisation strategies for HEIs are shaped by global dynamics, national policy and local history. The importance of government policy and environmental factors suggests, 'practices of international recruitment are shaped by a combination of proactive and reactive responses to wider transformations in the higher education landscape' (Mosneaga & Agergaard, 2012, p. 533). This means that HEIs are altering their international student recruitment practices to manage change in the environment. In a case study comparison of two Danish institutions, Mosneaga and Agergaard (2012) found that international students are a necessary strategic interest related to internationalisation and HEIs formulate strategies based on indirect and direct government control. In fact, in different parts of the world, approaches to internationalisation are shaped uniquely by politics and discourse (Brandenburg et al., 2014; Rumbley, Altbach, & Reisberg, 2012). This context is necessary to understand how HEIs experience and adapt to changes in political and market forces that impact internationalisation policies, such as international student recruitment. Context shapes institutional capabilities and is necessary to understand international student recruitment as strategy and practice within HEIs. In particular, is it essential to consider how practitioners view influences on their practice of international student recruitment.

Internationalisation can be defined as an activity that is recognised in practices such as the recruitment of international students (Mosneaga & Agergaard, 2012). As such, Mosneaga and Agergaard (2012) describe international student recruitment as 'doing' internationalisation. Internationalisation is an increasingly important dimension of higher education and its institutions. Internationalisation is becoming more complex and confusing as higher education policy is changing at both the institutional and national levels (Rumbley et al., 2012). In this chapter, internationalisation is viewed as an activity and that international student recruitment is a by-product of this activity. The link between internationalisation strategy and international student recruitment is not well understood. Some studies show that HEIs adopt innovative strategies to market themselves to prospective students (Zinn & Johansson, 2015) and, therefore, recruitment has become an important issue and a necessary practice for many HEIs. International student recruitment are a set of activities that is demonstrated through recruitment planning and tactics and is a derived from internationalisation strategies within institutions (Mosneaga & Agergaard, 2012). Mosneaga and Agergaard (2012) see international student recruitment as the 'doing internationalisation'. The literature points to extensive research into student decision-making and complex choice models related to student choice of HEIs (Szekeres, 2010; Tatar & Oktay, 2006); however, the literature on HEIs' international student recruitment practice is limited. This is, in part, because of the competitive nature of international student recruitment and the propriety nature of their operations.

100   Melissa James

Prospective international students desire to undertake higher education in countries other than their own in pursuit of a degree, particularly that of an English-speaking country (Szekeres, 2010; Tatar & Oktay, 2006). The top four countries in the world for international student study are the United States, Canada, the United Kingdom, and Australia, all of which are primarily English speaking countries (Goralski & Tootoonchi, 2015). As these countries are the 'top' in the world for international student recruitment, they compete with one another when it comes to enrolling international students. Competition exists between both HEIs and nations and is shifting the way these HEIs are perceived and how they operate (Marginson, 2011). During the mid-sixteenth century, HEIs attracted international students; however, the rapid increase in globalisation and internationalisation has led to dynamic changes (Wilkins & Huisman, 2011). Today, more and more students are seeking opportunities to pursue higher education in other countries (Global Affairs Canada, 2017). According to the OECD, the global demand for international higher education is set to grow from nearly 4.1 million students in 2010 to 7.2 million students in 2025 (OECD, 2015). As competition intensifies to acquire the talents and resources of mobile students, countries are developing rigourous strategies and policies that are supported by financial investments to increase enrolment to their institutions (Goralski & Tootoonchi, 2015). Globally, many institutions are facing similar policy priorities in higher education resulting in HEIs around the world pursuing international student recruitment opportunities (Marginson, 2011). This chapter addresses the gap in understanding international student recruitment practice by examining national policy, competition and institutional strategic plans and the impact of these forces on international student recruitment practice. This chapter considers the perspectives of a wide range of actors that brings understanding and meaning to the practice. Previous studies have not compared perspectives of practitioners who have different roles and responsibilities for the recruitment of international students or practitioners from institutions in different countries.

Previous research demonstrates that institutions require certain capabilities to recruit students from international markets. Ross et al. (2013) found that HEIs require market orientation to achieve diversity in student cohorts and to respond to decreases in government funding. Ross et al. argue that, '[…]until HE institutions realize the barriers to market performance that having traditional bureaucratic structures creates, then their sustainability may well be threatened' (Ross et al., 2013, p. 235). This suggests that if institutions do not understand the internal factors and dynamics that pose challenges to operating in international markets, their ability to be successful is limited. At the same time, the focus of higher education marketing research tends to be on the consumer or student perspective of international marketing and there is little research on higher education recruitment practice or the perceptions of managers on strategy (Asaad, Melewar, & Cohen, 2015). As such, it is important to understand the various aspects of international student recruitment to contextualise and examine these capabilities in HEIs. It is found that the role of practitioners is critically important to international student recruitment, particularly through coordination (Asaad et al., 2015; Hemsley-Brown & Oplatka, 2010; Ross et al., 2013). Practitioners demonstrate

Exploring Institutional Culture and Its Impact on International Student **101**

coordination through their level of communication, cooperation and problem-solving. For institutions to be successful in international student recruitment, communication, problem-solving and shared work-related goals amongst practitioners is necessary (Asaad et al., 2015). Different departments of the institution need to understand one another's goals and have a similar understanding of the various tasks and roles necessary to achieve institutional outcomes. This understanding of international student recruitment means effectiveness requires monitoring of communications between departments and outlining goals regarding markets (Nagy & Berács, 2012). HEIs capabilities may also be recognised in the absence or presence of shared goals and motives that highlight the true nature of institutional coordination and performance (Nagy & Berács, 2012).

> Universities are social units with potentially some organizational phenomena such as communication channels, cooperation, interfunctional conflict and shared work-related goals (based on Cadogan et al., 1999). The presence or lack of these organizational themes shape export coordination. (Asaad et al., 2015, p. 132)

This understanding is important as goals and motives contribute to intended and unintended outcomes and impact institutional performance in international markets. By using activity theory to explore the perspectives of practitioners of international student recruitment, this chapter explores their views of the perceived level of coordination occurring within these HEIs. This chapter goes further than merely exploring practitioners' views; it sheds light on why HEIs behave in certain ways that contribute or hinder their practice.

Methodology

This chapter explores how HEI international student recruitment practitioners develop, perceive and manage their practice. By examining the recruitment of international students in three universities from the United Kingdom, Canada and Hong Kong, this study explores the perspectives of strategy practitioners, those who develop and implement international student recruitment activity at various levels of the hierarchy. The institutions are Lancaster University, UK, University of Prince Edward Island (UPEI), Canada, and one anonymous institution which is called UNIA in this chapter. In this chapter, various actors in each institution are the subjects of the activity systems, who have different roles within the hierarchy of each institution. The majority of literature suggests the concept of strategy as a 'top-down' process, which is why the main focus of strategy as practice literature is usually on top managers, their demographics and their decision-making processes (Hambrick & Mason, 1984). This chapter purposively expands the definition of strategy practitioners to include different contributors to institutional strategy and practice such as staff, as they are significant to the institution's survival and shape practice. As Jarzabkowski, Balogun, and Seidl (2007) argue, it is important to identify other actors involved in shaping strategy, besides top managers. Each case study site presents unique policy, history and

102   Melissa James

culture; and by situating the case study sites in different jurisdictions, this chapter examines the internal operations of HEIs as they participate in international student recruitment.

The third generation of activity theory (Engeström, 2001) is used a research tool, in this chapter, as it examines the activity of international student recruitment. It explores international student recruitment as a mediated activity and seeks to understand practitioners' views of institutional strategic plans, competition and national policies and how their practice is shaped by institutional values, history and culture. Using activity systems encourages examining relational or mediating forces between subjects and objects. Tools, rules, division of labour and the community shape practice and form a model to examine the mediation of these constituents on practice. The activity system approach was used in this chapter to conceptualise institutional strategic plans, national policies, and competition as mediating international student recruitment. This was an important construct to understand the effects of these forces on international student recruitment. This approach assesses coordination, communication, role and goal clarity, and market responsiveness capability within each practice and the opportunities to improve international student recruitment (Nagy & Berács, 2012).

Research Design

The case study method is used to explore practices of international student recruitment at three HEIs and examines the perspectives of participants thereby creating a cross-case study analysis. Case study research, although criticised by some for lacking objectivity or rigor, supports the investigation of international student recruitment, as a real-world construct (McCutcheon & Meredith, 1993). Case study research is useful for institutional management as it allows for several data sources in real-world contexts, where there was no previous research before (Jensen & Rodgers, 2001). There are few empirical studies on HEIs, and the case study approach provides the flexibility to examine multiple sources and to gather appropriate qualitative data for the study.

The case study institutions were selected using purposive and convenience sampling based on three criteria: (1) diversity in enrolment size (UPEI < 5,000 students, Lancaster University > 12,000 students, and UNIA >12,000 students; (2) geographic differences that generate international perspectives from the participants and provide unique settings for each of the institutions from a national policy perspective; and (3) history and experience in conducting student international recruitment. At the same time, there are differences in each institution that were embraced for comparison purposes. UPEI and Lancaster University are relatively young institutions established in the 1960s while the HKU is over 100 years old. An important factor in choosing the case studies was to compare different national and historical settings that shape international student recruitment. While each institution showed that 18%–26% of their student population is international, practitioners may view their practices differently and face similar or different challenges in their practice. These unique circumstances contribute to our understanding of student recruitment practice in each case by recognising

Exploring Institutional Culture and Its Impact on International Student **103**

that internationalisation is occurring differently within each of these case studies (Anonymous, 2017; Lancaster University, 2013; University of Prince Edward Island, 2013a, 2013b).

The sample consisted of participants within each institution who are involved in the development of international student recruitment strategies or the implementation of international student recruitment. Within each institution, the sample was purposive in that only those individuals who contributed to strategy development or implementation role in the recruitment of international students were invited to participate – that is, the subjects of the activity system are strategy practitioners. These strategy practitioners were those involved in top management (called senior leaders), administrators, recruiters and support staff that assist in strategy development and implementation of international student recruitment at each institution. Senior leaders are those who were responsible for strategy development and resource allocation while administrators were responsible for oversight and implementation. Recruiters regularly interacted with prospective students while support staff conducted supported these efforts through tasks such as research and marketing. The size of the sample varied according to the number of individuals involved in international recruitment in either a strategic, implementation or support role until a saturation point was reached, meaning a sufficient number of participants representing the functional areas of the collective activity were interviewed (Guba & Lincoln, 1994). This point was measured in all institutions, as there were a finite number of potential participants. The title of the individual, along with a description of their role was used to determine whether or not a participant met the criteria for selection. As such, the study involved 5interviews at the UNIA case study (population 5); 8 at the UPEI case study (population 11); and 15 interviews at Lancaster University (population 22). This variation in size was reflective, not only of the level of effort and resources dedicated to international student recruitment but also how the institutions assigned responsibilities. These differences in roles and participation required a thoughtful approach to the selection of participants, the interviews and the analysis. In total, the study involved 28 interviews across the three case study locations. The interviews were conducted in-person and audio-recorded.

The Results

Engeström (2001) finds that exploring the perspectives of subjects can assist to identify the objects of their practice, the true meaning of the system (Engeström, 2001). When different objects exist amongst practitioners, tensions occur that can provide opportunities for learning and growth (Engeström, 2001). Using Engeström's approach, the perspectives of the strategy practitioners were explored to identify the influences on their practices and how these influences shape their capability to recruit students internationally. This chapter supports Engeström's method of examining practice by finding the practitioners in each case study accounted influences on their practice in similar and different ways. In each case, practitioners viewed national policies and competition as the 'playing field' for their work. They recognised that national policies influence international students' access to overseas education and that student decision-making is influenced

104   Melissa James

by visas, post-study work permits and cost. At the same time, they recognise that irrespective of these policies, higher education is a competitive space and they must compete for international students to achieve enrolment targets, brand positioning, attract talent and reap economic benefits for their communities. However, the participants' views of their institutional strategic plans show that these plans influence their practice differently in each institution. This is an important finding, as previous studies (Asaad et al., 2015; Ross et al., 2013) found that institutional capability to coordinate resources, establish goals, and communicate amongst teams is instrumental to effective international student recruitment. By examining institutional strategic plans as a tool or resource for international student recruitment, this study shows that institutional behaviour is unique. These findings show institutional capability is influenced by institutional culture and history and found three different cultural typologies that shaped institutional capability. Each of these cultural typologies influenced institutional coordination of resources, the establishment of goals for international student recruitment, and defined the extent of the international student recruitment roles within the institution. These cultural typologies are defined as *cooperative, compliant* and *isolating*. A cooperative typology is an institution that demonstrates a high level of coordination, communication, allocates resources to the practice, establishes goals and provides role clarity. On the other hand, an isolating cultural typology demonstrates a lack of communication and coordination within the institution, lacks identifiable international student recruitment or institutional goals and resources and tasks are assigned within the department or unit without context for the decision-making. This typology results in a practice that lacks understanding of their role. The compliant cultural typology demonstrates a mix or aspects of these behaviours. The compliant typology lacks role definition and implements tasks that create role confusion amongst recruiters. The compliant typology results in international student recruitment practice this is task-oriented and lacks connections to the institutional goals. Fig. 1 provides an outline of each typology and highlights the impact of these cultures on international student recruitment capabilities; coordination, resource deployment and goal and role clarity (see Fig. 1 for cultural typologies). This next section highlights the key characteristics of each typology that was discovered in each case study site.

Cooperative

The UK case study demonstrated a comprehensive approach to international recruitment by embedding responsibility for internationalisation within the faculties. The institution experienced a change in organisational structure that centralised international student recruitment into one department. At the same time, the institution began to instil an international focus within the administration and academia. The institution was striving to be internationally relevant and to advance in the league table rankings. This international focus and institutional structure demonstrated an organised approach to achieving institutional goals. In this case, faculty were engaged in internationalisation activities and this acknowledged, to a certain extent, the importance of the institution's culture, history and practices. Involving academic, staff and administration in international activities gave the study participants appreciation for

Exploring Institutional Culture and Its Impact on International Student **105**

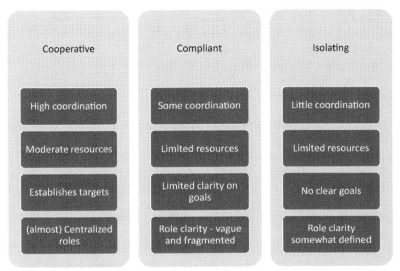

Figure 1. Cultural Typologies

the institution's strategies and goals. While issues still existed, engaging the academic faculties in the recruitment strategy appeared to assist the institution in advancing its agenda to be a globally relevant institution. However, the institution's Management School was an exception to the centralised model. Given its historical recruitment success and the high level of demand from international students, participants recognised that coordination and goals were critical to the institution but at the same time, recognition of the history of the institution was also required to successfully achieve outcomes. *'Culture trumps strategy sometimes. [But] there is an appreciation for what's better provisioned from the centre [central administration]'* (interviewee 26, senior leader, Lancaster).

In the UK case, the combination of faculty autonomy and negotiated centralisation of international student recruitment supported the expansion of programmes, offshore campuses and international recruitment efforts. This suggests that aligning agendas within the system, *while respecting history and culture* of an institution, may advance international and international student recruitment agendas. As such, the UK case study can be described as *cooperative* as it organised and deployed resources, communicated with various institutional communities, and articulated its institutional goals campus-wide.

Compliant

At the Hong Kong institution, faculty admission requirements and quality standards determined much of the activity associated with international student recruitment and created a practice that focussed on admissions.

> It's still the faculties who have the final decision of whether they want to admit the students or not. So, we let them have all the

106   Melissa James

> background of particular qualifications and things like that, to convince them that they're admitting the students of the right calibre that is comparable to the local standard. (Interviewee 13, UNIA recruiter)

The Hong Kong case study recruiters viewed their goals as competing for top students and promoting the institution's brand globally, in accordance with the institution's strategy to be internationally recognised as a diverse institution. International student enrolments were based on a quota system established by the University Grants Committee (UGC), a government organisation. The quota limited the annual number of international students to 20% of undergraduate enrolment with half of the quota designated for students from mainland China and the other half for students from the rest of the globe. For study participants, it was crucial to balance the quota established by the UGC.

> We have to be accountable to meet the quotas that are set aside by our Government. So we kind of have to work, have strategies to make sure we meet the quota and make sure we don't over enrol or under enrol, to make sure we fit all the policies. (Interviewee 13, UNIA recruiter)

While the quota clearly established targets in the Hong Kong case, it created tension because recruiters had to manage limited seats for prospective students by modifying target markets (to meet student allocations from mainland China and other international markets) and to work internally to ensure compliance with the UGC. The quota dramatically shaped the recruitment practice and placed more importance on the admissions process than the recruitment process. Recruiters were strongly motived to compete as a top-ranked institution with an international focus. However, they believed the institution was restricting international student recruitment's ability to compete by focussing the resources and attention to admissions. Furthermore, they felt the institution did not provide role clarity and that the recruitment and admissions team were assigned multiple tasks outside of their job descriptions.

> The flexibility within the bureaucracy is not there to support the flexibility that we need within international student recruitment. The university is not going to change a policy just for the international students when it has a [much larger] class. (Interviewee 10, UNIA recruiter)

The strategic plan initiated the international agenda for UNIA and gave importance to the brand and international student recruitment. However, within the context of international student recruitment, the lack of communication created a void in role and goal clarity for the practitioners.

> Sometimes I don't know if it's my goal to diversify or if it is the university's goal to keep very high standards? That wasn't

Exploring Institutional Culture and Its Impact on International Student   **107**

communicated to our level. We are working with bits and pieces of the strategic planning but it's a very small part of it. (Interviewee 12, UNIA recruiter)

The international student recruitment practice is defined as *compliant* and task oriented as participants sought ways to compete on an international scale while managing the expectations of faculty and the quota system. The practice was coordinated to manage admissions but lacked other aspects of international student recruitment capabilities such as role and goal clarity, resource allocation and establishing goals beyond admissions.

Isolating

In the Canadian case study, respondents were highly engaged in their practice and provided detailed accounts of the recruiting of international students. The respondents, based on their roles within the institution, had different perspectives on the practice and as a result, their interpretation of their institutional direction and strategy varied. Senior leaders had an understanding of institutional goals and resource allocation whereas the recruiters seemed to grasp the importance of their practice to the institution, they had little understanding of the goals for the practice. However, those in the recruitment team felt isolated from the larger university community. For example, participants indicated that faculty were vital to the success of international recruitment in terms of student experience, particularly as it pertains to student persistence and retention, but not for attracting prospective students. With respect to international recruitment activity, faculty were perceived as passive members of the community. *No one approaches us to say 'hey, you're recruiters. You are the way we're getting students internationally. That's the money maker* (Interviewee 4, UPEI recruiter). Faculty were engaged in recruitment activity sporadically and with little planning. At times recruiters consulted faculty when they needed to understand programmes and particular programme details; faculty members also occasionally participated in recruitment trips. In general, faculty held a responsive position; they were not actively involved in the strategic planning or implementation of recruitment activity.

At the same time, senior leaders did not communicate the goals to the recruiters. In this context, recruiters worked to attract as many applications from the best possible students by outperforming other 'competitive' institutions. They felt responsible for communicating the benefits of attending their institution over another. Yet, while they felt pressured to increase application or enrolment numbers, there was a disconnect between what those numbers were and how they related to their performance in international recruitment. *I don't actually know how many students we actually enrolled in September. I'd like to know more about how many people, specifically what am I getting from these different areas that I recruit from* (Interviewee 4, UPEI recruiter). This lack of communication and coordination resulted in the international student recruitment team operating in an *isolated* environment. The institutional capabilities to recruit internationally are restricted without clarity on goals, coordination outside the department, and appropriate resource allocation for the practice (see Fig. 1).

108   Melissa James

Discussion and Conclusion

This chapter shows that the practice of international student recruitment is influenced by the unique institutional culture of each case study site that results in three typologies: cooperative, compliant and isolating. In each case study, there was a community of actors engaged at different levels of international recruitment practice, strategy and implementation. Participants suggested there were differences amongst the three case study sites namely in coordination amongst teams within institutions, clarity of goals and roles, and how resources are allocated to the practice. Role clarity is found to be complex in both larger systems (e.g. the Hong Kong institution) and smaller systems (e.g. the Canadian institution), due to power relationships or lack of communication within an institution. Furthermore, each case study experienced significant growth in international applications, yet infrastructure and support systems (resource allocation) did not appear to keep pace with the increased demand. For instance, in Hong Kong, participants suggested that the appropriation of resources to admissions rather than international student recruitment was a source of dissonance within the recruitment activity. As a result, resources were stretched, leading to multiple roles for any one actor or placing emphasis on admissions rather than recruitment. While all three institutional strategies focussed on internationalisation, the resources did not always align to the strategy and this limits institutional capability in recruiting students from international markets.

All participants in this study deemed their institutions to be relatively new to the international recruitment 'game' and suggested that many other institutions were investing in advanced marketing techniques. *Some universities are so aggressive in their marketing; they use all the latest technology and geofencing and all that kind of stuff. We're not aggressive enough* (Interviewee 20, Lancaster, recruiter). This is not a surprise, but it places importance on institutional capability in international student recruitment to compete in a globally competitive environment. Studies such as these add insights into how institutions may improve their international student recruitment practice by highlighting institutional behaviours and culture and how they impact the practice (see Fig. 1). They viewed these two factors as influencing their practice as a 'playing field' – a reality shared by institutions globally. However, the unique cultures of each institution shaped the practice differently in each case study location. The different cultures resulted in three cultural typologies – cooperative, compliant and isolating based on institutional history and behaviour (Fig. 1). Institutional leaders and practitioners need to be cognisant of their institutional culture to understand how practices and practitioners are shaped by culture. In some cases, institutional culture may be impeding institutional capability and it is critical that institutions focus on their internal operations by recognising how culture shapes practice.

There are some possible directions for further research. This chapter showed that there is value in examining institutional culture and how it shapes practice. Further studies that shed light on how institutional culture shapes different types of practices may help institutions improve. Expanding the research to different jurisdictions and including a broad range of actors will improve understanding

Exploring Institutional Culture and Its Impact on International Student **109**

of international student recruitment practice but more importantly, add insights into the complexity facing higher education and its practitioners as they operate in public and market domains.

References

Anonymous. (2017).
Asaad, Y., Melewar, T. C., & Cohen, G. (2015). Export market orientation behavior of universities: The British scenario. *Journal of Marketing for Higher Education, 25*(1), 127–154. doi:10.1080/08841241.2015.1031315
Brandenburg,U., Berghoff, S., Taboadela,O., Bischof,L., Gajowniczek, J., Gehlke,A., ... & Vancea,M. L. (2014). The Erasmus impact study: Effects of mobility on the skills and employability of students and the internationalisation of higher education institutions. Luxembourg: Publications Office of the European Union.
Choudaha, R., Chang, L., & Kono, Y. (2013). International student mobility trends 2013: Towards responsive recruitment strategies. *World Education Services* (pp. 1–21). Retrieved from https://www.eurashe.eu/library/modernising-phe/mobility/data/WG4%20R%20International%20Student%20Mobility%20Trends%202013.pdf
Engeström, Y. (2001). Expansive learning at work: Toward an activity theoretical reconceptualization. *Journal of Education and Work, 14*(1), 133–156. doi:10.1080/13639080020028747
Findlay, A. M., McCollum, D., & Packwood, H. (2017). Marketization, marketing and the production of international student migration. *International Migration, 55*, 139–155.
Global Affairs Canada. (2017). Economic impact of international education in Canada – 2017 update. Retrieved from http://www.international.gc.ca/education/report-rapport/impact-2016/sec-2.aspx?lang=en
Goralski, M. A., & Tootoonchi, A. (2015). Recruitment of international students to the United States: Implications for institutions of higher education. *International Journal of Education, 10*(1), 53–66.
Guba, E. G., & Lincoln, Y. S. (1994). Competing paradigms in qualitative research. [Database] *Handbook of Qualitative Research, 2*(163–194), 105.
Hambrick, D. C., & Mason, P. A. (1984). Upper echelons: The organization as a reflection of its top managers. *Academy of Management Review, 9*(2), 193–206.
Hemsley-Brown, J., & Oplatka, I. (2010). Market orientation in universities: A comparative study of two national higher education systems. *International Journal of Educational Management, 24*(3), 204–220.
Jarzabkowski, P., Balogun, J., & Seidl, D. (2007). Strategizing: The challenges of a practice perspective. *Human Relations, 60*(1), 5–27.
Jensen, J. L., & Rodgers, R. (2001). Cumulating the intellectual gold of case study research. *Public Administration Review, 61*(2), 235–246. doi:10.1111/0033-3352.00025
Knight, J. (2015). New rationales driving internationalization. *International Higher Education, 34*. doi:10.6017/ihe.2004.34.7404
Lancaster University. (2013). Our strategy 2020. Lancaster, UK. Retrieved from http://www.lancaster.ac. uk/about-us/strategic-plan/. Accessed on January 12, 2017.
Marginson, S. (2011). Higher education and public good. *Higher Education Quarterly, 65*(4), 411–433.
McCutcheon, D. M., & Meredith, J. R. (1993). Conducting case study research in operations management. *Journal of Operations Management, 11*(3), 239–256. doi: 10.1016/0272-6963(93)90002-7

110 Melissa James

Mosneaga, A., & Agergaard, J. (2012). Agents of internationalisation? Danish universities' practices for attracting international students. *Globalisation, Societies and Education, 10*(4), 519–538.

Nagy, G., & Berács, J. (2012). Antecedents to the export market orientation of Hungarian higher education institutions, and their export performance consequences. *Journal of Marketing for Higher Education, 22*(2), 231–256. doi:10.1080/08841241.2012.738716

O'Connor, S. (2018). Problematising strategic internationalisation: Tensions and conflicts between international student recruitment and integration policy in Ireland. *Globalisation, Societies and Education, 16*(3), 339–352.

OECD. (2015). *Education at a glance 2012: OECD indicators.* Paris: OECD Publishing.

Onk, V. B., & Joseph, M. (2017). International Student Recruitment Techniques: A preliminary analysis. *Journal of Academic Administration in Higher Education, 13*(1), 25–34.

Ross, M., Grace, D., & Shao, W. (2013). Come on higher ed... get with the program! A study of market orientation in international student recruitment. *Educational Review, 65*(2), 219–240. doi:10.1080/00131911.2012

Rumbley, L., Altbach, P., & Reisberg, L. (2012). Internationalization within the higher education context. In D. K. Deardorff, H. de Wit, J. Heyl, & T. Adams (Eds.), *The SAGE handbook of international higher education* (pp. 3–27). Thousand Oaks, CA: Sage Publications.

Szekeres, J. (2010). Sustaining student numbers in the competitive marketplace. *Journal of Higher Education Policy and Management, 32*(5), 429–439. doi:10.1080/1360080X.2010.511

Tatar, E., & Oktay, M. (2006). Search, choice and persistence for higher education: A case study in Turkey. *Eurasia Journal of Mathematics, Science and Technology Education, 2*(2), 115–129.

University of Prince Edward Island. (2013a). UPEI strategic plan, Charlottetown, Canada. Retrieved from https://www.upei.ca/about-upei/upei-strategic-plan-2013-2018. Accessed on January 6, 2017.

University of Prince Edward Island. (2013b). UPEI short-term enrolment plan, Charlottetown, Canada. Retrieved from http://files.upei.ca/publications/upei_short-term_enrolment.pdf. Accessed on January 6, 2017.

Walker, P. (2013). International student policies in UK higher education from colonialism to the coalition: Developments and consequences. *Journal of Studies in International Education, 18*(4), 325–344.

Wilkins, S., & Huisman, J. (2011). Student recruitment at international branch campuses: Can they compete in the global market? *Journal of Studies in International Education, 15*(3), 299–316. doi: 10.1177/1028315310385

Zinn, M., & Johansson, H. (2015). *Student recruitment for the mobile generation: An exploratory study of mobile marketing practices in the international higher education industry.* Master's thesis, Jonkoping International Business School, Jonkoping University, Jonkoping.

Chapter 7

Recruiting Educational Tourists from Countries Under International Sanctions: The Case of Iranian Education Market

Cahit Ezel

Abstract

Iran, with its young and highly literate population, constitutes one of the main higher education markets in the Middle East region. Having now developed a highly comprehensive higher education sector, a result of the efforts to advance the higher education system following the Islamic Revolution in 1979, it is of no surprise that more than four million Iranians are currently enrolled in higher education institutions in Iran. Regardless of these developments, however, meeting the increasing demand for tertiary education has been a challenge leading to a large number of Iranians pursuing tertiary education opportunities overseas. This has created a vast and promising market for student importing countries, which has proved to be too difficult for international student recruiters to penetrate due to international sanctions imposed on Iran and local economic problems coupled with certain restrictions imposed internally by the ruling authorities. Despite the challenges of not being politically recognised as legitimate except by Turkey, North Cyprus has been one of the most popular destinations for Iranian students particularly in the last decade. Relative to its size, North Cyprus has proved to be one of the most internationalised higher education system in the world with more than 30,000 international students from more than 100 different countries and more significantly, Iranian students constitute one of the largest cohort. This chapter explores the student recruitment process from Iran with a specific focus on the external and internal challenges faced by the students as well as by the recruiters. North Cyprus is particularly evaluated as a case study to present how some challenges may have been overcome and student flow can be

---

Global Perspectives on Recruiting International Students: Challenges and Opportunities, 111–124
Copyright © 2021 by Emerald Publishing Limited
All rights of reproduction in any form reserved
doi:10.1108/978-1-83982-518-720211007

112   Cahit Ezel

achieved even to a country that has been struggling against the externalities of international political non-recognition.

Keywords: International sanctions; international student; internationalisation of higher education; Iran; North Cyprus; student recruitment

Introduction

Development of the global higher education sector, the changes in the preferences of the students and the demand from the labour market have paved the way for developing new and alternative services by the host countries as well as host higher education institutions (HEIs). In a way, the tertiary education sector is encouraged by recent developments and changes to be more responsive to the increasing competitiveness in different markets. Intensification of demand for more educated people around the globe has encouraged or in some cases forced people to enrol HEIs. In simple terms, the recent changes have, thus, fuelled the need for the provision of tertiary education not only in terms of capacity but also in terms of diversity of academic and non-academic services to respond to the demand from the students and the labour market.

Generally speaking, prospective students either enrol in local HEIs or choose to travel abroad for tertiary education which can be encouraged or forced by several factors (Mazzarol & Soutar, 2012). Students who choose to travel abroad are either not content with the higher education system at home country or they try endlessly to enrol in a local HEI without success due to limited capacity, strict admission conditions, or other factors which can be socio-economic, political or completely personal. Some students may also choose to study abroad because the academic program they wish to study is not locally available or offered so limited that admission is almost impossible. The choice of studying abroad may also be influenced by the perception that overseas degrees are better, more demanded by the local job market or preferring to enrol in world-wide prestigious universities (Ezel & Arasli, 2019).

International student mobility is mounting at a steady rate. Moreover, students' choice of the host country has diversified in recent years such that students are in search of different countries for tertiary education and not focussing on what is called the core student receiving countries such as the United States, United Kingdom, Canada and Australia. The number of international students studying in various countries increased two-fold from 2.5 million in 2007 (Altbach, Reisberg, & Rumbley, 2009) to an overwhelming 5 million in 2014 (ICEFa, 2015), and estimates indicate that the increasing trend will reach 8 million by 2025 (Tremblay, Lalancette, & Roseveare, 2012). The growth in international student mobility trends in recent years can be accounted for by the changes in the economic factors both at the student importing and student-exporting countries. Moreover, political relations amongst countries have encouraged (or sometimes discouraged) the movement of students. Moreover, more and more countries have adopted policies to develop their higher education systems and, thus, supported their HEIs through financial or other policies (British Council, 2016). Last but not least, new players have entered the market and new alternatives have emerged for the students in less familiar destinations.

Intensifying demand for tertiary education has encouraged or even some cases obliged particularly the governments in some countries to enhance the provision of higher education services. In recent years, many public and private HEIs have been established to meet particularly the growing domestic demand. For example, in Turkey, between 2004 and 2014, the total number of universities increased from 73 to 180 during which the number of public universities doubled and the private (foundation universities) almost quadrupled (Tekneci, 2016). Historically the mobility of students was from East to West; however, in recent years, the higher education sector has also shown remarkable progress in less popular countries intensifying the competition in the higher education market. A local student has more choices nowadays but at the same time, more options are available for those who are willing to study abroad. The increase in demand for tertiary education has intensified the competition and, thus, has raised awareness regarding student recruitment. Host countries and their HEIs nowadays are under pressure to recruit students not only from large student-exporting countries but also intensifying their effort to tap the resources in countries which had been ignored or neglected. Iran is one of these countries where a large stock of prospective students is willing to study abroad. This has turned Iran to a vast and promising market for students importing host countries, which has proved to be too difficult for international student recruiters to penetrate due to international sanctions imposed on Iran and local economic problems coupled with certain restrictions imposed internally by the ruling authorities.

This chapter explores the student recruitment process from Iran with a specific focus on the external and internal challenges influencing the student recruitment process along with the factors affecting the decision making the process of Iranian students to study abroad. It does so using data from primary and secondary sources.

Student Recruitment: Definition and Practices

Student recruitment can be best described as the process of searching and identifying the potential students who are willing to study at home or abroad and informing them about the various features such as academic and non-academic services of a university to convince them to enrol to the educational programs offered by that institution. The student recruitment process is mostly carried out amongst the prospective candidates who have recently completed their secondary education and willing to move on to gain knowledge and skills. On the other hand, university graduates who are interested in pursuing a higher degree to specialise or career change are also targeted.

Nowadays, the competition for attracting more and more prospective students has intensified amongst countries as well as amongst the HEIs. Core countries such as United States, Canada, United Kingdom and Australia have been the most popular countries in attracting prospective students; however, in recent years, countries from other parts of the world have also joined the competitive student market and developed their infrastructure and policies to attract students from leading student-exporting countries (Ezel & Arasli, 2019).

Competition at the country level is escalating due to the fact that higher education has become a lucrative service sector such as tourism. The 'consumers' (prospective students) travel to the host country to consume the core service (education) but on the side, they consume other goods and services produced by the host institution or country such as accommodation, transportation, communication, food, entertainments and so forth. On the other hand, competition has also intensified amongst the HEIs operating within host countries. In many countries besides public universities, private HEIs have also emerged increasing the number of options available for prospective local and international students. Therefore, nowadays individual HEIs are under extreme pressure to attract particularly internationals students who usually pay much higher tuition fees compare to locals and contribute to the local economy through their spending on various goods and services. Lack of sufficient funding from governments leaves no option for many HEIs to become self-sufficient particularly in financial terms to survive. Therefore, recruiting students particularly from large student-exporting countries has become the key process to bring in much needed financial resources.

Internationalisation of Higher Education in Iran

Iran, with its large, young and highly literate population, is one of the largest higher education markets in the Middle East. Having now developed a highly comprehensive higher education sector, a result of the efforts to advance the higher education system following the Islamic Revolution in 1979 (Ghavidel & Jahani, 2015), it is of no surprise that more than four million Iranians are currently enrolled in HEIs in Iran (ICEFb, 2015). Regardless of these developments, however, meeting the increasing demand for tertiary education which can be accounted for by labour market demand and increasing the young population has been a challenge. Insufficient capacity at the local higher education sector and for many other reasons, a considerably large number of Iranian students are pursuing opportunities overseas tertiary education. Naturally, Iran has received the attention of students importing countries and efforts have been underway to attract more Iranian students. However, despite all the interest and efforts to tap the lucrative higher education market of Iran, several issues have impeded the efforts of the HEIs and other similar agents. In other words, this vast and promising market for student importing countries has proved to be too difficult for international student recruiters to penetrate not only due to international sanctions imposed on Iran but also due to certain problems prevailing within the country itself.

According to recent statistics, the total number of Iranian students abroad is 52,521 (UNESCO, 2020). Almost one-fifth study in the United States (11,708). Despite the long-lasting political problems between the two countries, the United States has always been one of the most popular host countries amongst Iranian students. The United States is followed by Turkey (6,099) which is a neighbouring country to Iran and has close historical, political, and cultural and as well as social ties. Turkey is followed by Germany (4,846), Italy (4,265), Canada (3,884) and Malaysia (3,109). The remaining students travel to different European and Eastern countries.

Challenges and Opportunities of Student Recruitment in Iran from International and North Cyprus Perspective

Iran is a vast country with a population of more than 80 million people (World Bank, 2020) which according to recent statistics are considered as very young. Around one-quarter of the population is below age 15 and around 14% is between 15 and 24 (CIA, 2020). The young population coupled with very high literacy rate excerpt pressure on the education infrastructure; particularly on HEIs. Lack of capacity in local Iranian universities coupled with the tough entry requirements push some young Iranians to seek alternatives overseas. Iran has become a lucrative market for many counties that are keen to attract overseas students. Being a popular student-exporting country attracted the attention in international arena, however, there are many constraints obstructing host countries to penetrate to such a lucrative market. This study aims to identify these obstacles and present an overview of key players in the international higher education market.

The key obstacle regarding student recruitment in Iran is political. More precisely, all the challenges are somehow related to the international sanctions imposed by powerful Western countries and key international organisations. Below, these challenges will be explained in detail.

Many sanctions have been imposed against Iran by different countries (the United States and some European Union member countries in particular) and international organisations (e.g. United Nations) since 1979 for some different reasons ranging from support for terrorism to continuing uranium enrichment program. To name a few, the sanctions included freezing Iranian assets, trade embargo (restrictions on imports and exports) and excluding Iran from the international banking system and, thus, restricting money transfer. The sanctions were lifted or eased from time to time, but in recent years, particularly the United States has intensified the sanctions heavily.

The sanctions inevitably have harmed the Iranian economy. Iranian economy heavily relies on hydrocarbon production, agriculture and the service sector (World Bank, 2020). The government revenues greatly relies on oil and gas returns; however, as a result of the sanctions, Iranian economy has been facing serious repercussions. The loss of oil revenues coupled with the loss of export earnings of other products has caused serious economic problems such as high inflation, unemployment and a decline in foreign currency reserves. The impact of sanctions has been felt in the higher education sector as well; particularly the students willing to study abroad have faced serious challenges that are not purely limited to economic factors.

The visa issue is one of the main challenges. Certain countries are very popular amongst Iranian students as host countries such as the United States (still the most demanded country despite the problems and sanctions) and Canada. These countries have no active embassies in Iran; therefore, students who are keen to

116   Cahit Ezel

travel to them for tertiary education are ought to travel to another country (e.g. Turkey) to apply for a visa. Travelling to another country for visa application costs time and money to the applicants; they may end up staying in that particular country some time to complete the application and the interview processes and collect the visa. Moreover, there is no assurance that all visa applicants would be granted visas by the host countries and in case of rejection, the applicant would lose a serious amount of money and time even before starting the journey. This may deter some prospective students to follow such a costly path and instead look for other options. Moreover, visa-related problems sometimes exacerbate when the families of the students wish to visit their children in the host country where they pursue their studies. Culturally speaking, Iranian families are usually very much interested to visit their children and see with their own eyes the environment they are living in. In such cases, the family needs to go through the same procedure and spent a serious amount of time and money and take the risk of visa rejection. All these factors are considered when students choose a host country.

The second serious factor that obstructs recruiting students from Iran is related to money transfer restrictions resulted from imposed sanctions by the United States and the UN aiming to curtail access to the international financial system by Iran (Financial Times, 2008). The most striking negative impact of the financial transaction restrictions has been felt by the Iranian students studying (or planning to study) abroad. One of the obstacles is transferring tuition fees to the universities directly by the students or their families. Students who got admission cannot make direct money transfer from Iran to many countries therefore they end up using the 'dealers' who transfer the money from an account outside Iran on behalf of the student and charge the student certain percentage as money transfer fee like ordinary banks. Another option is to open a bank account in another country and transfer from that account to the university's account and by-pass the restrictions. Not all prospective students have access to this network and opportunities. Students also face similar problems when their families send them money for non-academic related expenses such as accommodation, transportation, food and entertainment. Each time money is to be transferred, the network has to be utilised which can be very costly since the agents who transfer the money on behalf of the sender charge a commission fee. Moreover, international credit cards such as Master and Visa do not work in Iran since Iran is not part of the international banking system. Iranian banks issue debit cards that are only valid in Iran and cannot be used at all for international payments or overseas. The problem becomes even more formidable when the constant devaluation of Iranian currency (Rial) against major currencies is considered. Iranian currency is on constant devaluation and, thus, its value is falling against major foreign currencies such as US Dollars and Euro. Students studying abroad or those who are planning to travel for tertiary education are facing serious financial challenges especially those who rely on their families for funding. The cost of foreign currency is going up constantly, therefore, putting additional pressure on the families' budget.

The third formidable challenge is academically related issues. The most notable of these is the impact of international sanctions on academic publications in scientific journals. Iran is amongst the countries that are affected by the trade sanctions imposed by the United States and EU (Elsevier, 2020). Some institutions or individuals are included in the 'list of sanctioned persons' and, therefore, these individuals or authors from these institutions (according to the US laws) are excluded from publishing (Seeley, 2013). Moreover, some journals demand publication fees carry out the review process and publish academic work. Iranian students and academicians have limited access to these types of journals since money transfer through banks or credit card payments are restricted.

On the other hand, degrees granted by certain HEIs in Iran are not recognised internationally; particularly in the United States. According to Rasouli (2020), Imam Sadiq University is one of the examples. Imam Sadiq University is a private HEI established in 1982 in Tehran as a private university. It is regarded as one of the elite HEIs in Iran and offers degrees in undergraduate and postgraduate levels in fields such as political science, economics, law, management and communication (ISU, 2020). Its notable alumni range from politicians to diplomats who have had impressive positions in the government. Graduates of this university, for example, cannot pursue their education in the United States, since the degrees they issued are not recognised. Another academically related obstacle is the limited access to internationally recognised English language proficiency exams. Even though prospective Iranian students are facing a formidable challenge to have access to overseas tertiary education, a considerable number of students are travelling every year not only to core student host countries but also to countries that have become popular in the international higher education system. Almost all these students travel to the countries where English is the native language (such as United States, Canada, United Kingdom or Australia) or to certain countries (such as Malaysia, Turkey, Russia and North Cyprus) where tertiary education in the English language is offered so that they do not have to learn the local language to pursue their education. To prove their English proficiency and also for visa purposes students are obliged to take these tests which are very difficult to access in Iran. Therefore, many students travel to neighbouring countries (such as Turkey) to take the tests which can be accessed through a direct flight from Iran (limited number of airline companies have a direct flight to and from Iran) and visa is easy to take or not asked at all. This is not a practical way of taking the test since the students have to travel and stay over for some time until the results are out. This puts an additional financial burden on their shoulders and also is very time-consuming. A prospective student may have good qualifications and even publications and can easily get admission from an international university; however, if the level of English proficiency cannot be documented, he or she may be rejected by the applied university or the process is deferred until all documents are completed.

All these factors briefly explained above limits the access of Iranian students to overseas universities. In some cases, they can have all the required admission conditions or already granted the admission but their visas are voided in the last minute; even when they are en route to the host country destination or upon their arrival (Fischer, 2019; Zraick, 2019).

Iran is one of the countries which attracts the attention of student importing countries. Considering the number of students travelling overseas for tertiary education under the current restrictions imposed directly or indirectly by the political sanctions Iran is still a very important and promising country for international student recruiting institutions as well as countries. These restrictions are imposed by powerful countries, therefore, cannot be eased or lifted by less influential countries and individual institutions. Therefore, the interested parties can only formulate other ways of going around these restrictions and, thus, attracting Iranian students.

The sanctions and their adverse impact on travelling to core countries such as the United States, Canada, Unite Kingdom and similar Western countries for tertiary education have in a way compelled the prospective Iranian students to look for alternative countries.

About a decade ago, around 150,000 students were leaving Iran to study outside per year and about 85,000 chose the United States as a host country (Rasouli, 2020). Nowadays, these numbers are much lower and continuing to decrease due to local economic problems as well as restrictions and challenges resulting from the sanctions. Nowadays in the United States and Canada, all together it is around 37,000 (Rasouli, 2020). According to the recent statistics (UNESCO, 2020), the figures are less. Despite the challenges and obstacles why these countries are still very popular amongst Iranian students? Rasouli (2020) argues that

> In Iranian culture, in our mind, for Iranians, the overseas country is the USA, Canada, and maybe the UK. Other countries are not very much considered as foreign. Turkey of the UAE is not another country. This is a cultural thing.

However, the recent developments did not leave any chance to the prospective students but to look for alternative destinations. Countries such as Turkey, China, Malaysia, Philippines, India, and Pakistan have become popular host countries amongst the students. Of course, other factors have influenced the changes in student flow trends. As stated above, one of the formidable challenges that Iranian students encounter is to have access to visas. In Turkey's case, for example, a visa for Iranian students is not required. Once acceptance is granted students can travel to Turkey by air or road and commence their studies. Iranian students in Turkey doubled in the last couple of years and nowadays they are above 6,000. Another important obstacle valid for many Western countries does not exist in Turkey. Iranians can easily exchange Rial to Turkish Lira in Turkey and, thus, eliminate the problem of finding foreign currency which is very scarce and expensive in Iran. Rasouli (2020) reported that there is an agreement between an Iranian bank (Tejarat Bank) and the Turkish Ziraat Bankası so students or their families can easily exchange Rial with Turkish Lira. Moreover, compared to many universities in Western countries Turkish universities are not very expensive.

Turkey is not the only popular destination in recent years. In Asia region, countries like India, Pakistan, Malaysia and the Philippines are very popular for economic as well as other reasons such as easy access to visas, relatively easy money transfer options, and programs offered in the English language. However, due to some complaints regarding the quality of education (Rasouli, 2020), these host countries have become less and less popular and new destinations have emerged such as Russia, Estonia, Ukraine and China. Russia, Estonia and Ukraine compared to China, has not become a popular destination amongst the Iranian students either due to harsh weather conditions or because of language-related issues. However, the demand for China is increasing for several reasons. First of all, it is not an expensive country to live and study compared to many Western countries. Moreover, China has good relations with Iran on many grounds (Cohen, 2020; Farnaz & Myers, 2020) and international sanctions do not pose any serious problems particularly in money transfer related issues. Many Iranian businessmen have investments in China or have established trade relations and money is easily transferred between two countries. Iranian students can get a visa for China without any delays or serious complications and also there are a serious number of reputable universities in China which offer programs in the English language and, thus, does not require knowledge and proficiency of the Chinese language to pursue tertiary education.

North Cyprus and Iranian Students: A Success Story

The first attempt to establish an HEI in North Cyprus dates back to the late 1970s. Since the establishment of the Higher Technological Institute in 1979—which was transformed into a state university in 1986 and assumed the name Eastern Mediterranean University—the higher education sector has been steadily developing. Almost all of the North Cyprus HEIs are privately owned and they are under strict control and audit of North Cyprus Higher Education Association (YODAK) and Higher Education Council of Turkey (YOK). In 2018, the total number reached to 17 and some further applications to open new universities pending approval (Mertkan, 2018). The student population, which is predominantly of Turkish and Turkish Cypriot origin, has recently not only shown extraordinary progress in numbers but also diversified in terms of nationality. In 2012–2013 Academic year, more than 51,000 students were pursuing their education in North Cyprus universities. Turkish Cypriot, Turkish and International students were representing 21%, 60% and 19% of the total population, respectively (MNEC, 2018; SPO, 2016). Following impressive progress, the total number of students pursuing their tertiary education in North Cyprus universities has reached 104,000 in the 2019–2020 academic year. Around half of this population comes from Turkey and the remaining is divided between Turkish Cypriot (12,000) and international students (42,000). The international students come from almost 100 different countries; however, students from particular Africa, Middle-East and Central Asian countries constitute the significant majority within the total population. Top 12 student sending countries—Nigeria, Jordan, Syria, Pakistan, Zimbabwe, Cameroon, Iran, Iraq, Libya, Egypt, Palestine and D.P.R. of Congo—constitute around 70% in aggregate (30,000) of the international students.

Despite the gradual decline in recent years, the Iranian student population has always been in the top five list. Regardless of all challenges, North Cyprus has been an attractive host country destination for many Iranian students quite

120   Cahit Ezel

some time. In the late 1980s, very small number of Iranian students arrived North Cyprus for tertiary education. Since then the Iranian student population number has increased and nowadays they constitute one of the largest student groups in the North Cyprus higher education sector. North Cyprus has even become a home to many Iranian students who have completed their education in different North Cyprus universities. Some of the graduates have settled in North Cyprus and set up their businesses and more strikingly some graduates joined the higher education system as lecturers and researchers. The question of why and how Iran has become such a lucrative market for North Cyprus universities and what challenges have overcome to attract more than 2,000 of them. More importantly, how did North Cyprus universities have managed to attract so many Iranian students despite the sanctions and all other challenges? It is worth mentioning that North Cyprus is not politically recognised in the international arena except by Turkey. Despite the political non-recognition, the higher education sector in North Cyprus has flourished and the universities have been attracting students not only from Turkey but also from almost 100 different countries amongst which Iranians constitute one of the largest cohorts of overseas students. How this success has been achieved despite the challenges prevailing on both sides?

As explained in the previous section, one of the challenges faced by Iranian students is the visa issue. In North Cyprus, Iranian students do not need to make a visa application before their arrival. The students who have got the admission can travel to the island (via Turkey by air or sea) and get a student visa at the airport upon arrival with the acceptance offer letter (an official document issued by the host university proving that the student has been accepted and enrolled to the university and is eligible to commence his or her studies). After they complete all the registration process at the host university, they complete the immigration procedure (called *Muhaceret*). Once all process is completed, the student has a multiple-entry visa for a specific period. The process is relatively very simple, hassle-free, and much less costly compared to many other visa processes imposed by other countries. Moreover, the visa process for the students' families or spouses is the same making North Cyprus even more attractive for them since they can easily visit their children or families whenever they wish to do so.

Another attraction of North Cyprus is the distance. Students can reach North Cyprus in a very short time by airways operating between Iran and Turkey. If for example, a student is travelling from Tehran, he or she can fly to Istanbul and then change to a flight to North Cyprus via transit so that he or she does not have to go through the Turkish customs. There are at least two Turkish airways companies operating on this route and the flights are frequent. The alternative route is to travel to Turkey from Iran by road or railways and then take a flight or ferry to North Cyprus. The proximity of two countries and the availability of alternative travelling modes coupled with visa-free travel are the factors that make North Cyprus attractive.

North Cyprus universities offer academic programs from different disciplines ranging from social sciences to engineering. A diverse range of programs is offered undergraduate and postgraduate levels where most of them are taught in the English language. To follow any program in the English language requires a certain level of English language proficiency where the standards are set by the relevant academic units of the respective universities. Students who had already acquired the relevant internationally recognised certificates such as TOEFL or IELTS produce these documents during the application process and get an exemption from the language training programs. If these documents had not been acquired before the application process or if the language proficiency of the students is not a sufficient level to follow the admitted program, then the student sits for an exam at the university to evaluate his or her English proficiency level. Depending on the score, the student either commences the program directly or is asked to follow the English language training offered by the Foreign Languages and English Preparatory School. This system makes the lives of the students very easy since they face problems in taking internationally recognised exams in Iran due to issues previously explained. Moreover, the system allows them to further develop their language skills at a reasonable cost. Through this system, the challenges faced by the Iranian students regarding English language proficiency are by-passed.

Financial issues also seriously challenge Iranian students travelling abroad for tertiary education. One of the advantages of studying in North Cyprus from a financial point of view is that money transfer to North Cyprus is relatively easy. Due to sanctions money transfer does not take place through banks but mostly through money exchange businesses established in North Cyprus by people who have connections in Iran. The brokers transfer the required amount to North Cyprus directly to the student for a commission (usually for 2%–3% commission fee). Briefly, the sanctions are by-passed and the students do not face any problems receiving money from his or her family. Because most of the students are self-financed (family support), through this well-established system both the students and families do not confront serious financial issues.

Finally, there are socio-cultural issues that make North Cyprus an attractive place for Iranians to pursue higher education. One issue is the fact that the culture has similarities in terms of beliefs and values and also in terms of food culture. Moreover, there is a well-established Iranian community in North Cyprus which is not limited to the considerable number of existing students but also Iranians who had settled in North Cyprus either doing business or working in different establishments including local universities. Moreover, in Iran, there exist very large Turkic-speaking people (including Azeri, Turkmens and some tribal groups) who are considered as the second largest ethnic group. Students particularly from this group easily adapt to the society in North Cyprus and do not face serious culture shock since they have many similarities and they speak the Turkish language (though with different dialect). According to Rasouli (2020), Iranian students also feel safe in North Cyprus and they do not experience any racism-related issues or discrimination in their daily lives.

Concluding Remarks

In this chapter, the challenges encountered in student recruitment from Iran are presented. Iran is a vast country inhabiting more than 80 million people substantial share of which is considered young. Moreover, Iranian people are highly literate and pay utmost attention to higher education. After the revolution in 1979, the consecutive governments in Iran have formulated policies to spread the provision of higher education to different parts of the country and to diversify the programs offered to meet the demand of the labour market. Consequently, more and more people have had access to tertiary education at Iranian HEIs; however, the demand for overseas education has also intensified despite the adverse impact of international sanctions and economic problems prevailing at home. The figures reveal that Iranian students still willing to travel abroad for tertiary education despite the challenges. More and more students could be recruited from Iran by overseas universities if certain obstacles are removed.

The Visa issue is one of the priorities. Countries willing to recruit more students from Iran need to change their visa regime and alleviate the bureaucratic formalities and strict measures in place. Countries such as Turkey, North Cyprus, China and recently Georgia are in demand because of their visa regime for Iranians. Moreover, the visa regime needs to be relaxed for the spouses and close family members since it is a common practice amongst Iranians to visit the country where their children study. Some countries have developed new policies such as granting a resident permit for people who buy immovable properties (there is a minimum price limit) or make investments at a certain minimum amount. Through this policy, for example, Turkey has attracted not only a considerable number of ordinary Iranian citizens but also students. Although it is an EU country and subject to many international sanctions, the number of Iranian students in South Cyprus increased from 10 to 140 in 2019 to 2020 (Rasouli, 2020) because of a similar policy.

Offering academic programs in the English language is also a big attraction for Iranian students. Countries other than the United States, Canada, Australia, United Kingdom and New Zealand where English is the native language need to offer programs where the medium of instruction is in English if they want to attract more Iranian students. English is the most popular language amongst Iranians nowadays and they are not very much interested to learn a new language unless they have no other choice. Countries such as India, Pakistan, Malaysia and the Philippines used to be very popular amongst young Iranians as the host countries for some time simply because many programs were offered in the English language.

Money transfer is also a serious problem for Iranians. Finding practical solutions to this problem will not only assist to attract more students but also will encourage Iranians to establish business relations and also make investments and, thus, transferring capital to the host country. For example, many Iranians have purchased immovable properties in North Cyprus in recent years not only for providing accommodation to their children but also for investment purposes.

Establishing solid and long-lasting academic collaboration between host universities and Iranian universities is proved to be a rewarding policy. Although Iran has a well-developed higher education sector and a serious number of universities are in operation, because of demand (owing to a large number of young population), many students cannot have access to certain programs. For example, programs such as pharmacy and dentistry are in high demand but the places offered by local universities cannot match it. As an example, Eastern Mediterranean University in North Cyprus has established programs in collaboration with Iranian universities, and currently, these programs are highly demanded by Iranian students. The academic collaborations can be enriched by organising joint academic events such as conferences or joint research projects. Such activities will enhance the visibility of the host university in Iran and, thus, would assist promotion activities amongst young Iranian students.

Core countries such as the United States, Canada and, to some extent, the United Kingdom has always been on the top of the list for Iranians prospective students but due to the problems explained in this chapter, it is getting more difficult day by day to travel to these very popular countries for tertiary education. This is an opportunity for many other non-core countries to tap this lucrative market by providing certain incentives such as relaxing visa regime, providing scholarships or establishing good relationships with the Iranian authorities and universities. The case of North Cyprus has proved that even as a country struggling with political non-recognition in the international arena have managed to achieve remarkable success in recruiting a considerable number of Iranian students by adapting the right policies.

References

Altbach, P. G., Reisberg, L., & Rumbley, L. E. (2009). *Trends in global higher education: Tracking an academic revolution*. A report prepared for the UNESCO 2009 World Conference on Higher Education. Paris: UNESCO.

British Council. (2016). *The shape of global higher education: National policies framework for international engagement*. United Kingdom: British Council.

CIA. (2020, July 31). *Iran*. The World Fact Book. Retrieved from https://www.cia.gov/library/publications/the-world-factbook/geos/ir.html

Cohen, A. (2020, July 17). *China and Iran Approach Massice $400 Billion Deal*. Forbes. Retrieved from https://www.forbes.com/sites/arielcohen/2020/07/17/china-and-iran-approach-massive-400-billion-deal/#c3a12252a168

Elsevier. (2020, June 8). *Trade sanctions and publishing*. New York, NY: Elsevier. Retrieved from https://www.elsevier.com/about/policies/trade-sanctions

Ezel, C., & Arasli, H. (2019). Movement from emerging economies to small island states: Motivations of Nigerian educational tourists in North Cyprus. *Island Studies Journal, 14*(1). doi: 10.24043/isj.87

Farnaz, F., & Myers, S. L. (2020, July 11). Defying U.S., China and Iran Near Trade and Military Partnership. *The New York Times*. Retrieved from https://www.nytimes.com/2020/07/11/world/asia/china-iran-trade-military-deal.html

Financial Times. (2008, April 14). How Iranians are avoiding sanctions. *Financial Times*. Retrieved from https://www.ft.com/content/6ca69788-0a48-11dd-b5b1-0000779fd2ac

Fischer, K. (2019, October 12). *Iranian student's visa voided en route to US. But why?* University World News. Retrieved from https://www.universityworldnews.com/post.php?story=20191011090621776

Ghavidel, S., & Jahani, T. (2015). Higher education demand estimation & prediction by 2025 in Iran. *Journal of Applied Research in Higher Education, 7*(2), 194–210. doi:10.1108/JARHE-04-2013-0021

124 *Cahit Ezel*

ICEFa. (2015, November 5). *The state of international student mobility in 2015*. ICEF Monitor. Retrieved from https://monitor.icef.com/2015/11/the-state-of-international-student-mobility-in-2015/

ICEFb. (2015, December 1). *Iran's university enrolment is booming. Now what?* ICEF Monitor. Retrieved from https://monitor.icef.com/2015/12/irans-university-enrolment-is-booming-now-what/

ISU. (2020, July 29). *All about ISU*. Tehran: Imam Sadiq University. Retrieved from https://isu.ac.ir/index.php?sid=1&slc_lang=en

Mazzarol, T., & Soutar, G. N. (2012). Revisiting the global market for higher education. *Asia Pacific Journal of Marketing and Logistics*, *24*(5), 717–737. doi:10.1108/13555851211278079

Mertkan, S. (2018). Higher education systems and institutions, Northern part of Cyprus. In P. Teixeira & J. C. Shin (Eds.), *Encyclopedia of international higher education systems*. Dordrecht: Springer. doi:10.1007/978-94-017-9553-1_430-1

MNEC. (2018). *2017–2018 Statistical yearbook*. Turkish Republic of Northern Cyprus: Ministry of National Education and Culture.

Rasouli, A. (2020, July 25). *Student recruitment in Iran* (C. Ezel, Interviewer). Famagusta: Turkish Republic of Northern Cyprus.

Seeley, M. (2013, May 9). *Trade sanctions against Iran affect publishers*. New York, NY: Elsevier. Retrieved from https://www.elsevier.com/connect/trade-sanctions-against-iran-affect-publishers

SPO. (2016). *Economic and social indicators*. Turkish Republic of Northern Cyprus: State Planning Organization.

Tekneci, P. D. (2016). Evolution of Turkish Higher Education System in the last decade. *Journal of Higher Education and Science*, *6*(3), 277–286. doi:10.5961/jhes.2016.164

Tremblay, K., Lalancette, D., & Roseveare, D. (2012). *Assessment of higher education learning outcomes: Feasibility study report*. Paris: OECD Publishing.

UNESCO. (2020). *Global flow of tertiary-level students*. Montreal: UNESCO UIS. Retrieved from http://uis.unesco.org/en/uis-student-flow

World Bank. (2020, May 1). Islamic Republic of Iran. Retrieved from World Bank: https://www.worldbank.org/en/country/iran/overview

Zraick, K. (2019, September 20). Iranian students set to start at U.S. universities are barred from country. *The New York Times*. Retrieved from https://www.nytimes.com/2019/09/20/us/iranian-students-visas.html

Chapter 8

Geopolitics and Global Events: International Student Recruitment in a Time of Disruption

Joseph M. Stokes

Abstract

International Education is worth billions of dollars to the world economy, and many countries such as the United States, United Kingdom, Canada and Australia have government initiatives that look to stimulate and guide international student mobility, research and technology transfer. The involvement of the state into student mobility does not come without risk.

Government foreign policy and international relations between sending countries and English-speaking study destinations threatens to upset the historical norms of international mobility. What is more, world events such as the global pandemic of 2020, will have a profound impact on the future of international education, and may change the international landscape altogether. This chapter will frame the challenges facing institutions who benefit from international mobility in the context of geopolitics and world events. It will explore how institutions can leverage strategic enrolment management tactics to help mitigate enrolment risks posed by global disruption.

Keywords: Student recruitment; international mobility; geopolitics; strategic enrolment management; SEM; pandemic

Introduction

International student mobility is estimated to be worth more than $300 billion to the world economy, and with shifting market share, the competition to attract students can be significant (Choudaha, 2019). Indeed, international recruitment

---

Global Perspectives on Recruiting International Students: Challenges and Opportunities, 125–138
Copyright © 2021 by Emerald Publishing Limited
All rights of reproduction in any form reserved
doi:10.1108/978-1-83982-518-720211008

126 Joseph M. Stokes

has become an important part of the business models at many universities around the world. Specifically, in the United States, Australia, Canada and the United Kingdom, where students flock to the reputations of highly regarded education systems, and in many cases, the prospect of the work and immigration pathways that are tied to enrolment and credential completion. The reliance on international students in these receiving countries has allowed for institutional operating budgets to become dependent on tuition and partnership dollars and has created massive amounts of commerce for agencies who specialise in the recruitment of foreign students. With over 1.5 million international students in the Unites States and Canada alone, this reliance is palpable (Dennis, 2020; Immigration, Refugees and Citizenship Canada, 2020).

With heavy reliance comes easy disruption, and geopolitical forces, global events and the world economy can have a large impact on international student mobility. In the last decade, racially motivated violence, international relations and, most recently, the global pandemic of 2020 have all contributed to shifts in international mobility. Although, the United States, Australia, Canada and the United Kingdom receive the majority of international students seeking English tertiary education, geopolitical factors could place this control in jeopardy in the long term, or at the very least influence the global pecking order in international study destinations. This chapter will explore the current realities of international student mobility in predominately English-speaking study destinations, and the geopolitical factors that influence international student recruitment. It will explore how international relations, global events and the world economy can influence student enrolment management and discuss possible solutions to mitigate the volatility of international student mobility and the challenges facing international student recruitment, and enrolment management.

Global Mobility and Institutional Dependence

To understand the international mobility landscape, it is important to consider first the scale of international student mobility and perhaps the easiest place to start is with India and China. Together, these two countries account more than a third of the world population and are major sending countries to English-speaking study destinations. According to the 2017 UNESCO data for the global flow of tertiary-level students, India and mainland China accounted for the top two sending countries in the United States (464,564), Canada (98,322), Australia (180,474) and the United Kingdom (112,964), collectively representing over 850,000 students abroad or 68% of the total outbound students from these two countries. In a global context, this represents 16% of all students studying abroad, a staggering number considering these students are coming from only two source countries.

Chinese and Indian students seek international tertiary education for multiple reasons, but importantly both countries have a developing middle class and a higher education system that lacks the capacity for the current demand for higher education (Chao, Hegarty, Angelidis, & Lu, 2017; King & Sondhi, 2018; Yang, 2002). Although China and India represent a large piece of the global international student picture, other countries such as Vietnam, Nigeria and Saudi Arabia are sending a significant number of students abroad annually. These markets continue to influence the international mobility landscape, but are not as entrenched in the enrolments of English-speaking receiving countries as India and China.

Perhaps no better is the reliance on one source country exemplified than at the University of Toronto, located in Ontario, Canada. A Top 20 global university according to the Times Higher Education (2019), the institution has a world-class research reputation and attracts more international students than any other university in the country. Students come from all over the globe to benefit from the perceived value of one of the best universities in the world, and more students are coming from China, then anywhere else. The University of Toronto has over 16,000 international students across three campuses and over 65% of their international undergraduate population comes from China (Takagi, 2019). With an operating budget of CAD$2.7 billion annually, the University of Toronto sees over CAD$700 million come from international students each year and more than half of that amount is coming from China.

This dependence is not unique to the University of Toronto. New York University in the United States has close to 19,000 international enrolments, a number that has increased close to 190% in the last decade (New York University, 2019). With almost 9,000 international students hailing from China and over 3,000 coming from India, NYU's reputation as the institution with the largest international enrolment in the United States is largely based on two source countries. Similarly, Australian universities have made higher education one of the largest exports in their economy. According to Welch (2019), Chinese students make up over 30% of the revenues at the top tier Group of Eight universities, and institutions such as the University of Melbourne and the University of Sydney both see tuition revenues in excess of AU$750 million annually from international students.

The growth in international enrolments has left many institutions open to significant budgetary risks, and some higher education leaders have taken steps to attempt to mitigate these risks. In 2018, the University of Illinois at Urbana Champaign (UIUC) purchased a USD$60 million insurance policy to protect the university form the risks of a significant drop in Chinese enrolments. With Chinese enrolment making up about a fifth of total enrolments at UIUC, the move was seen as prudent by some in the sector (Bothwell, 2018) and today with the future impact of the global pandemic due to COVID-19, the move seems almost prophetic. Elsewhere, some institutions have committed to strategic reductions in international students from specific countries. Centennial College in Ontario, Canada is so heavily reliant on international students that they make up almost half of their student population and over CAD$200 million in revenue (Teotonio, Keung, & LaFleche, 2019). With over 57% of total international enrolment from India, Centennial has committed to reducing Indian enrolments so that by 2022, they represent no more than a third of the international student population.

Other universities have relied on outsourcing their international enrolment management by developing partnerships that manage complex enrolment pipelines in order to keep the needed flow of international students coming. Companies

128   Joseph M. Stokes

such as Navitas and Study Group have partnered with dozens of universities throughout Australia, the United Kingdom, the United States and Canada by offering university preparatory programs that allow a pathway to undergraduate enrolment for students who are not directly admissible to the partner institution. These companies rely on massive agent networks that recruit students from developing countries for significant profits. A publicly traded company, Navitas realised a gross revenue of over AU\$930 Million in 2018 (Navitas Limited, 2018).

The enrolment and corresponding revenue dependence on large international source countries can pose a major risk to institutional operating budgets, and it is not surprising that institutions have begun to look at tactics in risk mitigation. Notwithstanding, there are certainly many examples of why international student dependence has become so potentially volatile and one simply needs to explore the last decade of global events to see how much fluctuation could be possible in the years to come.

Geopolitics and Uncertainty

In May 2009, thousands of Indian students gathered at Federation Square in Melbourne Australia to protest recent racially motivated violence against Indian students across the country. This tipping point came after a violent attack on Shravan Kumar, who was stabbed with a screwdriver while attending a birthday party, characterising a history of racial targeting of Indian students across the country. The rally, which was organised by the Federation of Indian Students in Australia (FISA), was a poignant display of the concerns that Indian students felt for their safety and treatment while studying abroad. The Australian government was quick to respond. Penny Wong, Australia's only Asian-born cabinet member, attempted to reframe the violent attacks by calling them isolated, and maintaining that Australia was largely a tolerant nation (Times of India, 2009). The government reaction was likely meant to assuage escalation of the protest sentiment, but it may have also had a more global message aimed at abating fears for the thousands of prospective students considering Australia as a study destination. It would have little effect, and by 2010, a steep decline in Indian student enrolments had begun as prospective students feared for their safety. The Australian government was forced to send special delegations to India to try and salvage their important education export industry, but by 2012, Indian enrolments in Australia would decrease by 55% from their height in 2009 (Baas, 2014).

The safety and social acceptance of international students in their receiving country can be a major influencer in study abroad decision making, and with the rise of populism in the Western world, some receiving countries may be becoming less attractive study destinations. In 2016, the United Kingdom held a referendum where the voting public chose to exit from the European Union. Labelled 'Brexit', this decision has had a tangible effect on international enrolments in the United Kingdom with the prospect of decreased international mobility, reduced research and collaboration and the rise of nationalistic sentiments. Although China (including Hong Kong SAR) and India are the two largest sending countries in the United Kingdom, almost 30% (143,025) of total international enrolments come from the European Union; since the Brexit vote, these numbers have largely stagnated (Universities UK, 2020). As a result, international student growth in the United Kingdom has been modest when compared to the United States, Canada and Australia (Universities UK, 2020). The Brexit move has reduced an important factor for the UK's international mobility landscape, namely, student diversity. The decrease in sending market diversity has led to increased reliance on India and China, leaving the United Kingdom vulnerable to the effects of single market reactions to government relations, and international events.

Government actions like the Brexit vote can have clear ripple effects on international student mobility and sometimes governments themselves may influence international mobility simply through the way in which they are perceived by the global community. Seven months after the Brexit vote, Donald Trump would become the 45th president of the United States. With a campaign based on nationalistic messaging and a commitment to cracking down on individuals who were in the United States illegally, some forecast that the Trump era would be a deterrent for international students considering the United States as a study destination (Bartram, 2018; C. Rose-Redwood & R. Rose-Redwood, 2017). In fact, 7 days after assuming office, Trump would sign an executive order that would ban entry to the United States from seven Muslim-majority countries. The Trump administration would go further by tightening visa restrictions, which has had some impact on international student mobility. It would be logical to think that this type of action would have a profound effect on the desirability of the United States as a study destination. Certainly, the previous examples from Australia and the United Kingdom should be a warning sign of what is to come. However, as Usher (2019), explained there has only been a small downturn in international students travelling to the United States and the high US tuition costs could be as much to blame as factors affecting the countries perceived desirability as a welcoming study destination.

Canada has possibly benefited from the instability in other English-speaking traditional study destinations. In 2020, Canada was the third most popular international study destination in the world, with 642,000 international students, a number that has tripled in the last decade (El-Assal, 2020). Although this number includes students at all education levels, many of the students enrolled in the secondary school system will ultimately matriculate to Canadian higher education institutions. While it is possible that Canada has become a more attractive study destination because of the geopolitical factors affecting Australia, the United States and United Kingdom, Canada has not been without its own challenges as an international study destination.

In the spring of 2018, attacks on civil liberties by the Kingdom of Saudi Arabia were causing strains with Western democracies who were quick to condemn the Kingdom's actions (Dangerfield 2018; Washington Post, 2018). After months of tension, Canada rebuked the Saudi government over Twitter for the detention of various women's rights activists including Samar Badawi, a Saudi human rights activist that had been involved in both the women's suffrage and women's right to drive campaigns. The Kingdom responded by criticising Canada's record on the unsolved deaths of Indigenous women, causing tensions to escalate. However, it

130 Joseph M. Stokes

was a subsequent tweet by then Foreign Affairs Minister, Chrystia Freeland, that similarly questioned the Saudi civil liberty suppression that allowed the situation to explode.

The Saudi reaction was swift and far reaching. The Kingdom expelled the Canadian Ambassador from Riyadh, banned flights and Canadian imports, and recalled all Saudi nationals studying in Canada immediately. The latter was tremendously impactful for Canadian universities as some 7,000 Saudi students, many of whom were studying on the Kingdom-sponsored King Abdulla Scholarship Program, were enrolled at institutions across the country (Canadian Bureau of International Education (CBIE), 2018). By the start of the 2018 academic year in September, a vast majority of Saudi students had been pulled out of their programs and forced to travel home, leaving student degree completion in limbo, and many Canadian universities scrambling to deal with the financial gap caused by the exodus.

Why do events such as the Saudi student departure in Canada, the FISA rallies in Australia or, Brexit, have such a profound impact on certain segments of international enrolments, whereas the rising xenophobia in the United States has arguably not had the same impact on the desirability of the United States as a study destination? Perhaps, the simple answer is that these swings in international student mobility, are complex and often unpredictable. Sometimes there has been dramatic and immediate reactions to geopolitical events, and sometimes not. If the effect of government policy on international mobility is this volatile and unreliable, what can be said about global events for which there is often no warning, and even less control?

Global Events and the COVID-19 Pandemic

There have been many global events in the last decade that have influenced international student mobility and tertiary education systems. Various natural disasters have caused death, damaged economies and destroyed infrastructure, creating hurdles for international mobility. For example, the Tohoku earthquake and tsunami that ravaged Japan's east coast was responsible for both devastating loss of human life and economic damage in Japan. In the aftermath, the six universities in the city of Sendai had laboratories and classrooms destroyed, while other institutions were turned into disaster relief centres. Even universities in Tokyo some 300 km south were dealing with rolling blackouts and computer network instability (McNeil, 2011). With the resulting nuclear incident at the Fukushima Daiichi power plant, students and faculty from Europe and North America, simply returned home instead of waiting out the recovery process with the risk of a potential nuclear disaster.

In 2017, hurricanes Irma and Maria ripped through the Caribbean within weeks of each other, causing widespread devastation. Students who were planning on leaving for international study destinations on the islands that suffered the most, such as Dominica, Antigua & Barbuda and Puerto Rico, were largely stranded. Moreover, the existing education infrastructure on these islands was destroyed. Ross University on the island of Dominica was forced to temporarily relocate to Lincoln Memorial University in Knoxville Tennessee (Gallagher, 2017) and universities in Puerto Rico were so badly damaged that some students simply left to peruse their studies elsewhere (Cleveland, 2018). In the devastation, some institutions such as Ontario Tech University in Canada gave full bursaries to select students who were unable to study in their home countries and who had faced significant financial hardships because of the disaster. In a blink of an eye a system can change, institutions can fail, while others assist in picking up the pieces.

Global events can cause sudden and unpredictable disruption to international student mobility creating unknown challenges for institutions who are deeply reliant on international student revenues. Currently the world is entering a new reality with the global pandemic caused by COVID-19. The rapid infections that have resulted from SARS-CoV-2, the virus that causes the disease COVID-19, has changed the international student mobility landscape for the foreseeable future. Countries have closed their boarders, airliners are largely grounded, and the prospect of international students attending English-speaking study destinations in 2020 seems uncertain.

The Australian university system is in total crisis, as the pandemic hit in the fall term of the 2020 academic year, and international students returned quickly to their home countries. The question now remains, will the students come back? With a heavy reliance on international students, Australia's top universities, called the Group of Eight, risk a financial uncertainty that could cripple their research and put normal operations into question. Although Australia has largely eliminated the virus, and with the prospect of a July reopening, China has warned their citizens about possible racial targeting of Asian students in the wake of pandemic (McGuirk, 2020). If Chinese student enrolments decrease at the same rate as Indian students did during the period of racial tensions that began in 2009, the Australian university system will face massive budget shortfalls.

In the United States and United Kingdom, the pandemic is not under the same control as Australia, and there exists much uncertainty if boarder restrictions will be lifted in time for a fall semester start. In Canada, most universities have opted to instruct students online, and the Canadian government has announced that it will allow students to study from their home countries without the need of a study permits. It is very likely that regardless of what happens in the coming months, the state of international mobility will be severely changed by the pandemic.

Not only is international student mobility in question from the standpoint of border and health safety, but the state of the world economy may leave many students who were previously seeking tertiary education abroad looking inward to their domestic education systems. Markets that were previously price sensitive will increase in sensitivity, and even China may face a decline in students seeking to study abroad. With the pandemic lockdown, many advanced and developing economies have come to a standstill, and the massive health and economic stimulus packages will have a lasting impact on economies as the world looks to move forward from COVID-19. As the International Monetary Fund (2020) observed, the new reality will require a global cooperation to overcome both the health and financial crisis wrought by the pandemic. Whether this same global unison

132 Joseph M. Stokes

extends to international mobility for tertiary education remains to be seen, but it is likely that the face of internationalisation in higher education will, at least in the short term, be very different. Arguably the state of international mobility in general may never return to the pre-pandemic state.

International Strategic Enrolment Management (ISEM): Competitiveness in the New Reality

Despite recent disruption, the tertiary education systems in traditional English-speaking study destinations are still increasingly dependent on international students. The disruptions that have resulted from geopolitics and global events are examples of just how dangerous this dependence can be for university business models. With an unknown end to the COVID-19 pandemic, institutions face a grim reality in a new economic volatility that promises to upend the education export industry in Australia, the United Kingdom, Canada and the United States. If institutions that have relied on international students are to survive, they will have to reinvent their approach to managing international enrolments. Indeed an International Strategic Enrolment Management (ISEM) approach that addresses multiple factors influencing the recruitment, retention and post-graduation outcomes of students will be needed in order to ensure the viability of many institutions international initiatives.

Student Recruitment and Diversification

In the current reality, increased student recruitment will be extremely important for institutions who want to continue enrolling international students. If there are fewer international students travelling abroad for tertiary education, institutions with higher reputations and rankings will likely continue to control their desired market share, while tier 2 and 3 universities will have a smaller pool to draw from. This could increase the pressure in what is already a fiercely competitive industry and as Cantwell (2015) suggested, institutions that cannot enrol a substantial number of international students see little return on investment. Indeed, some institutions may choose to exit from actively recruiting international enrolments altogether. With the fallout from COVID-19, universities will likely have to look beyond the capabilities of their internal recruitment staff as travel becomes more difficult and costly. Moreover, staff safety and the associated risk and liability with sending employees into areas recovering from the pandemic will certainly be challenging. The use of agent networks will likely become increasingly important, as outsourcing recruitment activity becomes a more viable option for managing countries that have travel restrictions, and because the cost of transcontinental travel is expected to increase (Drescher, 2020). Companies that run in-country, full-service recruitment and admissions operations may be a viable option to work alongside existing agent networks. Additionally, institutions that have not traditionally worked with recruitment agencies will need to seriously reconsider their position, as navigating off-shore recruitment becomes increasingly challenging as the world works through the pandemic.

Furthermore, the global economic recovery from COVID-19 may have an impact on tuition price sensitivity, and the need for increased scholarships and aid packages will become an imperative for institutions that wish to compete in a landscape with fewer students going abroad. This will be an especially important factor for US universities that have higher overall tuition costs than competing English-speaking study destinations. Specifically, non-elite institutions will need to balance their international tuition with the perceived value of their academic credentials, or be prepared to offer tuition discounting or other incentives.

Fewer international students seeking education in Australia, the United Kingdom, Canada and the United States will also make the need for market diversification more important than ever. Institutions cannot continue to rely on China and India to dominate international enrolments without leaving open significant enrolment continuity risks. Recruitment offices will need to increase spending in order to develop new and existing markets, and invest in a longer term strategy for enrolment diversification. This will be especially true if the pandemic shifts the way in which Chinese and, to a lesser extent, Indian students view their domestic education systems. If more students from these two countries look to domestic universities as a viable option, the flow of qualified students to English study destinations could rapidly decrease. Of course, the Chinese and Indian education systems cannot handle the current demands for higher education in their respective countries, and this could squeeze out students who may be underqualified for study in other jurisdictions. Such an outcome could give rise to more pathway programs offered by the likes of Navitas and Study Group, as universities grapple with under-prepared international students with a desire for tertiary education abroad. Perhaps most important is that as institutions shift to develop new markets, it is regions such as Africa (excluding the Middle East) that may prove the most important.

With the exception of Nigeria, which has just over 85,000 students abroad (UNESCO, 2020) or just under 2% of global students seeking tertiary education, most other African countries have very small numbers of outbound students. Consider populous countries such as Ethiopia, the Democratic Republic of Congo and Tanzania, with a combined population of over 250 million, the number of students from these countries seeking tertiary education abroad was just over 25,000 in 2017; less than a third of Nigeria's outbound students despite a larger total population (UNESCO, 2020).

Notwithstanding, Africa is poised for change, and regionally, they are one of the world's fastest growing economies (AfDB/OECD/UNDP, 2017). With a total population of over 1.2 billion, and a host of countries with rapidly developing economies, many African countries could look to traditional English study destinations within the not-so-distant future. Here lies an opportunity for diversification, as Africa is both rich with diversity but also presents many different countries with varying needs. Some African students may be looking for immigration pathways, but others will be interested in gaining skills that will be valuable when they return to their home countries so that they can assist in domestic economic transformation.

134 Joseph M. Stokes

Managing market development strategies to diversify enrolments form new and emerging markets, while dealing with a possible decline in students seeking tertiary education will be a complex endeavour. Universities will need to explore expanding off-shore recruitment representation and regard closely how they promote partnership creation, government relations and other market development tactics. This may require institutions to invest in more strategic-minded individuals that can manage relationships with in-country representatives and partnership development with key stakeholders. This could mean that campuses will require fewer traditional recruitment representatives who travel extensively and specialise in grass roots relationship development. With the high cost of tuition at many institutions, recruitment offices will also need to work with financial aid teams and central administration to develop tuition discounting strategies, or regional approaches to developing fee schedules. Ultimately, however, recruitment diversification is not an ISEM strategy that can happen in isolation, perhaps even more important to consider is how institutions redefine their value proposition. In the case of top-ranked universities, students will continue to find value in the perceived excellence that is accompanied by a top international ranking. For universities that are not a top 100 school, the factors that differentiate student experience and the evidence-based career outcomes of graduates can position an institution for enrolment success.

Student Support, Development and Career Outcomes

ISEM is more than simply recruiting quality international students. Other factors that affect enrolment management, including student retention and post-graduation success, can ultimately help differentiate an institutional brand perception, and in turn help recruitment efforts. However, in the United States, both student persistence to degree completion and the prospect of finding work after graduation have become challenging. Many US institutions have significant program attrition, and persisting from year 1 to year 2 of undergraduate study is a noteworthy problem. For students enrolled in a STEM (science, technology, engineering or math) major, year 2 persistence rates are only 62% (ACT, 2019). With the average international student paying almost USD$27,000 per year in tuition at a 4-year public US college (College Board, 2019), there is clearly work that can be done to increase the perceived value proposition. Similarly, the prospect of working in the United States after graduation has become more difficult, with H1-B visa denials at 24% in 2018 (National Foundation for American Policy, 2019), international students are faced with the prospect of both uncertain degree completion rates, as well as tenuous employability.

As geopolitical factors and world events complicate the international mobility landscape, it behoves institutions to invest in significant student development programs that will strengthen both the likelihood of degree attainment, as well as student employability after graduation. As Habley, Bloom, and Robbins (2012) have suggested, there are various retention strategies that have been shown to influences student success. If services such as academic advising and first-year transition programs are developed to focus specifically on international students, institutions may be able to increase the degree attainment for students studying abroad. Moreover, it is likely that institutions will need to continue to invest in diagnostic testing and early warning interventions in order to mitigate international student attrition.

Developing strong connections to career outcomes after graduation may also be a tactic that will increase the value proposition for students seeking tertiary education abroad. The United States, Canada, Australia and most recently the United Kingdom, have all developed programs that allow for recent foreign graduates to attain a temporary work permit, but having the prospect of potential employment may simply not be enough in an increasingly competitive landscape. Institutions will need to make connections between program outcomes and work attainment a priority factor in program development and review. Specialised resources to help students navigate immigrations laws and the various employment systems may not simply continue to be a service offered by higher education institutions, but rather an expectation of the international students choosing a study destination. In short, the mechanisms by which international students are brought to English-speaking study destinations have become much more complex. Institutions who desire to increase international enrolments will not be able to simply rely on recruitment, but they will require sound ISEM strategies that evaluate international enrolment management tactics from the prospective student stage to an employed graduate.

A Path Forward

Geopolitics and world events have proven to influence international enrolment management, and as the world recovers from the COVID-19 pandemic, the risk of disruption is that much greater. With greater disruption, comes greater risk for institutions that wish to continue to encourage international enrolments. Universities will need to make difficult choices in how they resource recruitment efforts and student development initiatives, but perhaps one of the most obvious tactics for mitigating risk is for institutions to start divesting international tuition revenues from operating budgets, and saving funds for capital and infrastructure projects that are not tied to annual operating costs. For universities with massive international populations such as NYU, the University of Toronto or the University of Melbourne, this may be a difficult task. However, even if institutions reduced the percentage of international tuition dollars that support operating expenditures a small amount each year it could go a long way in providing a defence against the unknown fluctuations caused by geopolitical factors and global events.

In addition to divesting international tuition from operating dollars, institutions could reinvest international tuition revenues into success initiatives focussed on international students. By developing better career outcomes that assist work permit conversions to immigration, as well as career attainment in students' home countries, institutions can differentiate their international destination profile through evidence-based success. As institutions move to differentiate their value proposition for foreign students, international recruitment tactics will have

136   Joseph M. Stokes

to change. Institutions that were concerned with using international students to simply fill enrolment gaps will likely not be able to continue to look to India and China alone. ISEM plans will require detailed market development strategies that look beyond institution and agent driven recruitment, and also focus on partnerships and joint programming with various international markets. Indeed, the international student recruitment landscape may never be the same, as we move past the global pandemic, and the risk of geopolitical, and world events on international student mobility will be higher than ever. Part of the path forward for all institutions from English destination countries will be to evaluate if internationalisation continues to be an imperative. Some institutions may simply decide that it is not.

References

ACT. (2019). *ACT technical manual.* Iowa City, IA.

AfDB/OECD/UNDP. (2017). *African Economic Outlook 2017: Entrepreneurship and industrialisation.* Paris: OECD Publishing. doi:10.1787/aeo-2017-en

Baas, M. (2014). Victims or profiteers? Issues of migration, racism and violence among Indian students in Melbourne. *Asia Pacific Viewpoint, 55*(2), 212–225.

Bartram, B. (2018). International students in the era of Trump and Brexit: Implications, constructions and trends. *Journal of International Students, 8*(4), 1479–1482.

Bothwell, E. (2018, November 29). Insuring gainst drop in Chinese students. *Times Higher Education.* Retrieved from insidehighered.com

Canadian Bureau of International Education (CBIE). (2018). *International Students in Canada.* Ottawa: CBIE. Retrieved from https://cbie.ca/what-we-do/research/library/

Cantwell, B. (2019). Are international students cash cows? Examining the relationship between new international undergraduate enrollments and institutional revenue at public colleges and universities in the US. *Journal of International Students, 512,* 512–525.

Chao, C. N., Hegarty, N., Angelidis, J., & Lu, V. F. (2019). Chinese students' motivations for studying in the United States. *Journal of International Students, 7*(2), 257–269.

Choudaha, R. (2019). *Beyond $300 Billion: The global impact of international students.* Eindhoven: Studyportals.

Cleveland, C. (2018). Without researchers or funds, Puerto Rico universities grapple with future after Hurricane Maria. *Cronkite News.* Retrieved from https://cronkitenews.azpbs.org/2018/05/04/puerto-rico-universities-grapple-with-future-after-hurricane-maria/

College Board. (2019). *Trends in college pricing, 2019.* New York: College Board.

Dangerfield, K. (2018, August 9). *Saudi Arabia-Canada spat: Here's everything to know about the feud.* Global News. Retrieved from https://globalnews.ca/news/4378208/canada-saudi-arabia-spat/

Davis, T. M. (2000). *Open Doors: Report on International Educational Exchange.*

Dennis, M. (2020). 2019 Open doors report on international educational exchange. *Journal of International Students, 10*(2), 1–3.

Drescher, C. (2020, May 13). How expensive will air travel be after the COVID-19 crisis? *CNN Travel.* Retrieved from https://www.cnn.com/travel/article/air-travel-expensive-coronavirus/index.html

El-Assal, K. (2020). 642,000 International students: Canada now ranks 3rd globally in foreign student attraction. *CIC News*. Retrieved from https://www.cicnews.com/2020/02/642000-international-students-canada-now-ranks-3rd-globally-in-foreign-student-attraction-0213763.html#gs.7w4rx1

Gallagher, F. (2017, December 1). Medical student sailing toward degree after Hurricane Maria destroyed his university in Dominica. *ABC News*. Retrieved from https://abcnews.go.com/International/medical-student-sailing-degree-hurricane-maria-destroyed-university/story?id=51504714#:~:text=Classrooms%20at%20Ross%20University%20in%20Dominica%20were%20destroyed%20by%20Hurricane%20Maria.&text=In%20the%20new%20year%2C%20Ross,LMU)%20in%20Knoxville%2C%20Tennessee.

Habley, W. R., Bloom, J. L., & Robbins, S. (2012). *Increasing persistence: Research-based strategies for college student success*. New York, NY: John Wiley & Sons.

Immigration, Refugees and Citizenship Canada. (2020, March 12). Temporary residence: study permit holders. Retrieved from https://open.canada.ca/data/en/dataset/90115b00-f9b8-49e8-afa3-b4cff8facaee

International Monetary Fund. (2020). *World economic outlook, April 2020: The great lockdown*. Retrieved from https://www.imf.org/en/Publications/WEO/Issues/2020/04/14/weo-april-2020

King, R., & Sondhi, G. (2018). International student migration: A comparison of UK and Indian students' motivations for studying abroad. *Globalisation, Societies and Education, 16*(2), 176–191.

McGuirk, R. (2020, June 12). Australia prepares to open its doors to international students in July. *Global News*. Retrieved from https://globalnews.ca/news/7058456/coronavirus-australia-schools-return/

McNeil, D. (2011, March 14). Japan's universities struggle to recover from earthquake and tsunami. *Chronicle of Higher Education*. Retrieved from https://www.chronicle.com/article/Japans-Universities-Struggle/126733

National Foundation for American Policy. (2019). *H1-B denial rates past and present*. Arlington, VA: National Foundation for American Policy.

Navitas Limited. (2018). *Life changing opportunities to learn: Navitas limited annual report 2018*. Retrieved from http://www.annualreports.com/HostedData/AnnualReports/PDF/ASX_NVT_2018.pdf

New York University. (2019). *Annual Report 2018-19 academic year*. NYU OGS Communications. Retrieved from https://www.nyu.edu/content/dam/nyu/globalServices/documents/annualreport/annualReport2018-19.pdf

Rose-Redwood, C., & Rose-Redwood, R. (2017). Rethinking the politics of the international student experience in the age of Trump. *Journal of International Students, 7*(3), I–IX.

Takagi, A. (2019, February 24). U of T receives more money from international students than from Ontario government. *The Varsity*. Retrieved from https://thevarsity.ca/2019/02/24/u-of-t-receives-more-money-from-international-students-than-from-ontario-government/

Teotonio, I., Keung, N., & LaFleche, G. (2019, September 25). 'I've given up everything.' Explosive growth in international students comes at a steep cost. *St Catherine's Standard*. Retrieved from stcatherinesstandard.ca

Times Higher Education. (2019, September 11). World University Rankings. Retrieved from https://www.timeshighereducation.com/world-university-rankings/2020/world-ranking#!/page/0/length/25/sort_by/rank/sort_order/asc/cols/scores

Times of India. (2009, June 1). Thousands rally against racism in Melbourne. *Times of India*. Retrieved from https://timesofindia.indiatimes.com/Thousands-rally-against-racism-in-Melbourne/articleshow/4599752.cms

138   Joseph M. Stokes

UNESCO Institute for Statistics (UIS) Database. (May 2020). Retrieved from http://data.uis.unesco.org

Universities UK. (2020, March 1). *International student recruitment data.* Universities UK. Retrieved from https://www.universitiesuk.ac.uk/International/Pages/intl-student recruitmentdata.aspx#:~:text=In%202018%2F19%20there%20were,over%20the%20equivalent%20time%20period

Usher, A. (2019). Has President Trump scared away all the foreign students? The facts behind fears of a higher-education revenue recession. *Education Next, 19*(4), 40–47.

Washington Post. (2018, August 4). *The Saudi crown prince is throwing women in jail for speaking up.* Washington Post. Retrieved from https://www.washingtonpost.com/opinions/the-saudi-crown-prince-is-throwing-women-in-jail-for-speaking-up/2018/08/04/8aec4b6c-9696-11e8-810c-5fa705927d54_story.html

Welch, A. (2019). Australia's China Question. *International Higher Education, 98,* 22–23.

Yang, F. (2002). Education in China. *Educational Philosophy and Theory, 34*(2), 135–144.

Chapter 9

Challenges to Admission for Indonesian Sponsored Applicants to a US Graduate Program in Education

Adrian Rodgers

Abstract

This chapter examines a 5-year case (Stake, 2005) which examines the structure and culture of the graduate admissions process of Indonesian applicants to a College of Education degree program in the Midwest United States. This chapter focusses on what steps are involved in the sponsorship, application and admission of international applicants to a graduate program. It was determined that the sponsorship of in-bound international students is a highly detailed and complex process engaging multiple agencies on tight timelines. This process is further complicated by single points of failure, slow decision-making and structural barriers. It was determined that because there are internal unpublicised ways to address some challenges, it is helpful to recruit and retain highly knowledgeable advocates to support the process.

Keywords: Admissions; college of education; Fulbright; graduate admissions; Indonesia; US University

Introduction

Identifying qualified international applicants, matching them to a sponsor, and then applying to and matriculating into a university program is an incredibly challenging enterprise (Lee, 2014) filled with issues related to the structure of administering the details and navigating varying cultural expectations of different individuals and organisations (Abelmann & Kang, 2014; Marginson, 2014).

Global Perspectives on Recruiting International Students: Challenges and Opportunities, 139–153
Copyright © 2021 by Emerald Publishing Limited
All rights of reproduction in any form reserved
doi:10.1108/978-1-83982-518-720211009

140 *Adrian Rodgers*

This chapter uses a case approach (Stake, 2005) and examines the structure and culture of the graduate admissions process of Indonesian applicants to a College of Education degree program in the Midwest United States. Indonesia was chosen as a focus because it is the fourth most populated country in the world, the most populous Muslim country and forecast to move to the fifth largest GDP by 2030 (PricewaterhouseCoopers, 2017). Additionally, the university in this case, subsequently referred to using the pseudonym 'the case university', had a 60-year relationship with Indonesian applicants and a number of partnerships there which supported entree.

This case is intended to help graduate students applying for programs or researching international education, staff involved in sponsoring and facilitating international university admissions, faculty involved in admission decision-making, senior administrators who decide on the organisation and structure of sponsored programs and university admissions, and government officials under which sponsored programs operate. This chapter aims to answer:

1. What steps are involved in the sponsorship, application and admission of international applicants to a graduate program?
2. What challenges does the admissions structure pose for matriculation into a degree program?
3. What challenges does the admissions culture pose for the matriculation into a degree program?

Unpacking the Application Process

Although there are many supports for international applicants (Redding, 2013), graduate school applications require highly specific matches between the applicant and the program. A private pay student is free to consider their interests, research faculty working in that area, and then contact prospective graduate schools. Sponsored students are limited to the pool of universities who the sponsor is willing to pay. How sponsors select applicants they are willing to fund, how those applicants identify potential degree programs, and how universities select applicants and support them through matriculation in to the first day of class, is something of a Black Box.

Bryk (2007), writing in the context of school reform, used the term 'Black Box' to label support processes that are not yet fully understood. By this, Bryk meant that administrators know what they want to do (fund Indonesian graduate students at American Universities) and know how they will attempt this (identify a strong applicant pool, provide pre-application mentoring, such as test preparation, and fund successful applicants), but they do not know all of the processes which happen internally at the university by which the applicant moves to admission. Likewise, the university faculty and administrators know what they want to do (attract the best and brightest), and know how they will attempt this (rigorous screening of applications), but they do not know all of the processes which happen external to the university by which the applicant came to them.

Bryk (2007) also notes that stakeholders know little about things like the use of time, the interaction between stakeholders, what participants need to know and be able to do, the role trust and perceived quality plays in relationships; and the supports needed. This illustrates Bryk's (2007) claim that it is essential for stakeholders to be self-critical about what they think they know as they build deeper levels of reflection and action.

In order to understand steps involved in the sponsorship, application, and admission of international applicants to a graduate program, Fullan's (2007, p. 292) components of 'structure and culture' can be used. Fullan (2007, p. 149) explains that the structural component is concerned with time, roles, communication structures and empowerment while culture includes social and human resources.

In writing about international education, Sutton and Obst (2011) also support the value of an analytic frame which uses structure and culture. In terms of structure, they focus on strategy, models, design and agreements. In terms of culture, they consider recommendations, transformation, partnership and development.

Gathering and Analysing Information from Stakeholders in Sponsored Admissions

To better understand the Black Box of sponsored international university admissions, it is essential to meet all the stakeholders.

Stakeholders

There are a large number of highly embedded stakeholders engaged in sponsored international admissions with very specific roles.

The Author

The author is a mid-career faculty member in Education at a research-intensive university in the United States. After the retirement of a full-time staff person responsible for Indonesian partnerships, the author was compensated for 3 years to lead Indonesian, and subsequently other, international engagement. This position was more like a coordinator and not in an administrative capacity such as a Department Chair or Associate Dean. After compensation ended, the author continued for 2 more years responding to inquiries from applicants regarding the admissions process.

Foreign Sponsors

Foreign sponsors are the Non-Governmental Organisations (NGOs) and Governments who fund part or all of the applicants' fees related to the application and tuition but are not wholly Indonesian funded. Some rely on government funds or are partnerships with governments and others are independent. In Indonesia, scholarship programs that would support instruction in different disciplines

142   Adrian Rodgers

but with English as the language of instruction includes JASSO (Japan), Stuned (Netherlands), AusAid (Australia) and the British Council (United Kingdom). Although such a large number of programs seems daunting, researching them is often an essential first step of the applicant which is likely to be undertaken independently.

Many US-destined applicants seek Fulbright funding, an expansive US international in-bound and out-bound academic funding program. LASPAU and AmidEast work with Fulbright in some countries, but for this case, the Indonesian stakeholder which administered US Fulbright funds was the Jakarta-based American Indonesian Exchange Foundation (AMINEF). Their out-bound graduate degree funding featured an ambitious recruitment program with visits to universities across the archipelago, multi-layered rigorous selection and pre-application supports including mentoring in the preparation of application materials, and payment of fees to take English and Graduate Records Exam (GRE) tests. Financial supports from Fulbright vary by country and can change over time. For example, the AMINEF sponsorship featured $40,000/year/3 years for PhD study.

Other sponsors for US-destined Indonesians include the US Agency for International Development (USAID) which has partnered with the Indonesian International Education Foundation (IIEF) who have traditionally been a testing organisation. Funding for degree-seeking applicants was not offered annually by USAID, but arose in response to perceived critical needs related to infrastructure development. IIEF helped with screening and application preparation.

Governments in Indonesia

The Indonesian federal government also sponsored seeking applicants. Historically, the Direktorat Jenderal Pendidikan Tinggi (DIKTI—the Department of Higher Education) had funded scholarships and that department shifted from the Ministry of Education to the Ministry of Science and Technology and back again. The Ministry of Religious Affairs which governs some Islamic Universities also has funded sponsorships. More recently, funds for sponsorships have moved from DIKTI to the Lembaga Pengelola Dana Pendidikan (LPDP, 2019) program administered by the Ministry of the Treasury. Initially, when funding was moved from DIKTI to LPDP, the LPDP program published two lengthy lists of Indonesian and international universities to which the sponsorships could be applied. Between 2015 and 2018, the LPDP list became increasingly limited but was expanded somewhat in 2019 (LPDP, 2019). LPDP publishes both a Regular list which applies to the vast majority of applicants and also a lengthier Affirmasi (Affirmation) list which includes more universities for applicants from rural Sumatra, Kalimantan and eastern Indonesia. The LPDP scholarship included full funding for 2 years (Masters) and 4 years (PhD) for those accepted into the program. For this case, applicants were funded by AMINEF, USAID, DIKTI and subsequently LPDP.

In addition to the Indonesian government, the US Embassy in Indonesia plays an important role in the application and matriculation of applicants to the United

States. The Bureau of Cultural Affairs at the US Embassy in Jakarta liased with the Indonesian federal government to consider joint efforts, and to support US universities as a destination for Indonesians. The Embassy and the US Secretary of State are also stakeholders in EducationUSA and @America which supported the matriculation of Indonesian students to the United States, with the latter acting as a 'walk in retail shopping mall' location to support Indonesian engagement at the individual level with the United States. Additionally, the US Embassy also played an essential role in visa application processing, including the dispelling of myths regarding difficulty obtaining a student visa.

Applicants

All the applicants were sponsored, Indonesian degree-seeking Masters and Doctoral students in Education at the case university. Almost all were employed but on-leave from their Indonesian jobs where they often worked as junior lecturers at universities with a salary of about $300/month. While it would make sense that the advice to any applicant would be to 'apply for everything', it was found individual applicant dispositions or attributes could cause those interested to pursue a graduate degree could have their goals steered by current events and peers. A breaking TV news such as a school shooting in the United States may steer an applicant to the United Kingdom, until a stabbing in London steered them to France, until a prohibition on hijabs steered them to Japan. In other cases, an applicant considered Japan or the Netherlands if they had a Test of English as a Foreign Language (TOEFL) score that made them ineligible to the United States because some Japanese or Dutch universities accepted lower scores. Applicants to the case university had decided on the United States as their first choice and almost always had the requisite English score. Over the course of 5 years, the author met with over 300 potential applicants prior to their decision to seek funding and facilitated 25 admissions into the degree program. Of all 300, not one prospective applicant had sufficient private funds to undertake even one year of study, yet alone 2–4.

US Agents and Partners

In addition to sponsors and governments, partners were sometimes involved in applications. In international education, on the one hand, 'agents' often means for-profit companies that facilitate admission and they were not used by the case university. Partners, on the other hand, had contracts with sponsors to perform tasks in the destination or origin country. For example, the Institute of International Education in New York (IIE—not to be confused with IIEF in Jakarta), acted to help the placement of AMINEF-funded applicants.

The Case University

The case university is a large research-intensive university in the United States which utilised ground-level decision-making. Many administrative decisions were

144   Adrian Rodgers

made at the level of the 15 colleges (equivalent to Faculties in other countries' university systems), with operational decisions and degree programs situated in well over 100 departments. This enormous institution was supported by a number of offices:

Graduate Admissions: Gathered individual department level admissions requirements, housed the online admissions system, released applications for departmental review, forwarded departmental decisions to the applicant and completed financial reviews.

Graduate School: Enforced admissions policies and matched fees for sponsored students with insufficient funds.

Undergraduate Admissions: Recruited domestic and international admissions including overseas recruitment, which featured private pay applicants from high income families focussed on business, law and sciences, but not education.

Department: Checked files for omissions, presented files to program faculty and alerted Graduate Admissions to faculty decisions.

Faculty: Housed in the department, reviewed the applicants' file and decided on admission, denial, or referral to another program, including provisional, conditional and 'recommend admission' for other semesters, and assigned a faculty advisor.

Clubs: The case university had both an alumni club in Indonesia and a student club at the university.

Information Gathered and Analysed

For this case, the author focussed on developing a comprehensive understanding of procedures in the admission process from every stakeholder. Additionally, there was great interest in exceptional cases where admissions systems acted as a barrier to the matriculation of the applicant. This information served as two sets of protocols: The protocols of each stakeholder and the procedures they must follow which comprised the structure of the admissions process, and cases where applicant files went awry. An autoethnographic approach was used, whereby the author was highly embedded in the admissions process, meeting with applicants, sponsors, admissions staff and faculty over a multi-year period to develop a deep understanding of the sponsorship and application process for international graduate students. Maréchal (2010, p. 43) explained that 'autoethnography is a form or method of research that involves self-observation and reflexive investigation in the context of ethnographic field work and writing' and Ellis (2004, p. xix) defined it as 'research, writing, story, and method that connect the autobiographical and personal to the cultural, social, and political'. Each protocol was examined from a structural and cultural perspective.

Findings

The simple act of applying is quite complex given the large number of stakeholders. Large numbers of communications flowed back and forth between individuals and groups within and between organisations who do not typically work with one another. The practices of different sponsors were quite different. This section considers those processes and what occurred over the course of the case.

Nineteen Steps of a Sample Application

Even before the application begins, sponsors undertook rigorous selection processes including on campus visits, pre-application intake, screening, testing, interviews, mentoring of documents including the research statement, final selection and submission of documents. After the year-long first phase screening was completed, the year-long second phase admission process began and is summarised in Table 1 that I created. Table 1 is called 'transactions process' because it lists each time a file or decision must flow from one individual or group to another.

Following phase 2, the sponsor, applicant, and university continued the matriculation process between May and August in phase 3 which included the

Table 1. Admission Transactions Process for an AMINEF Applicant with Approximate Dates.

Process	Description
1.Applicant to AMINEF (July)	Vita, GRE/TOEFL scores, Statement of intent, Writing sample, Transcript, Passport page, References, List of Universities AND program areas to which the applicant applied are submitted
2.AMINEF Jakarta to IIE in New York (August)	After checking completeness, file was forwarded to the US partner
3.IIE to multiple universities (September–October)	IIE staff researched university www sites, completed the application selecting the program of study indicated by the applicant, and paid the application fee for up to 5 universities. The contact address in the applicant file is IIEs
4.University Graduate Admissions to Department (November)	Case university Graduate Admissions maintained the online admissions system and released the applicant file to the Department
5.Department to Faculty (December–January)	Department staff reviewed the file for completeness, request omitted data, and forwarded completed files to faculty
6.Faculty to Department (January–February)	Faculty reviewed completed files to determine the applicant quality, the 'fit' with the program, and whether there is a faculty member available and willing to advise and notified the Department of the decision including provisions, conditions, and 'recommended admissions' (rec admits)
7.Department to Graduate Admissions (March)	Applicants were informed of Departmental recommendation to accept

(Continued)

146   *Adrian Rodgers*

Table 1. (*Continued*)

Process	Description
8. Department to Graduate School (March)	Departmental staff wrote a letter to the Graduate School requesting additional funds
9.Graduate School to Graduate Admissions (March)	Graduate School requested Graduate Admissions to identify amount of sponsorship
10. Graduate Admissions to IIE (March)	Scholarship terms including amount and number of years was requested
11. IIE to Graduate Admissions (March)	The terms were received
12. Graduate Admissions to Graduate School (March)	The terms were submitted so the size of the Graduate School match could be calculated
13. Graduate School to Graduate Admissions (March)	Graduate Admissions and the Department were informed of the size of the matching funds
14. Graduate Admissions to IIE (April)	Financial and other reviews were completed and IIE was notified of full acceptance
15. IIE to AMINEF (April)	IIE informed AMINEF of the acceptance
16. AMINEF to applicant (April)	AMINEF informed the student of the acceptance—the student decided to either accept or wait to see if other offers from other universities were made
17. Applicant to AMINEF (April)	The student informed AMINEF of their decision
18. AMINEF to IIE (April)	AMINEF informed IIE of the student decision
19. IIE to multiple universities (April–May)	IIE clicked 'accept' on the accepted university and withdrew the applications from other universities

visa application, uploading of data to the US government data system known as SEVIS, visa interview and granting of the visa, airline ticket issuance, housing decisions, travel, settling in funds, tax ID number issuance and bank account establishment, tuition payment, orientation including health screening, and first day of class attendance.

Although Table 1 depicted the process for an AMINEF-funded applicant, the process for an LPDP applicant was more complex. Because the LPDP program was global and not directed to a particular country, applicants had to complete the application process and fee payment themselves with the promise they would be reimbursed after acceptance. Over the years, LPDP changed its policy, sometimes recommending the applicant obtain admission before applying for the scholarship, sometimes after, and, at one point, recommending but not requiring the university have an MOU with LPDP.

Challenges in the Structure of the Application Process

There were a number of challenges posed by the application process.

Systems Challenges

One challenge was that there was no flow chart or procedural list as depicted in Table 1. Although the case university had electronic systems for leave requests and travel requests, which automatically forwarded a file to the next level for review, no such system existed for the admissions process. Therefore, it was up to employees to act on the files, sometimes prompted by e-mails. Additionally, acting expeditiously was essential in the admissions process. Steps 1–19 in Table 1 must be accomplished in approximately 20 weeks, and steps 6–19 must be accomplished in about 10 weeks. That means each step must be accomplished in 3.5 business days, so if a staffer was on vacation, sick, or busy with other work it meant files could sit without action. In summary, some of the offices involved in processing the applications featured a 'single point of failure.'

A second challenge was uncertainty in administrative processes. The AMINEF procedures remained largely unchanged, but LPDP processes over the course of the case changed frequently. For example, at the inception of the LPDP funding program, four competitions per year were held to recruit applicants. Over time, this changed to one competition per year, but on a schedule that favoured admissions to a southern hemisphere university where the first semester starts in January creating challenges for northern hemisphere universities where the first semester starts around September. LPDP also annually changed the university placements it was willing to fund creating uncertainty as to how a university could recruit prospective applicants. Indeed, at the end of the case, the university was no longer on the LPDP regular list but was on the LPDP affirmation list for Indonesians from more rural areas which effected the applicants that faculty at the university tried to recruit.

Lastly, LPDP decision-making was also something of a black box. It was learned through sources that LPDP categorised applications (e.g. by science, the arts and business) and then created caps for each category. This meant that although a strong applicant might be rejected for one competition because the cap was reached in that competition, they could apply again and if they were accepted before the cap was reached on a subsequent competition, they would be successful. This process was not publicised although it was helpful information for stakeholders to know.

Structural Barriers to Application

At some points during the case, the LPDP funding scheme reimbursed applicants for expenses for tests such as the TOEFL and the GRE. This meant

148   Adrian Rodgers

the applicant had to pay those costs up front at about $150/test and when applicants are only making $300/month that's a prohibitive expense. For those from rural areas, travel to the test site could be several hundred dollars. This meant the best and brightest could not always be recruited because of the challenge posed by relatively small dollar assessments required at the beginning of the process.

Identifying and Correcting Handling Errors

Although a massive amount of time, energy and money went into the identification and recruitment of applicants, seemingly small handling errors jeopardised the candidacy of applicants. One challenge were errors in the formatting of reference letters. Especially for LPDP funded applicants who were 'on their own' in terms of completing their application, some reference letters lacked letterhead or a signature. Applicants would also sometimes upload their three reference letters as 1 pdf document, but when the Department staff who reviewed the file saw 1 pdf they believed the application to be incomplete because there was only one attachment (even though it contained all three letters). Not all staff would open the pdf to check the contents.

Another challenge was English scores. Generally, two scores were commonly used for admission: the internet-Based TOEFL (iBT) and the International English Language Testing System (IELTS). It's difficult to compare test scores exactly, but the creators of the iBT suggest that an IELTS score of 6.5 is equivalent to an iBT of 79–93, and an IELTS score of 7 is equivalent to an iBT of 94–101 (Educational Testing Service, 2010). The case university had a different requirement with a minimum of 79 on the iBT or 7.0 on the IELTS. This created issues for applicants. For example, IIE forwarded a 6.5 score for an applicant even though that score was not admissible at the case university even though it had an equivalent iBT score that was acceptable. Also, LPDP applicants often took the IELTS test even though for admission to the case university the iBT had a comparatively lower requirement. There were solutions to address these situations, such as requesting a new or updated test or a provisional admit decision pending an updated score; however, these solutions required faculty or staff initiative and they did not always know to request updates or make provisional acceptances.

Lastly, a challenge was created when not all faculty or staff knew the procedures for sponsored applicants. For example, when time was running out for an applicant to accept their admission offer, one staffer asked why the applicant did not just accept the offer, not realising that, for an AMINEF-funded applicant, steps 14–19 in Table 1 had to occur.

Insider Unpublicised Practices to Address Barriers to Admission

In understanding the flow of applications from one process to the next, it was determined that a challenge was posed by the structure of the department's organisation of its program. For example, at the case university, there are six different foci that are all related to literacy which an applicant can choose (e.g. children's literacy, early childhood reading and writing, secondary reading and writing and so on). They were not actually different program areas, but for the purposes of the organisation of the online application system, they were deemed different 'subplans'. Because of online system limitations, an applicant could apply to only one sub-plan and applicants from Indonesia interested in studying literacy with English as the language of instruction invariably chose 'foreign and second language education' (FSLED) even if they were interested in classroom literacy and not second language acquisition. There were actually many other foci that were a much better fit for them, but they basically indicated to IIE to 'check the wrong box' not realising that there was a better fit. The problem with this was that FSLED was an oversubscribed program with intense competition for entry. The remaining foci were all limited in that the applicants had to meet rigorous expectations, but they were not competitive in terms of seats available. Furthermore, once accepted to the degree students could take any course in any foci area and work with faculty across foci areas. This cap on numbers by the FSLED foci area was not publicised. Additionally, if a focus area rejected an application, it was rare that the file was referred to another foci area. Instead, a denial resulted in an automatic rejection. These localised departmental practices created invisible barriers for applicants and could undo all of the work which had been invested into the applicant simply because of a sub-plan coding error.

Another challenge was posed by the funding timeline of the LPDP scheme which caused applicants to miss the case university's application deadline. Although applicants could apply to the university for the following year, by this time the LPDP scholarship offer expired. Requests were made of the Department to allow two international applicant deadlines per year to accommodate LPDP funding but that was rejected for multiple reasons. Finally, a central administrator explained that faculty could tag a file with a 'recommended admission date' which could override the usual timeline so that an applicant could start their program in January instead of September which better aligned with the LPDP funding timeline. This is a second example of deeply embedded knowledge known by a limited number of stakeholders that had to be learned to accommodate the needs of sponsored students.

Challenges in the Culture Surrounding the Application Process

There were a number of challenges posed by the application process.

Embedded Cultural Issues of the Case University

One challenge was the decentralised nature of university culture. There were no formalised mechanisms by which faculty or staff talked with one another, especially between different offices. For example, Undergraduate Admissions staff travelled to Indonesia to recruit applicants from High Schools, but they did not talk to faculty or Graduate Admissions staff. The Graduate Admissions office did not have a recruiting budget and saw recruitment as the work of the College or faculty. In one case, faculty from the same College who did not know each other

150   Adrian Rodgers

learned they were doing overseas work when they coincidentally bumped into each other at a hotel breakfast in the overseas country and one of them was wearing a university logo T Shirt. In another case, an Undergraduate Admissions staff member and a faculty member learned that they were staying at the same hotel on the same day in Jakarta after they returned from their trips and were talking about another matter. To remediate this, inquiries were made to multiple officials about how information could be gathered to identify what staff and faculty were travelling to Indonesia with the goal of creating more communication across offices. For months, officials were unsure how to identify that information, until randomly the official who had the information was asked, whereupon a 2-year history of university-funded travellers to Indonesia was generated in less than 3 minutes. Additionally, other university affiliated groups like the Alumni and Student Clubs also did not communicate with each other.

Faculty Culture

Reviewing Indonesian sponsored applicants posed three challenges for faculty. The first was the content of the Statement of Intent which faculty thought should be narrowly focussed explaining how the applicant's interest aligned with the foci area of the Department. Faculty also took great interest when particular faculty members were mentioned by name in the Statement because this assisted with Advisor assignments. This was something that AMINEF applicants were unable to do since they could only write one statement which was sent to all five universities, so they were unable to customise their Statement to a particular program nor could they specifically name the program to which they were applying since different universities used different program names. This caused confusion as to what foci with which the applicant best fit.

A second challenge was reference letters. When Indonesian faculty wrote reference letters they often used a check list or wrote a 3–4 sentence statement which the case university faculty felt did not give them enough insight into the quality of the applicant. Indonesian reference writers also dwelt on personal characteristics or mentioned 'God's will' which was appropriate for entry to Indonesian institutions but which was not valued by the faculty at the case university.

A last challenge was posed by the GRE score. For some time during the case, the university required a score but did not require a minimum. Subsequently the university dropped the requirement, but the Department maintained the GRE requirement but without a minimum. It was often the case that many quality Indonesian applicants who subsequently matriculated and did well had abysmal scores below the 15th percentile. Although some applicants were selected, other applicants in some foci areas were not and the GRE scores was a contributor to that.

Communications

Communications between offices also contributed to cultural challenges. For a part of the case, IIE did not communicate the size of the award at the time of application which meant the information had to be subsequently requested. This added extra steps delaying the decision-making process. IIE also preferred that the university not directly communicate with the applicant, in part to provide one communications channel.

Since applicants were sometimes unsure of the status of their application, they sometimes turned to one another to get updates as to what peers had received acceptances. This folk theory was helpful in some cases but also acted as a source of misinformation. For example, some applicants told their peers that 'you should only apply to a university where the tuition and living expenses are less than $40,000/year (the award amount) or you will have to pay the rest'. This informal advice did not take into account that the university had a match system to 'top up' scholarships which was not known by the applicants.

Discussion

The case university engagement with Indonesia, especially when it comes to admissions, is a case of success despite being neither efficient nor strategic. It is founded on immense effort by applicants, organisations and staff, which all hinge on expeditious handling of files and one short meeting where faculty decide whether or not to take on an applicant for a 3–5-year period of study. Given the immense energy that has gone into this enterprise, a lot could be done to both better showcase the quality of the applicant and to ensure that every applicant gets the scrutiny which they earned by paying their application fee.

In some ways, the structure of the approach taken by the case university resembles what Fullan (1993, p. 31) famously called 'ready-fire-aim'. When Fullan wrote that, he meant it in a helpful way suggesting that sometimes you just have to pull the trigger to get things moving. However, once international engagement is moving one must aim and that is something that can only be calculated by senior administration, hopefully with advisement from individuals who actually do the work in the overseas country. As Fullan (1993), in relating an analysis by Pascale (1990, p. 126) explains, 'when there is consensus above, and pressure below, things happen'. Thus, both senior administrators who set the vision and the ground-level staff who do the work need to be acting in concert. Structural changes that would help leadership and ground-level faculty and staff aim would include the development of flow charts and online streaming systems to move applications from one stakeholder to the next, the use of two or more annual funding competitions when a country is sending students to northern and southern hemisphere destinations, and alignment in the setting of TOEFL equivalents,

More collaboration between all stakeholders is necessary which could take the form of high-level meetings between sponsors, governmental agencies, and university administrators (Gonzalez & Sutton, 2013) or be as simple as a group Facebook where in-country staff collaborate. It's essential in this work that the United States university not view its role as one of 'taking the best and brightest,' but instead think more deeply about its engagement to create win–win (Sutton & Obst, 2011; Walker, 2014). One way to do this would be to recognise one or more faculty and staff as a change agent who could advocate for supporting

152   Adrian Rodgers

coordinated engagement with deeper significance (Lunenberg, 2010). A part of the role of such a change agent would surely be to educate stakeholders in essential components. This could include expectations for writing reference letters, efficacy of GRE scores on predicting student success, identifying what foci areas are oversubscribed and limited by number, knowing admissions 'tricks' like being able to re-set an admissions deadline by 'recommending admission' to a different semester, and bringing together Alumni and Student clubs to support the identification of and mentoring of applicants, supporting them when they arrive, and returning them home after graduation to become future alumni members and leaders in their country.

In writing about educational reform, Bryk (2007) has suggested that there is a critical distinction between useful tools or routines and routinised practice, and between critical observation to deconstruct unwarranted beliefs and critical observation intended to manipulate practitioners into replicating simplistic practices (Bryk, 2007). What is important about this assertion is that building another administrative structure like a Sponsored Programs Office is not as powerful as capitalising on the faculty and staff whose work is embedded in overseas countries and whose knowledge can contribute to a richer adjudication of the applicant.

Conclusion

This chapter aims to unlock the Black Box of international admissions by providing a rich description of stakeholders and processes in one case using structure and culture as an analytic frame. Obviously, the details of this case will not be generalisable across other institutions, countries and sponsors, but the opportunity to give careful thought to how an institution strategizes its approach by accounting for structure and culture should be transferrable to a wide range of circumstances. Through deep reflection by administrators and ground-level faculty and staff who 'do the work', more impactful approaches can be crafted.

References

Abelmann, N., & Kang, J. (2014). A fraught exchange? US media on Chinese international undergraduates and the American university. *Journal of Studies in International Education*, *18*(4), 382–397.

Bryk, A. (2007, June). Lessons learned and new directions for research and practice improvement. Paper presented at the annual meeting of the Teacher Leader Institute and North American Leadership Academy, Vienna, VA.

Educational Testing Service. (2010). *Linking TOEFL iBT scores to IELTS scores: A research report*. Princeton, NJ: ETS.

Ellis, C. (2004). *The Ethnographic I: A methodological novel about autoethnography*. Walnut Creek, CA: AltaMira Press.

Fullan, M. (1993). *Change forces: Probing the depth of educational reform*. New York, NY: Falmer Press.

Fullan, M. (2007). *The new meaning of educational change* (4th ed.). New York, NY: Teachers College Press.

Gonzalez, G. M., & Sutton, M. (2013). The role of supportive leaders at top performing universities: Best practice lessons from American institutions for Indonesian higher education. *International Journal of Leadership and Change, 1*(1), 5–13.

Lee, C. (2014). An investigation of factors determining the study abroad destination choice: A case study of Taiwan. *Journal of Studies in International Education, 18*(4), 362–381.

LPDP. (2019). *PT Luar Negeri: Panduan Daftar Perguruan Tinggi Tujuan LPDP Program Beasiswa Reguler 2019*. Jakarta: LPDP.

Lunenberg, F. C. (2010). Managing change: The role of the change agent. *International Journal of Management, Business, and Administration, 13*(1), 1–6.

Maréchal, G. (2010). Autoethnography. In A. J. Mills, G. Durepos, & E. Wiebe (Eds.), *Encyclopedia of case study research* (Vol. 2, pp. 43–45). Thousand Oaks, CA: Sage.

Marginson, S. (2014). Student self-formation in international education. *Journal of Studies in International Education, 18*(1), 6–22.

Pascale, P. (1990). *Managing on the edge*. New York, NY: Touchstone.

PricewaterhouseCoopers. (2017). *The long view: How will the global economic order change by 2050?* London: PwC.

Redding, A. B. (2013). Supporting international applicants and promoting an ethical model of global college admission. *Journal of College Admission, 219*, 8–15.

Sutton, S. B., & Obst, D. (2011). *Developing strategic international partnerships: Models for initiating and sustaining innovative institutional linkages*. New York, NY: IIE.

Walker, P. (2014). International student policies in UK higher education from colonialism to the coalition: Developments and consequences. *Journal of Studies in International Education, 18*(4), 325–344.

Chapter 10

The Qualitative Study of Factors Influencing to International Students' Satisfaction: The Case of a Private University in Turkey

Ayşe Collins, Zeynep Goknil Sanal and Aygil Takır

Abstract

The purpose of this qualitative study was to determine international students' satisfaction on the quality of a private university in Turkey and the factors which influence their satisfaction. The study also investigated international students' suggestions to improve their studies and life in Turkey. For these purposes, focus group interviews were conducted with 27 international students. Deductive coding was used to analyse collected data. The findings show that international students' satisfaction is shaped by a number of different factors including, perceived quality of teaching, living and support service experiences and scholarships. Results also showed that participants considered extracurricular activities as an important part of their experiences when it comes to improving their campus life and learning experience.

Keywords: Higher education; student satisfaction; student dissatisfaction; university services; factors influencing satisfaction; experiences; qualitative study

Introduction

Turkish higher education was heavily influenced by the neo-liberal political economies which were spreading rapidly all over the world in the early 1980s. Law No. 2547, highlighted for the first time the concept of '*higher education*', established

---

Global Perspectives on Recruiting International Students: Challenges and Opportunities, 155–172
Copyright © 2021 by Emerald Publishing Limited
All rights of reproduction in any form reserved
doi:10.1108/978-1-83982-518-720211010

156 Ayşe Collins et al.

the Council of Higher Education (YÖK) in order to direct important activity-planning, organisation, governance, instruction and research of higher education institutions in Turkey. In addition, this law provided for the establishment of private universities run by non-profit foundations (Akar, 2010). Law No. 2547 can be viewed as one of the main turning points that drove Turkish higher education institutions into the global higher education market, despite being modified throughout the years. Currently, there are 130 public and 73 private universities in Turkey with nearly 154,505 international students in the 2018–2019 academic year (YÖK, 2019). As service providers, higher education institutions are placing greater emphasis on students' needs and expectations. Of course, this becomes even more important for self-funded private universities whereby their main source of income is from students' tuition fees. Compared to domestic students, foreign students generate more income for the universities that host them, thus, it is important for universities to become more active in the international education market (Akar, 2010). Furthermore, international students enhance academic institutions in terms of diversifying the campus (National Association for Foreign Student Affairs – NAFSA, 2015). One of the ways of becoming more active in the international education market is being aware of students' satisfaction with the services of university. Private universities have to carefully consider their marketing effort in the open market environment because of intense competition. This has forced universities to plan for strategies that satisfy the needs and expectations of their international students by maintaining high-quality university services. Students' satisfaction on the quality of university services and positive experiences in the university can be served as a useful measurement of institutional quality in Turkey. The satisfaction levels of international students play crucial roles in the recruitment and enrolment process, not only during students' tenure on campus, but well into their careers (WES, 2016). As known from the huge literature (Chen, 2006; Harahap & Amanah, 2019; Harahap, Hurriyati, Gaffar, Wibowo, & Amanah, 2017; Ngamkamollert & Ruangkanjanases, 2015; Seng, 2013; Smith & Ennew, 2000; WES, 2016) word-of-mouth plays an important role in making an institution 'preferred'. In order to ensure that more prospective international students select Turkey as their educational destination, satisfying the current students is the best and most effective way to promote education. Therefore, it is critical to identify factors that influence international students' satisfaction of educational services. The main goal of this study is to determine international students' satisfaction on the quality of a private university in Turkey and the factors which influence their satisfaction. Meanwhile, the study also seeks international students' suggestions for pre-marketing improvements that could be made to assist international students and to improve their studies/life in Turkey.

Literature Review

The review of literature reveals a lack of consensus on the definition of satisfaction and how it measures. In the broad sense, Giese and Cote (2000) defined satisfaction as a 'summary, affective and variable intensity response centred on specific aspects of acquisition and/or consumption and which takes place at the precise

The Qualitative Study of Factors Influencing to International Students' **157**

moment when the individual evaluates the object'. Elliot and Healy (2001) adapt this definition to students and define student satisfaction as *'a short-term attitude resulting from an evaluation of a student's educational experience'* in the context of higher education. Although there is no consensus on its definition, there is agreement with regard to its multi-dimensional nature (De Lourdes Machado, Brites, Magalhães, & Sá, 2011; Hartman & Schmidt, 1995). Based on numerous studies, satisfaction with higher education service is proposed in dimensions such as facilities, teaching staff, teaching methods, environment, enrolment and support services (Navarro, Iglesias, & Torres, 2005). All these dimensions, which can be extensively controlled by universities, could be considered determinants of their students' satisfaction (De Lourdes Machado et al., 2011).

Satisfaction with an institution/university includes a combination of *academic factors* as well as areas related to *campus services*. Aldemir and Gülcan (2004) state that *institutional factors, extracurricular factors* and *expectations* are three major groups of factors that seem to affect student satisfaction. Institutional factors consist of *academic* (quality of education, communication with instructors inside and outside the classroom, curriculum, textbooks and other teaching materials and student evaluations of instructors) and *administrative factors* (university administrators' philosophy, practices). The extracurricular activities are all social, health, cultural and sport activities, as well as transport and board (Donald & Denison, 1996; Harvey, 2001). Expectations relate to the students' faculty choice and probability of finding a job after graduation and hopes from higher education. Another classification about groups of factors that affect satisfaction includes *core level service* and *augmented level services* (Elsharnouby, 2015). The core level service is education itself (teaching quality, faculty expertise and knowledge and administrative staff reliability (Clemes, Ozanne, & Tram, 2001). Augmented level services include physical environment quality, learning environment, social factors, and campus climate (Clemes et al., 2001; Elsharnouby, 2015).

No matter how these factors are classified, it is important to consider both academic and campus services together in determining student satisfaction. Parahoo, Harvey, and Tamin (2013) stated the importance of this as

> [...] the concept of student experience related not only to interactions with faculty, courses, and overall learning experiences, but also to other aspects that fall within the domain of student life such as administrative service, staff, physical characteristics of academic facilities, social environment, and advising support

Therefore, higher-quality in administrative factors may result in a better student experience, which in turn would generate increased satisfaction (Elsharnouby, 2015).

Many researchers noted that the stress that international students experience inclines to centre on *academic situations* (Zhai, 2002). In other words, academic support plays a key role in the experiences of international students as they navigate their way through university life (Trice & Yoo, 2007). International students found academic demands heavy and extremely stressful (Rienties, Beausaert,

158 Ayşe Collins et al.

Grohner, Niemantsverdriet, & Kommers, 2012; Zhai, 2002). For this reason, they may need some specific academic support (Curtin, Stewart, & Ostrove, 2013) such as orientation programs addressing academic and cultural differences (Zhai, 2002), counselling services or faculty support (Curtin et al., 2013; Trice & Yoo, 2007).

Like satisfaction, there are a number of factors that influence international students' dissatisfaction. On the one hand, factors like health issues, financial difficulties, family-related problems are coming from outside the institutions (Thompson & Prieto 2013). On the other hand, factors like perceived lack of quality of education, high tuition fees, disappointing learning environment, inflexible schedule and bad location of institution are directly linked with the institutions (Tandilashvili, 2019). Furthermore, the level of dissatisfaction also depends on the slight possibility of employment after graduation (Gbadosami & De Jager, 2010).

Studying aboard is an exciting goal for many international students. However, despite their positive social and economic contributions, international students often experience some challenges. Titrek, Hashimi, Ali, and Nguluma (2016) indicated that the challenges for international students may differ from region to region depending on the country where they are pursuing their education. Indeed, international students face some common concerns and difficulties such as facilities (accommodation, transportation, food and libraries), social environment (culture, communication and language difficulties), academic difficulties (the academic system, lectures and methodology, and faculty supervisors), and the international office program (lack of entertaining activities) (Rawjee & Reddy, 2012; Talebloo & Baki, 2013). The literature shows that many international students try their best to overcome the challenges facing them, but still some challenges occur and measures should be taken to deal with them (Titrek et al., 2016).

Methodology

A qualitative approach was employed for this research and focus groups were selected as an appropriate method for developing an understanding of international students' satisfaction on the quality of a private university in Turkey and the factors which influence their satisfaction. Focus group interview was a valuable data collection method for this study, providing a rich and detailed set of data about the satisfaction of international students (Stewart & Shamdasani, 1990). Two types of qualitative data were collected from these focus groups, interviewer field notes and transcripts of group interviews.

The first stage of the research started with designing and conducting group interviews. Deciding what to ask and how many questions to asked is very important for focus group interviews. For data collection purposes, an interview schedule form was prepared by the researchers including six open-ended questions to provide more in-depth responses. The six questions given below were prepared to attain information related to:

1. The experience they were most satisfied with and the reason.
2. The experience they were most dissatisfied with and the reason.

The Qualitative Study of Factors Influencing to International Students'   *159*

3. Their worries about studying in a different country.
4. How the marketing/feedback compared with their experiences after arriving.
5. Their suggestions about pre-marketing improvements that could be made to assist international students.
6. Their suggestions for improving their studies/life in Turkey right now.

The researchers created an information letter that explained the main aim and the process of the focus group interviews and consent forms. A pilot study was conducted with a group of two international students to understand the appropriateness of the questions prior to the focus group interviews.

The university enrolment population was approximately 13,000 students, of which 923 were international students. In selecting participants for the study, maximum variation sampling method (Lincoln & Guba, 1985) was used to allow for maximum variation in international students' countries (Pakistan, Uzbekistan, Malaysia, Taiwan, Iran, Finland and South Korea), language, religion and culture. Twenty-seven international students volunteered to be interviewed out of the sample. The time and location of the focus groups were decided considering convenience for the participants.

The researchers started the focus group sessions by giving information about the process of the interviews, stating the purpose of the research briefly and having the participants sign consent forms. The researchers also emphasised the rules of confidentiality. Next, the researchers introduced the questions one by one in the same order as in the interview form. To facilitate interaction between the group members, the researchers constantly provided probes and pauses, and to involve people in the discussion without expressing, making or suggesting any reactions to the answers received (Anderson, 1990). The focus group interviews were held in English and conducted within one hour. All the focus group discussions were recorded and the interviewer also took notes.

The process of data analysis began immediately after all the focus group sessions had ended. Deductive analysis was used for data analysis. In this analysis approach, the data obtained are summarised and interpreted according to the previously determined themes (Yıldırım & Şimşek, 2006). First of all, a framework for data analysis was created by using focus group interview questions. In this framework, it was decided to organise and present the data under the themes of '*The experiences of international students were most satisfying*', '*The experiences of international students were most unsatisfying*', '*worries about studying in a different country*', '*How the marketing/feedback compared with international students' experiences after arriving?*', '*International students' suggestions about pre-marketing improvements that could be made to assist international students*' and '*International students' suggestions for improving their studies/life in Turkey right now*'. The data obtained from the focus group interviews were read and arranged according to this framework. In order to strengthen the reliability of the qualitative analysis results, the data were coded by the researchers separately and then compared.

The researchers followed ethical standards to ensure that the research did not abuse the privilege of access to participants (Gubrium & Sankar, 1994). The research objectives were explained verbally and in writing. Each participant was

160   *Ayşe Collins et al.*

informed of all data collection devices and activities (a consent form was signed by each participant). The results, transcriptions, written interpretations and reports were stored in a locked place and made available to each participant at request. Each participant was assigned a code and all other identifiable data was changed to protect the identity of each participant.

Results and Discussions

This section discusses the findings and results of the qualitative analysis of the focus group interview data. The five main themes emerging from this study are as follows.

1. The Experiences International Students were Most Satisfied with and the Reasons for their Satisfaction:

The study identified the main factors contributing positively to the overall satisfaction of international students: satisfaction in education quality (teachers and teaching), the university's ability to effectively communicate with students, satisfaction in living arrangements, students' ability to understand the English language, socialising with peers, and the source of economic support (scholarships).

The teachers/teaching was found to be satisfactory by four of the students. For example, one of the students conveyed his/her experience as:

> I remember first pre-registration period in the department. I did not know anyone, none of the teachers, I did not know how to login into the system and I just found a teacher and he said you'll do that and that, he explained everything in detail. (S2)

As known from the literature, communication with the instructor in and outside the classroom (Fredericksen, Pickett, Shea, Pelz, & Swan, 2000; Hong, 2002) relates to students' satisfaction and is validated by this study.

Another student explained his/her satisfaction with the professor's guidance related to his/her ideas:

> First one is the freedom the professor gives me whenever I come up with some idea and I say I want to do it no matter it works out or no. He supports me he guides me a little if he thinks it is not going to work out but still tries to make me … and let me see the result myself. He doesn't just reject me and I really appreciate that […]. (S5)

These results showed that it is important for university administrations to employ highly qualified instructors.

Meanwhile, the atmosphere was found to be satisfactory by two respondents, one of whom expressed his/her satisfaction upon arrival as:

> The atmosphere is so good and convenient for students to study and people are so friendly. I appreciate the kindness of the people. (S18)

The Qualitative Study of Factors Influencing to International Students' **161**

Others said,

> [...] here it was very easy it is something usual here and you don't feel like you are foreigner. It gives you a good feeling. The atmosphere is good. There are many foreigner students here. It makes you feel good. (S11)

> I am not sure, but it is about the people in universities. I feel like this is heaven and it is very different from the other parts of Turkey. (S5)

Two students said they were satisfied with the admission process and orientation:

> [...] So, whenever we were being admitted here giving our international exams the international office was always near-by us and answering to our questions all the time.... The first orientation week was great. So the international students were not losing themselves in the first week just 'where it is, where it is?'.... So I was satisfied with this period. (S27)

> I chose [this university] was because I also actually...scholarships for foreigners offered by the Turkish government but I only got the information and the mail after I was accepted to [other universities] and at that time when they sent the mail I already got the student ID card of [this university]. (S6)

The other factors were mentioned by individual students. One of the students mentioned that s/he was satisfied with the facilities:

> I was so happy to be here since the facility is better than my university because my university is also a private university and fee is also high but in [this university] they have better facilities. (S18)

One student said that the use of English in this university was satisfactory:

> I went to...different universities and speaking English was difficult for them so I could not get help on the campus from the students but in here it was very easy. It is something usual here and you don't feel like you are foreigner. It gives you a good feeling [...]. (S22)

These results imply that quality of education has a strong influence on student satisfaction together with living and support service experiences. These findings highlight the fact that the quality of teaching is perceived to be the most important factor influencing international student satisfaction. Because of the student diversity, lecturers need to use a variety of teaching methods to provide for the diverse learning demands of international students. The results of this

162   Ayşe Collins et al.

study validate that universities should recognise the importance of factors like the university's atmosphere, admission, facilities, language and economic options. This finding is more or less similar to the findings of other researchers (Aldemir & Gülcan, 2004). The results also show the provision of financial services such as scholarships as one of the important factors of the international students' perceived service quality satisfaction, which validates the Hill (1995) study.

Student orientation programs were also mentioned by the participants of the study as an important part of the support services required by international students. The study conducted by Zhai (2002) had similar findings.

2. The Experiences International Students were Least Satisfied (Dissatisfied) with and the Reasons for their Dissatisfaction:

There was also a wide range of factors that the international students were dissatisfied with including faculty (teachers/teaching, guidance), the language barrier (some courses/clubs are only in Turkish), facilities (lack of lifts in the dorms, lack of cafes near the dorms, insufficiency of transportation), lack of available work/internships, university policies regarding departments (some departments are given priority), payments (Turkish students can pay in instalments but international students cannot) and tests/exams.

The only factors mentioned by multiple students were dissatisfaction with the teachers/teaching mentioned by three students and language barrier mentioned by two. Therefore, the results of the study showed that the dissatisfaction of international students is directly linked to the university.

One of the students who said s/he was dissatisfied with the teachers explained why:

> [...] sometimes I think that the lecturer didn't teach us how to do but the lecturer teaches us on how to do his/her work not on how to do the assignment not on the knowledge....The outcome would be learning but in the process we don't learn anything....Only 20 percent knowledge 80 percent how to do it. (S7)

Several students were dissatisfied with the lack of English use in class, in the clubs and socially. Some of their quotations are given below:

> Sometimes like even the instructor like do not mean to understand what the question is. There are times like for example English professors. Like a lot of times they just don't speak English and I was very disappointed. (S14)

> There are clubs in [this university]...basically they operate completely in Turkish. Most of the meetings I was, knowing that I am an international student, I asked them if they could speak English I can help you and learn from it, but most of the people did not understand English here so they said we are not going to start

The Qualitative Study of Factors Influencing to International Students' **163**

speaking English just for one person, so I asked all of them and they all agreed that they knew English, but they did not talk it because if the person is speaking Turkish that is better because they'll understand it more. (S10)

[…] there is no lift in the dormitories we bring 30 or 40 kgs of bags and there is no lift to take us up to level 5[…] (S19)

One student mentioned that s/he was dissatisfied with the lack of available work/internships:

I am dissatisfied that we don't get any opportunity to work in Turkey. During or after our studies, so the university does not support us with internships to have the opportunity to work […]. (S8)

As known from the literature, the level of dissatisfaction depends on the slight possibility of employment after graduation (Gbadosami & De Jager, 2010). According to the results of this study, dissatisfaction also depends on possibility of internship opportunities during the program.

Another student expressed his/her dissatisfaction with university policy:

Mine is a little bit about the university policy. So, my field sort of belongs to humanities faculty…I feel that there is an unfair treatment between engineering departments and other departments. (S9)

As a result, the findings of this study show that while the majority of students were satisfied with their overall experience in this university, some were not.

3. Worries of International Students about Studying in a Different Country:

When asked about their worries, the students also revealed a wide range of factors which worried them including the language barrier, potential financial problems, cultural differences, differences in university schedules, grades, being able to graduate and teachers/teaching. Two of the students said that they did not have any worries.

The language barrier was mentioned by three students and two students mentioned that they were worried about potential financial problems. Several of the students mentioned their worries about the language barrier prior to coming to this university.

[…] my biggest worry was that I would not communicate with Turkish or other international students and I would have a small confined [fellow citizen] group of friends. (S1)

Language skills are a significant source of dissatisfaction for international students because of the effect that communication ability can have on social life

164   *Ayşe Collins et al.*

(Chen, 2006). This finding of the study validates the Özoglu, Gür, and Coskun (2015) study which reported that international students' Turkish language proficiency is the most challenging issue during their academic life in Turkey. Language difficulties pose a communication barrier for many international students, who, as a result, fail to cope with social life (Cathavart, Dixon-Dawson, & Hall, 2005). As a consequence, social difficulties influence their integration. According to Allhouse (2013), international students who participated too much in events organised by student associations were found to have more confidence in their daily and academic language than other students. This indicates that there should be services within the universities or host countries that help students develop their language and, thus, improve their well-being.

Some others mentioned their financial worries:

> My first worry was financial. Whether the finance that I had in my scholarship were enough for my accommodation and daily life [...]. (S2)

Financial concerns are a practical and critical issue in international students' daily lives (Smith & Khawaja, 2011; Yakunina, Weigold, & McCarthy, 2010; Yeh & Inose, 2003). As Chen (1999) mentioned, without adequate financial resources, basic survival becomes an issue. This finding of the study validates Akdağ's (2014) study which shows that international students who receive scholarships from Turkey, spend it on their basic needs like nutrition, accommodation and clothing. It is thought that financial problems that international students experience may be overcome by satisfying part-time work provided by the university and more scholarships. But this is also a reason for dissatisfaction as mentioned earlier.

Meanwhile, several students said that there was an incoherence in the time schedules of this university and their home university:

> [...] 3 terms in one year [in home university] so you would complete your degree early....14 weeks here is better because we don't pressure ourselves much, but when we go back we are going to start at week 4 because our university they start the semester in early January, but we will go there at the end of January. (S20)

4. Students' Comparison Between Marketing Process and Experiences after Arrival:

When asked how the marketing/feedback compared with their experiences after arriving, the students had a variety of views ranging from the need for more promotion, especially through social media and/or the engagement of agencies and the need to mention potential problems that students may be faced with and/or provide more information. The responses of the students reflected contradictory views. While most of the students expressed that the marketing and reality matched almost perfectly, one student said that reality had nothing to do with the marketing and another said that reality exceeded expectations.

The Qualitative Study of Factors Influencing to International Students' **165**

Some of the responses expressing their views included:

> The facility is more than we expected. We thought it would be like our previous university but it was more...Our university is one of the top private universities. But this is better than there. (S20)

> I was positively surprised, I think. Yeah, to see the conditions of the dorms, and the free transportation. (S12)

> I was expecting like the accommodation is like so, is not in a very good condition but when I arrived here it was good [...]. (S13)

Only one student said that marketing did not match the reality:

> Only thing that is not true is the marketed. The language barrier. The faculty is superior, I really like my department all the things are true except for the language barrier. (S11)

The results of this study showed that international students were mostly satisfied with their experiences after arriving in Turkey. The results showed that accuracy of the information received about academic and social life provided by the university on social media, web, etc. has effect on their satisfaction. This validates the Alemu and Cordier (2017) study which found international students' satisfaction in information accuracy received about academic and social life increase their overall satisfaction.

5. Student Suggestions about Improving the Marketing Process:

Not many of the students provided suggestions related to marketing. Those that did suggested that there be more detailed information such as department specific marketing and more details about the expected study experience.

> I think there is no department marketing only...university marketing and I think it is big enough to do department specific marketing, every department can do their own marketing for the international students. If that can happen, every department can talk about their achievements and what they can do for the students. I think that would be helpful. (S23)

Of course, engaging in international education by increasing international student enrolments has made a significant financial contribution to universities. In today's climate it is important for institutions to use marketing techniques (such as attracting international candidates on social media, overarching student union, making a multilingual website, etc.) and students expect institutions to advertise and create an awareness of their offerings (Russell, 2005). In this respect, this finding of the study may support all these marketing strategies by considering department-based advertising.

166   *Ayşe Collins et al.*

One other participant mentioned the importance of the scholarship:

> The thing is in the pre-marketing they can tell you more about your scholarships....There are so many conditions there you have to attend every class you have to do this and that all the things so basically. When we come here, we have to know the reality about all the things so they can tell you those things to make better choices. (S25)

Chen's (2008) study showed that scholarship or financial aid by itself will not be enough to induce enrolments of the international students. The core competencies – faculty, quality, research capabilities and reputation – play far more important roles in attracting international students. Thus, this recommendation of the participant is actually a secondary core competency of international students' choice of university.

Student Suggestions about Improving Campus Life and Learning Experience:

The suggestions made by the international students may be grouped into three different clusters: a cluster of suggestions related to the social activities of the university, a cluster made up of the suggestion related to administration and teaching and a final cluster related to the facilities available on campus.

The suggestions related to the social activities included the need for more trips/tour/activities to be arranged and announced effectively so that all students including international students learned about them, buddy groups which may contribute to the socialisation and assistance of international students, moving the activity times of the clubs to earlier hours so that students who live in the city could participate. Some of these suggestions are provided below:

> I do hope for more tours from our department in this city because we actually we don't know this city....They should be well prepared and organize well before we came and organize a lot of things. Like trips cultural nights and dinners. We came here because we wanted to learn the culture of Turkish people. (S19)

> [...] when the international students come, so the buddy groups will like assist you. Like caring of you but not all the time because students in [this university] also have...so the buddy groups are where you, to know how the conditions are. I think the buddy group can actually, it can build a relationship longer. (S15)

As mentioned above, extracurricular activities (e.g. school-sponsored events, participation in athletics, buddy groups, etc.) are physically or mentally stimulating to the individual and contain some structural parameters. Results showed that participants of this study suggested some extracurricular activities for improving the campus life and learning experience of international students. In literature, there are many studies (Arambewela & Hall, 2009; Mazzarol & Soutar, 2002) which show the importance of the extracurricular activities on international students' satisfaction. This finding of the study validates all of these studies.

Most of the suggestions were related to administration and teaching and included using ice-breakers in class, providing more exercise notes, eliminating useless courses, not permitting the use of Turkish in courses or providing separate courses for international students including Turkish language courses, the need to care about the students and provide more useful information and the need to end discrimination against international students while also providing department specific marketing.

> Improving the language barrier. You cannot force someone to speak Turkish but at least academics like music faculty all the clubs basically ... can make them completely English by making some rules and those rules have to be followed by anyone not to be objected the rule about the...Most of the teachers talk and teach in English they cannot argue it so why not make those rules also for the clubs and all the things. (S10)

> For me, if in the class increase the projects, they combine in all the students means each group they have an international student. So, they will learn how to communicate, how to adapt, how to socialize [...] (S16)

Integrating international students in the classroom through quality education practices and teaching expertise has become a priority for many institutions (Hellsten & Prescott, 2004). It was evident that aspects of teaching such as the quality of lectures, instructor's feedback, availability of resources and staff might be the sources of the satisfaction of international students supported by the results of this study. Student-centred teaching methods are considered important for improving the learning experiences of international students. Like in Seng's (2013) study, students prefer lecturers who were knowledgeable, have a good command of English and well equipped with industry experience.

As known from the literature, international students' experiences are influenced by a number of individual and social resources such as language skills and perceived discrimination (Lee, 2008; Mai, 2005; Sherry, Thomas, & Chui, 2010). The results of this study also validate all of these findings.

The final cluster related to campus facilities included factors such as the establishment of co-ed dorms and the improvement of services in the cafeteria such as the widening the periods in which the meals are available and allowing students to get refills.

> [...] the "yemekhane" [cafeteria] can be improved sometimes. I am not sure the regulation is still like that you cannot have another meal in two hours right after you finish one...people sometimes cannot really get or feel full after just one. (S9)

168 *Ayşe Collins et al.*

Positive campus experiences reflect on institutional quality (Elliot & Healy, 2001), therefore, institutions should not only emphasise students' social values, capabilities and skills but also their campus experiences (Ginsberg, 1991). This finding of the study is important because there are many studies (Banwet & Datta, 2003; Douglas, Douglas, & Barnes, 2006; Elliot & Healy, 2001) which report the contribution of positive campus experiences to international student satisfaction.

Conclusions

The results indicate that generally the international students are satisfied with the service quality provided by the university. It can be concluded that the university has successfully implemented its strategic improvement of service quality. However, it is important to build a positive market perception of Turkish universities. It will influence customers' intention and brand awareness of the quality of Turkish universities to attract international students. On the other hand, students express their dissatisfaction regarding faculty, language, facilities, lack of available work. All these results show that the satisfaction of international students is a complex phenomenon consisting of several factors. Differences in satisfaction levels of international students are likely determined by a range of factors, including faculty, staff, cultural barriers, linguistic problems and financial struggles. Understanding these differences or factors at one's specific institution is vital for international students. Of course, institutions cannot address all the challenges that international students face, but they can take steps to ease the impact of key challenges such as cost (WES, 2016). As mentioned by the participants of this study, the Turkish government already provides scholarships for international students; however, institutions may also develop funding opportunities for qualified students through scholarships. Furthermore, universities may provide part-time jobs for international students.

According to the results of the study, it may be recommended that universities provide opportunities for international students to attend some extra-curricular activities (sports, arts, interest groups, volunteer work, etc.). Extra-curricular activities based on language practice may lead to developing the communication skills of international students in the Turkish Language. These activities may enable students to develop better communication skills and this in turn may improve their integration with local students and make the whole transition process much easier. In order to recruit through positive word-of-mouth endorsements, universities need to deliver a high-quality social experience together with a high-quality educational experience.

The Ministry of Trade in Turkey provides half of all the transportation, accommodation and advertising expenses universities incur in their marketing efforts abroad (Özoglu et al., 2015). All these efforts allow higher education institutions to attend international education fairs and exhibitions outside Turkey and engage in marketing activities. Of course, these types of activities assist Turkey's higher education institutions in attracting more international students. Furthermore, almost every higher education institution in Turkey often uses webpages and multiple social media platforms in the attempt to further market their brand,

The Qualitative Study of Factors Influencing to International Students' **169**

to increase applications and engagement with their applicants. As producers and deliverers of services, universities should provide accurate information about their service quality for international students, furthermore, they should improve the educational processes such as cultivating service quality and understand the patterns that underlie the students' attitudes and meanings to receive their services. This will allow universities to anticipate their students' needs and respond to them efficiently (Watjatrakul, 2014).

It is critical to implement strategies to maximise visibility and increase engagement for universities on social media. By choosing the right content topics for posts, universities can achieve higher visibility and engagement on social media. According to literature, there are content categories in social media that, when used, increase engagement of the students: athletics, news related, school spirit, admissions and promotions (Peruta & Shields, 2018). Of course, it is challenging for the social media managers of universities to create content that satisfies all the needs of an international student. Choosing the right content topics (useful and accurate information) for posts, along with strong visual media to accompany the posts in order to provide them with content that they need when choosing a university seems to be very important for international students. Furthermore, their satisfaction with information about the accuracy of academic and social life is very important for a sustainable increase in international students.

For future research, it is important to repeat the study with a more diverse and larger population which represents international students from other countries or with other universities in Turkey, attended by international students. Future research may also be conducted to explore the satisfaction of international students using quantitative data collection methods. These data would provide useful information for the administrators of universities in Turkey who are interested in hosting international students and policy makers who are influential in the administration of scholarships, or the overall international student policies of Turkey.

References

Akar, H. (2010). Globalization and its challenges for developing countries: The case of Turkish higher education. *Asia Pacific Education Review*, *11*(3), 447–457.

Akdağ, M. (2014). *Türkiye Bursları Kapsamında Yükseköğrenim İçin Türkiye'ye Gelen Öğrencilerin Sorunları ve Bu Sorunlara İlişkin Çözüm Önerileri. Yayımlanmamış Yüksek Lisans Tezi*. Ankara: Ankara Üniversitesi, Eğitim Bilimleri Enstitüsü.

Aldemir, C., & Gülcan, Y. (2004). Student satisfaction in higher education: A Turkish case. *Higher Education Management and Policy*, *16*(2), 109–122.

Alemu, A. M., & Cordier, J. (2017). Factors influencing international student satisfaction in Korean universities. *International Journal of Educational Development*, *57*, 54–64.

Allhouse, M. (2013). International student engagement with student union activities as a way to increase sense of belonging, improve cultural integration and aid language confidence. *International Student Experience Journal*, *1*(2), 1–5.

Anderson, G. (1990). *Fundamentals of educational research*. London: The Falmer Press.

Arambewela, R., & Hall, J. (2009). An empirical model of international student satisfaction. *Asia Pacific Journal of Marketing and Logistics*, *21*(4), 555–569.

170 Ayşe Collins et al.

Banwet, D. K., & Datta, B. (2003). A study of the effect of perceived lecture quality on post-lecture intentions. *Work Study*, *52*(5), 234–243.

Cathavart, A., Dixon-Dawson, J., & Hall, R. (2005). There are too Many Chinese Students. How Am I Meant to Learn? Reflections on Cross Cultural Group Working in a British University. Paper Presented at the Chinese and South East Asian Learner: The Transition to UK Higher Education, Southampton Solent University, Southampton, England, 14–15 September 2005, pp. 29–39.

Chen, C. P. (1999). Professional issues: Common stressors among international college students: Research and counselling implications. *Journal of College Counselling*, *2*(1), 49–65.

Chen, C. H. (2006). *Word-of-mouth information gathering: An exploratory study of Asian international students searching for Australian higher education services*. Unpublished Doctoral dissertation, Queensland University of Technology.

Chen, L. H. (2008). Internationalization or international marketing? Two frameworks for understanding international students' choice of Canadian universities. *Journal of Marketing for Higher Education*, *18*(1), 1–33.

Clemes, M. D., Ozanne, L. K., & Tram, L. (2001). An examination of students' perceptions of service quality in higher education. *Journal of Marketing for Higher Education*, *10*(3), 1–20.

Curtin, N., Stewart, A. J., & Ostrove, J. M. (2013). Fostering academic self-concept advisor support and sense of belonging among international and domestic graduate students. *American Educational Research Journal*, *50*(1), 108–137.

De Lourdes Machado, M., Brites, R., Magalhães, A., & Sá, M. J. (2011). Satisfaction with higher education: Critical data for student development. *European Journal of Education*, *46*(3), 415–432.

Donald, J. G., & Denison, D. B. (1996). Evaluating undergraduate education: The use of broad indicators. *Assessment and Evaluation in Higher Education*, *21*(1), 23–39.

Douglas, J., Douglas, A., & Barnes, B. (2006). Measuring student satisfaction at a UK university. *Quality Assurance in Education*, *14*(3), 251–267.

Elliot, K., & Healy, M. (2001). Key factors influencing student satisfaction related to recruitment and retention. *Journal of Marketing for Higher Education*, *10*, 1–11.

Elsharnouby, T. H. (2015). Student co-creation behaviour in higher education: The role of satisfaction with the university experience. *Journal of Marketing for Higher Education*, *25*(2), 238–262.

Fredericksen, E., Pickett, A., Shea, P., Pelz, W., & Swan, K. (2000). Factors influencing faculty satisfaction with asynchronous teaching and learning in the SUNY learning network. *Journal of Asynchronous Learning Networks*, *4*(3), 245–278.

Gbadosami, G., & De Jager, J. (2010). Specific remedy for specific problem: Measuring service quality in South African higher education. *Higher Education*, *60*(3), 251–267.

Giese, J., & Cote, J. (2000). Defining customer satisfaction. *Academy of Marketing Science Review*, *00*(01), 1–34.

Ginsberg, M. B. (1991). *Understanding educational reforms in global context*. Garland, NY: Economy, Ideology and the State.

Gubrium, J. F., & Sankar, A. (Eds.). (1994). *Qualitative methods in aging research*. Thousand Oaks, CA: Sage.

Harahap, D. A., & Amanah, D. (2019). Assessment in choosing higher education: A case of Indonesia. *Journal of International Business, Economics and Entrepreneurship (JIBE)*, *4*(1), 10–21.

Harahap, D. A., Hurriyati, R., Gaffar, V., Wibowo, L. A., & Amanah, D. (2017). Effect of Word of Mouth on Students Decision to Choose Studies in College. In *1st International Conference on Islamic Economics, Business, and Philanthropy (ICIEBP 2017)* (pp. 793-797).

Hartman, D., & Schmidt, S. (1995). Understanding student/alumni satisfaction from a consumer's perspective: The effects of institutional performance and program outcomes. *Research in Higher Education, 36,* 197–217.

Harvey, L. (2001). Defining and measuring employability. *Quality in Higher Education, 7*(2), 97–109.

Hellsten, M., & Prescott, A. (2004). Learning at university: The international student experience. *International Education Journal, 5*(3), 344–351.

Hill, F. M. (1995). Managing service quality in higher education: The role of the student as primary consumer. *Quality Assurance in Education, 3*(3), 10–21.

Hong, K. S. (2002). Relationships between students' and instructional variables with satisfaction and learning from a Web-based course. *The Internet and Higher Education, 5*(3), 267–281.

Kondakci, Y. (2011). Student mobility reviewed: Attraction and satisfaction of international students in Turkey. *Higher Education, 62*(5), 573.

Lee, J. (2008). *Stress and coping experiences of international students with language barriers during the acculturation process.* Gainesville, FL: University of Florida.

Lincoln, Y. S., & Guba, E. G. (1985). Naturalistic inquiry. Beverly Hills, CA: Sage.

Mai,L. (2005). A comparative study between UK and US: The student satisfaction in higher education and its influential factors. *Journal of Marketing Management, 21,* 859–878.

Mazzarol,T., & Soutar,G. (2002). Push-Pull factors influencing international students destination choice. *International Journal of Educational Management, 16,* 82–90. http://dx.doi.org/10.1108/09513540210418403

NAFSA: Association of International Educators. (2015). Welcoming foreign students to U.S. institutions is vital to American public policy. Retrieved from https://www.nafsa.org/_/File/_/2016_campaign_issuebrief.pdf

Navarro, M., Iglesias, M., & Torres, P. (2005). A new management element for universities: Satisfaction with the offered courses. *International Journal of Educational Management, 19,* 505–526.

Ngamkamollert, T., & Ruangkanjanases, A. (2015). Factors influencing foreign students' satisfaction toward international program in Thai universities. *International Journal of Information and Education Technology, 5*(3), 170.

Özoglu, M., Gür, B. S., & Coskun, I. (2015). Factors influencing international students' choice to study in Turkey and challenges they experience in Turkey. *Research in Comparative and International Education, 10*(2), 223–237.

Parahoo, S. K., Harvey, H. L., & Tamim, R. M. (2013). Factors influencing student satisfaction in universities in the Gulf region: Does gender of students matter? *Journal of Marketing for Higher Education, 23*(2), 135–154.

Paswan, A. K., & Ganesh, G. (2009). Higher education institutions: Satisfaction and loyalty among international students. *Journal of Marketing for Higher Education, 19*(1), 65–84.

Peruta, A., & Shields, A. B. (2018). Marketing your university on social media: A content analysis of Facebook post types and formats. *Journal of Marketing for Higher Education, 28*(2), 175–191.

Rawjee, V. P., & Reddy, K. (2012). Exchange student communication challenges. A case study of a University in South Africa Design. A paper presented in international conference on communication, media, technology and design (ICCMTD), Istanbul, Turkey, 9–11 May 2012.

Rienties, B., Beausaert, S., Grohnert, T., Niemantsverdriet, S., & Kommers, P. (2012). Understanding academic performance of international students: The role of ethnicity, academic and social integration. *Higher Education, 63*(6), 685–700.

Russell, M. (2005). Marketing education: A review of service quality perceptions among international students. *International Journal of Contemporary Hospitality Management, *17*(1), 65–77.

172 Ayşe Collins et al.

Seng, E. L. K. (2013). A qualitative study of factors contributing to international students' satisfaction of institutional quality. *Asian Social Science*, *9*(13), 126.

Sherry, M., Thomas, P., & Chui, W. H. (2010). International students: A vulnerable student population. *Higher Education*, *60*(1), 33–46.

Smith, R., & Ennew, C. (2000). Service quality and its impact on word of mouth communication in higher education, Paper presented at the academy of marketing annual conference, University of Derby, Derby, 5–7 July.

Smith, R. A., & Khawaja, N. G. (2011). A review of the acculturation experiences of international students. *International Journal of Intercultural Relations*, *35*(6), 699–713.

Stewart, D. W., & Shamdasani, P. N. (1990). *Focus groups: Theory and practices*. Newbury Park, CA: Sage.

Talebloo, B., & Bin Baki, R. (2013). Challenges faced by international postgraduate students during their first year of study. *International Journal of Humanity and Social Science*, *3*(13), 138–145.

Tandilashvili, N. (2019, July). Factors influencing student satisfaction in higher education. The case of a Georgian State University. In *Proceedings of the 13th International RAIS Conference on Social Sciences and Humanities* (pp. 39–54). Rockville, MD: Scientia Moralitas Research Institute.

Thompson, L. R., & Prieto, L. C. (2013). Improving retention among college students: Investigating the utilization of virtualized advising. *Academy of Educational Leadership Journal*, *17*(4), 13.

Titrek, O., Hashimi, S. H., Ali, S., & Nguluma, H. F. (2016). Challenges faced by international students in Turkey. *The Anthropologist*, *24*(1), 148–156.

Trice, A. G., & Yoo, J. E. (2007). International graduate students' perceptions of their academic experience. *Journal of Research in International Education*, *6*(1), 41–66.

Watjatrakul, B. (2014). Factors affecting students' intentions to study at universities adopting the student-as-customer concept. *International Journal Education Management*, *28*(6), 676–693.

WES: World Education Services. (2016). Improving the International Student Experience: Implications for Recruitment and Support. Retrieved from https://knowledge. wes.org/rs/317-CTM-316/images/08%20-%20Improving%20Experience%20-%20v FINAL.pdf

Yakunina, E. S., Weigold, I. K., & McCarthy, A. S. (2010). Group counseling with international students: Practical, ethical, and cultural considerations. *Journal of College Student Psychotherapy*, *25*(1), 67–78.

Yeh, C. J., & Inose, M. (2003). International students reported English fluency, social support satisfaction, and social connectedness as predictors of acculturative stress. *Counselling Psychology Quarterly*, *16*(1), 15–28.

Yıldırım, A., & Şimşek, H. (2000). *Nitel Araştırmanın Planlanması, Sosyal Bilimlerde Nitel Araştırma Yöntemleri* Ankara: Seçkin Yayınları.

Zhai, L. (2002). Studying international students: Adjustment issues and social support, ERIC Document 474481.

Zhai, L. (2004). Studying international students: Adjustment issues and social support. *Journal of International Agricultural and Extension Education*, *11*(1), 97–104.

Chapter 11

Are Chinese Students Studying at European Universities Satisfied? Performance and Challenges

Marta Melguizo-Garde and Ana Yetano

Abstract

International education is one of the largest and fastest growing economic sectors in the world. Degree-seeking students have become a large and growing export opportunity. Asian countries, especially China, are amongst the top countries sending students out, as a result, most countries aim to attract their students. Nevertheless, moving from Asian countries to the western ones is not an easy move. Chinese students face different types of challenges that need to be analysed to smooth their adaptation. This chapter analyses their performance, satisfaction and the challenges – pedagogical, language, cultural – they face to deploy the appropriate strategies to reduce failure and drop-out. Results show that the first 2 years are key for they adaptation. Language is the main barrier, it seems that the time devoted prior to their universities studies and their integration with national students is still a pending task.

Keywords: Chinese students; Business School; satisfaction; performance; Europe; challenges

Introduction

International education is one of the largest and fastest growing economic sectors in the world. Asian countries, especially China and India, constitute the main source of international students (Daller & Wang, 2017). According to the Ministry of Education in China, the total number of students taking university studies

---

Global Perspectives on Recruiting International Students: Challenges and Opportunities, 173–186
Copyright © 2021 by Emerald Publishing Limited
All rights of reproduction in any form reserved
doi:10.1108/978-1-83982-518-720211011

174   Marta Melguizo-Garde and Ana Yetano

abroad was 662,100 in 2018 (a number that increases more than 11% per year).[1] These students are degree-seeking ones, by contrast to exchange program students that spend a year or a semester abroad. Attracting the best international students has become a large and growing global export opportunity, while their countries normally hope that these students will return home to contribute to their home economy (Chao, 2015).

Spain is amongst the major exporters of education worldwide along with countries greater in size and population, such as the United States, Canada, Australia and Great Britain (Grasset & García-Menéndez, 2018). Moreover, from 2002 till 2019, there has been a 250% increase in foreign students in Spain (see Table 1). Besides the importance of the figures, it is worth pointing out Spain has 5% of foreign students, a percentage that is below those of other EU 27 countries, such as Germany (23%) and France (17%), creating room for improvement as well as the need for developing the appropriate strategies in order to attract international students while securing their success.[2]

According to official statistics, the greatest number of study visas issued by Spain are for Chinese students, followed by students from the United States, Colombia, Ecuador and other Latin-American countries (see Table 1). Amongst those study visas, during recent years, the greatest increase has been for university studies (both at public and private institutions). According to ICEX in 2019,[3] 8,068 Chinese students decided to do their graduate studies in Spain. According to the Spanish Ministry of Education,[4] these students mainly choose Business studies, Spanish studies or Tourism, and the reason for choosing Spain not only is its culture but also the potential that Spanish has as a language, being the 4th most spoken language in the world (1st English, 2nd Chinese and 3rd Hindi[5]). As a result, Chinese students not only represent an important number of current students but also mean a population with a great potential to increase the number of international students in Spain.

In addition, of the importance of the culture and the language, it should be recognised that in 2017, the Chinese and Spanish governments signed an agreement of mutual recognition of Diplomas, and that additionally the access to the graduate programs changed in 2014, allowing non-Spanish students access to a university without a prior content evaluation. Now, they only requirement needed is to finish high school studies to have access to a University. This access structure (general agreement) is accompanied by the good perspectives of the Latin-American markets

---

[1]http://edu.sina.com.cn/a/2019-03-28/doc-ihtxyzsm1115517.shtml. Accessed on July 26, 2020.

[2]Own elaboration with data from Eurostat for the last year published in July 2020 (year 2018).

[3]https://www.icex.es/icex/es/Navegacion-zona-contacto/revista-el-exportador/mercados/REP2019812478.html. Accessed on July 24, 2019.

[4]http://www.educacionyfp.gob.es/china/publicaciones-materiales/publicaciones.html. Accessed on July 25, 2020.

[5]Ethnologue 2019, 23rd Edition. https://www.ethnologue.com/guides/ethnologue200

Are Chinese Students Studying at European Universities Satisfied? 175

Table 1. Foreign Students Studying in Spain and the Countries of Origin.

Year	Total	China		USA		Colombia		Ecuador		México		Perú		Marruecos	
2019	59,275	8,068	14%	6,754	11%	4,983	8%	3,375	6%	2,854	5%	2,781	5%	2,664	4%
2018	56,951	8,445	15%	6,850	12%	4,540	8%	3,545	6%	2,913	5%	2,371	4%	1,846	3%
2017	55,953	8,604	15%	6,435	12%	4,131	7%	3,658	7%	2,953	5%	2,380	4%	1,800	3%
2016	54,739	8,152	15%	6,308	12%	4,191	8%	3,362	6%	3,178	6%	2,001	4%	1,742	3%
2015	49,669	6,444	13%	5,629	11%	3,975	8%	2,853	6%	3,325	7%	1,949	4%	1,614	3%
2014	49,053	6,254	13%	5,345	11%	3,789	8%	2,168	4%	3,184	6%	1,879	4%	1,798	4%
2013	44,519	5,713	13%	4,685	11%	3,876	9%	1,725	4%	2,918	7%	1,846	4%	1,856	4%
2012	42,864	3,985	9%	4,074	10%	4,177	10%	1,456	3%	3,484	8%	1,702	4%	1,773	4%
2011	51,804	4,176	8%	7,371	14%	5,403	10%	1,266	2%	5,126	10%	2,230	4%	1,473	3%
2010	46,914	4,018	9%	4,588	10%	5,434	12%	853	2%	4,506	10%	2,419	5%	1,827	4%
2009	44,465	3,485	8%	3,962	9%	4,988	11%	606	1%	4,919	11%	2,227	5%	2,593	6%
2008	41,829	2,500	6%	3,272	8%	4,799	11%	535	1%	5,272	13%	2,129	5%	2,678	6%
2007	39,974	1,625	4%	2,840	7%	4,598	12%	557	1%	5,618	14%	2,177	5%	3,245	8%
2006	33,267	908	3%	2,455	7%	3,605	11%	564	2%	5,261	16%	1,808	5%	2,257	7%
2005	30,640	724	2%	2,183	7%	3,077	10%	605	2%	5,468	18%	1,383	5%	2,289	7%
2004	35,545	938	3%	2,407	7%	4,113	12%	598	2%	6,410	18%	1,454	4%	3,374	9%
2003	30,253	647	2%	1,933	6%	3,797	13%	451	1%	4,778	16%	1,115	4%	3,015	10%
2002	23,737	395	2%	1,591	7%	2,812	12%	341	1%	3,728	16%	832	4%	2,250	9%

Source: Own elaboration with data from the Spanish Immigration web.[6]

[6] http://extranjeros.mitramiss.gob.es/es/Estadisticas/operaciones/con-autorizacion/index.html. Accessed on July 24, 2020.

176   Marta Melguizo-Garde and Ana Yetano

(where Spanish is a key language). Furthermore, other factors are important such as general safety, as being part of the EU, the climate, as having good diplomatic and commercial relationships, and as having a lower cost of living than in countries such as the United Kingdom or the United States. The majority of families who are sending their children abroad to study belong to the country's burgeoning middle class (general employees and middle managers or entrepreneurs). The Ministry of Education in China indicates that 90% of the Chinese students pay for their studies abroad.[7] Most of them are representative of a generation of the Chinese single children, they are expected to be winners (Zhao, 2019), so their parents search abroad for the opportunities to study what they have not had at Chinese universities, searching for affordable options. It should be highlighted that around 250,000 Chinese students do not qualify in the university access exam (Gaokao) to study in China[8] and that in the case of 65% of these students, the decision of country, program and/or university is made by the parents (Bodycott & Lai, 2012).

The aim of this work is to analyse the performance, the challenges and the satisfaction of Chinese students in a Spanish School of Economics and Business. This will serve as a measure of the academic and internationalisation policy success and to give directions for future improvements. Economics and Business studies were chosen because, as it has been argued, for Chinese students business studies are their preferred field of study (28% of Chinese students studying abroad choose them) (Chao, 2015). For doing so, we will analyse the characteristics of these students, main barriers found by them, their academic performance and their levels of satisfaction. This will allow us to identify the main difficulties they are having, their impact in internationalisation policies, as well as, to identify areas of improvement to overcome their main difficulties. The statistical and qualitative analysis shows that Chinese international students have difficulties in their adaptation to the Spanish learning environment and campus life. The language barrier is the most important one.

The rest of the chapter is structured as follows. First, the School of Economics and Business environment is presented. Then, the challenges faced by Chinese students identified by previous studies are analysed. Methodology and analysis of results are the next sections. The chapter ends with the conclusions drawn from this work.

Chinese Students at Business and Economics Schools in Spain: The Case of the University of Zaragoza

Zaragoza is considered a medium size city, in European terms (600,000 inhabitants), with short distances and easiness to find accommodation. The School of Economics and Business (named *Facultad de Economía y Empresa*-FECEM) has

---

[7]http://edu.sina.com.cn/a/2019-03-28/doc-ihtxyzsm1115517.shtml. Accessed on July 26, 2020.

[8]https://www.icex.es/icex/es/Navegacion-zona-contacto/revista-el-exportador/mercados/REP2019812478.html. Accessed on July 24, 2019.

a long research tradition and exchange experience, with around 160 incoming and 170 outgoing students every year for yearly programs, such as Erasmus students but also from programs with Latin America, North America, Oceania and other Asian countries. Not surprisingly, exchange students consider their experience in Zaragoza quite satisfying. However, in order to continuously create enriching experiences for foreign students, it is necessary to analyse their experiences considering the particularities of each group. Thus, this research focusses on Chinese students' performance and satisfaction and links up with other with prior studies of Chinese students in other countries (Bartlett, Han, & Bartlett, 2018; Henze & Zhu, 2012; Mazzarol, Soutar, Smart, & Choo, 2001) and with Spanish language teaching in Spain (Pérez Milans, 2006).

The FECEM takes part in a strategy for the whole University to attract Chinese students, as almost any university around the globe. However, this strategy is far younger at the University of Zaragoza than those in the United Kingdom and Australia. In addition, the environment of the Chinese community studying in Spanish universities (at least in the public ones) is different to those of the United Kingdom or Australia. As show by Doe, Lyden, Jaikaran-Doe, and Wang (2018), the Chinese make a significant contribution to the income stream of higher education institutions in Australia and, in some classes, there are more international students than local students. By contrast at the FECEM the percentage of Chinese students is quite low and in the maximum number of 80 students per class the percentage is required to be lower than 15. The FECEM has around 800 new students every year and most of them are national, from the region or the closest regions.

The first students came to the FECEM during the academic year 2013–2014, with two students of the Bachelor in Economics. However, in 2019–2020, there were already 34 new students: 12 for the Bachelor in Economics, 9 for the Bachelor in Business Administration, 10 for the Bachelor in Finance and Accounting and 3 for the Bachelor in Market and Marketing Research. Since then, there has been a slow but continuous increase. However, an important number dropped out during the first 2 years, the main reason being not having passed any course or just one (see below in the analysis of results). Most Chinese students are degree-seeking students, and their mobility has differences with year exchange programs, such as the duration and the lack of grants.

At the FECEM, many Chinese students came under a program named 'X+1', specifically designed for them due to pre-established agreements with Chinese Universities. This program accepts students that carry out a year of studies in China, recognising part of the courses done in China due to a prior agreement of recognition. The ECTS (European Credits Transfer System) recognised are between 30 and 40 ECTS (out of the 240 ECTS of a Bachelor program), depending on the studies done previously in China and the agreement with FECEM. In China, they study Spanish, English and certain Business courses. In their first year at FECEM, they continue to study Spanish in order to reach the B1 language level required to be enrolled at the FECEM, and at the same time do two courses of their chosen undergraduate program. In the second year, they enrol full-time on their undergraduate program that should last 4 years. As will be shown, performance during their first and second year is not satisfactory, creating dropouts. Understanding the potential reasons for the high initial failure rate for students and implementing appropriate support structures are important strategies towards ensuring the wellbeing of international students transitioning to Spanish and the longevity of the programs X+1. Therefore, the characteristics of the FECEM creates a perfect setting to study the challenges Chinese students and deploy an appropriate strategy and avoid the future failures of others.

Chinese Students: Their Challenges and Satisfaction

Education is a top priority for Chinese families. As a result of the economic achievement of the country and the small nuclear family size due to the one child policy in place during many years, sending children abroad to study at international universities has become an affordable and desired expense (Chao, 2015; Liu, 2016; Yan, 2015). Additionally, other drawbacks in the Chinese educational system, such as corruption and briberies make many Chinese parents believe that to send their kids abroad for their university studies is better for their future (Chao, 2015; Liu, 2016; Yan, 2015). As the number of Chinese students studying in western universities has been increasing every year, both students and university teachers of host universities have faced challenges that require attention to understand how to deal with and ease the problems these students encounter (Bordovskaia, Anderson, Bochkina, & Petanova, 2018; Doe et al., 2018). To better identify effective ways to serve this population is not only an educational strategy, but also an international trade strategy (Chao,2015).

Despite the importance given to moving from China to Western countries, it is not in fact an easy move for students. Once they move to Western countries to study, they will face language, personal, psychological, pedagogical, organisational and cultural factors that will influence their success (Bamford, 2008; Bordovskaia et al., 2018; Doe et al., 2018; Gu, 2011). In the following lines, general problems, rather than individual ones, are discussed, as well as the importance of paying attention to satisfaction levels.

Pedagogical

The first thing to consider is the problem related with the academic adaptation. A problem faced by Chinese students studying in Western universities is the difference in the forms and requirements of instruction, the norms and methods of pedagogical interaction in a new socio-cultural environment (Bordovskaia et al., 2018). The educational principles are an important first difference, Chinese education is deeply imbued with traditional Confucian values and norms of interaction. In this model, a key factor is the emphasis on education as a means of conveying the cultural tradition and a hierarchical relationship. By contrast, Western education is focussed on autonomy in learning, critical thinking and participation in critical discussions (Bordovskaia et al., 2018; Doe et al., 2018; Wong, 2004). From the start in China, students are expected to be passive learners, in an environment where attendance is mandated. In addition, students learn to respect their academics and not to question the validity of their teachings (Doe et al., 2018).

Chinese universities typically follow more of a parent-child relationship between the teacher and student (Wong, 2004). As shown by Doe et al. (2018), the challenge for academics is to prepare these students for the very different student-centred teaching and learning style they encounter when transferring to a Western model.

Language

Chinese students enter a new linguistic environment with a level of language that may not be the one required for the university environment. Often, they do not have the level of linguistic understanding to comprehend all the academic information of their university subjects (Bordovskaia et al., 2018; Doe et al., 2018; Gao, 2005). As noted in studies of English speaking countries, being able to speak and understand the language of instruction becomes a major concern for them at the majority of the host institutions (Daller & Wang, 2017). Similarly, as argued by Doe et al. (2018) academics have problems in engaging Chinese students because most of them are not able to understand what is being said in class. Teaching methods can also affect or increase language problems. Many Chinese students may be able to follow lectures when notes are posted in advance, others may try to use a cell phone to translate technical terms while the lecturer is speaking (Doe et al., 2018) but debates and discussions are more difficult to follow for them. Moreover, university lecturers noticed that a large number of international students are unable to understand many learning and teaching activities even if they have passed the required language ability test (Daller & Wang, 2017). It has been found that students learn to pass language tests rather than learning to use the language itself. Thus, alternative test formats have been claimed to increase their success with communication skills (Daller & Wang, 2017).

Cultural Adaptation

The third problem is related with the cultural adaptation, as it has been termed 'cultural shock' or 'acculturative stress' (Berry, 2005; Bordovskaia et al., 2018). Berry (2005) indicates that 'acculturative stress' refers to the interaction between two cultures that produces a stress phenomenon. As noted by Bordovskaia et al. (2018), there is dynamic interplay when the intercultural encounter takes place, which has been shown by several studies of the socio-cultural adaptation of Chinese students. Doe et al. (2018) show that two-thirds of Chinese students have experienced loneliness and/or isolation, especially during the initial stage. Similarly, Spencer-Oatey, Dauber, Jing, and Lifei (2017) found that Chinese students were dissatisfied with their friendships and that they have challenges when socialising with students of other nationalities.

Satisfaction

Satisfaction and loyalty towards the higher education institutions and/or their academic studies are key elements of education research (Subrahmanyam & Raja Shekhar, 2017), considering current students and graduates (Borraz-Mora, Hernandez-Ortega, & Melguizo-Garde, 2019; Doña & Luque, 2020). Both satisfaction and loyalty are even more important when paying attention to the Chinese degree-seeking students and the problems they face. Student satisfaction improves the institution reputation and attracts more students (Espinoza, González, McGinn, Castillo, & Sandoval, 2019), which, as has been argued, is a key goal of universities with regard the Chinese degree-seeking students.

Methodology

For the purpose of the study, two sources of information have been used. On the one hand, the performance of the Chinese students enrolled in the FECEM of the program X+1 is analysed. Taking into account the year of enrolment, the length of their studies or when they drop-out. Additionally, the number of ECTS pass before dropping out have been considered. Chinese enrolled on the program X+1, during the first year, are focussed on continuing studying Spanish and they need to pass 12 ECTS, but later, the normal workload is of 60 ECTS per year. On the other hand, a questionnaire has been carried out on all the Chinese students enrolled at the FECEM during the course 2019–2020 (entering though the program X+1 or general agreement). The objective of the questionnaire was to analyse their satisfaction and the main challenges they face.

The questionnaire was answered in 2019 by 35 students out of 65, this represents a response rate of 54%, 20 (57%) were women and 15 (43%) were men. In order not to have language problems with the responses, the questionnaire was given both in Spanish and Chinese.

Analysis of Results

Who Are the Chinese Students at FECEM?

At the beginning of the academic year 2019–2020, there were 65 Chinese students enrolled at the FECEM, 38 (58%) were women and 27 (42%) men. Of those 65 Chinese students, 45 (70%) came under the program X+1 agreements with several Chinese universities and 20 (30%) came under the Spanish general agreement of access to the university. It is important to highlight that while the program X+1 requires a B1 level of Spanish and to take some courses, the general agreement does not require any prior level or course. It also should be highlighted that while the program X+1 has a specific agreement to be enrolled guaranteeing their access if they pass the exam. The general agreement students should compete with national students. Table 2 shows that the distribution of students amongst the different Bachelor programs is quite similar, except for MMR. For the analysis of the performance, we will focus on the program X+1 students that represent the main way of entrance of Chinese students and have a more traceable record.

Performance of the Program X+1 Students

Table 3 shows the dropouts of the students under the program X+1 from 2013/14 till 2019/2020, without considering the 15 new students of the last year because they have no possibility of dropping out yet . A total of 84 students have been enrolled at SEB under the program X+1, 62% of which have dropped out of their

Table 2. Distribution of Students by Bachelor Programs and Origin.

	BAM		ECO		FIAcc		MMR	
	N	*%*	*N*	*%*	*N*	*%*	*N*	*%*
Total Chinese students	**18**	**28**	**21**	**32**	**17**	**26**	**9**	**14**
General agreements	1	2	9	14	8	12	2	3
Answers to the questionnaire	–		4	11	4	11	–	
Program X+1 agreements	17	26	12	18	9	14	7	11
Answers to the questionnaire	7	20	10	29	5	14	5	14

Source: Own elaboration. BAM (Business Administration and Management), ECO (Economics), FIAcc (Finance and Accounting) and MMR (Marketing and Market Research).

studies. This was usually done during the first 2 years as a consequence of not being able to pass more than 12 ECTS, in most cases they passed 6 or 0. Only 1 student of 2013/2014, 1 of 2014/2015 and 1 of 2015/2016 have finished their studies. It took them 5 years, one year more than planned, besides they have already recognised around 30 ECTS. Drop-out rates seem lower for the year 2018/2019 due to the time that it takes from the moment they enrol for the first time until dropping out which is usually 2 years.

Performance of the students that continue show that once they are able to pass the first 2 years their performance increases, nevertheless, except for the first year (2013/2014), the pace is quite slow (Table 4). It should be also highlighted that there are important differences amongst students and the variance is quite high. Additionally, it should be pointed out that performance seems to be improving for the students that have enrolled during the last 2 years, once the language requirement level was in place.

Questionnaire to Chinese Students

Spanish Language Learning and Use. For all the students surveyed, Chinese is their mother tongue. Surprisingly, given the big differences between Spanish and Chinese, 17 (49%) have studied Spanish for a short period of time before

Table 3. Program X+1 Drop-out Rates.

	2013/14		2014/2015		2015/2016		2016/2017		2017/2018		2018/2019		TOTAL	
	N	*%*	*N*	*%*	*N*	*%*	*N*	*%*	*N*	*%*	*N*	*%*	*N*	*%*
	2		17		22		19		5		19		84	
Drop-out	1	50	14	82	17	77	14	74	3	60	3	16	52	62
Continue			2	12	4	18	5	26	2	40	16	84	29	34
Finishes	1	50	1	6	1	5							3	4

Source: Own elaboration.

182 Marta Melguizo-Garde and Ana Yetano

Table 4. Performance of Continuing Students Globally and Per Year of Enrolment.

	2013/ 2014	2014/ 2015	2015/ 2016	2016/ 2017	2017/ 2018	2018/ 2019	2019/ 2020
Average of credits after the first year	12	4	9.6	2.4	9	18	17.2
Average of credits after the second year	48	20	26.4	18	51	52.5	
Increase	36	16	16.8	15.6	42	34.5	
Average of credits after the third year	90	50	48	40.8	87		
Increase	42	30	21.6	22.8	36		
Average of credits after the fourth year	143	88	82.8	71.8			
Increase	53	38	34.8	31			

Source: Own elaboration.

coming to Spain (a year in 88% of the cases) and 10 (29%) have started studying Spanish once they have enrolled at the University. The rest have started months later after coming to Spain: these do not belong to the program X+1. Since they arrived in Spain, most of them have been living in Zaragoza, the majority, 23 (66%), live only with other Chinese students. The other students are equally divided between those that live only with Spanish and those that live with Spanish and Chinese. Not surprisingly, five of those that live with Spanish roommates use Spanish rather than Chinese more time. Of those that use equally Chinese and Spanish, the majority live with other Chinese. Finally, 22 (60%) use Chinese more than Spanish. It should be highlighted that 7 (20%) indicate they use Spanish less than 21% of the day and one says that he hardly uses Spanish. The level of Spanish use is highly related to their level of integration.

Regarding Spanish most of them indicate having a medium level. Only one of them affirms having a high level of Spanish in all the competences except speaking (where a medium level is declared). The speaking competence is the most difficult part (37% indicate a low level of speaking). By contrast, they find reading the easiest competence. In fact, only one declares a low level of reading (a student that indicates a low level for all the competences) and nine consider their reading skills high. Results for listening are slightly lower than for reading. Despite the apparently low level of Spanish language only 27 (77%) continue with Spanish language courses. Most of them (56%) study at least 2 hours per week, and the rest around 1 hour.

Teaching Methods and Learning Habits. Regarding study habits, 9 students (26%) claim that they only study in Chinese, 18 (51%) do it only in Spanish and the rest study combining both languages. All of them use institutional mail to check university news. Additionally, they informed us that they use their own social networks like WeChat instead of WhatsApp, which is used most commonly by Spanish students, so this aspect creates certain difficulties to establish a communication channel amongst all the students. This includes taking part in group tasks with Spanish students, a difficulty that has been highlighted by some of them. They make up a strong community, and they highlight that they are always helped by other Chinese students when dealing with paperwork.

Considering the greater difficulties of the Bachelor program, 12 of them indicate that they understand the lecturer. There are three that add that difficulties come when the vocabulary is quite specific and three that indicate that it is more difficult when there are no notes nor a PowerPoint to follow. They usually prefer analytical courses and practical classes.

Satisfaction and Loyalty

Chinese students were asked to rate whether they were satisfied with their degree and whether it was meeting their expectations. Both questions gave an average of 8.5 out of 10. Regarding loyalty, Chinese students were asked if they would choose the same studies again, whether they would recommend them to other Chinese colleagues, or whether they would speak positively of the degree to his/her friends and acquaintances. The average attained for the three statements was 9.5 out of 10. In the open questions, it was indicated that recommending the university was due to reasons such as the good educational level, the polite attention of the lecturers, the affordable cost of living and the importance of Spanish.

Conclusions

The aim of this chapter was to analyse the satisfaction, the performance of and the aspects Chinese students face when entering a Spanish university, and to deploy the appropriate strategies to increase their numbers by making a more friendly environment. The most important barrier is the language, as has been indicated by them. As found in prior studies, their background in Spanish is usually not longer than a year. This fact creates difficulties to have the appropriate knowledge for academic learning. It should be noted that while Chinese students of the program X+1 are required to have a B1 level, the Erasmus program recommends a B2 level for successful mobility. In fact, the B1 level requirement was implemented only 2 years ago, to highlight the importance of the required language level and to increase their performance. Another measure to confront the language problems is the recommendation to the students to participate as listeners while they are taking the Spanish courses, so they can start to learn the technical Spanish required for their undergraduate studies. Some Chinese students have been following this recommendation during the last year, so during the following year, we will be able to see the effects. Moreover, initially Law and Economic History where the recommended courses for the first year and now they are mathematical and accounting courses. This may have influenced in the performance of the students enrolled in 2018/2019, only 15% have dropped out, and of those that

184   Marta Melguizo-Garde and Ana Yetano

continue, all except one have passed at least 30 ECTS. This fact confirms that the first strategy should be oriented towards language improvement and to enforce certain levels of language acquisition. In addition to the measures implemented, it has been recommended to implement Business Spanish courses in additional to the general Spanish courses. Given the performance of the last 2 years (to be analysed again in the future), the language requirement level seems to have also discouraged those students with lower levels to move to other possible universities. Moreover, the increase in the demand for study visas, which are renovated every year, also suggests that the students remain in Spain for more time.

Language problems are highly related with socialisation problems. As it has been shown, many Chinese students tend to isolate themselves within the Chinese community. This considerably reduces the use of Spanish during the day, making it more difficult to achieve proficiency. University housing services and agencies should make an effort to guarantee that their roommates are not only Chinese and that, if possible, there are Spanish roommates too. At this point, the University has a program that helps Chinese students to find a Spanish family for their first 6 months, but some additional effort is needed after this period to avoid the easiness of moving into flats with only Chinese students, which is the most common behaviour.

The strength of the Chinese community confirms (Zhao, 2019) findings, regarding the strength of their national identity, and even the increase of it, when studying abroad. However, it is a double-edged sword. On the one hand, it helps them with isolation problems, it aids them to know how to cope with paperwork and daily living problems. In fact, as the satisfaction and loyalty analysis has shown, they feel positive about their selection of studies and would recommend them. On the other hand, it slows down their Spanish learning and their integration into the FECEM community. Thus, to increase the socialisation of students, it is necessary to involve them with other students aside of the Chinese community and in the activities of the FECEM. In order to do this, communication amongst students is crucial. Nevertheless, to have proper communication, a main strategy needs to be adopted. Institutional mailing could be used as the official channel, but this should be complemented by contacting Chinese representatives to disseminate the important information using their own social networks. Additionally, a Spanish representative should act as connection with the Chinese students, to be able to plan activities together. In fact, contacting the representative of Chinese students was the most effective channel to obtain responses for the questionnaire. This effectiveness should be an opportunity to also connect representatives of both communities of students. These two sides of the coin should be balanced, the strong community may help with cultural and even language problems, so it should be valued, and their link with the FECEM community, a pending task, may help them with socialisation issues. Another possibility would be to encourage language conversation exchange programs where non-university students who are learning Chinese in government programs or at local academies are put into contact with these Chinese students. This would give them more chance to improve their fluency.

Seminars with Chinese students and problem-solving sessions can be a useful way to integrate them too. The decision-making considerations Chinese students choose for studying at the FECEM is an interesting topic for educators and researchers to explore. It is a topic that could be an icebreaker for these seminars and to improve the knowledge of their challenges. A buddy program like those of exchange programs could facilitate the link between the Chinese community and the Spanish students. At this point, the FECEM has implemented tutoring and mentor programs. The former involves a lecture that aims to facilitate the paperwork, organisation and teaching problems of these students, especially during the first year. The latter is a Chinese student already enrolled on his fourth year who can also help with doubts that they may feel uncomfortable asking a Spanish lecturer about.

Results have also shown commonalities with prior studies regarding the teaching methods. Chinese students do not feel the high hierarchy of the Chinese educational systems, and they see it as positive because it allows them to feel freer to make questions. Nevertheless, their prior background also emerges, as they do not feel confident with critical thinking and problems with different solutions.

The study of the performance and challenges of the Chinese community at the FECEM has confirmed the language, cultural and pedagogical problems that arise when they come to Western universities. Nevertheless, the existence of a small community has allowed the FECEM to implement measures that little by little help them to cope with these challenges. The increase in the language level required, the tutor and mentor programs and the adaptation of the courses to be taken on the first year are almost cost-free measures for a small community that improves performance. In future years, additional measures taken will be analysed to see whether they also increase performance. It should be highlighted that measures should be taken during the first 2 years, as they are critical to guaranteeing the success of the students and his/her satisfaction. As shown by He and Hutson (2018) revisit existing orientation, first-year, and intensive language programs designed for international students are key for success. Measures that, with a small community, are easier to implement and less costly.

References

Bamford, J. (2008). Strategies for the improvement of international students' academic and cultural experiences of studying in the UK. *Hospitality, Leisure, Sport and Tourism Network: Enchancing Series: Internationalisation*, November 2008 (pp. 1–10).

Bartlett, M. E., Han, W., & Bartlett, J. E. (2018). Perceptions of mainland Chinese students toward obtaining higher education in the United States. *Journal of International Students, 8*(2), 623–637. doi:10.5281/zenodo.1249045

Berry, J. W. (2005). Acculturation: Living successfully in two cultures. *International Journal of Intercultural Relations, 29*(6 SPEC. ISS.), 697–712. doi:10.1016/j.ijintrel.2005.07.013

Bodycott, P., & Lai, A. (2012). The influence and implications of Chinese culture in the decision to undertake cross-border higher education. *Journal of Studies in International Education, 16*(3), 252–270. doi:10.1177/1028315311418517

Bordovskaia, N. V., Anderson, C., Bochkina, N., & Petanova, E. I. (2018). The adaptive capabilities of Chinese students studying in Chinese, British and Russian Universities. *International Journal of Higher Education, 7*(4), 1. doi:10.5430/ijhe.v7n4p1

Borraz-Mora, J., Hernandez-Ortega, B., & Melguizo-Garde, M. (2020). The influence of generic-academic competences on satisfaction and loyalty: The view of two key actors in higher education. *Journal of Higher Education Policy and Management*, *42*(5), 563–578. doi:10.1080/1360080X.2019.1689802

Chao, C. (2015). Decision making for Chinese students to receive their higher education in the U.S. *International Journal of Higher Education*, *5*(1), 28–37. doi:10.5430/ijhe.v5n1p28

Daller, M., & Wang, Y. (2017). Predicting study success of international students at English-speaking universities. *Applied Linguistic Review*, *8*(4), 355–374.

Doe, P. E., Lyden, S., Jaikaran-Doe, S., & Wang, X. (2018). Enhancing Chinese Students' learning in an Australian 2+2 Undergraduate Engineering Program. *International Journal of Higher Education*, *7*(5), 86. doi:10.5430/ijhe.v7n5p86

Doña, L., & Luque, T. (2020). How loyal can a graduate ever be? The influence of motivation and employment on student loyalty. *Studies in Higher Education*, *45*(2), 353–374. doi:10.1080/03075079.2018.1532987

Espinoza, O., González, L. E., McGinn, N., Castillo, D., & Sandoval, L. (2019). Factors that affect post-graduation satisfaction of Chilean university students. *Studies in Higher Education*, *44*(6), 1023–1038. doi:10.1080/03075079.2017.1407306

Gao, X. (2005). A tale of two mainland Chinese learners. *Asian EFL Journal*, *7*(2), 1–20.

Grasset, C., & García-Menéndez, B. (2018). *The economic impact of international students in Spain*. Spain Education Programs. Retrieved from http://www.spaineduprograms.es/wp-content/uploads/Economic-Impact-of-International-Students-in-Spain-2018-FINAL.pdf

Gu, Q. (2011). An emotional journey of change: The case of Chinese students in UK higher education. In L. Jin & M. Cortazzi (Eds.), *Researching Chinese learners*. London: Palgrave Macmillan. doi:10.1057/9780230299481_10

He, Y., & Hutson, B. (2018). Exploring and leveraging Chinese international students' strengths for success. *Journal of International Students*, *8*(1), 87–108. doi:10.5281/zenodo.1101037

Henze, J., & Zhu, J. (2012). Current research on Chinese students studying abroad. *Research in Comparative and International Education*, *7*(1), 90–104. doi:10.2304/rcie.2012.7.1.90

Liu, W. (2016). The international mobility of Chinese students: A cultural perspective. *Canadian Journal of Higher Education*, *46*(4), 41–59.

Mazzarol, T., Soutar, G., Smart, D., & Choo, S. (2001). Perceptions, information and choice: Understanding how Chinese students select a country for overseas study. In *Australian Education International* (June 2014). Canberra: Australian Education International Department of Education, Training and Youth Affairs.

Pérez Milans, M. (2006). Spanish education and Chinese immigrants in a new multicultural context: Cross-cultural and interactive perspectives in the study of language teaching methods. *Journal of Multicultural Discourses*, *1*(1), 60–85. doi:10.1080/10382040608668532

Spencer-Oatey, H., Dauber, D., Jing, J., & Lifei, W. (2017). Chinese students' social integration into the university community: Hearing the students' voices. *Higher Education*, *74*(5), 739–756. doi:10.1007/s10734-016-0074-0

Subrahmanyam, A., & Raja Shekhar, B. (2017). Where do you find loyalty in the contemporary university scene? *Journal of Applied Research in Higher Education*, *9*(3), 378–393. doi:10.1108/JARHE-01-2016-0004

Wong, J. K. K. (2004). Are the learning styles of Asian international students culturally or contextually based? *International Education Journal*, *4*(4), 154–166.

Yan, A. (2015). Why Chinese parents are sending their children abroad to study at a younger age | South China Morning Post. *Scmp*. Retrieved from http://www.scmp.com/news/china/article/1747075/why-mainland-parents-are-sending-their-children-abroad-study-younger-age

Zhao, K. (2019). Made in contemporary China: Exploring the national identity of Chinese international undergraduate students in the US. *Studies in Higher Education*, *0*(0), 1–13. doi:10.1080/03075079.2019.1615046

Chapter 12

How to Integrate International Students into the Local Society and How That Will Affect Their Satisfaction Level

Janet M. Howes

Abstract

International students face challenges when they attend a university outside their home country. Some of those challenges can be language barriers, expectations of professors, university rules and living situation. All of these can add strain to an already stressful situation of studying abroad. Student integration into a local society can offset some of the anxiety of studying overseas (Mattis, 2019). Students who have made friends are comfortable living within the locale in which they are studying and have reported more satisfaction than those students who have not integrated into a local society (Fischer, 2012).

This chapter will study the ways in which students should work to integrate themselves into the local society and how the university and professors can help international students find a way to become familiar and content within the local society. Learning the regional language, culture and social activities help enhance the student's satisfaction.

Keywords: Activities; assignments; culture; host; international; language; local; participation; satisfaction; society; tutors; volunteers

International students face challenges when they attend a university outside their home country. Some of those challenges can be language barriers, expectations of professors, university rules and living situations. All of these can add strain to

---

Global Perspectives on Recruiting International Students: Challenges and Opportunities, 187–196
Copyright © 2021 by Emerald Publishing Limited
All rights of reproduction in any form reserved
doi:10.1108/978-1-83982-518-720211012

188   *Janet M. Howes*

an already stressful situation of studying abroad. Student integration into a local society can offset some of the anxiety of studying overseas (Mattis, 2019). Making friends helps international students feel comfortable while living and studying abroad (Fischer, 2012).

This chapter will study the ways in which students should work to integrate themselves into the local society and how the university administration and professors can help international students find a way to become familiar and content within the local community. Learning the regional language, culture and social activities help enhance the students' satisfaction.

Studying Abroad

International Education Programs have been growing steadily over the past several years. In 1975, approximately 0.8 million students studied in foreign countries. By 2012, that number rose to 4.5 million study abroad students. With the interest of students going overseas to study that number is expected to rise to 8 million students studying abroad by 2025 (Organisation for Economic Co-operation and Development, 2019; University of Oxford, 2015).

University age students both international and domestic are comfortable in studying at the university level (Hodges, 2007; Ward, 2001). Leaving family and friends is not a major stress factor as the students are looking forward to learning in a new environment. Some factors that do constitute stress for international and domestic students are educational work load, pressure to meet deadlines, and health issues (Kosheleva, Amarnor, & Chernobilsky, 2015). For students studying abroad, other stressors may apply. Learning a new language, communication skills, bicultural competency and meeting people add to the experience of studying overseas (Musgrave-Marquart, Bromley, & Dalley, 1997; Nailevna, 2017; Noh & Kaspar, 2003; Poyrazli & Grahame, 2007).

As students move on to their university education, coping mechanisms may change as they may lose some support figures. Moving away from friends and family means the students must work to create new friendships and support structures (Kosheleva et al., 2015). The friendships students make in the early weeks of their education may become the most lasting friendships with the strongest ties (Peacock & Harrison, 2009). Once arriving in the foreign country, the students must adjust to their new environment and make their way around a new city and university grounds.

International Educational Experiences

Many universities have an office or department for international studies. Some departments have study abroad programs in which students may take classes at universities in a country other than their own. These experiences can be educational and compelling for students in higher education. Through an International Studies Program or Office of International Education, students may learn about study abroad experiences by attending seminars in which former study abroad students speak about their international educational experiences or students may

How to Integrate International Students into the Local Society   **189**

attend preparation modules in which the students learn what to expect when they study in a different country.

Host Universities

Travelling can be an exciting adventure. Seeing new places, meeting new people and getting a glimpse of the culture can be exhilarating. Adding education to the itinerary for a university student may make for a stressful situation. Students must learn the new university policies, study under unfamiliar professors and work with other students whom they do not know and may not understand the local language. The host university may offset some of the stress by offering students opportunities to visit the city in which the university is located. Guided tours of the city, including local markets in which the students may shop, restaurants for dining and entertainment venues within the city help the students feel more at ease (Fischer, 2012). Ride share opportunities can be important for students to travel from place to place. Uber or Lift, taxi and bus services or bicycles are valuable for students to be able to travel about the city when they cannot reach their destination by walking. Opportunities for students to travel within the city to learn and experience the culture in which they are studying may lead to student satisfaction (Hendrickson, 2018).

Housing

Living arrangements for international students will play an important factor in the students' satisfaction. Living with local students may increase the international students' satisfaction as exposure to the local culture will offer opportunities for international students to immerse themselves within their host community (Hendrickson, 2018; Savicki, 2010). Close contact with local students and host families may establish cross cultural friendships. Host families play an important role in including international students within the familial structure (Jackson, 2009; Kudo & Simkin, 2003; Schmidt-Rinehart & Knight, 2004). Inclusive living and social occurrences may lead to a satisfying experience for the international students. Local host students can give the international students inclusive living and social occurrences which may result in positive experiences (Kim, 2001).

International students residing in dormitories should be introduced to upper level students who may act as a guide for the visiting students (Hodges, 2007). The guide would familiarise the international students to life on campus, clubs, extracurricular activities, and share some meals in the dining hall.

Professors and the Educational Experiences

Studying a subject in one university may not transfer to the same education in another university. Students who study abroad need to research the host university and courses to be sure that the information they will receive in the host university will translate to the education they will receive in their home university. Once the university and degree program are chosen, the courses which the

190   Janet M. Howes

students will attend need to be selected. Some courses may be similar to what the students would study at the home university and some courses may vary in subject matter and level of higher education.

Professors who have international students attending class could design assignments which enhance the learning experience for the visiting students. Assignments which require researching the local community or host country may help the students understand the local culture. Assignments can be general in nature such as 'research business management techniques within specific countries' to more specific assignments such as 'compare the management techniques of a company/organisation in the host country to a company/organisation in the students' home country'. Researching and presenting the information can be educational and enlightening for all students in the class and help the international student become more familiar with their chosen host country.

Having students form groups in which all students collaborate on assignments can help ease the burden of meeting other students (Rienties & Nolan, 2014). Often, students will opt to work with people they know. International students may be inclined to congregate with other international students and local students may do the same (Fischer, 2012; Mattis, 2019; Ward, 2001). International students can be placed in groups with local students in order to enable all students the chance to meet each other (Campbell, 2012; Hodges, 2007). The group will work together towards the end product. Any class discussions in which the students are encouraged to speak will enable them to voice their thoughts on topics discussed.

Having students introduce themselves and presenting information to the class expediates students in becoming familiar with each other and practicing communication and social skills. This will benefit all students by showing similarities and differences in education, culture and communication skills. Friendships between students often grow from classroom experiences (Hendrickson, 2018; Kudo & Simkin, 2003).

Assignments

An assignment which benefits all students may be a presentation of the students' home countries and cultures. This is a great way for all students to learn about each other's culture. Having discussions about the similarities and differences in culture can enlighten all students in the class.

Assignments involving interviewing a local person and visiting a local business will give the students an opportunity to venture off campus and connect them to the local community. Having students perform this assignment in teams with domestic university students may create friendships, bonding opportunities and occasions for practicing the local language.

An assignment may include finding the similarities and differences between two countries. This can be an interesting assignment for students to learn the local culture and compare it to their home culture.

Assignments which are collaborative in nature will introduce the new students to the host university course(s) and students.

Tutors

In the case where international students need extra help with class work, tutors become an essential part of the study abroad experience. Working with a multinational tutor may ease the strain of studying abroad. Working in small groups will aid students in meeting one another and finding common interests. International students who are matched with domestic students in small groups may create intercultural friendships. Volunteer tutors who offer academic assistance to students reflect openness and acceptance (Hendrickson, 2018). Campbell (2012) recommends tutoring in small groups may create dyadic relationships. Students who are tutored by a local person may find communal networks which build intercultural relationships and advance their social and communication skills.

Language Barriers

As students study in foreign countries, often the classes are taught in the host country language. Universities can help students with language barriers by offering to teach them the host country language. At some universities, students may be expected to know the official language of the host country (Kosheleva et al., 2015; Nailevna, 2017). Offering basic courses in the host country official language may aid students in understanding the spoken language and assist in communication skills (Hegarty, 2014; Mattis, 2019). Learning a new language can be a daunting task where the language of the country may not be the first language spoken by the visiting students. Professors can help international students by being open to the fact that the students may struggle with the language and it may take time for the students to express themselves. Giving assignments in which students must meet local people and practice the language may aid students in developing communication competence (Ward, 2001).

When classes are taught in the host country language, international students may struggle with communication. Often these students spend a great deal of time translating the lectures into their home language which can be stressful (Kosheleva et al., 2015; Nailevna, 2017). Taking a foreign language course before studying abroad can help improve communications skills. It may be possible to take a language course once the students are settled at the university (Scholarship Positions, 2019). Foreign language translation devices range from 50 dollars to 200 dollars. Universities can invest in translation devices for students while they are studying at the host university or students may want to purchase one before they travel to the host country (SpaceMazing, 2020).

Social Activities and Volunteer Participation

Whether on campus or off, social activities help students have a sense of belonging to a community. Social activities can include eating out with friends, listening to music, watching a film, play, dance or musical act. Physical activities may include participating in sports. These are circumstances in which students meet each other as well as getting physical exercise and socialising. Professors and

192   Janet M. Howes

administration staff can persuade students to join clubs or organisations to learn more about campus life and make friends.

On campus events run by student organisations expose students to others with similar interests. Some universities have an international student organisation which helps visiting students meet people from the host country as well as other countries and, thus, expanding the social group in which students may reside. Having on campus festivals such as an International Day which promotes cultures, religions and global topics exposes all students to other societies and customs which in turn encourage global citizenship (Hodges, 2007).

Many times social networks and international connections are built through campus club memberships where international students learn language patterns, create a sense of belonging, gain a global perspective and increase campus life satisfaction (Mittelmeier & Kennedy, 2016; Montgomery & McDowell, 2009; Neri & Ville, 2008; Toyokawa & Toyokawa, 2002). Initially, when students gather together they will cluster in groups of people with which they are familiar (Fischer, 2012; Mattis, 2019; Ward, 2001). Club leaders should work to integrate all students within the community and increase club membership by making all students feel welcome.

Ward (2001) stated study abroad students are interested and open to intercultural interactions. When joining a club, opportunities may arise in which students find themselves volunteering at events off campus within the local society. These are great opportunities for students to immerse themselves in the local community and culture. Students have found these opportunities rewarding and studies show that the local community benefits from the students valuable assistance (Hart, Sheehy-Skeffington, & Charles, 2007).

Bartram (2007) suggested that organised extracurricular activities should carry merit in the study abroad programs in order to facilitate international students' integration into the local culture. University staff and professors should endorse these organisations for all students as club membership stimulates socialisation and communication.

Collegiate and Club Sports

Playing collegiate sport is set up through the coaches recruiting students from their high schools or previous educational institutions. Often times this is done months before the students choose to attend a certain university. Collegiate sport involvement may not be available to students studying abroad. However, international students may find themselves in a position where they can ask for permission to join a collegiate team to either play on the team or simply practice with the team in order to stay in shape for their return to their home university. If permission is granted for the athlete to participate on a sport team, the athlete will have an opportunity to meet other students with similar interests and, thus, find a way to belong to a group.

In cases where student athletes are not allowed to join a team or their particular sport does not exist at the university, students may be able to set up a club sport. This is done by meeting with the Athletic Director of the university and asking for information on how to start a club sport. If a club sport exists on the campus already, it may be helpful for the student athlete to meet with the club sport coach and ask for permission to join the team while the student is studying at that university. The Athletic Director can introduce the athlete to the coach and let the relationship progress from there.

Student Satisfaction with Experiences

International study can be a challenging and rewarding experience. Students have reported satisfaction with their study abroad experiences when university administration has offered peer guides, language classes and social activities (Hendrickson, 2018; Mattis, 2019). Students who feel connected with the city in which they are studying report more satisfaction with the inclusiveness of the experience (Fischer, 2012). Involvement in the culture of the host city which includes dining, shopping and exploring the city is reported as satisfiers for international students who feel welcomed (Hendrickson, 2018).

Given the opportunity to live in campus residence halls with domestic students leads to less feelings of isolation than living on their own. Visiting students should be matched with local upper level students who will act as peer student guides. These guides are a source of companionship and extend an opportunity for international students to ask questions and get acquainted with their surroundings. Students who feel included in overall university life report satisfaction with the study abroad experience (Hodges, 2007).

Pairing local students with international students in classes creates an atmosphere for discussion and extends students the opportunity to learn language patterns and social customs. Students report being happier with their academic experiences when they are welcomed into the class (Hodges, 2007). Interaction with local tutors or multinational tutors may lead to satisfaction and potential international friendships (Hendrickson, 2018; Hodges, 2007). Tutors represent an inclusiveness which international students may need while away from friends and family. University staff should match up students early in the experience to ensure more satisfied encounters for the international students to feel included in the community and contentment with interactions with other students (Hendrickson, 2018). Positive outcomes of peer tutors include social adjustment, higher academic achievement and more satisfaction with the educational experience (Hendrickson, 2018). Students learn communication and social interaction skills (Campbell, 2012).

Basic host language courses support students in understanding the spoken language and assist in communication skills (Hegarty, 2014; Mattis, 2019). International students report confidence when they feel they have sufficient host language skills and are willing to communicate with others (Hodges, 2007).

Students who participate in social activities and sports on and off campus report higher satisfaction rates that those who do not participate (Hart et al., 2007; Ward, 2001). Clubs and social events offer students a way to build local contacts, integrate with the culture, gain confidence, make friends and creates a sense of belonging. These are sources of satisfaction for international students (Neri & Ville, 2008; Savicki, 2010; Toyokawa & Toyokawa, 2002). Off campus volunteer occasions provide students connections to local people, culture, language

194   *Janet M. Howes*

and customs. These experiences have proven to be beneficial to both the international students and local community (Hart et al., 2007; Ward, 2001). International festivals and cultural awareness days give both domestic and international students an opportunity to meet and discuss various societies and societal norms and present information on global citizenship (Hodges, 2007).

Conclusion

Studying abroad can be an exciting opportunity and educational experience for young adults. Preparing students for this opportunity takes time. Proper knowledge of the expectations may make for a better and more satisfying experience. Home universities need to properly educate the students on the culture and expectations of the host country in which they will be studying. Host universities play an important role in educating the students, making them feel welcomed and ensuring the students receive a proper education and experience.

Feeling welcomed while living on campus leads to a more satisfied experience. Students given a peer guide when they first move onto campus may have a better experience getting acquainted with the university and grounds. Living in campus dormitories offers students the chance to live amongst host country students and learn language patterns and customs. Less feelings of isolation occur when international students spend time with host country peers in residence halls.

Educational opportunities in which students work together in classrooms propose a unique prospect to meet fellow classmates and discuss theories and opinions. Classroom discussions lead to openness and students feeling welcomed. Professors can integrate their classrooms with group work and discussions where open dialogue is encouraged while helping the international students become familiar with the subject matter and feel at ease in the classroom. When needed, pairing international students with domestic or multinational tutors supports visiting students in learning language patterns, developing social skills and obtaining higher academic achievement.

Communication barriers are a source of stress for many international students. Basic host country language courses can ease the stress of communicating in a new language. Students who have a basic knowledge of the language may feel more confident which leads to satisfaction with the study abroad experience.

Social activities and sport involvement create an atmosphere of belonging which international students need while away from their friends and families. On campus clubs and off campus volunteer opportunities have positive effects on students and communities alike. These encounters may affect students long after their international education is completed. Creating a global awareness of students needs while on campus leads to satisfied students and a more fulfilling experience.

As in any travel and educational experience, knowledge of expectations helps ease the anxiety which comes from making the leap to studying in a foreign country. Administration staff, university professors and local students can help ease the stress of an international education and increase student satisfaction with the study abroad experience.

References

Bartram, B. (2007). The sociocultural needs of international students in higher education: A comparison of staff and student views. *Journal of Studies in International Education, 11*(2), 205–214. doi:10.1177/1028315306297731

Campbell, N. (2012). Promoting intercultural contact on campus: A project to connect and engage international and host students. *Journal of Studies in International Education, 16*(3), 205–227. doi: 10.1177/1028315311403936

Fischer, K. (2012). Many foreign students are friendless in the U.S., Study finds. *The Chronicle of Higher Education.* Retrieved from https://www.chronicle.com/article/Many-Foreign-Students-Find/132275

Hart, C., Sheehy-Skeffington, J., & Charles, I. (2007). *International students and local communities – A research project by HOST UK.* Hatfield: Host UK.

Hegarty, N. (2014). Where we are now – The presence and importance of international students to universities in the United States. *Journal of International Students, 4*(3), 223–235.

Hendrickson, B. (2018). Intercultural connectors: Explaining the influence of extracurricular activities and tutor programs on international student friendship network development. *International Journal of Intercultural Relations, 63*, 1–16. doi:10.1016/j.ijintrel.2017.11.002

Hodges, L. (2007). *Foreign students: Overlooked and over here.* Independent.co.uk. Retrieved from https://www.independent.co.uk/news/education/higher/foreign-students-overlooked-and-over-here-403595.html

Jackson, J. (2009). Intercultural learning on short-term sojourns. *Intercultural Education, 20*(Suppl. 1), S59–S71. doi:10.1080/14675980903370870

Kim, Y. Y. (2001). *Becoming intercultural: An integrative theory of communication and cross-cultural adaptation.* Thousand Oaks, CA; Sage Publications.

Kosheleva, E. Y, Amarnor, A. J, & Chernobilsky, E. (2015). Stress factors among international and domestic students in Russia. *Procedia – Social and Behavioral Sciences, 200*, 460–466. doi: 10.1016/j.sbspro.2015.08.096

Kudo, K., & Simkin, K. A. (2003). Intercultural friendship formation: The case of Japanese students at an Australian university. *Journal of Intercultural Studies, 24*(2), 91–114. doi:10.1080/0725686032000165351

Mattis, G. (2019). *How to improve international student's academic and cultural experiences.* QS Quacquarelli Symonds 1. Retrieved from https://www.qs.com/improve-international-students-academic-cultural-experiences/

Mittelmeier, J., & Kennedy, J. J. (2016). Adapting together: Chinese student experience and acceptance at an American university. In D. Jindal-Snape & B. Rienties (Eds.), *Multi-dimensional transitions of international students to higher education.* New Perspectives on Learning and Instruction (pp. 161–180). London: Routledge.

Montgomery, C., & McDowell, L. (2009). Social networks and the international student experience: An international community of practice? *Journal of Studies in International Education, 13*(4), 455–466. doi:10.1177/1028315308321994

Musgrave-Marquart, D., Bromley, S. P., & Dalley, M. B. (1997). Personality, academic attribution, and substance use as predictors of academic achievement in college students. *Journal of Social Behavior & Personality, 12*(2), 501–511.

Nailevna, T. A. (2017). Acculturation and psychological adjustment of foreign students (the experience of Elabuga Institute of Kazan Federal University). *Procedia – Social and Behavioral Sciences, 237*, 1173–1178.

Neri, F., & Ville, S. (2008). Social capital renewal and the academic performance of international students in Australia. *The Journal of Socio-Economics, 37*(4), 1515–1538. doi:10.1016/j.socec.2007.03.010

196 Janet M. Howes

Noh, S., & Kaspar, V. (2003). Perceived discrimination and depression: Moderating effects of coping, acculturation, and ethnic support. *American Journal of Public Health, 93*(2), 232–238. doi:10.2105/ajph.93.2.232

Organisation for Economic Co-operation and Development. (2019). oecd.org. Retrieved from https://www.oecd.org/unitedstates/

Peacock, N., & Harrison, N. (2009). "It's so much easier to go with what's easy" "mindfulness" and the discourse between home and international students in the United Kingdom. *Journal of Studies in International Education, 13*(4), 487–508. doi:10.1177/1028315308319508

Poyrazli, S., & Grahame, K. M. (2007). Barriers to adjustment: Needs of international students within a semi-urban campus community. *Journal of Instructional Psychology, 24,* 28–45.

Rienties, B., & Nolan, E. M. (2014). Understanding friendship and learning networks of international and host students using longitudinal Social Network Analysis. *International Journal of Intercultural Relations, 41,* 165–180. doi:10.1016/j.ijintrel.2013.12.003

Savicki, V. (2010). An analysis of the contact types of study abroad students: The peer cohort, the host culture and the electronic presence of the home culture in relation to readiness and outcomes. *Frontiers: The Interdisciplinary Journal of Study Abroad, 19,* 61–86.

Schmidt-Rinehart, B. C., & Knight, S. M. (2004). The homestay component of study abroad: Three perspectives. *Foreign Language Annals, 37*(2), 254–262. doi:10.1111/j.1944-9720.2004.tb02198.x

Scholarship Positions. (2019, July 1). Anxiety for International Students Living Abroad. Retrieved from https://scholarship-positions.com/anxiety-for-international-students-living-abroad/2019/07/01/

SpaceMazing. (2020, March 10). SpaceMazing.com. Retrieved from https://spacemazing.com/best-language-translator-device/

Toyokawa, T., & Toyokawa, N. (2002). Extracurricular activities and the adjustment of Asian international students: A study of Japanese students. *International Journal of Intercultural Relations, 26*(4), 363–379. doi:10.1016/S0147-1767(02)00010-X

University of Oxford. (2015). *International trends in higher education.* www.ox.ac.uk. Retrieved from https://www.ox.ac.uk/sites/files/oxford/International%20Trends%20in%20Higher%20Education%202015.pdf

Ward, C. (2001). *The impact of international students on domestic students and host institutions.* Victoria: New Zealand Ministry of Education.

Chapter 13

Living Closely Together but in Parallel - Multi-dimensional Challenges to the Integration of International Students in a Danish 'Muscle' Town.

Annette Aagaard Thuesen and Eva Mærsk

Abstract

Esbjerg is located in the Wadden Sea region and is a regional centre with approximately 72,000 inhabitants. Commercially, the city has recently ranked first amongst major Danish cities in the creation of jobs. However, in Denmark, it is mainly other cities that attract younger students, and Esbjerg has some of the same structural problems due to outmigration as Danish rural areas in general. It is, therefore, important for Esbjerg to be able to attract international students so that businesses and institutions in the region can recruit skilled employees. In this book chapter, the authors aim to reanalyse data from 10 semi-structured interviews with international students at higher education institutions in Esbjerg conducted in 2016. The authors position their empirical findings within the literature on international student integration to investigate the obstacles to international student integration into study, business and leisure life in Esbjerg and potential solutions given Esbjerg's peripheral location. The chapter, thus, aims to improve the understanding of cultural, work-related and everyday life challenges that are present in university town environments where international students study, mainly from the perspective of students.

Keywords: International student integration; housing; 'stay-home culture'; higher education; student jobs and internships; peripheral town

---

Global Perspectives on Recruiting International Students: Challenges and Opportunities, 197–213
Copyright © 2021 by Emerald Publishing Limited
All rights of reproduction in any form reserved
doi:10.1108/978-1-83982-518-720211013

198 *Annette Aagaard Thuesen and Eva Mærsk*

Living closely together but in parallel - multi-dimensional challenges to the integration of international students in a Danish 'muscle' town

Introduction

At the end of February 2020, Wadden Sea National Park held its 10th annual research meeting. Scientists from all over Denmark gathered in Esbjerg to hear about research results on the Wadden Sea area. One of the presenters discussed developments in the number of breeding birds. The birds had been monitored using systematic bird counts. The censuses showed that the number of breeding birds in the Wadden Sea is in decline. The speaker stated that it is important to know more about the conditions that make the waders come to the area and want to stay.

When one of the authors of this chapter delivered a presentation later that day about young students in the largest city in the Wadden Sea area – Esbjerg – she referred directly back to the research on waders: it is important to know more about the conditions that make *young people* want to stay in this area, just as it is important to know this information about the waders. At a recent educational conference held amongst actors with an interest in the educational field in Esbjerg, the CEO of one of the major local firms also emphasised the need to better understand young people's selection of a town in which to study for Esbjerg to be able to develop into a successful educational region.

Current statistical data on the net inflow of 20–24-year-olds in five Danish municipalities show that compared to the other major cities in Denmark, Esbjerg is losing this population segment. In 2018, the population of 20–24-year-olds in Esbjerg decreased by 243 persons (StatBank Denmark, 2019) (Table 1). This decrease was in sharp contrast to the trend in larger university towns, where the yearly net inflow of persons in this age group increased to just under 2,000 (Aalborg and Odense), just over 3,000 (Aarhus) and just under 10,000 (Copenhagen) in 2018.

Such a development creates a population gap and is of great importance for the demographic development and tax base of Esbjerg Municipality and for opportunities to ensure that there is enough manpower for the area's businesses. Consequently, measures are being taken to attract more Danish students to Esbjerg, but initiatives have also been launched to increase benefits for international students who choose to study in Esbjerg.

Just as the wadden see birds come from far away, this chapter focusses on how university towns can work to better retain *students who come from far away*. We achieve this aim by analysing interviews with international students living in Esbjerg and by answering the following questions:

What are the obstacles to international student integration into the study, business and leisure life of Esbjerg, and what are plausible solutions given Esbjerg's peripheral location?

Recruitment of International Students: Challenges and Opportunities   **199**

Table 1. Net Inflow of 20–24-Year-Olds in Five Danish Municipalities (Own Original Work-Based on StatBank Denmark, 2019)

Municipality	Net Inflow 2008	Net Inflow 2018
Copenhagen	7,058	9,024
Aarhus	1,085	3,352
Aalborg	736	1,795
Odense	701	1,693
Esbjerg	−186	−243

The chapter proceeds in the following way. First, we present international literature on the research topic. This is followed by a short context and methods section explaining the Danish and Esbjerg international student situation and the data collection procedure. Then, we present the analysis of semi-structured interviews with 10 international students. We end with a discussion and conclusions on the obstacles and solutions to improve the integration of international students in the Esbjerg region.

Obstacles Observed in the International Literature

A wide range of literature addresses the retention of students during their study period, but for regions such as Esbjerg, the retention of students in the region *after* graduation and integration in the regional job market is also important. This is of course also related to international students' experience, learning and creation of networks during their study time. We, thus, present literature from both inside and outside the classroom but exclude literature that addresses the initial recruitment of international students and the role of international agents in recruitment strategies to attract the best international students in a globalised competition. Importantly, much of the international student literature is from contexts other than Denmark, such as the United States, Australia, the United Kingdom and Canada, because of the high numbers of international students in these countries. There is also a large amount of literature focussing on students from Asian and Middle Eastern countries, as the largest number of international students come from these countries.

Insufficient Cultural Mixing and the Need for a More Responsive Study Environment Amongst Academic Faculty, Counsellors and Students

Taha and Cox (2016) investigated international student networks through a case study in a UK university. They noted that international student research has been approached from mainly two perspectives – an 'adjustment to the home context' perspective and a 'diversity'/'multicultural' perspective – with both perspectives focussing on the within-class context. They described friend and work networks, with 'work networks' referring to networks associated with study work in class.

200 Annette Aagaard Thuesen and Eva Mærsk

Taha and Cox observed Haythornthwaite's (2008, p. 185) four types of networks (work, friendship, advice and support networks) amongst international students as well as changing clusters of relationships over time. They stated that the literature shows that co-nationals (those with the same language and culture) are the first preferred network for both international students and home students when working in class, which constitutes a 'failure of cultural mixing'. In addition, Taha and Cox (2016, p. 188) identified other factors, for example, the 'programme of study and learning motives and time'. They also highlighted the existence of the so-called invisible but important outside class networks, noting, 'Only work and friendship networks were based on others in the classroom. Personal support and advice networks showed continuity with pre-existing networks' (p. 191). Overall, Taha and Cox's study indicates the importance of proactively and continuously working with integration dynamics in class.

In a study with students from Alberta, Canada, Nunes and Arthur (2013, p. 36) interviewed 16 graduate students after graduation and 'explored the transition experiences of international students living their first-year after degree completion in Canada'. Nunes and Arthur (2013) found that these students did not note the importance of networks for jobs until after they had graduated and had difficulties entering the job market. The authors wrote, 'In hindsight, they recognised the importance of building networks and work experience as soon as possible' (p. 41). Generally, the international students they interviewed emphasised a need for employers to be more open-minded and open to diversity and to try to better value their international experience or different experience. The authors also suggested that career services personnel at higher education institutions should be more focussed on graduate students and their acquisition of work experience and networks before graduation. Regarding incoming students themselves, the interviewees recommended that they should use time to become acquainted with Canadian culture and people and the work environment. One specific interviewee recommended that international students 'do more volunteer work', develop their 'English language proficiency', 'find resources and information' and 'be brave' (p. 40). Concrete suggestions from Nunes and Arthur included the establishment of a database of companies interested in hiring and workshops to help students increase their skills and build their networks. According to Nunes and Arthur, counselling services should also to some degree cover international graduate student immigration and familial aspirations. The interviewees proposed peer mentoring programmes with the involvement of current international students to help incoming students focus on learning about the language, culture and work environment (p. 42).

Arthur (2017) indicated the importance of readiness to socially integrate international students amongst academic faculty, counsellors and local students. Academic faculty can facilitate international students' adjustment to the learning environment, provide an international curriculum, react when they observe international students having difficulties thriving, and provide networking opportunities and discuss questions related to post-graduate work experience (pp. 888–889). Counsellors should be aware of the diversity of international students and help international students in relation to both cross-cultural adjustment and culture shock through culturally responsive interventions. They should also help students who are suffering from acculturation stress and who lack social support to overcome barriers to engaging in the local community (pp. 889–891). Arthur (2017, p. 891) stated that international students 'are often far more motivated for cross-cultural peer interactions than local students'. Arthur referred to Kashima and Loh (2006) when he noted that consequently, 'friendship development may occur more frequently with co-nationals or other international students than with local students'. Despite a lack of a need to socialise with others beyond one's friends and family, the positioning of international students as others, an aversion to the exploration of diversity, different cultural norms regarding active and passive learning participation, etc., local students should, according to Arthur, therefore, try not to isolate and discriminate international students academically and socially. Instead, local students should see interaction with international students as an opportunity to enhance their global knowledge locally, and opportunities on campus for interactions between international and local students should be fostered. As Arthur stated,

> Becoming an international student is more than a geographical transition; all students are international learners when they actively seek opportunities to learn from the diversity found in educational contexts. (p. 892)

Although Arthur concluded that there are many macro, family, institutional and personal processes affecting the decision to become an international student, the international study experience itself, and the decision to stay or leave after graduation, his article concentrated on reviewing literature concerning the study period. However, Arthur also concluded that the emphasis on the recruitment of international student must be coordinated with resources that create supportive academic and interpersonal experiences for international students specifically as well as for locals to move away from a 'them joining us' approach because 'all students gain from a careful preparation of the campus community, including curriculum content, pedagogical practices, and support services required for internationalization' (Arthur, 2017, p. 892). Arthur stated that 'international students are a relatively untapped source of learning about an increasingly connected and global society' (pp. 892–993).

Financial, Internship-related and Work-related Obstacles Due to a Non-responsive Labour Market

In the American context, Rubin (2014) reported that students often feel turned away by companies and institutions when trying to enter the local labour market through internships and jobs. She stated that in regions relying on international students, it is important to have specific organisations working to connect international students to internships and post-graduation employment and help international offices in their attempts to achieve the same objective. Rubin (2014, p. 33) cited a director of international programmes and services who emphasised

202   Annette Aagaard Thuesen and Eva Mærsk

that a high retention rate indicates success regarding the 'institution's level of internationalisation or level of accommodating cultural difference'. Interestingly, Rubin referred to a large survey on student retention in educational institutions, which generated responses from 480 educational professionals and 517 international students from 100 institutions; the survey showed that students mainly noted financial and internship/job-related obstacles to retention, while a large number of responses from educational professionals noted the school reputation, finances and academics.

Blackmore and Rahmini (2019) interviewed 34 Australian employers in multinational, medium and small firms and found that despite a common discourse on workforce diversity in relation to gender, cultural and linguistic capital, unconscious biases existed in recruitment practices. These biases reproduced a monocultural environment in organisations, which 'screened out' rather than included people without proper 'Western worker habitus', thus, undermining diversity and promoting specific cultural norms of the organisation. The authors described this screening out process as being based on a 'best fit' rationale. Even though the employers emphasised that graduates must be able to 'think outside of the box', 'different forms of cultural and linguistic capital were not considered to lead to innovation or new perspectives' (p. 442). Blackmore and Rahmini explained that international graduate applicants especially had difficulties being accepted into small firms due to concerns that they would not fit in and would not be ready to work with clients or in groups (p. 443). The authors stated that few international graduates were directly recruited into the most popular workplaces, and the

> [...]few who were recruited had either gone through a rigorous selection process which [...] effectively excluded most international graduates or had undertaken significant long-term strategic planning – such as returning to their home country to gain work experience, being fluent in English prior to coming to Australia, and working in jobs out of their specialism and moving horizontally and cross-nationally, thus acquiring those forms of social capital that led to achieving their desired employment destination.

Context and Methods

The Danish and Esbjerg policy context

Esbjerg developed around the harbour located in the northern part of the Wadden Sea region, first, as a fishing port and then as an export harbour for agricultural products. This development was followed by extensive offshore oil activities. Today, the Esbjerg region has succeeded in its green transition, becoming a leading town in this area, for example, through its large wind energy industry. Recently, Esbjerg was amongst the leading Danish cities in the creation of jobs (OECD, 2019).

In Esbjerg, the recruitment of international students is a responsibility that is divided between higher education institutions, which market their educational

Recruitment of International Students: Challenges and Opportunities **203**

services to international students and help with their housing situations; the municipality, which aids students in practical matters and acts as host; and businesses, which provide job and apprenticeship opportunities. At the national Danish level, international student integration is a political issue, too. Recently, a matter of national political concern has been that one-fourth of students from English-language graduate programmes have left Denmark within 2 years after completing their education and that only about one in three continue to work in Denmark after 2 years (Uddannelses- og Forskningsministeriet, 2018). The concern stems from the fact that English-speaking students receive an education and that some also receive funding from the Danish student grants and loans scheme (abbreviated 'SU' in Danish) paid by Danish taxpayers. Calculations have been made that show that the presence of international students at higher education institutions in Denmark *can* result in economic gains for Danish society. However, the so-called 'dimensioning' initiatives to reduce the number of international students at specific institutions have been especially targeted at institutions with large proportions of international students. For institutions to avoid being affected by 'dimensioning', they must show that their students manage to obtain a job.

Methods

Ten semi-structured interviews with international students were conducted from April to September 2016 as part of a larger study on young students' experience of moving to Esbjerg; in this larger study, interviews were conducted with 30 students in total (Thuesen et al., 2016, 2020). The interviews were transcribed and coded in the computer program NVivo 11 as part of writing of a previous report, which made it easy to revisit the data to write this chapter focussing only on the group of international students. The international students mainly came from other European countries. The participants did not receive any payment or gifts for their participation, and we talked to them in their own study environment, which supported the reliability of the results. The rationale for the use of a qualitative approach stemmed from our objective to gain a thorough understanding of international students' everyday challenges and goals.

Results

A Good Welcome from Higher Education Institutions and the Municipality

The international students have experienced a good reception in Esbjerg, including practical assistance for housing from higher education institutions, which have often found homes for them. This has helped make the decision to relocate easier and helped the students feel more secure:

> Yeah, that was important. When you are moving abroad and this service at the university says, "Oh, we will look for accommodation for you", then it is more okay. [...] That is an important part of saying "Okay, I'm doing it!".

204 Annette Aagaard Thuesen and Eva Mærsk

The students note that the reception from educational institutions, from both administrative staff and teachers and from the Study City of Esbjerg, which is a collaboration between the educational institutions and the Esbjerg Business Development organisation, has been good. However, some students emphasise that a more intense effort could be made in the initial days of international students' arrival, when there is an opportunity for deeper integration because everyone is in a seeking phase.

In general, the interviewees are satisfied with their opportunities to create networks at educational institutions. For example, one interviewee says,

> When I was coming [...], I was completely alone, so I was [like], "Oh, I'll never meet other people". But everyone here came with the same kind of situation, so we just met in the common areas and wanted to socialize together. So, it was not a problem in the end at all.

Another foreign student describes being impressed by the amount of introductory aid given and notes that he is not sure if Danish students receive the same help. He says,

> [...]This welcome day and this teaching [us] all the things in the university, how it works... Perhaps it is because we are foreigners and they also do this in [my country] with the foreigners, I'm not sure. But when I started university, I was eighteen, and everything was completely new, and you did not have any idea [about] what should I do, who should I talk to if I have a problem... Here, they told us exactly where to go and what to do. I think the welcome from the university is perfect; they showed us the building, [and] we had a barbeque to welcome everybody. No complaints about that, completely the opposite[...].

A third international student confirms that the international students are given substantial help from the educational institution:

> [...] Everything I manage through the university, the international office from [...] the university was guiding us all the time and helping us with all the personal matters and the guidance we were seeking.

A fourth international student similarly states that it was easy to create networks after arrival. She says,

> It was actually surprisingly easy. [...] I had really good flat mates in the house, [and] they introduced me to everyone, to their friends... And then I think my classmates are really open-minded, so I think I know enough people, and also I am attending Danish classes,

Recruitment of International Students: Challenges and Opportunities   205

and there I met some girls who I found out was living in the place where I am living, so I have a bunch of friends, and it is really nice.

Several of the foreign students mention that an app provided by the municipality, 'Esbjerg live'; the annual welcome meeting with the mayor; and the welcome pack for newcomers from Esbjerg Municipality are good resources, and some students also compare these resources to those provided in other Danish municipalities where they have lived. Regarding the municipal welcome package, one student says,

> I remember we got some free tickets for newcomers; it was pretty nice to go, like to the swimming pool and the aquarium with seals and some museums around, so it was kind of to introduce myself the city and to get an idea of what are the options.

Another aspect that students cite as beneficial but that also highlights culture differences and presents students with an initial obstacle is the variety of learning styles that international students encounter in Denmark. One student states,

> The university [...] was quite a shock for me because I am used to universities with thousands of students, and this is more familiar, and the way of education [here] is different from what I am used to because we can talk to each other, and we are working in groups, and we can talk to the teachers if we have some problems [...].

One student describes not being accustomed to taking oral exams, which involve people listening to you, while another student positively remarks on 'the way the educational system is working here in Denmark, where you have projects with the companies and every semester you have another project'.

Studying Together but Living Apart

Regarding negative aspects of the housing situation in Esbjerg, it is most often mentioned in the interviews that foreign students live by themselves, and, thus, there is a tendency for their networks including both international and Danish student to not to be particularly developed. While some interviewees do not perceive this to be particularly problematic, others note that it can be a challenge to interact with Danes and to try to learn the language.

The tendency for international students and Danish students to form their own respective networks is mentioned by an international student who, when asked, if he has succeeded in creating a network in Esbjerg, answers,

> Yeah, I think so. But mostly with international students.

However, some of the international students say that they are trying to form connections with Danes. One student attends gymnastics classes, but she has only 'accidentally' talked to someone in this context. Other students are more positive

206 *Annette Aagaard Thuesen and Eva Mærsk*

and say they interact with Danes by going to the swimming pool and by engaging in Danish teaching. Another interviewee hopes she will interact with Danes in a creative course that she has recently signed up to attend in her spare time. Nevertheless, a majority of students note the separation between Danish and foreign students, as stated in the following student's comment:

> I have Danish friends, but they are only my colleagues; we study together. They are my only Danish friends, actually. I do not have any Danish friends outside [the university]. But among international students, I have many friends, because we are living together.

One of the foreign students stands out due to her deliberate attempts to engage in the local community by establishing new sports classes in Esbjerg that she will coach; meanwhile, another student has not yet made such attempts. The following quotes illustrate their distinct approaches:

> [...] Sometimes it can be difficult to be part of a community, so I wanted to give something back, and what I did was, I started [sports] classes as an instructor [...], where I meet people. It is like fitness. I was a fitness instructor, so I just had to meet people... The fact that I try to do some work to be part of the community is what created this, that I feel some kind of belonging. Still, I think that me not speaking Danish is a barrier, not that everybody speaks Danish [...], but I still feel that this language barrier somehow exists for me to be a fully accepted member... [...]. I think that if I learn the language, it would be much easier and more productive somehow.

> It is like, I am living in the university, not in Esbjerg, that is my feeling.

As an international student in a non-English-speaking country, integrating is a challenge that is not facilitated by the residential segregation between Danish and international students. While distributing Danish and international students amongst the same residential locations may seem like an easy solution, it is not necessarily easy because of the different price levels of possible student accommodation: it is stressed in the interviews that the residences where international students live are less expensive than Danish student residences and have shared kitchens, while Danish students have better economic situations, want their own kitchens, etc.

Little Focus on Settling Amongst Free-flying Young People in Transition

Foreign students generally seem undecided regarding whether they will ultimately settle in Esbjerg, somewhere else in Denmark, their home country or somewhere else entirely. One student says that being an international student in the Erasmus Programmes involves staying only one year in the host country, and another

Recruitment of International Students: Challenges and Opportunities   207

student says that his continued presence in Esbjerg depends on whether the people he knows will also be staying:

> [...] If the people are here, then I will feel like staying here, but if they move, I would probably do that as well.

When asked if she feels a connection with Esbjerg, another interviewer says,

> I basically don't feel a sense of belonging anywhere, which I think can be explained by the fact that I left my country when I was like really, I was around eighteen years old, and before that, I was in a neighbouring country [...] since I was fifteen, which kind of … I have been travelling and working in different places after that, which kind of takes the sense of belonging away … for me, because if I had a sense of belonging somewhere, it would mean that every time I go to a new place, it will be painful, so I don't feel that sense anywhere, not even in my home country, when I go back [...], I feel like I am a foreigner there[...]

However, the same student answers positively to the question of whether she wants to associate herself with Esbjerg, partly due to the welcome the city gave her. She says,

> I think mostly, if I want to settle, like my mind comes to the idea that I want to settle, then I could do that here in Esbjerg, especially with the community newcomer service here, I kind of have the feeling [...] that here, the municipality of Esbjerg and the people around are trying to welcome foreigners, and I think I could find my place here if I decided to. The thing is, I'm not sure if I want to.

Another foreign student, however, claims a strong connection to his home area by virtue of the networks built over many years and says,

> You always miss your country. I have friends there I have known for 16-17 years, of course I miss them. When I talk to them, I share my experiences here, and they tell me what they are doing [...].

Thus, there are challenges associated with foreign students' possession of networks in several places or development of a very mobile lifestyle.

The Game-changing Potential of Internships and Jobs

Generally, the interviewed international students are positive about securing an internship or job in Esbjerg. One student was even informed before moving to Esbjerg that 'in Esbjerg, there would be more job opportunities and internship

208   *Annette Aagaard Thuesen and Eva Mærsk*

opportunities than in other cities in Jutland... […]'. However, this student has not succeeded in finding a job and says '[…]I do not know if it is my bad luck […] that I do not have […] a student job or that I did not find an internship'. Others mention that international students have problems approaching firms, which makes them leave Esbjerg after graduation:

> […] Internships are quite difficult. I applied many companies and still didn't get any positive response, and many of them didn't reply […], so I am still looking. I guess the school should help more about the internship, because nobody found one.

> […] On the other hand, there are some good jobs, which are mostly for the engineers. I think that is a huge problem and people are struggling financially. Because if you have the SU and a job, it is really easy, but I do not know many who have a steady job here; that is a problem in Esbjerg, I would say.

> Maybe that is one area that the municipality can think about and do better, to attract and keep people in the city, because after I graduate, if I cannot find a job, then there is no point for me to stay here.

> I feel like I have a good profile, and I have experience in my domain. But I know that a big part of the internship and study jobs is networking, and as a foreigner, my networking is not that great.

One interviewee suggests that firms should be more open to international students and mentions an example of a large company where the interviewee applied for a position at a graduate programme in English that ultimately hired seven Danes, which made the student wonder why the firm called the graduate programme an international programme and emphasised the discovery of different and new markets. Interviewees also recommend that small firms in particular should be assisted in overcoming barriers to employing international students so that small firms can also gain from new perspectives that are introduced by international students.

Generally, the interviewees offer many recommendations regarding what the municipality and educational institutions can do to improve the integration of international students:

> Share experiences about in which companies students have previously had internships, if they have any relations because if they personally could help you, then... maybe some event that tells you how to write your CVs, how to apply internships, […], and some contacts to companies... we just go on the internet and look randomly.

> [...]Most people, when they go to the university, they do that because they want to find a job related to their studies, so if the university in cooperation with the municipality and the local businesses try to find a way to ensure that more people are getting some kind of experience with internships, that could help.

Due to international students' financial situations, it is suggested that they should have the possibility of having paid internships. In addition, because international students face more obstacles to integration into the job market than local students, it is recommended that they have the opportunity to stay slightly longer in their student accommodations and perhaps be provided with additional help to enter the local job market during this period.

Discussion and Conclusion

This chapter aimed to explore the obstacles to international student integration into study, business and leisure life in Esbjerg and plausible solutions given Esbjerg's peripheral location. The literature has highlighted a variety of challenges to and solutions for improving the integration of international students, which we have compiled in Table 2 along with the content of the empirical data from Esbjerg. Both the literature and the empirical data indicate that international students often have very few location-specific insider advantages, which is a term that Fischer and Malmberg (2001) use to refer to place-bound advantages accumulating over time, such as a large social network in a specific town or knowledge about job or housing markets in a region. International students' 'outsider advantages' *could* include their diversity and global outlook, but this diversity is not often capitalised and thus ultimately is viewed as a disadvantage.

It seems, however, that a large part of the introductory procedures arranged by educational institutions and the municipality of Esbjerg generally work very well. Thus, a formal structure for welcoming procedures has been established, which facilitates the initial period when international students must build location-specific insider advantages. In this period, public institutions assume the role of host and provide support in a neoliberal worldwide economy in which international students are a factor of production in line with other goods. However, some barriers can also be identified in the reception of international students. In particular, two aspects indicate that further change is needed for Esbjerg to become a successful location for international student integration. First, the fact that international students often do not live in the same accommodations as Danish students fundamentally diminishes the possibility of out-of-class integration and, thus, accentuates the challenges of the insufficient cultural mixing of international and national students that has been proposed in the literature. Second, the 'stay-home culture' amongst Danes makes the integration of international students difficult and reduces the effect of the efforts of municipal and educational institutions. This stay-home culture, together with the status of Esbjerg as a young university town that has not yet built up the characteristics of university towns, such as

Table 2. Comparing Obstacles and Recommendations from the Literature with the Esbjerg Case (Own Original Work).

Solutions (Literature)	Solutions in Esbjerg (Interviews)
Co-nationals are the favoured network for both int. and local students	The initial good introduction of int. students does not continue throughout the semester
Personal support and advice networks maintain pre-existing networks	Int. students and local students do not live in the same places
Int. students realise too late that they should build networks and work experience	Int. students mainly form friendships with other international students
Local students are not interested in cross-cultural interactions and position int. students as others	Lack of open café facilities in the educational institutions in the afternoons/evenings/weekends leads to a closed 'stay-home culture'
There are diverse norms regarding active/passive participation in learning activities	There is not much integration with people in the local community people
Financial sacrifices are involved in studying abroad	Int. students can stay only 3 months in their student residences after graduation and travel home after failing the first job search
Students feel turned away by companies/institutions when entering the labour market for internships/jobs	There is an impression of too few activities taking place and low actual use
A 'best fit rationale' reproduces a monocultural environment in organisations and workplaces	There are no possibilities for paid internships due to national educational rules
There is a lack of valuation of different cultural and linguistic capital	Int. students have difficulties in finding internships and study-related jobs, especially in small firms
Small firms in particular are not open to diversity	There is a lack of knowledge of career advice personnel at educational institutions but good knowledge of electronic job portals
Integration dynamics should be addressed in class	Local people should show int. students around and help them build their networks
Int. students should seek knowledge on the local culture, volunteer, learn English and 'be brave'	The initial welcoming activities should be repeated to ensure that int. students stay connected to more than just other int. students

Solutions (Literature)	Solutions in Esbjerg (Interviews)
Local students should not isolate and discriminate against int. students academically and socially – int. students can provide local students with an opportunity to enhance their global knowledge locally	The fact that everyone is actively seeking integration in the beginning should be used actively to promote community integration outside university
Peer mentoring programmes with current int. students should be established for incoming students	Int. students should engage more in sports; creative hobbies; non-profit organisations; and trips to nature, surrounding towns and cultural attractions
Acad. faculty should provide international curriculum, react when int. students do not thrive, and include post-graduate work-related topics in class	Academic staff should proactively profit more from the opportunities from an active pedagogical approach and group work for integration between int. students and local students
Counsellors should address cross-cultural adjustments through culturally responsive interventions and, to some degree, address int. students' immigration and familial aspirations	Int. students should have the opportunity to learn the language
Specific organisations should work to connect int. students to internships and post-graduation employment	Better housing situations during the post-graduate period should be secured to encourage free-flying young people to settle
Workshops should be held to market int. student's skills and provide networking opportunities	Paid internships should be provided, and electronic job portals should be used to market internships and jobs in English explicitly to int. students
A database of companies interested in hiring int. students should be established and maintained	Educational services in Esbjerg should be marketed more—e.g. green energy activities, group work and active and participative learning environment

collective cultural values of and demand for knowledge-intensive labour in firms other than purely private and business-oriented firms, means that some of the solutions for integration of international students must be found in this cultural field. Thus, even though host institutions work to reduce the initial challenges of international students, additional agency from international students is required if they are to be integrated and remain, as neither businesses nor locals adequately

212   *Annette Aagaard Thuesen and Eva Mærsk*

facilitate this integration. The town of Esbjerg bears the image of being a 'muscle' town with many jobs in the energy sector, but even students within environmental and energy fields of study state that they struggle to find apprenticeships and student jobs. This is evidence that cultural and language barriers to integration play a key role in challenging the integration of international students.

As the empirical data show, integration also does not occur easily when the mindset of international students is considered. International students in Esbjerg are basically free-flying, very mobile young people who, in order to decide to stay, must be restrained by something. The restraints imposed by the crisis following the COVID-19 pandemic could provide an opportunity for international students to obtain a job in the Esbjerg area. Young southern Europeans face the prospect of the job markets in their home countries, where it will be difficult to gain a foothold because of the second economic crisis in 10 years. However, proper retention requires the further merging of gown and town (Martin, Smith, & Phillips, 2005), involving ordinary 'educational knowledge-resistant' people in Esbjerg and the entire base of small businesses in the local area.

Almost all the literature emphasises what different actors should do individually and in groups. However, solutions will be found through collaborative innovation rather than reliance on single partners, since all challenges and solutions are interrelated in the wicked problem of international student integration. There are no one-size-fits-all solutions to the integration of international students. The overcoming of 'invisible walls' must include many different initiatives (Martin et al., 2005, p. 13). Esbjerg has the chance to build a new culture with equal amounts of input from the university, businesses, the local government and the local community. International student integration is an internationally acknowledged and researched issue. The literature has indicated the following solutions to international student integration: international student agency + mentoring amongst the community, national students and international students + firm openness. We identified additional specific challenging aspects of international student integration and thereby identified causes of the suboptimal international student integration, which we add to this literature; these aspects must be considered in future research: stay-home culture + knowledge economy-resistant culture + segregated housing + invisible walls (constructed by firms and the local community).

References

Arthur, N. (2017). Supporting international students through strengthening their social resources. *Studies in Higher Education*, *42*(5), 887–894. doi:10.1080/03075079.2017.1293876

Blackmore, J., & Rahmini, M. (2019). How 'best fit' excludes international graduates from employment in Australia: A Bourdieusian perspective. *Journal of Education and Work*, *32*(5), 436–448. doi:10.1080/13639080.2019.1679729

Fischer, P. A., & Malmberg, G. (2001). Settled people don't move: On life course and (im-)mobility in Sweden. *International Journal of Population Geography*, *7*, 357–371. DOI:

Haythornthwaite, C. (2008). Learning relations and networks in web-based communities. *International Journal of Web Based Communities*, 4(2), 140–158.

Kashima, E. S., & Loh, E. (2006). International students' acculturation: Effects of international, conational, and local ties and need for closure. *International Journal of Intercultural Relations*, 30(4), 471–85. doi:10.1016/j.ijintrel.2005.12.00

Martin, L. L., Smith, H., & Phillips, S. (2015). Bridging 'Town & Gown' through innovative university-community partnerships. *The Innovation Journal: The Public Sector Innovation Journal*, 10(2), 2–16.

Nunes, S., & Arthur, N. (2013). International students' experiences of integrating into the workforce. *Journal of Employment Counseling*, 50, 34–45. doi:10.1002/j.2161-1920.2013.00023.x

OECD. (2019). Education at a Glance 2019: OECD Indicators. Paris: OECD Publishing.

Rubin, K. (2014). Retaining international students. *International Educator*, Sept + Oct, 30–37.

StatBank Denmark. (2019). Statistikbanken.dk/FLY66.

Taha, N., & Cox, A. (2016). International students' networks: A case study in a UK university. *Studies in Higher Education*, 41(1), 182–198. doi:10.1080/03075079.2014.927851

Thuesen, A., Mærsk, E., & Randløv, H. R. (2016). *Når unge uddannelsessøgende flytter mod vest. Esbjerg: Danish Centre for Rural Research, University of Southern Denmark.* CLF Report 57/2016.

Thuesen, A., Mærsk, E., & Randløv, H. R. (2020). Moving to the 'Wild West' – Clarifying the first-hand experiences and second-hand perceptions of a Danish University Town on the periphery. *European Planning Studies*, 28, 1–19. doi: 10.1080/09654313.2019.1709417

Uddannelses- og Forskningsministeriet. (2018). *Offentlige indtægter og udgifter ved internationale studerende.* København: Uddannelses- og Forskningsministeriet.

Chapter 14

The Impact of Cultural Adjustment on International Student Recruitment and First-Year Success

Clayton Smith

Abstract

This chapter explores the impact of cultural adjustment on international student recruitment and first-year success. The research design consists of a full-year cohort follow-up qualitative methodology study using both undergraduate and graduate students, as well as a two-part interview process and survey of both faculty and service providers, which included 100 research participants. Researchers identified factors associated with international student recruitment and success and how they are being addressed by the research site institution. Recommendations for professional practice are discussed, along with potential areas for further research.

Keywords: International students; student recruitment; student retention; student success; cultural adjustment; institutional supports

Background

The recent growth in international student enrolment in Canadian and US colleges and universities has resulted in institutions becoming more culturally and ethnoculturally diverse (Canadian Bureau of International Education, 2016; Institute of International Education, 2019). This has led to institutions being challenged to meet the various needs international students have as they adjust culturally to their new educational communities (Teotonio, Keung, & LaFleche, 2019).

Cultural adjustment is something international students will experience throughout their educational journey. It begins during the student recruitment

---

Global Perspectives on Recruiting International Students: Challenges and Opportunities, 215–229
Copyright © 2021 by Emerald Publishing Limited
All rights of reproduction in any form reserved
doi:10.1108/978-1-83982-518-720211014

period and continues through the student's first year on campus, and, for many, goes on into subsequent years of study. Acculturation stress is often caused by insufficient English, cultural shock, academic difficulties, limited integration with domestic peers and perceived discrimination (Xue, 2018). It is the result of international students possessing different value systems, communication patterns, sign and symbols of social contact and interpersonal relationship patterns (Wu, Garza, & Guzman, 2015). Nearly all international students will be challenged by studying in a different academic environment. Their instructors will use new methods of teaching, which will, for many, be in a foreign language. They will also have to change their learning strategies and preferences in this new learning environment.

Adapting to a new culture takes both time and effort. In order to ensure that students successfully navigate the cultural adjustment process, institutions need to confront the challenges faced by international students and support them throughout their student experience. The purpose of this chapter is to explore the impact of cultural adjustment on international student recruitment and first-year student success. The following two research questions guided this study:

1. What is the impact of cultural adjustment on international student recruitment and first-year student success?
2. What are the promising practices for supporting international students as they transition from first contact until the end of their first-year of studies at postsecondary educational institutions?

Literature Review

North American postsecondary educational institutions have demonstrated that they can attract international students by developing strong strategic enrolment-management initiatives. However, to achieve diversity, inclusivity and internationalisation, institutions must also enhance the international student experience. This will require paying more attention to international student success factors so that faculty, staff and students can support the adjustment of new international students.

Brown and Holloway (2008) describe adjustment as 'a dynamic and multi-faceted process, fluctuating throughout the sojourn as a result of a host of individual, cultural and external factors' (p. 243). Some of the academic challenges international students face in their educational journey include language challenges (Zhang & Zhou, 2010), exclusion from group discussions (Yates & Thi Quynnh Trang, 2012), culturally related learning differences (Koul & Fisher, 2005), academic support issues (Zhang & Zhou, 2010) and adjustments to new educational systems (Hofstede, 1997). They also experience several non-academic challenges, including cultural adjustment (Zhang & Zhou, 2010), social issues (Fritz, Chin, & DeMarini, 2008; Zhang & Goodson, 2011) and finances (Choudaha & Schulmann, 2014).

Cultural Adjustment for International Students

Cultural differences are important issues that can influence the learning process for international students. Cultural adjustment is 'a process of multiple interacting factors distinguished by different behavioral, cognitive, affective and demographic attributes and by different levels, varying from cultural assimilation to cultural transmutation' that involves both acculturation and assimilation (Kagan & Cohen, 1990, p. 133). Several stressors, including academic pressure, financial stress, homesickness, perceived discrimination, social disconnectedness, and culture shock, relate negatively to cross-cultural adjustment amongst international students (Yoko & Hosoda, 2014). Taken together, they make it difficult for international students to integrate socially with host faculty, staff and students.

The way learners absorb content is different according to their cultural background (Foster & Stapleton, 2012). It is also important to consider that international students prefer the teaching practices and approaches that they are accustomed to in their home countries (McKinnon, 2013). This suggests that any other approach used by instructors can cause an estrangement to international students, seeming foreign and incompatible.

One example is the Asian educational system, especially the Chinese system, which follows Confucianism values. These values, when reflected in the classroom, provide students with a learning environment quite different from what is found in North American institutions. Confucianism gives professors the authority to be the holders of knowledge; their wisdom must never be questioned. Chinese students tend not to question their instructors and maintain silence for most of the class (Le Ha & Li, 2012). The learning styles and preferences of Chinese students may also be affected by the exam culture, that is, their learning strategies are more related to memorisation, in order to get excellent marks on their exams (Lee, 1996). Therefore, Asian students require more direction from their instructors when studying abroad (Liang & McQueen, 1999).

Institutional Supports for International Students

Many institutions help international students adjust to their new environment as a way of reducing their stressors. Research shows that international students who increase their interaction with host students achieve a sense of belonging (Klomega, 2006), and the development of culturally specific social skills tends to make it easier for international students to engage in cross-cultural interactions with host students (Furnham & Boehner, 1982).

One of the tasks that institutions should consider is the reduction of the stressors that challenge cultural adjustment. Institutional help can take many forms. For example, instructors need to understand the preferred learning and interaction styles of international students, and consider embracing teaching practices that have high levels of student satisfaction and student perceptions of learning in such areas as academic integrity, assessment, assignments, clarifying expectations, communicating outside of the classroom, lecture design and delivery, along with verbal communications and visual communications (Smith et al., 2019). Counsellors

218   Clayton Smith

could also play a key role by helping students who lack social networks with homesickness and culture shock (Laboy Gonzalez, 2006; Nilsson & Anderson, 2004). Institutions could also provide sensitivity training to its faculty and staff to reduce potential discrimination and prejudice against international students.

A recent study (Rhein, 2018), completed at an African university, found that institutions can limit some of the negative aspects of cultural adjustment through the presence of supportive people, service and academic facility availability, and political stability. Individual qualities, such as self-determination and inner strength, also were found to impact cultural adjustment. Researchers identified several possible solutions institutions could adopt that include implementing comprehensive orientation programs, expanding support networks for international students, enhancing information dissemination regarding available services on and off-campus, and empowering students with knowledge and skills to cope with the psychological challenges of adjustment.

Little research has been conducted on the impact of cultural adjustment during the international student recruitment process. Pre-departure orientation and bias preparation courses are suggested as one method to assist in the reduction of ethnicity-based adjustment demands during the recruitment process (Rhein, 2018). Choudaha (2013, p. 11) suggests that

> Social media is an emerging and evolving channel, which is quickly becoming indispensable in international student recruitment. Like any new change, it faces several challenges and opportunities. However, institutions that embrace this change in an informed and entrepreneurial manner will create a significant competitive advantage. The key is to experiment, engage and evolve in a credible and effective manner.

International student recruitment requires a personal approach, which is not sufficiently highlighted in the literature. Onk and Joseph (2017) encourage the development of a multicultural atmosphere that includes classes, professors and study materials. Özturgu (2013) put it well when he wrote, 'Without a personal approach to recruitment and retention, international students will not necessarily be simply attracted to "an American university" but rather, will explore other study abroad opportunities that are easily available around the world' (Özturgu, 2013, pp. 11–12).

Method

The research design consisted of a full-year cohort follow-up qualitative methodology study using both undergraduate and graduate students that included a two-part interview process and survey of both faculty and service providers (Smith & Demjanenko, 2011). A pilot study was completed as an initial process of discovery and exploration of the issues.

Participants

Research participants are faculty, service providers and international students who work or study at a mid-sized, comprehensive university in Ontario, Canada.

They included students from a wide array of countries of origin, study levels, programs, study times, study stages and ages. A total of 100 research participants participated in the quantitative portion of the research study, while 47 research participants participated in the qualitative portion of the study.

Procedures

Step 1: A pilot study was conducted where the researchers interviewed service providers and international students to explore the factors affecting international student success. Research instruments were subsequently developed to learn more about these factors and how they affect international student persistence.

Step 2: The student participants of this study were recruited by e-mail to participate in the research project using individual e-mail invitations, a list-serve broadcast message, and referral email messages sent to international student-serving offices, international student campus groups and student government associations.

Step 3: The service providers and faculty participants of this study were recruited by individual email invitations,

Step 4: Focus groups and individual interviews lasted approximately one hour in length. They were digitally recorded, and then transcribed, after which the recordings were destroyed.

Step 5: Data were coded and analysed, which resulted in a thematic analysis.

Results

In this study, researchers identified factors associated with international student success and how they are being addressed by the research site institution. Emergent themes are presented.

Factors Associated with International Student Success

Study findings identify five key barriers to international student success and retention. They include culture, facilities and services, language, racism and discrimination, and frustration, disorientation and confusion. Culture was identified by all three respondent groups, while language, racism and discrimination were mentioned by two of the three groups (faculty and service providers). International students also viewed frustration, disorientation and confusion, along with facilities and services, as major barriers. Each of the major barriers to student success connects to the cultural adjustment experiences international students encountered during their education abroad experience.

Language. Faculty reported language as one of the major issues arising for international students in their classes. A language problem often signals an inability to function in English and/or comprehension issues, which may result in poor communication with instructors and other students. This was especially true in some programs where students interact closely and care for individuals (e.g. nursing). Language challenges affect daily conversation, oral presentations in a course, communication with domestic and international students, as well as

220 *Clayton Smith*

preparation of an academic report or paper. Some faculty commented, however, that the issue of unsatisfactory communication by some international students was more an issue of self-consciousness and a need for reassurance. Therefore, it was more the case of the development of a strategy to overcome any residual issues related to communication rather than an issue of appropriate skills.

Some service providers report the difficulties international students experience in daily 'language and communication', noting that 'the language and cultural barriers are for a great many international students, a very tall barrier, even though they claim to be educated in English'. Some noted the importance of using inclusive language in their communication with international students. Another said that there are challenges with face-to-face communication. They said that by simplifying their speech and written information, most issues can be resolved.

One instructor described an ideal English-language building class as one that helps international students to build adequate language skills in preparation for a typical university classroom, which incorporates listening to lectures, readings, and writing. In this class, students would learn skills which may not be easily transferable from one culture to another and which may take time to master. For instance, it could focus on how to synthesise and summarise information, as well as reading between the lines, and emphasise group work, with exercise of learning how to listen, how to take notes, and learning how to make inferences from what they are reading.

Culture. An important barrier for new international students is the expectation that they will integrate into, and participate in, mainstream society, which places a heavy burden on students to adapt to the host culture. Moreover, international students are expected to do most of the cultural adjusting, which furthers the Western mindset of placing the responsibility and blame in case of failure on the student. This often results in international students feeling lonely, tired, and having difficulty making friends. One faculty member commented that

> the university, and also the local student organizations, can do something to reach out to the students who come from a different culture, because when you come from a different culture you feel disoriented,

reserved, unsure and ill-informed, and they do not know the boundaries of the new culture.

Some service providers reported that they enjoy interacting with international students. Some ways in which they attempt to be culturally sensitive to students from other countries include keeping current of their religious holidays, making allowance for prayer times, trying to understand the international students' 'perspective, which is often informed by their culture', staying informed and aware of the 'political and socio economic issues related to their countries', using culturally sensitive language and mannerisms, and approaching 'problem-solving and counselling with a sense of cultural understanding'. Generally, they described a need to assist students beyond orientation and perhaps in a structured manner throughout the initial first year(s).

The Impact of Cultural Adjustment on International Student Recruitment   221

Cultural adjustment takes several forms. This ranges from food to weather, which, for some, results in frequent illnesses during the first couple of months in Canada. Some instructors reported that some international students 'bargain for marks' with their professors and engage in behaviour that is not typical in Canadian institutions of higher education.

Faculty observe that international students are frequently more silent than domestic students in their courses. They tend to befriend and socialise primarily with other international students from their own, or similar, cultural backgrounds. Faculty respondents dealt with these behaviours by planning for group work, organising mixed groups of domestic and international students, asking students to present their work in oral presentations, talking to international students individually and encouraging them to communication with people they may not typically reach out to. Additional ways instructors help with cultural adjustment include:

- inviting guest speakers from different organisations to help students understand the Canadian school system;
- using 'universal examples' in their teaching;
- adjusting their vocabulary and jokes during lectures and for the purpose of making themselves understood;
- highlighting a global perspective in their classes and assigned group formations;
- scheduling assignments away from important holidays of the religious or ethnic group in their classes; and
- helping students on a one-to-one basis as faculty are approached for help.

Faculty reported that some international students do not ask for help when they begin to struggle academically or personally for cultural reasons. This may be particularly true if an international student comes from a culture where 'people think they look bad if they say something wrong', or if they ask for help. This may sometimes lead to missed opportunities to help a student in time, or before an academic crisis develops because of inaction. One instructor said that international students learn differently than Canadian students, and that learning, and teaching styles may add to the academic difficulties of incoming international students, particularly when the learning in some countries differs from the student-centred method preferred in the Canadian education system.

Racism and Discrimination.   Many international students experience adverse treatment, both on and off-campus. One student reported that a roommate had used the 'n' word in reference to him, further stating that, 'yeah, that was wrong, but I got along with him. It was a challenge'. Some students also reported that they 'felt' racism from professors, teaching assistants (TAs) and/or graduate assistants (GAs) in their courses, stating that at times it was difficult to get help and that professors, TAs and GAs may not be as helpful to them as they were to other students. Racism and discrimination 'just made it difficult...just made the day completely bad for me'.

One instructor commented that 'classmates of international students frequently are rude to international students in group work' and that international

222   Clayton Smith

student 'complaints about the selection of grad students follow the racial demographics of certain professors, and the allocated Gas'. Some faculty described this as a 'social phenomenon' that will take time to address.

Some faculty advocated for a holistic approach of teaching and learning involving 'educating people [faculty, staff, students] from different service departments', and in general, training university staff to have the ability to deal with international students in a culturally sensitive way. This would help them grow personally and professionally. They further said that the main goal of retraining service staff is to 'bring awareness', to change the 'habitual way of doing things' and to appreciate having international students on campus, and the richness they add to the university culture.

Frustration, Disorientation and Confusion.   International students described their experiences as positive, but also 'different and challenging'. Some said their initial arrival was marred by 'difficulty' and 'frustration'. Others were appreciative of the support they received.

Some international students described their first days as 'awful'. Specifically, they noted that: they could not properly orient themselves using the campus map; they could not find the supermarket or convenience shops to purchase food; and that they had trouble adjusting to the cool environment inside university buildings and the hot climate outdoors. One student reported that he 'stayed hungry the first day' because he did not know where to find food, while another said he was 'very sick' the first few months, partially because of poor nutrition and the change from an indoor to outdoor climate.

Students identified a discrepancy between the information they were given during recruitment and the environment they encountered upon arrival. While they were given correct information prior to their arrival, they also commented that they were not given 'enough information' or enough 'details' about the state of daily living in residence. Some noted that pictures of the city and the university did not accurately portray their lived experiences.

Students reported that what helped them adjust to the new culture and life in Canada was a combination of:

- 'friends', which was typically qualified as other international students they met in their classes or in residence;
- their religious beliefs and convictions, as well as the ability to practice their faith;
- the assistance, help and kindness of people they had met, such as their roommates, teachers and friends;
- guidance and information provided by the international office; and
- support and encouragement from their family.

Recommendations students made for improving their arrival experience included having staff available during the weekends, expanding support beyond taking students to the international office, beginning orientation during their beginning days and encouraging students to arrive three weeks early, so they can 'used to their environment a bit, settle down, and get comfortable' prior to the

The Impact of Cultural Adjustment on International Student Recruitment   **223**

beginning of the school year. Other students identified issues specific to their accommodations, including the availability of fresh halal food, relationships with roommates, the layout of a typical dorm room, shared co-ed bathrooms and co-ed floors. The main reason for discomfort was religious beliefs and being able to practice their religion in comfort and ease.

Facilities and Services.   Some of the facilities and services that were helpful in transitioning to their new university included recreational, library, academic writing, and academic advising supports. Standing out amongst the list of helpful facilities and services is the work done by the international office, which students described as 'a home' away from home. For some, the international office is a place to 'hang-out', 'study' and spend time outside of their residences. One student described the international office as 'your mother and your father...that's where you go for help'.

Additionally, students reported that the lack of proper or readily available facilities to cook in residence soured their experiences. They identified that residence meals typically consisted of 'fast food', which is not normally consumed on a regular basis in their home countries or cultures. Furthermore, some reported that their residence accommodations were equipped with one 'microwave on each floor' and a 'kitchen in the basement'. Some described this as inadequate for the maintenance of a healthy diet and lifestyle.

Some students felt dissatisfied with tuition fees, residence fees and mandatory meal plans. There were suggestions for how to improve their experience that included offering a greater number of scholarships, more financial assistance programs and an increased number of campus work opportunities specifically for international students. In addition, some students expressed dissatisfaction with the transportation system in the city and the availability and regularity of busing in the outside-of-campus community, claiming that they felt isolated on campus.

Institutional Supports for International Students

This study identified several ways institutions can provide support for international students as they transition into their new university. The backbone of these supports rests on the value the department places on the contribution of international students towards a global perspective at the institutional and departmental levels. While there are several common threads in the type or style of support these departments offer to international students in their programs, the most prevalent is a multi-layered approach. Students are supported on a one-to-one level over an extended period.

Part of this support includes the monitoring of student progress, building a team effort that incorporates the international student within the team framework, as well as referral and support of students to appropriate providers. More specifically, successful example strategies include: transition courses that help students adjust to a Western academic system, funding tutoring for students in need, monitoring student progress based on attendance or course progression, fostering a structured environment, establishing regular small-group meetings with students, individual support for each student, community building activities, prompt referrals to various campus services as needs arise, building a relationship

224   *Clayton Smith*

with the student, developing a learning plan with the student, providing opportunities for coaching and mentoring of students by students, connecting students with their own community of supports and creating smaller groups of students to build community. In addition, other department noted that they have made conscious efforts to adjust to the needs of the incoming student. Noting the value placed on a global perspective offered by a multicultural student body, some faculty have consciously adjusted their programs to meet their needs.

Successful academic supports included:

- Planning for cultural differences, cultural sensitivity and culturally specific learning when designing course instruction;
- Early intervention – course completion, program completion, progression towards graduation
- Academic improvements – writing, spoken English, presentation, research, university policy, knowledge base, math, academic integrity;
- Inspiring in-class interaction between domestic and international students;
- Improving the academic department/faculty culture in recruiting, accepting, welcoming, involving and servicing international students; and
- Enhancing in class culture in accepting, welcoming and involving international students.

Non-academic best practices included:

- Create training programs for service providers in cultural differences, cultural sensitivity and culturally specific learning;
- Develop international students' communication skills, socialisation skills and time with other students; and
- Enhance the department culture in service-provider departments in accepting, welcoming, involving and serving international students.

Discussion

This chapter explored the impact of cultural adjustment on international student recruitment and first-year retention. Following the guidance of Conrad and Morris (2010), it examined the international student experience at a single postsecondary educational institution. Findings from this study echoed several literature findings. First, each research participant group identified culture, language, racism and discrimination as important factors in international student retention. Second, student-focus-group participants added facilities, services, frustration, disorientation and confusion as additional factors. Third, the faculty and service providers described academic and non-academic institutional supports that, if implemented, would positively enhance the international student experience. International student success is a complex matter that appears to be affected by a combination of dynamic and interacting factors, including social, linguistic, economic, cultural, academic, familial and environmental variables.

The Impact of Cultural Adjustment on International Student Recruitment   **225**

One student called for the creation of 'a home away from home'. Building a sense of community and cultural adjustment of international students go together and work to positively reinforce one another by providing support in-place of the absent presence of family. Acculturation results when institutions help students adjust to and function effectively and independently in a new society and culture (Berry, Kim, Minde, & Mok, 1987). It is only when this is achieved that students will fully complete their cultural adjustment. This calls on institutions to implement multiple levels of formal and informal supports to meet the needs of international students on a regular and one-on-one basis, and in smaller more organic groups, such as departments or other organisations that work to build a sense of community. Institutional support should have a solid and flexible structure to support students throughout their student experience, and especially during periods of academic and non-academic difficulties.

Student success is highly dependent on the institutional culture and how it supports the cultural adjustment of international students to their new learning environment. It needs to support the integration of international students with domestic students, faculty, service providers and the larger educational community. Furthermore, it must support the independent needs of each stakeholder in the process. This study delved deeply into the thoughts and feelings of these stakeholders on the activities and challenges they face daily, attempted to develop an understanding of the various stakeholders' views at a single postsecondary educational institution, as well as what is being done and could be done in the future to support this important work.

Recommendations

Postsecondary educational leaders looking to improve the cultural adjustment of their international students could benefit from a review of this study's research findings. Faculty should review the emergent themes that flow from the student-academic experience, while service providers should review the themes that came from students' non-academic experiences. Both groups should review the discussion on institutional support for international students. Taken together, they should help institutions become more accepting, welcoming and involving of international students

Faculty who teach international students should consider planning for cultural differences, cultural sensitivity and culturally specific learning when designing their courses. This should include academic improvements (e.g. academic integrity, mathematics, presentation, research, writing, spoken English), class culture, early intervention and in-class interactions between domestic and international students. They should also support improving the faculty/department culture to consider the factors associated with international student retention.

Service providers should consider helping international students acquire enhanced communication and socialisation skills. They should also encourage domestic and international students to interact with each other and enhance the department culture to make it supportive of the cultural adjustment being experienced by international students. Institutions should give service providers

226   *Clayton Smith*

with training in cultural differences, cultural sensitivity and culturally specific learning.

During the study, stakeholders identified several academic, non-academic and professional development forms of institutional support for supporting the cultural adjustment of international students. Table 1 provides a list of possible approaches and suggestions by type.

Table 1.   Possible Approaches and Suggestions for Supporting the Cultural Adjustment of International Students by Type.

Type	Approach or Suggestion
Academic	Provide an annual, or semester, academic advising review with individual international students to discuss program progress and other academic concerns
Academic	Offer proof reading and editing services with assignments and papers to international students (with a conscious effort towards academic integrity issues)
Academic and Non-Academic	Create a position in academic departments which hosts large numbers of internationals whose role would involve the care and attention to international students
Academic and Non-Academic	Provide a course for international students that would outline services and expectations (e.g. policies and regulations, academic integrity, health care, psychological services, food, entertainment, religious locations)
Non-Academic	Engage Canadian students to interact, in a larger capacity, with international students
Non-Academic	Increase the number of supports available to international students and distribute these supports throughout the academic year; and advertise these supports widely to international students, faculty, and staff
Non-Academic	Increase the number of financial supports through scholarships, bursaries, awards and work-study opportunities
Non-Academic	Require that international students arrive for a period prior to the start of classes
Non-Academic	Require that late-arrival international students begin studies the following term

Type	Approach or Suggestion
Non-Academic	Ensure that recruitment agencies provide accurate and complete information regarding the international student experience (e.g. co-op opportunities, living arrangements in residence, meal plans, potential employment opportunities upon graduation, etc.)
Non-Academic	Increase the availability of international student advisors and social space for congregating
Professional Development	Provide training for all faculty, staff, and domestic students in cultural sensitivity, cultural differences, and culturally specific learning

Conclusion and Further Research

The results of this study suggest that international student success and retention is a result of the fit among student, institution and sociocultural environment. This supports the findings of earlier studies (Conrad & Morris, 2010; Mallinckrodt & Sedlacek, 1987). An added complication that emerged in this study is the impact that growing number of international student enrolment has on the institution's ability to support a culture that is accepting, welcoming, involving and servicing of international students. In order to achieve this, institutions will need to move their focus away from retention rates towards retention risk factors (Conrad & Morris, 2010). This will require early prevention and efforts that support the cultural adjustment of international students throughout the student life cycle, from recruitment through to graduation. It also calls on institutions to 'understand the diverse needs and expectations of international students, collaborate on internationalisation efforts across departments, and invest in campus programs and services that improve student experiences' (Choudaha & Schulmann, 2014, p. 2).

As further research is contemplated, there is a need to learn about the experiences of international students during the pre-arrival period. Much of the international student recruitment literature is filled with enrolment management-focussed activities that successful recruiters use to recruit international students. More needs to be learned about the challenges, both academic and non-academic, faced by students during a time when institutional support is limited. It may also be helpful to examine the perspectives of educational agents and international student recruitment officers on this matter.

This study had limitations that need to be acknowledged, which may limit generalisation of the results. It was conducted at one mid-sized, Canadian university and incorporated responses from only 100 research participants, most of whom are faculty and service providers. While research findings help to understand factors associated with international student retention and institutional supports, care should be taken in generalising results beyond the research site.

228 Clayton Smith

Notwithstanding these limitations, this study demonstrates that there are cultural adjustment issues that international students face, along with successful practices institutions can adopt to support the adjustment process.

References

Berry, J., Kim, U., Minde, T., & Mok, D. (1987). Comparative studies of acculturative stress. *International Migration Review*, *21*, 491–511. doi:10.1177/019791838702100303

Brown, L., & Holloway, I. (2008). The adjustment journey of international postgraduate students at an English university: An ethnographic study. *Journal of Research in International Education*, *7*(2), 232–249. doi:10.1177/1475240908091306

Canadian Bureau of International Education. (2016). *A world of learning: Canada's performance and potential in international education*. Ottawa: Canadian Bureau of International Education.

Choudaha, R. (2013). *Social media in international student recruitment*. Association of International Education Administrators Issue Brief.

Choudaha, R., & Schulmann, P. (2014). *Bridging the gap: Recruitment and retention to improve student experiences*. Washington, DC: NAFSA, Association of International Educators.

Conrad, M., & Morris, K. (2010). *Shifting from retention rates to retention risk: An alternative approach for managing institutional student retention performance*. Toronto: Higher Education Quality Council of Ontario.

Foster, K. D., & Stapleton, D. M. (2012). Understanding Chinese students' learning needs in Western business classrooms. *International Journal of Teaching and Learning in Higher Education*, *24*(3), 301–313.

Fritz, M. V., Chin, D., & DeMarini, D. (2008). Stressors, anxiety, acculturation and adjustment among international and North American students. *International Journal of Teaching and Learning in Higher Education*, *24*(3), 301–313. doi:10.1016/j.ijintrel.2008.01.001

Furnham, A., & Boehner, S. (1982). Social difficulty in a foreign culture: An empirical analysis of culture shock. In S. Bocher (Ed.), *Cultures in contact: Studies in crosscultural interaction* (pp. 161–198). Elmwood, NY: Pergamon Press.

Hofstede, G. (1997). *Cultures and organizations: Software of the mind*. New York, NY: McGraw-Hill.

Institute of International Education. (2019). *Open doors 2019*. New York, NY: Institute of International Education.

Kagan, H. H., & Cohen, J. (1990). Cultural adjustment of international students. *Psychological Science*, *1*(2), 133–137. doi:10.1111/j.1467-9280.1990.tb00082.x

Klomega, R. Y. (2006). Social factors relating to alienation experienced by international students in the U.S. *College Student Journal*, *40*, 303–315.

Koul, R., & Fisher, D. (2005). Cultural background and students' perceptions of science classroom learning environment and teacher interpersonal behavior in Jammu, India. *Learning Environments Research*, *8*, 195–211. doi:10.1007/s10984-005-7252-9

Laboy Gonzalez, B. (2006). *Perceptions of university counseling services to foreign students* (Order No. 3220407). Available from ProQuest Dissertations & Theses Global. (304986100). Retrieved from https://search.proquest.com/docview/304986100?accountid=14789

Le Ha, P., & Li, B. (2012). Silence as right, choice, resistance and strategy among Chinese 'Me Generation' students: Implications for pedagogy. *Discourse: Studies in the Cultural Politics of Education*, *35*(2), 233–248. doi:10.1080/01596306.2012.745733

The Impact of Cultural Adjustment on International Student Recruitment **229**

Lee, W. O. (1996). The cultural context for Chinese learners: Conceptions of learning in the Confucian tradition. In D. Watkins & J. Biggs (Eds.), *The Chinese learner: Cultural, psychological and contextual influences* (pp. 25–41). Hong Kong: The Comparative Education Research Centre, Faculty of Education, University of Hong Kong.

Liang, A., & McQueen, R. J. (1999). Computer assisted adult interactive learning in a multi-cultural environment. *Adult Learning, 11*(1), 26–29. doi:10.1177/104515959901100108

Mallinckrodt, B., & Sedlacek, W. E. (1987). Student retention and the use of campus facilities by race. *NASPA Journal, 24*(3), 28–32.

McKinnon, S. (2013). A mismatch of expectations? An exploration of international students' perceptions of employability skills and work-related learning. In J. Ryan (Ed.), *Cross-cultural teaching and learning for home and international students: Internationalisation of pedagogy and curriculum in higher education* (pp. 211–224). London: Routledge.

Nilsson, J. E., & Anderson, M. Z. (2004). Supervising international students: The role of acculturation, role ambiguity, and multicultural discussions. *Professional Psychology: Research and Practice, 35*(3), 306–312. doi:10.1037/0735-7028.35.3.306

Onk, V. B., & Joseph, M. (2017). International student recruitment techniques: A preliminary analysis. *Journal of Academic Administration in Higher Education, 13*(1), 25–34.

Özturgu, O. (2013). Best practices in recruiting and retaining international students in the U.S. *Current Issues in Education, 16*(2), 1–22. Retrieved from https://cie.asu.edu/ojs/index.php/cieatasu/article/view/1213/495

Rhein, D. (2018). African American student sociocultural adjustment to Thai international higher education. *Globalisation, Societies, and Education, 16*(4), 381–394. doi:10.1080/14767724.2018.1440349

Smith, C., & Demjanenko, T. (2011). *Solving the international student retention puzzle.* Windsor, ON: University of Windsor.

Smith, C., Zhou, G., Potter, M., Wang, D., Pecoraro, M., & Paulino, R. (2019). Variability by individual student characteristics of student satisfaction with promising international student teaching practices. *Literacy Information and Computer Education Journal, 10*(2), 3160–3169. Retrieved from https://scholar.uwindsor.ca/education-pub/25

Teotonio, I., Keung, N., & LaFleche, G. (2019, September 25). I've given up everything. Explosive growth in international students comes at a steep cost. *The Standard.* Retrieved from https://www.stcatharinesstandard.ca/news-story/9613741-i-ve-given-up-everything-explosive-growth-in-international-students-comes-at-a-steep-cost/

Wu, H.-p., Garza, E., & Guzman, N. (2015). International student's challenge and adjustment to college. *Education Research International*, Article ID 202753. doi:10.1155/2015/202753

Xue, F. (2018). Factors that contribute to acculturative stress of Chinese international students. (2018). *Major Papers.* 30. Retrieved from https://scholar.uwindsor.ca/major-papers/30

Yates, L., & Thi Quynnh Trang, N. (2012). Beyond a discourse of deficit: The meaning of silence in the international classroom. *The International Education Journal: Comparative perspectives, 11*(1), 22–34.

Yoko, B., & Hosoda, M. (2014). Home away from home: Better understandings of the role of social support in predicting cross-cultural adjustment among international students. *College Student Journal, 48*(1), 1–15.

Zhang, J., & Goodson, P. (2011). Predictors of international students' psychosocial adjustment to life in the United States: A systematic review. *International Journal of Intercultural Relations, 35*(2), 139–162. doi:10.1016/j.ijintrel.2010.11.011

Zhang, Z., & Zhou, G. (2010). Understanding Chinese international students at a Canadian university: Perspectives, expectations, and experiences. *Comparative and International Education, 39*(3), 1–16.

Chapter 15

International Chinese Students' Cultural Experience and Cultural Support in the UK

Yimeng Zhang

Abstract

As the development of internationalisation in higher education, the mobility of international students around the world has been more active than ever. Chinese international student community is growing larger and larger in the popular destination countries like the United States, the United Kingdom, Australia and Canada.

Cultures vary from east to west; Chinese students might find it difficult to adjust in a new cultural environment. When international Chinese students are struggling with cultural adjustment issues, they might have difficulties finding the support that they need, as schools might not have culturally relevant international students support service. Using an exploratory case study approach, the researcher intends to investigate some uncommon issues that Chinese undergraduate students were facing in their cultural experience in the United Kingdom.

This research is aimed to raise the awareness for institutions to supply more through international students support service to reach a higher level of students' satisfaction.

Keywords: International students; Chinese international students; cultural shock; acculturation; cultural adjustment; international student support

Background

Even the smallest detail in a new cultural environment can be called a cultural experience. In this chapter, I will examine the cultural experience of international

---

Global Perspectives on Recruiting International Students: Challenges and Opportunities, 231–243
Copyright © 2021 by Emerald Publishing Limited
All rights of reproduction in any form reserved
doi:10.1108/978-1-83982-518-720211015

232   Yimeng Zhang

Chinese students as a process. The terms culture shock, cultural adaptation, cultural adjustment and acculturation can overlap and are sometimes used interchangeably, but I see them as parts of the overall cultural experience. Generally speaking, the journey from initial culture shock passing through cultural adjustment and acculturation and finally arriving at the cultural adaptation stage is the process by which sojourners become familiar and comfortable with a new culture while maintaining and balancing their home culture.

Sussman's (2000) definitions prove useful in expounding on the cultural experience that international students may undergo. First, culture shock is a psychological and physiological negative affective response that individuals face when faced with an unfamiliar culture, social norms and behaviour. Second, cultural adjustment is a relatively positive and motivational adjustment; this term refers to the cognitive and behavioural modifications that sojourners make to balance negative cultural impacts and experiences in a new environment. Third, acculturation generally describes a long-term cultural adaptation process, whether between minority cultures and the mainstream culture or immigrants' home cultures and the host country's culture. No clear separation between cultural adjustment and acculturation is intended in this study, but all terms may be considered as referring to the attempt to adjust to a cultural difference. Therefore, discussion about cultural adjustment will tend to focus on the adjustment, attempts and trials involved in the process, while considering acculturation will encompass the entire process and the overall result. Lastly, the term cultural adaptation refers to the successful or balanced cultural outcome after the cultural adjustment takes place whereby cognitive and behavioural modifications lead to positive consequences.

This study investigates undergraduate students' cultural experience. Compared to postgraduate students, younger students are more likely to undergo cultural difficulties due to their age and lack of independence, and they encounter a higher level of language difficulty and cultural stress (Yan & Berliner, 2011). In contrast to larger numbers of international students in the postgraduate sector, undergraduate international students in the United Kingdom seem to receive less attention. However, I think it is important for institutions to consider undergraduate students' cultural experience and their need for a support service for international students.

Methodology

Case Study Design

A case study is usually defined by the case, which can refer to an event, entity, issue, individual or unit of analysis (Yin, 2009). In this study, I define the case as international Chinese undergraduate students attending a university in the southern region of England. For confidential reasons, I will refer to this university as the University of the South.

Merriam (1998) and Stake (2005) suggested that a case study should be conducted over a span of time to allow the researcher to gain a deeper understanding of the case and individuals; thus, I proposed to conduct a longitudinal case study. Such a study can provide insight into the cultural adjustment of international students. As mentioned, in viewing cultural experience as a process rather than a single event, adapting a longitudinal case study enabled me to observe students' changes, transitions and shifts of cultural experience over time. In this case, I followed study participants over the length of an academic year (9 months) to observe and study their perspectives, attitudes and experiences.

The flexibility of the case study research design lends itself to a strategy to assemble data and draw interpretations (Yin, 1981). Thus, a case study can involve multiple resources and research methods to investigate the case in its context (Yin, 2009).

Data Collection

In this study, I gathered data through two stages, using two different methods. In the first stage, I designed a questionnaire with closed-ended questions and Likert scale questions that mainly focussed on understanding various types of international students' difficulties related to culture shock and cultural adjustment to provide a guideline for perfecting a support service for international students. Although the original goal in terms of online participants called for 100 undergraduate Chinese students pursuing studies in any institution in the United Kingdom, the study results reflected 96 valid responses out of a total of 132 responses. Participants were all undergraduate students from various universities in the United Kingdom. The survey was conducted online, and the link was sent via emails and social media.

The second stage aimed to provide an in-depth understanding of international Chinese students' needs. Twelve undergraduate Chinese students at the University of the South participated in this stage. Of these, nine were female and three were male. In terms of participants' level of study, four were in their third year of study, six were in the second year and two students were in the first year of study.

Pre-determined interview schedules were used to guide interviews and make sure all the desired elements would be covered in the interviews. Participants were encouraged to talk freely; however, irrelevant topics were carefully redirected. Although each interview was designed to last around 30 min, depending on each participant's willingness to talk, the duration varied from 25 min to an hour. Participants were able to choose to communicate in either English or Chinese in the interview: Two participants, therefore, chose to use English in the interviews, while 10 participants used a mixture of English and Chinese (though mostly Chinese) in the interviews. All the interviews were audiotaped and transcribed. For the sake of anonymity, randomly chosen English names were assigned to the participants.

Reflecting the longitudinal nature of the case study, the second stage of the study lasted for 9 months. Each participant engaged in three semi-structured interviews, one every 3 months. Between interviews, participants completed one short questionnaire with four open-ended questions each month asking them to record good and bad cultural events that happened to them, which allowed their cultural experience and cultural events to be brought up and reviewed in the next interview.

234 Yimeng Zhang

Data Analysis

The quantitative data from the survey were collected online and analysed as descriptive data. Rather than for the purpose of generalising, descriptive analysis of data is used for describing a particular group of participants in detail. As the first step in data analysis, this type of analysis can help the researcher to gather valuable information about participants (Loeb et al., 2017). The descriptive data from the survey supplied knowledge about the general cultural difficulties of international Chinese students in the United Kingdom and helped in identifying unexpected themes as well as adjusting the interview design.

The qualitative data were analysed using thematic analysis, which is used to identify, analyse and report patterns and themes in qualitative data (Braun & Clarke, 2006). I followed Braun and Clarke's (2006) six-step guideline for thematic analysis. First, I familiarised myself with the data by repeatedly listening to the audio recordings as well as reading the transcripts. Next, I was able to generate initial codes. Once sufficient initial codes existed, I could develop potential themes. Repeatedly returning to the original data, I then reviewed all the themes and was finally able to define and name all the themes. The final step involved generating a report to represent the participants' perspectives and perceptions.

During the thematic data analysis, I used Microsoft Word and Microsoft Excel to help in organising and recording all the codes and themes.

International Students' General Cultural Adjustment Difficulties

This survey-based study of international Chinese students' general experience with culture shock and difficulties in cultural adjustment while in the United Kingdom returned 96 valid responses. Amongst all the students, 54.2% (52 students) expressed that they had faced a noticeable number of cultural challenges and cultural difficulties.

One of the oftenest-mentioned challenges was the English language: of all participants, 57.3% (55 students) thought that overall English proficiency affected their cultural experience in the United Kingdom. Despite having completed a language test, language lessons and intensive English language preparation before they arrived in the United Kingdom, 28.1% (27 students) of the Chinese undergraduate international students surveyed still find trouble in using English in daily communication. Moreover, 54.2% (52 students) of the participating Chinese undergraduate students admitted to struggling with academic English, especially academic reading and writing.

As a complicating factor, the teaching styles and educational systems differ significantly in China and the United Kingdom. Consequently, 46.9% (45 students) of the Chinese undergraduate students who participated in the study reported that they are finding it difficult to become accustomed to the teaching style in a UK classroom. In addition, 52.1% (50 students) of the participants stressed difficulties they had encountered in understanding differences in assessment criteria as UK markers might seek different types of responses from students than their counterparts in China.

The participants also reported cultural difficulties and struggles in their daily lives. Of all respondents, 28.1% (27 students) admitted that they found separation from friends and families difficult. In other words, the students identified loneliness as a significant issue in being alone in the United Kingdom. Not only is being away from familiar surroundings and familiar people difficult, but also finding a local group that provides students a sense of belonging can be hard. On this topic, 38.5% (37 students) of the participants admitted to problems in finding emotional support locally. On a related note, 64.6% (62 students) of Chinese undergraduate students surveyed found it challenging to make friends with local students.

Small aspects of life can be troublesome as well. When discussing the aspect of nutrition and sustenance, 40.6% (39 students) of the Chinese undergraduate students in the study found that local cuisine, as well as the local eating habits in the United Kingdom, can be quite different from home and, therefore, difficult to adjust to. On the topic of health care, 50% (48 students) of participants found that the healthcare system in the United Kingdom can be confusing to international students; not only do students encounter problems in understanding the process in general, but understanding medical terms in particular can comprise a barrier. Thus, international students might have difficulties obtaining timely medical support as well as receiving appropriate necessary medical attention. The smallest daily errands could pose a challenge; for example, 28.1% (27 students) of the participants expressed concerns with such common tasks as opening a bank account, renting an apartment, shopping and avoiding fraud and scams, identifying these as challenging for international students to figure out all by themselves.

Considering the limited income that is a common factor for many students, budget issues also affect international students' cultural experience in the United Kingdom. In this survey, 59.4% (57 students) of the Chinese undergraduate students who participated pointed out that the expense of studying abroad can be high. As a result, students must pay careful attention to their spending at all times.

The Chinese undergraduate students surveyed frequently mentioned the cultural challenges and cultural difficulties under consideration here. Some students noted other difficulties as well, such as racial discrimination and stereotypes. Added to these were challenges inherent in using local public transport and locating themselves, difficulties in using institutional facilities, a lack of convenience in living and struggling to find local entertainment.

Current International Students' Support Services at the University of the South

According to the University of the South's official website, the institution offers a wide range of international student support services (The University of the South, 2020).

Examples are as follows:

- Before international students arrive, dedicated staff are made available to help answer questions about the visa application process and accommodation as

236 Yimeng Zhang

well as travel and healthcare information. Upon students' arrival, the university offers an airport pickup service from London.

- To help students settle in, the university posts online guides to familiarise international students with the process of clearance, opening a bank account and registering with a local health centre as well as registering with the police.
- To aid international students in integrating with the wider university community, the university offers different communities and social clubs as well as a student mentor system.

It appears that the University of the South offers sufficient support services for international students. However, international students still have difficulties in accessing these services and continue to struggle with cultural challenges and cultural difficulties. In the next section, I will discuss current issues regarding the international support services that emerged in the semi-structured interviews, and I will also offer suggestions for improving students' support systems.

Issues in International Students' Support Services

Defining 'International Student' and Finding Help

The United Nations Educational, Scientific and Cultural Organization (2020) defined the term 'international student' as characterising students who have crossed a national or territorial border to enrol in an educational organisation outside of their home country. Although this definition reflects how institutions define the term, much variation exists within the international student group itself. One of the Year 2 Chinese undergraduate participants stated her confusion in an interview, saying:

> I am classified as an international student, but I found it difficult to identify as an international student. Because if you think about it, what is an international student? An American student is an international student, an Australian student is an international student, but how can I be the same with them? (Sarah, personal communication)

It is indeed critical for international students to obtain support when studying in a foreign country. However, treating international students as a whole and ignoring their diversity might be troublesome as such a course raises the risk of neglecting these students' diverse needs. Institutions might find it salutary to consider offering more specific and targeted support services to international students according to their 'sub-groups'. In the area of international cultural adaptation support services, a 'one size fits all' solution is not possible (Schwartz, Unger, Zamboanga, & Szapocznik, 2010).

A more targeted approach to international student support will be especially beneficial to university newcomers who are suffering from culture shock and language challenges. As mentioned, despite the many available support services for international students, some students do not know how to utilise them.

Having been in the United Kingdom for 3 years, Lisa is now familiar with these student support services. Thinking back to when she first arrived in the United Kingdom, she spoke about how she found everything confusing, saying,

> When we first arrived, there were way too many introductory sessions and activities going on, I could not intake all of them. There were a lot of international students support services mentioned, but a lot of them were just so new and alien to me, I might just forget half of them after the session, the other half of them I just did not understand because of my poor English back then. (Lisa, personal communication)

Cultural differences can also show in varied social practice. Institutional support services in China can be very different from those found in the United Kingdom. Thus, Chinese students studying abroad might find looking for help difficult if they do not know what kinds of help are available.

> I could not even believe the kind of service exists. I suffer from dyslexia, and it has been bothering me for my entire life. I never enjoyed school when I was in China because all the teachers and students seemed to treat my condition as an excuse for laziness. Right here in the UK, lectures are more understanding than I can ever imagine. One of them recommended me to use professional counselling service provided by the school. It was very beneficial, and it was free, but I never even heard of it before I was told by my lecturer. (Yasmin, personal communication)

Due to differing cultural backgrounds, the many services and opportunities that universities offer can be confusing to international students, and it is unrealistic to expect such students to completely understand an institution's support system intended for international students in only a few introductory sessions. To ease the information overload for international newcomers, the school can offer a written form of introduction or offer a recorded session so students can revisit anytime when it is needed. Such a tool can be in the form of a brochure or a website where international students can take their time to read, understand and take in the information.

New students might have lower language proficiency and less confidence in their use of the language, a situation that might make them hesitant to ask questions or call for assistance. Thus, international students may find it helpful to look for answers in their mother tongue. As one part of this effort, institutions can set up international student ambassadors to offer help in students' native language.

Admittedly, due to the varied backgrounds of international students, institutions may find covering the needs of all international students difficult. That said, offering an international students' support service guide in multiple-language versions might help students more easily understand and utilise the school's facilities.

238 Yimeng Zhang

Student Perspective: 'I was not used to seek for help.'

Even though the significant efforts of host institutions to provide services and designate facilities and staff to help international students improve their study and quality of life in a new culture, Klein, Miller, and Alexander (1974) found that international students underutilise professional support services. Some students tend to find talking about their problems and concerns extremely awkward. Moreover, methods for seeking aid reflect cultural differences. Thus, institutions must consider the cultural differences that international students exhibit in seeking and asking for help within the support service sector established for their benefit.

When it comes to turning to institutions or other professional facilities for help, Chinese students' attitudes are not positive overall. For example, a Year 2 student participant stressed his concern during an interview, saying,

> Growing up my parents always tell me to not bother other people with my problems. And I always have the impressions that the school would not care so much about my little issues, so I just cannot be bothered to ask for help. Unless it is physical harms or anything major, I always want to solve problems myself or talk to my families or friends to figure things out. (Jason, personal communication)

This hesitancy in seeking help, especially within the East-Asian international student community, seems to stem from traditional beliefs and common practices in their cultures (Wilton & Constantine, 2003). One major reason for the negative attitudes of East-Asian international students towards seeking professional and institutional help is that any need for support and admitting personal problems are often associated with shame and weakness (Zhang & Dixon, 2003).

Cultures vary greatly in that each culture has a unique set of philosophies to guide and unify people within the cultural group. In East Asia, especially China, Confucianism shapes people's minds and their ways of thinking as well as daily practice. Traditional Chinese philosophy has historically taught people to emphasise the interpersonal harmony and obedience inherent in the social hierarchy. In other words, Confucian societies esteem collectivist accomplishments over personal value (Uba, 2003; Yao, 2000).

Individuals from a system involving a clear social hierarchy might see institutions as authorities demanding respect rather than established to be available for solving problems for international students. In light of placing value on the collective, Chinese international students might think that their personal feelings and issues are not a priority and, therefore, are not worthy of help. Valuing collectivism also implies the potential presence of a close-knit Chinese international student community where members will prefer to seek for support and help within the social community instead of looking for institutional and professional assistance (Kung, 2004).

Due to the significant cultural gaps between China and the United Kingdom, international Chinese students imbued with strong Chinese cultural values might find it difficult to embrace and adjust to British cultural values and social practice in the United Kingdom. As an added consequence, they might find it more diffi-cult to approach university services in search of professional help (Skinner, 2010). Thus, I have two suggestions for institutions to motivate Chinese international students to voluntarily look for help.

As a first step, institutions can promote their support services and promote a positive attitude towards helping international students. Educational organisations can approach international students using multiple methods to aid students in understanding the help available. To inform the students they serve, institutions can make use of social media, e-mails, posters and other methods to showcase the organisations' willingness to help international students to have a better cultural experience in the United Kingdom. As mentioned previously, using a multi-language approach to promote student support services can also make institutions more approachable to international students.

Second, international Chinese students are a major source of support for each other. Utilising Chinese students' community can motivate international students to seek help as well. Senior international students and alumni can be asked to share their experiences with new students to encourage new students to make use of international student support resources and school facilities. Those students who access any student support service can write testimonial stories to emphasise the trustworthiness of a particular service to other international students. Institutions can promote their student support services by cooperating with clubs and societies to make the support system less formal, encouraging more international students to explore their options.

Student Perspective: 'I don't want to be British.'

In 1997, Berry proposed a theory to explain how people negotiate between host and home cultures, identifying two dimensions of acculturation. First, the author mentioned the value of individuals maintaining their own cultural identity and characteristics. The second dimension involves the value of maintaining a relationship with the broader society and host culture.

According to the two dimensions, the following four strategies describe how people identify themselves between the host culture and their own culture: integration, separation, assimilation and marginalisation. Cultural integration is usually seen as the ideal situation for cultural adaptation for international students in the host country (Berry, 1997). Specifically, cultural integration refers to international students who value both home and host cultural interactions, allowing them to adapt to host cultural and social norms while maintaining their home cultures.

Considering cultural integration to be the only answer to the problems of international students is an item of debate. One Year 1 Chinese student participant stated her confusion regarding the concept of cultural integration in the following words:

> I kept hearing about learning English culture and adapting to English culture. I don't want to be a British, and therefore I don't have to act like one. It is good for me to know about the culture, but I

240 *Yimeng Zhang*

> don't want to change the way I act, because I am a Chinese even now I am in a foreign country. (Jessica, personal communication)

Adapting to a new cultural environment is a continuous, lengthy process. Sometimes, intercultural adaptation is not as simple as acquiring cross-cultural competence or having an open mind. Cultural adaptation is a painful internal battle between deep-rooted cultural values and values reflecting an individual's cultural identity in the context of an unfamiliar cultural environment and social system (Schwartz et al., 2010; Wang & Mallinckrodt, 2006).

Cultural integration is deemed an ideal situation for cultural adaptation because it balances the individual's home culture and host culture and allows the two cultures to coexist. On the other hand, even cultural integration requires international students to change their attitude towards their home culture and lose some home-cultural traits (deculturation) in learning and adapting to the host cultural environment (acculturation). Thus, the question arises as to whether this process is really necessary for international students. This is especially the case for international students who are eventually going back to their home country.

My suggestion to institutions is that international students themselves should be the ones who decide the success of intercultural adaptation. International students can choose to stay unchanged or immerse themselves in British culture. For their part, institutions simply need to make sure that no one forces cultural education and cultural adjustment aids on international students. Different intensity levels of cultural education and cultural adaptation aids should be available to serve the needs of varied international students.

As another complicating factor, when international students finish their studies and return to their home country, their successful cultural adaptation might become a burden. Because cultural adaptation leads to changes in an individual's cultural views, cultural values and cultural identity, these changes will affect the student's transition to the home country. Sussman (2000, 2002) suggested that exposing individuals to a new cultural environment causes their cultural identity to emerge and become salient during the cultural transition. Similar to identity salience when international students arrive in the host country, repatriation involves another cultural identity disturbance.

Michelle (Year 2) shared her experience when she returned to her hometown for a long summer holiday, saying, 'I feel more and more like an outsider even in my most familiar settings. I feel disjointed in every small aspect of life, even though they are things that I grow up with' (personal communication).

When international students return to their home countries after graduation, they might find themselves in another cultural outgroup. International students and their adapted ways of thinking, culturally appropriated behaviours and newly formed cultural identity do not fit within the home culture environment. Nor do their new attitudes apply to home-cultural norms. Accordingly, while institutions might not be able to offer much aid for international students who are on a break or becoming alumni, they can help by making students aware of the change and the reversed culture shock that the latter might face upon repatriation.

Student Perspective: 'They don't know about my culture.'

Internationalisation can be debatable. On a more positive note, the process involves hybridisation, heterogeneity and a celebration of variety and diversity.

The internationalisation of education shows both traits in terms of cultural exchange. On the one hand, international students enrich the local cultural environment. On the other hand, such intercultural exchange always seems one-dimensional. Chole (Year 3) expressed her struggle involving intercultural communication with the observation,

> It is frustrating sometimes. I tried my best to learn about the culture, to learn the lingos, idioms, the customs, the habits so I can communicate with my classmates and make some local friends. But I seemed to be the only one that's putting the efforts in, local people do not want to know about my culture. (personal communication)

The 'inter' in intercultural communication should suggest that cultural communication is mutual. However, it is difficult to call an intercultural communication 'mutual' when the cultural flow between the host and sojourners is unbalanced (Ellingsworth, 1988). A report by The British Council (Education Intelligence, 2014) showed that 56% of local students had little or no interaction with international students and only 10% of British students acknowledged international students' value in bringing new cultures and views.

The effort to learn other cultures is unbalanced between international students and local students. Enabling multicultural education for all students promises a way to correct this one-dimensional cultural learning and cultural exchange. That said, the emphasis on multicultural education should not only focus on international students' cultural adjustment and adaptation to the local cultural environment, but it should also concern respect for inclusivity and diversity (Bhatti & Leeman, 2011; Veugelers & Leeman, 2018).

Mutual understanding is the foundation of cross-cultural communication. Thus, multicultural education can teach students the basic cultural values of differing cultures so that home students can know more about international students and international students of different nationalities can understand each other better. Hopefully, understanding and respect for another culture will lead to an overall inclusive integration, which will promote acceptance of all cultures, nationalities, races, languages, religions and ethnicities while limiting racism, discrimination and stereotypes.

Limitations and Implications

This study showcases issues that exist at the University of the South regarding the institution's international student support services from the perspective of Chinese undergraduate students. Because the study design involved a rather small scale, the student participants' opinions might not cover all the potential issues

242   Yimeng Zhang

occurring in the wider community. In future, researchers can try to include more participants to illuminate more possibilities and varieties of topics.

As this study only focusses on one case, it might provide only contextual knowledge. As a matter of fact, this study might be able to serve as a starting point or springboard or laying the foundation for future research. Future researchers can, therefore, explore investing in and comparing multiple cases in the same study to provide multi-layered findings. Such comparison can cover varying university locations to examine the impact of urban and countryside differences in the cultural experience. As a complicating factor, international students of differing nationalities can have completely different cultural experience. Differences in age group, gender and background can also affect students' cultural experience. Consequently, researchers have a choice of many different directions to explore in future studies. Regardless of their chosen course of investigation, all the knowledge they gain promises to be equally valid, helping to enrich the literature.

References

Berry, J. W. (1997). Immigration, acculturation, and adaptation. *Applied Psychology*, *46*(1), 5–34.

Bhatti, G., & Leeman, Y. (2011). Convening a network within the European conference on educational research: A history of the social justice and intercultural education network. *Eerj*, *10*(1), 129–142.

Braun, V., & Clarke, V. (2006). Using thematic analysis in psychology. *Qualitative Research in Psychology*, *3*(2), 77–101.

Education Intelligence. (2014). *Report: Integration of international students | British Council*. Retrieved from https://www.britishcouncil.org/education/ihe/knowledge-centre/student-mobility/report-integration-international-students. Accessed on March 13, 2020.

Ellingsworth, H. W. (1988). A theory of adaptation in intercultural dyads. In Y. Y. Kim & W. B. Gudykunst (Eds.), *Theories in intercultural communication* (pp. 259–279). Beverly Hills, CA: Sage.

Klein, M. H., Miller, M. H., & Alexander, A. A. (1974). When young people go out in the world. In W. P. Lebra (Ed.), *Youth, socialization and mental health. Vol iii of Mental health research in Asia and the Pacific* (pp. 217–232). Honolulu, HI: University Press of Hawaii.

Knight, J. (2006). *Internationalization of higher education: New directions, new challenges. The 2005 IAU global survey report*. Paris: International Association of Universities.

Kung, W. W. (2004). Cultural and practical barriers to seeking mental health treatment for Chinese Americans. *Journal of Community Psychology*, *32*(1), 27–43.

Loeb, S., Dynarski, S., McFarland, D., Morris, P., Reardon, S., & Reber, S. (2017). *Descriptive analysis in education: A guide for researchers*. NCEE 2017-4023. National Center for Education Evaluation and Regional Assistance.

Merriam, S. B. (1998). *Qualitative research and case study applications in education. Revised and Expanded from "Case Study Research in Education*. San Francisco, CA: Jossey-Bass Publishers.

Schwartz, S., Unger, J., Zamboanga, B., & Szapocznik, J. (2010). Rethinking the concept of acculturation: Implications for theory and research. *American Psychologist*, *65*(4), 237–251. doi:10.1037/a0019330

Skinner, B. (2010). Online discussion: Can it help international students ease into British University life? *Journal of Studies in International Education, 14*(4), 335–354. doi:10.1177/1028315308327866

Stake, R. (2005). Qualitative case studies. In N. K. Denzin & Y. S. Lincoln (Eds.), *The Sage handbook of qualitative research*. London: Sage.

Sussman, N. M. (2000). The dynamic nature of cultural identity throughout cultural transitions: Why home is not so sweet. *Personality and Social Psychology Review, 4*(4), 355–373.

Sussman, N. M. (2002). Testing the cultural identity model of the cultural transition cycle: Sojourners return home. *International Journal of Intercultural Relations, 26*(4), 391–408.

The United Nations Educational, Scientific and Cultural Organization. (2020). International (or internationally mobile) students | UNESCO UIS. Retrieved from http://uis.unesco.org/en/glossary-term/international-or-internationally-mobile-students. Accessed on March 1, 2020.

The University of South. (2020). *International Student Support | International Student Support | University of South*. Retrieved from http://www.south.ac.uk/international-students/. Accessed on March 1, 2020.

Uba, L. (2003). *Asian Americans: Personality patterns, identity, and mental health*. New York, NY: Guilford Press.

Veugelers, W., & Leeman, Y. (2018). Pedagogical possibilities in culturally diverse educational contexts: Theory and practice of inclusive education in the Netherlands. In L. Claiborne & V. Balakrishnan (Eds.), *Difference, ethics and inclusive education: Changing global policy and practice*. Boston, MA: BrillSense Publishers.

Wang, D. C., & Mallinckrodt, B. (2006). Acculturation, attachment, and psychological adjustment of Chinese/Taiwanese international students. *Journal of Counseling Psychology, 53*(4), 422–433. doi:10.1037/0022-0167.53.4.422

Wilton, L., & Constantine, M. G. (2003). Length of residence, cultural adjustment difficulties, and psychological distress symptoms in Asian and Latin American international college students. *Journal of College Counseling, 6*(2), 177–186.

Yan, K., & Berliner, D. (2011). An examination of individual level factors in stress and coping processes: Perspectives of Chinese international students in the United States. *Journal of College Student Development, 52*(5), 523–542. doi:10.1353/csd.2011.0060

Yao, X. (2000). *An introduction to Confucianism*. Cambridge: Cambridge University.

Yin, R. K. (1981). The case study crisis: Some answers. *Administrative Science Quarterly, 26*(1), 58–65.

Yin, R. K. (2009). *Case study research: Design and methods (applied social research methods)*. London: Sage.

Zhang, N., & Dixon, D. N. (2003). Acculturation and attitudes of Asian international students toward seeking psychological help. *Multicultural Counseling and Development, 31*(3), 205–222.

Chapter 16

The Future of International Student Recruitment

Belal Shneikat

Abstract

Many universities in the world depend on tuition fees paid by international students as the main source of institutional operating budgets. The current study aims to predict the future of international student recruitment from education agents' perspectives. The study is qualitative and nineteen interviews were conducted. Results show why students contact international student recruiters before making their decisions regarding which HEIs they will join. Results also highlight the effect of COVID-19 on recruiting international students and finally, four predictions were suggested by interviewees regarding the future of this industry. Discussions and conclusion are presented.

Keywords: Education agents; international students; tuition fees; HEIs; COVID-19; North Cyprus

Introduction

Globalisation is described as continuous process of profound integration between different countries that have progressed in different stages since 1945 (Ostry, 1999). The idea of globalisation started with focus on reducing barriers to trade. After that the emphasis was on the liberalisation and free movement of capital (Ostry, 1999). The advancement of Information and Communication Technologies (ICTs) in 1990s contributed to the development of globalisation (Ostry, 1999). The advancement of ICT made it easy to manage multinational enterprises and global production networks, this resulted in stimulating technology, capital and trade. Globalisation is so related to education because World Trade

---

Global Perspectives on Recruiting International Students: Challenges and Opportunities, 245–256
Copyright © 2021 by Emerald Publishing Limited
All rights of reproduction in any form reserved
doi:10.1108/978-1-83982-518-720211016

Organisation (WTO) promoted globalisation by opening the door for all fields of social sciences including education (Stromquist, 2002).

The fierce competition in terms of quality and recruiting international students amongst Higher Education Institutions (HEIs) can be referred to globalisation; HEIs usually compete each other nationally and globally (Altinay & Shneikat, 2019). Moreover, systems and policies of HEIs have been changed by globalisation (Márquez, Torres, & Bondar, 2011). Given that, universities started having strategies for internationalisation (Altinay & Shneikat, 2019). The topic of internationalisation in higher education has gained attention by practitioners, policy makers and researchers lately in the twentieth century (de Wit, 2011; Knight, 2013). Therefore, internationalisation has become a vital issue in HEIs.

Knight (2004) defined internationalisation as a process of merging global, international, or intercultural dimensions into the objective or delivery of postsecondary education. This definition implies the importance of having education at an international university because labour markets look for university graduates who have the intercultural skills (e.g. speaking English language), knowledge and awareness (Altinay & Shneikat, 2019). Hence, many universities in the world started offering international programs in English language, international curriculum and usually have international academic staff members (Altinay & Shneikat, 2019). Indeed, the availability of English programs with international professors and curriculum make it possible for non-native English-speaking countries to recruit many international students.

Recruiting international students can offer cultural and economic benefits. Thus, it is not a surprise to witness competition between different countries to recruit international students. As an example, The Institute of International Education (Bhandari, 2011) reported a record number of more than 690,000 international students studying in the academic year 2009–2010 in different majors and universities across the United States. The Institute of International Education (IIE) reported in 2019 that number of international students in the United States hits all-time high. They reported around 1.1 million international students studying in the United States and this represents a 0.05 increase over the previous year (IIE, 2019). In England, the number of international students increased by 128% between 1955 and 1962 (Bolsmann & Miller, 2008). In the academic year of 1962–1963 when the number of international students was around 64,000, that was seen as a part of the diplomatic relationship between England and sending countries and source of revenue (Silver & Silver, 1997). However, in the recent years, around half a million international students were studying in the United Kingdom, accounting for 20% of total student population (Universities UK, 2019). It is worth mentioning here that some countries such as France, Germany and Turkey started offering international programs in English language to recruit more international students.

Since the 1960s, there has been a heated debate about vital role played by HEIs in leading a new stage of social development, which has been known recently as the knowledge society, the information age (Castells, 1996), postmodern society (Lyotard, 1984), the third wave (Toffler, 1980), post-industrial society (Bell, 1973), the knowledge economy (Drucker, 1969, as cited by Ziguras & Law, 2006). According to Ziguras and Law (2006), the knowledge that HEIs make and spread has become more integral to cultural & government production and economic development.

The aim of this chapter is to explore the future of recruiting international students from the perspective of international students' recruiters. The number of international students in the world was over 5.3 million in 2017 up from 2 million in 2000 (UNESCO, 2017). The emergence of distance learning and switching to online education due to COVID-19 have made the future of recruiting international students to be vague. Till now, nobody can predict the future of educational tourism due to lockdown in many countries and even some universities decided to resume face to face education for Fall semester 2020/2021 but they have cancelled their plans recently because a second wave of COVID-19 has already started in some countries in August and September 2020.

Literature Review

Adoption of distance learning in the universities resulted from the advancement in information technology and communication industry and this advancement stimulated researches in technology and instructional design (Reiser & Dempsey, 2007). Statistics show that demand on online education is increasing sharply and is expected to continue in the next few years (Mokhtar, Walworth, Hester, & Dyer, 2008). However, the demand on online education has increased sharply due to COVID-19. Many universities around the world decided to switch to online education because of the pandemic. The pandemic has imposed many changes on people in all over the world, one of these changes is how to deliver an educational content (Shah et al., 2020). As an example on the imposed changes, Coronavirus has disrupted medical education (Rose, 2020). Medical schools as a response to the pandemic shifted to online formats because the virus can be spread or acquired by medical students while being at hospitals or clinics (Rose, 2020).

Many universities around the world depend largely in their budgets on tuition fees paid by local and international students. For instance, the main source of institutional operating budgets for South Korean universities is tuition fees (Lee, Kim, & Lee, 2020). Since the pandemic has presented some economic challenges and since the overwhelming majority of universities around the world depend on the tuition fees of students, this has made the universities prone to economic challenges caused by COVID-19. Thatcher et al. (2020) highlight the impact of economic challenges on Australian universities. They expected that Australian universities will lose around $19 billion in 3 years because they depend on the international students' tuition fees. This loss is resultant from the travel ban imposed on certain nationalities because of the pandemic (Hurley & Dyke, 2020). However, if travel restriction to Australia continues, the long-term loss will be huge (Thatcher et al., 2020).

The overwhelming majority of universities in the world have networks of agents that promote HEIs in international markets. Recruitment agencies play a vital role in recruiting international students for the universities. Hence, international students' recruiters make great contributions to support the budgets of the

248 Belal Shneikat

universities. Education agents 'international student recruiters' serve as mediators between HEIs and prospective students. The idea of hiring education agents started when some countries adopted reforms 'neoliberalism' which resulted in identifying international students as a source of income (Xu, 2020). Collins (2012) highlighted the role of education agents in increasing the number of international students in New Zealand. He described the changes in legislations and neoliberalism adopted by New Zealand universities which enabled them to gain profits from international fee-paying students. Similarly, Raimo, Humfrey, and Huang (2014) stated that all UK universities depend largely on international student recruiters to achieve their economic goals.

Although some risks associated with relying in education agents (Raimo et al., 2014), HEIs do not have many options to recruit international students. Indeed, universities usually depend on social media platforms and education agents to recruit students. Social media platforms may not convince prospective students to join a certain university because all universities have accounts on social media. Hence, prospective students may not decide because they hear the same information on social media. Thus, education agents play a vital role in directing international students into particular HEIs (Collins, 2012). Indeed, universities need someone who speaks the local language of the prospective students to persuade them. Education agents affect the student decision regarding which institute they should join (Collins, 2012). Some agents have been students at the same universities they recruit for. Therefore, when they recruit students, they usually capitalise on their experience to convince prospective students to join. In addition, students usually prefer to listen from someone who has experience in that place.

Education agent usually provides information about overseas education system and application process (Collins, 2012; Roy, 2017). Because this industry is growing well, the market value of agencies is in hundreds of millions of USD (Nikula & Kivisto, 2018). There are some education agent companies that provide a wide range of services for students and, therefore, their annual revenues exceed $150 million (Xu, 2020). It is worth mentioning here that the size of agent companies differs largely, but in all cases, most of the education agent companies have less than 10 employees (ICEF Monitor, 2013 as cited by Xu, 2020). This reflects a fact that most of agents are entrepreneurs who take the advantage of ICT to gain more revenues with minimum cost. Only the United States was banning HEIs to hire education agents till 2013 (Xu, 2020), then they lift the ban and because of that, many US HEIs started depending on the services provided by the agents.

Methodology

Given the lack of literature on the future of international student recruitment, the current study was designed as a qualitative research to help in deriving potential hypotheses and significant themes for future studies as recommended by Shneikat and Ryan (2018). Silverman (2000) stated that qualitative methods offer a deeper understanding of the phenomena being studied. The study involved 19 semi-structured interviews with international student recruiters in the Middle East. Those agents recruit students for HEIs in the Middle East, Europe and North

America. The interviews were conducted individually via Messenger, WhatsApp and Imo. The author contacted the agents after getting their phone numbers from the websites of some universities in the Middle East and Europe. All interviews were conducted in English because all recruiters have good command of English as recommended by Abubakar and Shneikat (2017). All informants gave the permission to record the interviews with one condition that in transcribing manuscripts they would be given pseudonyms (Shneikat & Ryan, 2018). It was ensured that no information or opinion was provided beforehand to the respondents and they were asked to express their own views on each question provided (Karadal, Shneikat, Abubakar, & Bhatti, 2020).

The author built trust first with informants through introducing the research topic to them and its goals. After that, three questions were presented to the respondents. The questions are:

1. From your point of view, Why do students depend on education agents to decide which HEIs to join?
2. How has COVID-19 affected your ability to recruit students for overseas HEIs?
3. What are your expectations for the future?

Questions were developed based on literature review of education agents and new articles about the impact of Coronavirus on education. The questions then were sent to two professors in education and one education agent. All of them saw the questions relevant to the research topic and have the ability to generate excellent information that may clarify the future of recruiting international students. Lastly, pilot study with five education agent has been conducted and no changes were made based on the feedback.

Findings

The participants were 15 males and 4 females. This should be studied in the future researches to recognise the reasons behind the dominancy of males in this industry in the Middle East. The age of informants ranged between 28 and 62 years old. Fourteen respondents are married, three divorced and two are single. Eight employees have master degree, six PhD and five bachelor's degree. The work experience for the agents ranged between 2 and 31 years. Only three agents do not have employees and one agent has one employee. All other employees have three or more employees. Table 1 shows the demographics of education agents.

In regards to the question, Table 2 represents the breakdown of the text.

The agents in their answers for the first questions highlighted the distrust in social media as the first reason for seeking an advice from education agents. Indeed, not all advertisements on social media can be trusted especially when they ask you to pay. One of the informants said:

> Informant #7 '…. They come to my office because they don't trust social media and they are afraid of being scammed'.

250 *Belal Shneikat*

Table 1. Demographics (Own Original Work).

Respondent #	Age	Gender	Marital Status	Education	Work Experience	# of Employees
1	29	Female	Single	Master	2	–
2	28	Male	Single	Bachelor's degree	4	–
3	55	Male	Married	Master	27	12
4	62	Male	Married	Bachelor's degree	31	9
5	49	Male	Married	PhD	15	4
6	43	Male	Married	Master	17	5
7	38	Male	Married	PhD	9	4
8	59	Male	Married	PhD	21	4
9	45	Male	Married	Master	7	4
10	41	Female	Married	PhD	13	8
11	37	Male	Married	Bachelor's degree	11	5
12	60	Female	Married	Bachelor's degree	24	14
13	58	Male	Married	PhD	19	9
14	29	Male	Divorced	Master	3	–
15	36	Female	Divorced	Master	8	3
16	46	Male	Married	Master	13	7
17	45	Male	Married	Master	10	5
18	31	Female	Divorced	Bachelor's degree	4	1
19	44	Male	Married	PhD	11	6

Some agents highlighted the role of reputation. When you work in the market for many years and your customers talk to their family members and friends about your honesty and good services, this will attract new customers to your agency. A respondent stated that:

> Informant #4 '.... one customer same to me with his son asking about a university in the UK, he said that he heard about our office from his cousin who sent his son to Turkey through our office'.

Experience plays a role in attracting customers. Recruiting international students is not an easy process as some people think. Lack of experience makes

Table 2. Text Breakdown (Own Original Work).

Text Breakdown	#of Coding for Each Theme	#of Interviews Associated with Each Code
Question #1		
Distrust in social media	15	15
Reputation	9	8
Experience	3	2
Question #2		
Less students	16	15
Online education	14	14
Cost-benefit analysis	7	5
Question #3		
Online education	18	18
Social media	15	14
Unexpected competitors	10	10
Websites of the universities	6	5

a lot of troubles to students when they move abroad. One of the interviewees explained this point:

> Informant #12 'A guy called me in 2014 and said that he will send his son to study medicine in Kharkov and a education agent advised him to go there because of low tuition fees. I was shocked when he told me this, I said but there is a war now in that area!. The guy couldn't know what to say for a while and then said, but that education agent didn't tell me this [...]'

In regards to the second question, three themes emerged. The first theme, many education agents strongly believe that COVID-19 will not allow them to recruit many students as they used to do. An informant said:

> Informant #12 'Last year like this month, I applied for more than 150 students, till now only 37 students applied'.

Switching to online education in almost all countries around the world affected the ability of international student recruiters to apply for many students because most of international students go abroad not just for education, but they seek to enjoy and interact with a new culture. One of the respondents stated that:

> Informant #17 'switching to online education was a big problem for us because most of students go abroad to master their English language and enjoy their lives'.

252   Belal Shneikat

Some informants stated that switching to online education with fixed tuition fees has made their job difficult because students can study anywhere online with low tuition fees. One of the informants said:

> Informant #3 'some students calling and asking me if the study in Fall semester 2020-2021 will be online or face to face. When I tell them that it is most likely online, they ask me, what about tuition fees, is there any discount?. I say no, then they say why should we pay full tuition fees for online classes while we can study online at another university and pay less fees [...]'.

Regarding the third question, respondents expected online education to be prevalent in the near future especially if Coronavirus continues for two to three years. One of the respondents stated that:

> Informant #11 'If Coronavirus continues for some years, people will be accustomed to online education and it will be difficult for them to get back to face to face education'.

Respondents expected social media to play an important role in recruiting international students in the future. One of the interviewees explained this point:

> Informant #6 'Many people instead of coming to your office, they will contact you via Facebook or WhatsApp because they know that they will not be scammed since the accounts are yours'

Ten informants highlighted the 'unexpected competitors', one of the agents clarified this by saying:

> Informant #13 '[...]you do your best to serve students and enroll them at high-profile universities and in the second or third year they start working as an agent. They even start advertising on Facebook and Instagram that they get admissions for prospective students and are willing to serve students there for free. One student asked his friends on Facebook that if they know anybody who wants to study abroad, they shouldn't contact my office because I get commission while he is willing to offer the admission for them for free... This is unfair competition and I really didn't expect that student to be a competitor'.

Six respondents raised the issue of universities websites that they will start recruiting more international students in the future. One of them mentioned:

> Informant #14 'Universities started paying more attention to their websites and make them easy to use so students can apply directly to the universities without dealing with agents. Universities want to reduce the commission they pay for agents'.

Discussion

This study aimed to see the future directions of recruiting international students from education agent perspectives. The study recruited 19 education agents and conducted semi-structured interviews to serve the aim of the study. Three questions were presented to the respondents and some themes were extracted after breaking down the text.

Distrust in social media was the first reason that pushes students to seek advice from education agents. Kim and Ahmad (2012) highlighted the key role of trust in sharing some contents on social media. When people trust the source of information, they tend to share it with others. Since social media is used by all people including scammers, many people hesitate to act based on any information they get from social media. Scammers aim at extorting economic resources in a manipulative dynamic (Colluccia et al., 2020). Thus, they ask applicants to pay for admissions and this trigger distrust from students who deal with unknown figures. However, social media accounts with blue mark are trustable and some students contact universities via those pages.

Reputation and experience of international admission recruiters is important because it reduces the concerns of students. Reputation as stated by Kim and Lennon (2012) has a significant positive effect on consumers' emotion and significant negative effect on perceived risk. When a certain education agent has a reputation that means s/he has an experience and customers are happy with them. Thus, more students come to the agency seeking information about certain places or they apply for universities directly through that agency.

COVID-19 has affected negatively the education sector in certain countries that recruit many international students every year (Thatcher et al., 2020). Thus, it is expected that many universities in the west will have less international students for the academic year 2020/2021. Switching to online education has triggered several questions about the quality of education and student satisfaction. Online education seems to affect the quality of education and student satisfaction (Chen, 2020). Switching to online education was not voluntary, in fact, it was the only option to let students finish their semester. However, students complain from online classes because they paid full tuition fees to get face to face education (Anderson, 2020). Some student got loans to have face to face education and now they have online education. They could have joined any school that teach online with low tuition fees. These circumstances have pushed students to make cost–benefit analysis. Before, they were paying high school fees to get quality education, now the quality of online education is questionable everywhere.

Given that the advancement of ICT is expected to continue in the next few years. Online education will continue to have a bright future (Kim & Bonk, 2006). In addition, social media platforms might be the main source of recruiting international students in the next decade because current generation tend to depend more and more on social media to make decisions. Muskat et al. (2013) found that young generations in the United States were more than twice as likely as were old generations to consider others' suggestions as an influential factor in making decisions. One of the sources that can have influence on decisions of this generation is social media.

Conclusion

The current study seeks to predict the future of international student recruitment from educational agents' perspectives. The study employed 19 respondents and 3 open-ended questions were used in this study.

The findings show three reasons for students seeking information and applying for universities through agents. These factors are distrust in social media, reputation and experience. Three factors also emerged as the effects of COVID-19 on the recruitment of international students. These effects are less students, online education and cost–benefit analysis. Finally, four predictions for the future of international student recruitments have appeared.

International student recruiters should adopt quickly to the changes in the market and should take the advantage of ICT to increase the number of students they recruit. They should pay attention to the power of social media in recruiting international students and understand the needs of current generation who prefer to get services online.

This study was not without limitations. First, the author could not reach international student recruiters in other parts of the world. Thus, future studies may conduct researches in other regions. Second, the study only recruited 19 education agents. Hence, the generalisability of this study is questionable.

Future studies may focus on the economic aspects of international student recruitment and make qualitative and quantitative research in this area.

References

Abubakar, A. M., & Shneikat, B. H. T. (2017). eLancing motivations. *Online Information Review, 41*(1), 53–69.

Altinay, M., & Shneikat, B. (2019). Internationalization of higher education institutions in North Cyprus. *Policies and initiatives for the internationalization of higher education* (pp. 98–125). IGI Global. doi:10.4018/978-1-5225-5231-4.ch007

Anderson, G. (2020). Feeling Shortchanged. Retrieved from https://www.insidehighered.com/news/2020/04/13/students-say-online-classes-arent-what-they-paid

Bell, D. (1973). *The coming of post-industrial society*. New York, NY: Basic Books.

Bhandari, R. (2011). (Ed.). *Open Doors 2008: Report on international educational exchange*. New York, NY: Institute of International Education.

Bolsmann, C., & Miller, H. (2008). International student recruitment to universities in England: Discourse, rationales and globalization. *Globalization, Societies and Education, 6*(1), 75–88.

Castells, M. (1996). *The information age: Economy, society, and culture. Volume I The rise of the network society*. Oxford: Blackwell.

Collins, F. L. (2012). Organizing student mobility: Education agents and student migration to New Zealand. *Pacific Affairs, 85*(1), 137–160.

Colluccia, A., Pozza, A., Ferretti, F., Carabellese, F., Masi, A., & Gualtieri, G. (2020). Online Romance Scams: Relational dynamics and psychological characteristics of the victims and scammers. A scoping review. *Clinical Practice and Epidemiology in Mental Health: CP & EMH, 16*, 24.

De Wit, H. (2011). Globaization and internationalization of higher education (Introduction to online monograph). *Revista de Universidad y Sociedad del Conocimiento (RUSC)*, *8*(2), 241–248. Retrieved http://rusc.uoc.edu/ojs/index.php/rusc/article/view/v8n2-dewit/v8n2-dewit-eng> ISSN 1698-580X. Accessed on January 13, 2020.

Hurley, P., & Dyke, N. V. (2020). *Australian investment in education: Higher education*. Portland: Mitchell Institute. Retrieved from https://www.vu.edu.au/sites/default/files/australian-investment-in-education-highereducation-mitchell-institute.pdf?fbclid=IwAR38CBffBIK8N8XEWPBSXFkP0M2jv5GRoAkD5B8sXo0Y1zh-OsP863GIeY. Accessed on August 15, 2020.

ICEF Monitor. (2013). Seventh annual agent barometer provides agents' view of marketplace. Retrieved from http://monitor.icef.com/2013/11/seventh-annual-agentbarometer-provides-agents-view-of-marketplace/

Karadal, H., Shneikat, B. H. T., Abubakar, A. M., & Bhatti, O. K. (2020). Immigrant entrepreneurship: The case of Turkish entrepreneurs in United States. *Journal of the Knowledge Economy* Springer. doi:10.1007/s13132-020-00684-8

Kim, Y. A., & Ahmad, M. A. (2012). Trust, distrust and lack of confidence of users in online social media-sharing communities. *Knowledge-Based Systems*. doi:10.1016/j.knosys.2012.09.002

Kim, K. J., & Bonk, C. J. (2006). The future of online teaching and learning in higher education. *Educause Quarterly*, *29*(4), 22–30.

Kim, J., & Lennon, S. J. (2013). Effects of reputation and website quality on online consumers' emotion, perceived risk and purchase intention. *Journal of Research in Interactive Marketing*, *7*(1), 33–56.

Knight, J. (2004). Internationalization remodeled: Definition, approaches, and rationales. *Journal of Studies in International Education*, *8*(1), 5–31.

Knight, J. (2013). The changing landscape of higher education internationalization – For better or worse. *Perspectives: Policy and Practice in Higher Education*, *17*(3), 84–90.

Lee, Y. H., Kim, K. S., & Lee, K. H. (2020). The effect of tuition fee constraints on financial management: Evidence from Korean Private Universities. *Sustainability*, *12*(2), 50–66.

Lyotard, J. F. (1984). *The postmodern condition: A report on knowledge* (G. Bennington & B. Massumi, Trans.). Minneapolis, MN: University of Minnesota Press.

Márquez, B. L. D., Torres, N. E. H., & Bondar, Y. (2011). Internationalization of higher education: Theoretical and empirical investigation of its influence on university institution rankings. *Globalisation and Internationalisation of Higher Education*, *8*(2), 265–284.

Mokhtar, W., Walworth, M., Hester, J., & Dyer, G. (2008). Distance learning and student recruiting using an internet controlled robot. *The International Journal of Learning: Annual Review*, *15*(8), 277–286.

Muskat,M., Muskat,B., Zehrer,A., & Johns,R. (2013). Generation Y: evaluating services experiences through mobile ethnography. *Tourism Review*, *68*(3), 55–71

Nikula, P., & Kivisto, J. (2018). Hiring education agents for international student recruitment: Perspectives from agency theory. *Higher Education Policy*, *31*, 535–557. doi:10.1057/s41307-017-0070-8

Ostry, S. (1999, March). *Globalization and sovereignty. James R. Mallory Annual Lecture in Canadian Studies*. Montreal: McGill Institute for the Studies of Canada.

Raimo, V., Humfrey, C., & Huang, I. Y. (2014). Managing international student recruitment agents: Approaches, benefits and challenges. Retrieved from https://www.britishcouncil.org/sites/default/files/managing_education_agents_report_for_bc_2.pdf

Reiser, R. A., & Dempsey, J. V. (2007). *Trends and issues in instructional design and technology* (2nd ed.). Upper Saddle River, NJ: Pearson/Prentice-Hall.

Rose, S. (2020). Medical student education in the time of COVID-19. *JAMA*. Retrieved from https://jamanetwork.com/journals/jama/article-abstract/2764138

256 Belal Shneikat

Roy, M. (2017, June 6). Decoding international students' experiences with education agents: Insights for US institutions. *World Education News*. Retrieved from https://wenr.wes.org/2017/06/decoding-international-students-experiences-with-education-agents-insights-for-u-s-institutions

Shah, S., Diwan, S., Kohan, L., Rosenblum, D., Gharibo, C., Soin, A., ... Provenzano, D. A. (2020). The technological impact of COVID-19 on the future of education and health care delivery. *Pain Physician, 23*, S367–S380.

Shneikat, B., & Ryan, C. (2018). Syrian Refugees and their re-entry to 'normality': The role of service industries. *The Service Industries Journal, 38*(3–4), 201–227.

Silver, H., & Silver, P. (1997). *Students: Changing roles, changing lives*. Buckingham: Open University Press.

Silverman, D. (2000). *Doing qualitative research: A practical handbook*. London: Sage.

Stromquist, N. P. (2002). *Education in a globalized world: The connectivity of economic power, technology and knowledge*. Lanthan, MD: Rowman & Littlefield Publishers, Inc.

Thatcher, A., Zhang, M., Todoroski, H., Chau, A., Wang, J., & Liang, G. (2020). Predicating the impact of COVID-19 on Australian Universities. *Journal of Risk and Financial Management*, doi:10.3390/jrfm13090188

The Institute of International Education. (2019). Number of International Students in the United States Hits All-Time High. Retrieved from https://www.iie.org/Why IIE/Announcements/2019/11/Number-of-International-Students-in-the-United-States-Hits-All-TimeHigh#:~:text=The%20total%20number%20of%20international,total%20U.S.%20higher%20education%20population

Toffler, A. (1980). *The third wave*. New York, NY: William Morrow and Company.

UNESCO. (2017). Education: Outbound internationally mobile students by host region. Retrieved from http://data.uis.unesco.org/Index.aspx?queryid=172

Universities UK. (2019). International facts and figures. Retrieved from https://www.universitiesuk.ac.uk/International/Documents/2019/International%20facts%20and%20figures%20slides.pdf

Xu, H. (2020). *Recruitment of international students in Canadian Higher Education: Factors influencing students' perceptions and experiences*. Master Thesis, University of Prince Edward Island.

Ziguras, C., & Law, S. F. (2006). Recruiting international students as skilled migrants: The global 'skills race' as viewed from Australia and Malaysia. *Globalisation, Societies and Education, 4*(1), 59–76.

Index

Academic factors, 157
Academic institutional websites, 68
Academic situations, 157–158
Acculturation, 232
Acculturative stress, 179
Activity theory, 102
Admissions, 140
    application process, 140–141
    challenges in culture surrounding
        application process,
        149–151
    challenges in structure of
        application process, 147–149
    findings, 144–147
    gathering and analysing
        information from
        stakeholders in sponsored
        admissions, 141–144
    identifying and correcting handling
        errors, 148
    insider unpublicised practices,
        148–149
    nineteen steps of sample
        application, 145–147
    structural barriers to
        APPLICATION, 147–148
    systems challenges, 147
Affiliation with schools abroad, 31
American Indonesian Exchange
        Foundation (AMINEF),
        142
Amplification rate, 74
Applause rate, 74
Applicants, 143
Application process, 140–141
    challenges in culture surrounding,
        149–151
    challenges in structure of, 147–149

Assignments, 190
Attribution theory, 53–54
Augmented level services, 157
Australian university system, 131
Autoethnography, 144
Average variance extracted results
        (AVE results), 58

Beijing Olympic Games, 46
Bias preparation courses, 218
Bounce rate, 71
Boxer indemnity, 40–41
    grantees, 41–43
Brand awareness, 54–55
Brand equity approach, 52, 54
Brand familiarity, 56
Brand preference, 55
Brand recognisability, 52–53, 55–56
Brand recognition, 56
Brand reputation, 56
Brand signature, 53, 56–57, 59
Brexit, 128–129
Business and Economics Schools in
        Spain, 176–178

Canadian Bureau of International
        Education (CBIE), 130
Case study
    design, 232–233
    method, 102
Case university, 143–144
Challenges of Chinese students,
        178–180
Chinese international students, 232
    current international students'
        support services at
        University of South,
        235–236

258   Index

international students' general
cultural adjustment
difficulties, 234–235
issues in international students'
support services, 236–241
limitations and implications,
241–242
methodology, 232–234
Chinese Student Protection Act
(1992), 45
Chinese students, 37, 46, 174
at Business and Economics
Schools in Spain,
174–176
challenges and satisfaction,
178–180
at FECEM, 180
and professionals, 47
questionnaire to, 181–183
as spies, 46
stages of tourism development,
40
students in US, 39
in US under COVID, 40
Chinese Study Abroad Program, 39
Chung yu, 45
Club sports, 192–193
Collaboration with other HEI
abroad, 28
College of Education degree
program, 140
Collegiate sports, 192–193
Common method bias (CMB), 58
Communications, 26–27, 150–151
Complexity, 8
Confusion, 222–223
Conversation rate, 73
Conversion rate, 72
Cooperative typology, 104–105
Core level service, 157
Cost, 17, 23
of program, 11
Council of Higher Education
(YÖK), 156
COVID-19, 247

Cultural adaptation, 179, 232
Cultural adjustment, 215–216, 232
institutional supports for
international students,
217–218
for international students, 217
literature review, 216
method, 218–219
recommendations, 225–227
Cultural environment, 11–12, 25–26
Cultural experience, 231
Cultural/culture shock, 179, 232
Culture, 220–221

Danish policy context, 202–203
Deductive analysis, 159
Dimensioning, 203
Direktorat Jenderal Pendidikan
Tinggi (DIKTI), 142
Discrimination, 221–222
Disorientation, 222–223
Distance learning, 6
Diversification, 132–134
Domestic tourism, 5

Earned media, 73
Eastern Mediterranean University
(EMU), 14
accreditations awareness, 30
facilities and standard of
education, 31
Edu-tourism, 12–13
Education, 176 (*see also* Higher
education)
agents, 248
Educational destination image, 11
Educational experiences, 189–190
Educational tourism, 2–5, 38, 52
case study in Northern Cyprus,
14–31
determinants, 14
literature review, 4–14
tourism and, 38
Educational tourists, 15
decision, 7–8

factors influencing educational tourists' decision-making process, 8–12
key elements, 13
Embedded cultural issues of case university, 149–150
Engeström's approach, 103
Environmental factors, 99
Esbjerg, 198
policy context, 202–203
European Credits Transfer System (ECTS), 177
Exchange programs, 29–30
Expectations, 157
Experiences, 156
Extracurricular factors, 157

Facilities, 223
Factors influencing satisfaction, 156
Facultad de Economía y Empresa (FECEM), 176–177
Chinese students at, 180
Faculty culture, 150
Family Reunion Act (1965), 45
Federation of Indian Students in Australia (FISA), 128
Federation Square in Melbourne Australia, 128
Feedback, 30
First 52 Chinese students in 1978, 44–47
Fondo di Finanziamento Ordinario (FFO), 86
Foreign and second language education (FSLED), 147
Foreign sponsors, 141–142
Free-flying young people in transition, 206–207
Frustration, 222–223
Fulbright funding, 142

Game-changing potential of internships and jobs, 207–209

Geopolitics, 126
global events and COVID-19 pandemic, 130–132
global mobility and institutional dependence, 126–128
ISEM, 132–135
and uncertainty, 128–130
Germany
higher education sector in, 53
sales of e-trade in, 54
Global mobility, 126–128
Globalisation, 245–246 (*see also* Internationalisation)
of educational tourism, 7
processes, 82
Governments, 30
in Indonesia, 142–143
policy, 99
Graduate admissions, 140
Graduate assistants (GAs), 221
Graduate Records Exam (GRE), 140

Heterotrait–monotrait ratio of correlations (HTMT), 58
High-school institutions, 30
Higher education, 52, 66, 103, 155–156
internationalisation of higher education in Iran, 112–113
sector in Germany, 53
Higher Education Council of Turkey (YOK), 119
Higher education industry (HE industry), 2, 6–7
Higher education institution (HEI), 2–3, 66, 112, 246
capabilities, 101
countries and, 98
financial tenacity, 4
and municipality, 203–205
researchers in marketing, 12–13
Host universities, 189
Housing, 189, 203

260 Index

Imam Sadiq University, 117
Indonesia, 140
   governments in, 142–143
Indonesian International Education
     Foundation (IIEF), 142
Information and Communication
     Technologies (ICTs), 245,
     248
Information gathered and analysed, 144
Institute of International Education
     (IIE), 246
Institute of International Education
     in New York (IIE), 143
Institutional capability, 104
Institutional culture, 98
   compliant typology, 105–107
   cooperative typology, 104–105
   isolating typology, 107
   literature review, 99–101
   methodology, 101–102
   research design, 102–103
   results, 103–107
Institutional dependence, 126–128
Institutional factors, 157
Institutional policy, 99
Institutional supports for
     international students,
     217–218, 223–224
Intensification of global
     competitiveness, 82
International comparisons, 99
International education, 173
International educational experiences,
     188–189
International English Language
     Testing System (IELTS),
     121, 148
International environment, 21
International mobility, 126
International recruitment, 125–126
International sanctions, 113, 115
   challenges and opportunities of
     student recruitment in Iran,
     115–119
   internationalisation of higher
     education in Iran, 114–115

North Cyprus and Iranian
     students, 119–121
student recruitment, 113–114
International strategic enrolment
     management (ISEM),
     132–135
International student integration, 199
   cultural mixing and need
     for responsive study
     environment, 199–201
   Danish and Esbjerg policy context,
     202–203
   financial, internship-related and
     work-related obstacles,
     201–202
   methods, 203
   obstacles observed in international
     literature, 199
   results, 203–209
International student mobility, 112,
     125–126
International student recruitment, 99,
     107, 218, 246
   findings, 249–252
   literature review, 247–248
   methodology, 248–249
International students, 7, 66, 81–82,
     112, 187
   and academic institutional
     websites, 68
   cultural adjustment for, 217
   factors associated with
     international student
     success, 219–223
   general cultural adjustment
     difficulties, 234–235
   information searched online by,
     68–70
   institutional supports for, 217–218,
     223–224
   issues in international students'
     support services, 236–241
   places of origin, 66
   research implications, 75–76
   research method, 67
   social listening of, 73–75

studying abroad, 188–194
support services, 235–236
web analytics for understanding
    online behaviour of, 68–73
worries of, 163–164
International tourism, 5
Internationalisation, 99, 246
    case study, 86–92
    of educational tourism, 7
    of higher education in Iran,
        114–115
    at home, 83
    processes, 82
    strategies, 82–85
    of students, 84
    of teaching and learning, 82
Internet, 54
Internet-Based TOEFL (iBT), 148
Iran, 113
    challenges and opportunities of
        student recruitment in,
        115–119
    internationalisation of higher
        education in, 114–115
Iranian students, 119–121
Isolating typology, 107
Italian higher education system, 86–87
Italian public universities, evidence
        of strategic planning for
        internationalisation of
        students from, 87–91
Ivory Tower of American academies,
        39

Key performance indicators, 67, 71
Korean War, 39

Lancaster University, 102
Landing page, 71
Language, 179, 219–220
    barriers, 191
    skills, 163–164
Learning, internationalisation of, 82
Lembaga Pengelola Dana Pendidikan
        (LPDP), 142, 147–148
Location, 19–20, 24

Marketers, 2
Marketing, 99
Medium of instruction, 20–21, 25
Ministry for Education, Universities
        and Research (MIUR), 86
Motivation, 9
Motivators in selecting educational
        tourism destination, 18
Muhaceret, 119
Multicollinearity, 58

New York University, 127
Non-governmental organisations
        (NGOs), 141
Non-native English speakers (NNES),
        67
North Cyprus Higher Education
        Association (YODAK), 119
North(ern) Cyprus, 3–4
    case study in, 14–31
    international students in, 7
    and Iranian students, 119–121

Offline communication, 22
Online communication, 12, 21–22
Online marketing, 12–13, 29
Online media platform, 54
Online platforms, 54
Online purchasing, 54
Organization for Economic
        Co-operation and
        Development (OECD), 66
Owned media, 73

Paid media, 73
Pandemic, 126–127
Partial least squares structural
        equation modelling (PLS-
        SEM), 58
Pedagogical interaction, 178–179
Performance of Program X+1
        students, 180–181
Performance-based funding
        mechanisms in Italian
        Universities, 91–92
Post war cohort, 43

262 Index

Pre-departure orientation, 218
Private HEIs, 113
Professors, 189–190
Programming, 99
Public HEIs, 113
Public universities, 82, 86
Pull factors, 6, 8–10
Push factors, 6, 8–10

Qualitative study
experiences international students,
160–163
literature review, 156–158
methodology, 158–160
student suggestions, 165–168
students' comparison between
marketing process and
experiences after arrival,
164–165
worries of international students,
163–164
Quality of communication, 21–22, 29
Quality of education, 20, 24–25

Racism, 221–222
Recruiters, 103, 106

Safety, 20
Satisfaction, 156–158, 178–180
Scenery, 19
Scholarships, 30
Segmentation of sentiments, 75
Self-supported study, 44
Senior leaders, 103
Sentiment analysis, 75
Services, 223
Sign-gestalt paradigm, 9
Smart-PLS software, 57
Social activities, 191–192
Social development, 246
Social listening, 73–74
of international students, 73–75
Social media, 13, 51–52, 218
marketing, 55
monitoring, 73
platforms, 73

Social media marketing activities
(SMMAs), 52
effects, 53
literature review and research
hypotheses, 53–57
method and results, 57–59
Social network, 19, 24
influences from, 10
Society, 188
Stakeholders, 141
gathering and analysing
information from
stakeholders in sponsored
admissions, 141–144
Standardised root mean square
residual (SRMR), 59
State funding, 86
Stay-home culture, 209
Stone–Geisser's Q^2, 58–59
Strategic enrolment management,
132
Strategic performance objectives,
85
Strategic planning, 85
evidence of strategic planning for
internationalisation of
students, 87–91
Strategic plans, 82, 106
Student dissatisfaction, 158
Student internationalisation, 92–94
Student jobs and internships,
207–209
Student recruitment, 113–114,
132–134, 215–216
challenges and opportunities of
student recruitment in Iran,
115–119
Student retention, 225
Student satisfaction, 157
with experiences, 193–194
Student success, 216
Student support, development
and career outcomes,
134–135
Student's needs and wants, 28–29
Student's plea, 31

Index   263

Students' comparison between marketing process and experiences after arrival, 164–165
Studying aboard, 158, 188–194

Teaching, internationalisation of, 82
Teaching assistants (TAs), 221
Tertiary education sector, 112
Test of English as Foreign Language (TOEFL), 121, 143
Thematic analysis, 16
Times Higher Education (THE), 14
Top-down process, 101
Tourism, 4–5, 51
   actors, 3
   Boxer indemnity, 40–41
   in Chinese Study Abroad Program, 39
   and educational tourism, 38
   first 52 Chinese students in 1978, 44–47
   of foreign students, 37
   of international students, 37–38
   literature review, 39–40
   Mao's death, 43–44
   methodology, 38–39
   post war cohort, 43
   theoretical framework, 38
Traditional education marketing, 52
Transactions process, 145
Transformation, 6
Travelling, 9
Tuition fees, 28, 247
Turkish higher education, 155
Tutors, 191

Uncertainty, 128–130
UNIA, 101, 103

University Grants Committee (UGC), 106
University international education, 83, 85
University internationalisation, 83, 85
University leadership, 84
University of Illinois, 38
University of Illinois at Urbana Champaign (UIUC), 127
University of Prince Edward Island (UPEI), 101–103
University of Toronto, 127
University services, 156
University websites, 68
US Agency for International Development (USAID), 142
US agents and partners, 143
US Embassy
   in Indonesia, 142–143
   in Jakarta, 143
US–China educational exchange, 40

Volume, 74–75
Volunteer participation, 191–192

Wadden Sea National Park, 198
Water Taxi tour of New York Harbor, 46
Web analytics for understanding online behaviour of international students, 68–73
Web-2.0, 54
World Trade Organisation (WTO), 245–246

Zaragoza university, 176–178

Printed in the United States
by Baker & Taylor Publisher Services